This book is published strictly for historical purposes.
The Naval and Military Press Ltd
expressly bears no responsibility or liability of any type,
to any first, second or third party, for any harm,
injury or loss whatsoever.

DEAL THE FIRST DEADLY BLOW

		Paragraphs	Page
CHAPTER 1.	BAYONET		
Section I.	Introduction	1–4	3
II.	Positions	5, 6	4
III.	Movements	7, 8	10
IV.	Assault course	9–11	29
V.	Pugil training	12–17	32
VI.	Group assault tactics	18, 19	53
CHAPTER 2.	HAND-TO-HAND COMBAT		
Section I.	Introduction	20, 21	64
II.	Fundamentals	22–27	64
III.	Vulnerable points	28–34	69
IV.	Fall positions	35–42	98
V.	Basic throws and takedowns	43–49	104
VI.	Variations of basic throws and takedowns	50–53	124
VII.	Holds	54–61	132
VIII.	Escape from holds	62–73	145
IX.	Knife attack	74–79	176
X.	Bayonet disarming	80–85	192
XI.	Rifle and pistol disarming	86–98	213
XII.	Knife disarming	99–104	256
XIII.	Silencing sentries	105–110	275
XIV.	Prisoner searching	111–118	284
XV.	Securing and gagging prisoners	119–126	294
APPENDIX I.	REFERENCES		304
II.	BAYONET ASSAULT COURSE TARGETS, OBTACLES, AND SCORESHEETS		305
III.	ADVICE TO INSTRUCTORS OF BAYONET TRAINING		321
IV.	ADVICE TO INSTRUCTORS OF HAND-TO-HAND COMBAT		327
INDEX			331

The Naval & Military Press Ltd

Published by

The Naval & Military Press Ltd
Unit 5 Riverside, Brambleside
Bellbrook Industrial Estate
Uckfield, East Sussex
TN22 1QQ England

Tel: +44 (0)1825 749494

www.naval-military-press.com
www.nmarchive.com

*In reprinting in facsimile from the original, any imperfections are inevitably reproduced
and the quality may fall short of modern type and cartographic standards.*

FOREWORD

This manual is designed as a reference and training text for all personnel engaged in the training of combatives. It also serves as a guide for unit commanders and their personnel in understanding the purpose, scope, capabilities, limitations, and applications of combatives training. Combatives training demonstrates the techniques of bayonet fighting and hand-to-hand combat which can be successfully used to meet and defeat an opponent at close quarters. A healthy, competitive spirit will be developed through this training by aggressive and determined practice.

The manual describes methods of self-protection to use when you are unarmed or unable to use your weapon. If a situation does not permit you to fire your rifle, you still have a potent weapon in the bayonet. Hand-to-hand combat is a further means of defeating an enemy if you do not have a bayonet or rifle. The bayonet and hand-to-hand combat remain the final means of defeating an enemy.

Basic principles of bayonet fighting and hand-to-hand combat are similar. Both types of training stress maximum strength against an opponent's weakness. It is important that your balance be maintained at all times so that you can overcome an opponent's momentum or superior strength. In training, accuracy should come first. After the required accuracy is attained, speed will come through practice. It must be understood that in close combat the best available weapon must be used. Whether you use a bayonet or hand-to-hand combat, simple movements executed aggressively will result in victory.

CHAPTER 1
BAYONET

Section I. INTRODUCTION

1. Purpose and Scope

a. This chapter teaches you how to use the bayonet. It describes basic techniques, positions, movements, and procedures for training. The techniques outlined will help you develop confidence in your ability to successfully engage and defeat an opponent using your bayonet. You will be certain of your ability to use the weapon swiftly and accurately. By aggressive, determined practice, you will learn to react instinctively to any situation.

b. The material presented is applicable to both nuclear and nonnuclear warfare.

c. Users of this manual are encouraged to submit recommended changes or comments to improve it. Comments should be keyed to the specific page, paragraph, and line of the text in which the change is recommended. Reasons should be provided for each comment to insure understanding and complete evaluation. Comments should be forwarded direct to the Commandant, United States Army Infantry School, Fort Benning, Ga.

2. Uses of the Bayonet

a. Powerful new weapons, improved equipment, and new tactics have been introduced into modern warfare. However, firepower alone cannot drive a determined opponent from his position. He will often remain in his foxhole until driven out by close combat. The role of the individual soldier, particularly in the final phases of the assault, remains relatively unchanged. His mission is to destroy or capture the enemy. This mission remains the ultimate goal of all individual training. The bayonet, or the threat of it, is one of the final means of defeating an opponent in an assault.

b. At night, on infiltration missions, or whenever secrecy must be maintained, the bayonet is a silent weapon.

c. When close-in fighting makes the use of bullets or grenades impracticable, or when the situation does not permit the loading or reloading of the rifle, the bayonet is the most important weapon you have.

3. Principles of Bayonet Fighting

a. The bayonet is an offensive weapon to be used aggressively. Hesitation, delay, and maneuvering may mean sudden death.

b. As a bayonet fighter, you must attack in a fast, relentless assault until your opponent is destroyed. You should be alert to take advantage of any opening. If the enemy gives no opening, you must make one by parrying your opponent's weapon and then driving your blade or rifle butt into the opponent with killing force.

c. All areas of the body are likely targets for attack with the bayonet. The throat area, in particular, is a good spot to attack. An opponent will act by instinct to protect this area from a thrust. By threatening your opponent's throat with the bayonet point you will often cause him to drop his guard and leave other vulnerable parts of the body unprotected, namely the face, chest, abdomen, and groin.

4. Developing a Bayonet Fighter

a. Proper form with the rifle and bayonet, footwork, and accuracy are essential in training. These traits lead to coordination, balance, speed, strength, and endurance which characterize the expert bayonet fighter. Differences in individual body makeup may require slight changes from the bayonet techniques described in this manual; technique variations will be allowed if the individual's attack is effective.

b. All positions and movements described in this manual are for a right-handed man. A left-handed man, or a man who wishes to learn left-handed techniques, must use the opposite hand and foot for each phase of the described movements.

c. Illustrations in this manual show the M14 rifle with the sling tightened under the magazine. The sling is placed in this fashion only for uniformity. All positions and movements, however, can be executed with or without the magazine and with the sling tight or loose.

Section II. POSITIONS

5. General

Relax all muscles you do not use in a particular position. Hold the rifle firmly but do not be tense. Tense muscles cause fatigue and tend to slow you down. After proper training and through diligent practice, you will instinctively assume the basic positions of a bayonet fighter.

6. Basic Attack and Rest Positions

The basic attack positions in bayonet fighting are *guard, short guard,* and *high port.* The rest positions, used only on the training field, are *at ease* and *relax.*

a. Attack Positions.
(1) *Guard* (fig. 1). To simplify instruction, all movements in bayonet training begin from the guard position. You assume the guard position in the following manner:
  (*a*) Face your opponent.
  (*b*) Take a short step forward and to the side with your left foot so that your feet are comfortably apart. Your toes are pointed toward your opponent. Bend your knees slightly and lean your body slightly forward. Your hips are level.
  (*c*) Grasp the rifle with your left hand so that your palm is against the left side of the rifle at the most comfortable point forward of the balance point. Your left arm is bent slightly. With your right hand, grasp the small of the stock. Your right forefinger should not be inside the trigger guard. The underside and inside of your right forearm is held against the top of the stock. The base of the rifle butt is pressed snugly against the side of your hip. Hold the rifle firmly, but not rigidly, with both hands. The rifle is not canted either to the right or to the left. Point the bayonet at the base of your opponent's throat. To initiate this movement from order arms, throw your rifle forward into the air with the bayonet point toward your opponent. Catch the rifle with both hands. This movement must be swift and sure.
  (*d*) The weight of your body is balanced on both legs so you can move quickly in any direction.
  (*e*) Watch your opponent's bayonet and body simultaneously.
(2) *Short guard* (fig. 2). This is a convenient carrying position when moving through dense woods, brush, trenches, around buildings, or if you suddenly meet an enemy at close quarters. Assume the short guard position in the following manner:
  (*a*) From the guard position you bring the rifle back so that your right hand is at your right hip.
  (*b*) Drop the bayonet point level with your opponent's midsection.
(3) *High port* (fig. 3). Carry the rifle at high port when running during bayonet training. The high port is the most natural and commonly used position while moving and is used when jumping ditches or hurdling obstacles. The attack normally starts from the high port position during combat. Assume the position of high port as follows:
  (*a*) From the guard position you shift the rifle diagonally across your body without changing the position of your feet or hands.
  (*b*) Keep the rifle sling to the front.
  (*c*) Keep your left wrist level with your

Figure 1. Guard position.

Figure 2. Short guard position.

Figure 3. High port position.

Figure 4. Relax position.

Figure 5. At ease position.

left shoulder and in front of the shoulder.
(d) Keep the rifle butt to the right and alongside the right thigh.
(e) Keep your right elbow pressed firmly against your right side.

b. *Rest Positions.* The rest positions are used to give you a chance to relax during bayonet training. They also allow you to direct your attention toward the instructor as he discusses and demonstrates the positions and movements.

(1) *Relax* (fig. 4). To assume the relax position you straighten up and drop the rifle horizontally across the front of your body by extending your arms. The position of your feet and your grasp on the rifle do not change.

(2) *At ease* (fig. 5). To assume the at ease position you bring your feet on line and lower the rifle butt to the ground. Keep the butt alongside the right toe and on line with it. Hold the rifle with your right hand along the upper part of the handguard and extend the muzzle of the rifle forward of the body until the right arm is straight. This position is a modified parade rest position.

Section III. MOVEMENTS

7. General

You will eventually strike at openings without thinking and become aggressive in your attack once you have learned to relax and have developed instinctive reflexes. Your movements will not be done in any fixed order. You will achieve balance in all your movements, will be ready to strike instantly in any direction, and will keep striking until you have killed your opponent. The movements explained in this chapter will help you to become a bayonet fighter.

8. Basic Movements

The two basic movements used at the beginning of your instruction are the *whirl* and the *high port* and *crossover*. These movements help you become familiar with the rifle and bayonet and develop the instinct of reacting to simple commands. They also afford the instructor maximum control of the formation while on the training field. The movements used to disable or kill your opponent are the *long thrust*, the *short thrust*, the *vertical butt stroke*, the *horizontal butt stroke*, the *smash*, the *slash*, the *parry right*, and the *parry left*. At first you will learn these movements as separate actions. After further training, however, you must learn to execute these movements in a swift and continuous motion.

a. Whirl Movement (fig. 6). The whirl is executed from the guard position. Bring the rifle to the high port and whirl by pivoting on the ball of the leading foot in the direction of the leading foot. Remain at the high port until the whirl is completed. At the completion of the whirl take up the guard position.

b. High Port and Crossover Movement. While performing certain movements in bayonet training, two ranks will be moving toward each other. When the men in the ranks come too close to safely execute another movement then the high port and crossover is used. On the command HIGH PORT AND CROSSOVER, come to the high port position. Then move straight forward and pass your opponent so that your right shoulder passes his right shoulder. Continue moving forward for approximately six steps; halt and take up the guard position. Then, without any command, execute the whirl and again assume the guard position.

c. Long Thrust Series.
  (1) *Execution* (fig. 7).
   (a) When executing the long thrust from the normal guard position, bring your rear foot forward and lunge. Your entire body will be extended.
   (b) Complete the extension of your body as your rear foot strikes the ground. During this movement, drive the bayonet with great force straight at your opponent's throat or at an unguarded part of his body. To do this, grasp the rifle firmly with both hands, guiding it with your left hand. Extend your left arm quickly to its full length so that your bayonet darts toward the target. At the instant you are fully extended, hold the comb of the rifle stock inside of, and pressed against, your right forearm. Bend your front knee, lean your body well forward, and straighten your rear leg.
   (c) Look at the point of your opponent's body you are attacking throughout the movement.
   (d) Recover instantly after you complete the thrust; never linger in the extended position.
   (e) The long thrust is a power thrust which utilizes your maximum reach; however, you are in an awkward, extended position. You must recover your balance quickly. The power for the long thrust comes from coordination between your arms, shoulders, back, legs, and the weight of your body. The distance from which you begin the long thrust depends on your reach and on how rapidly you and your opponent are approaching each other. When you practice with the thrusting targets, you will learn the full distance that you can reach. It is important that

Figure 6. Whirl movement.

Figure 7. Long thrust (step one).

Figure 8. Recovery from long thrust (step two).

Figure 9. Withdrawal from long thrust (step three).

you know the limit of your reach and that you are able to judge from what distance you can begin your thrust and reach your target. You will be trained to execute the thrust with either foot forward.

(2) *Recovery* (fig. 8). Bring your trailing foot forward of your leading foot; at the same time shift your weight forward.

(3) *Withdrawal* (fig. 9).

 (a) Withdraw the bayonet by lifting your trailing foot slightly forward then kicking it sharply to the rear. At the same time, jerk the rifle back along a straight line using your body weight. Pull the rifle back until your left forearm hits the pit of your stomach.

 (b) Assume the guard position by snapping the rifle forward and bringing the toe of your right foot on line with the heel of your left foot.

d. *Short Thrust Series.*

(1) *Execution* (fig. 10).

 (a) To execute the short thrust from the high port position, move your lead foot forward while lunging. Your entire body will be extended.

 (b) Complete the extension of your body as your lead foot strikes the ground. During this movement, drive the bayonet with great force in a straight line at your opponent's throat or at an unguarded part of his body. To do this, grasp the rifle firmly with both hands, guiding it with your left hand. Extend your left arm quickly to its full length so that your bayonet darts toward the target. At the instant you are fully extended, hold the comb of the rifle stock inside of, and pressed against, your right forearm. Bend your front knee, lean your body well forward, and straighten your rear leg.

 (c) Look at the point of your opponent's body you are attacking throughout the movement.

 (d) This movement is a short, quick thrust. You do not use the maximum reach or full body weight as in the long thrust. You are not off balance and can quickly follow up with another movement.

(2) *Recovery* (fig. 11). To recover from the short thrust, advance your trailing foot to the rear and slightly to the right of your leading foot. Do not shift the weight of your body or change the position of your arms.

(3) *Withdrawal.* The withdrawal from the short thrust is the same as from the long thrust (fig. 9).

e. *Common Errors.*

(1) "Telegraphing" the thrust by drawing the rifle back just before delivering the thrust.

(2) Thrusting with only your arms. You should also use the power of your legs and body.

(3) Thrusting with a slight slash. This prevents straightforward penetration.

(4) Carrying the point of the bayonet too high or canting the rifle either right or left.

(5) Not bracing the rifle butt against the inside of the right forearm.

(6) Not leaning your body far enough forward.

(7) Taking too long a step, causing you to lose your balance.

(8) Not bending the front knee enough.

(9) Not keeping your eyes on the point of attack.

(10) Moving the rifle forward during recovery instead of holding it steady.

(11) Dropping the rifle butt during recovery.

(12) Not keeping your elbow straight when recovering.

(13) Not using force to withdraw. You should use your legs, the weight of your body, and the strength of your arms to withdraw the bayonet.

(14) Not withdrawing the bayonet straight back. Do not allow the rifle butt to drop.

Figure 10. Short thrust (step one).

Figure 11. Recovery from short thrust (step two).

f. Butt Strokes, Smashes, and Slashes.
  (1) *General.* You will not use the butt strokes, smashes, and slashes in combat when you can use a thrust. However, when there is not enough room to deliver a thrust, or immediately after your enemy has avoided a thrust, butt strokes and slashes can be used to great advantage. This is particularly true for close-in fighting. When using a butt stroke, you can often knee your opponent in the groin, trip him, or kick him on the leg. Butt strokes, smashes, and slashes can be used effectively while fighting in trenches, woods, and brush where your movements are restricted, or after you have missed with a thrust and need to continue the attack.
  (2) *Vertical butt stroke series.*
    (a) *Execution* (fig. 12). In making the vertical butt stroke from the guard position, step in with your rear foot and at the same time drive the rifle butt forward and upward in a vertical arc to your opponent's groin, solar plexus, or chin. Put the force of your body weight into the blow. You may also start the vertical butt stroke from a crouched position and hit low points on your opponent's body. In this position, you make a small, difficult target for your opponent to strike.
    (b) *Smash* (fig. 13). If your opponent moves backward and the vertical butt stroke misses, step forward quickly with your left foot and drive the rifle butt to his head. In doing this, extend your arms full forward and bring your right foot forward, stepping under the rifle to maintain your balance.
    (c) *Slash* (fig. 14). If your opponent falls or jumps out of butt range, continue to advance and slash diagonally downward with the bayonet. Aim the slash toward the junction of his neck and shoulder. Hit either this point or the head, throat, or arms. If the slash misses, it will bring you close to the guard position. Continue the attack aggressively.
  (3) *Horizontal butt stroke series.* In this series, the rifle and bayonet are moved horizontally instead of vertically.
    (a) *Execution* (fig. 15). In making the horizontal butt stroke from the high port position, drive in with force, advancing your rear foot. Swing the rifle butt diagonally through a horizontal arc to your opponent's head or body.
    (b) *Smash* (fig. 16). If the horizontal butt stroke misses because your opponent has moved backward, deliver a smash by stepping forward quickly with your left foot and driving the rifle butt to his head. Keep the rifle butt in the same horizontal position, extend your arms full forward, and bring your right foot forward, stepping under the rifle to maintain your balance.
    (c) *Slash* (fig. 17). If the smash misses, continue the attack with a slash, executing the movement the same as you did for the vertical butt stroke series.

g. Common Errors.
  (1) Not fully reaching out at your opponent.
  (2) Not putting the power of your arms and body weight into the movement.
  (3) Not keeping the plane of your bent right arm behind and parellel to the rifle and bayonet.
  (4) Not using all your speed.

h. Parries.
  (1) *General.* The parry is an offensive blow. You use it to create an opening by moving your opponent's bayonet out of the way. It is made by a forward and lateral movement of great force and speed. Attempt to make blade-to-blade contact, keeping your bayonet pointing directly at your opponent. Use your bayonet in a lateral movement only until your opponent's weapon is driven clear of your body.

Figure 12. Vertical butt stroke (step one).

Figure 18. Smash (step two).

Figure 14. Slash (step three).

Figure 15. Horizontal butt stroke (step one).

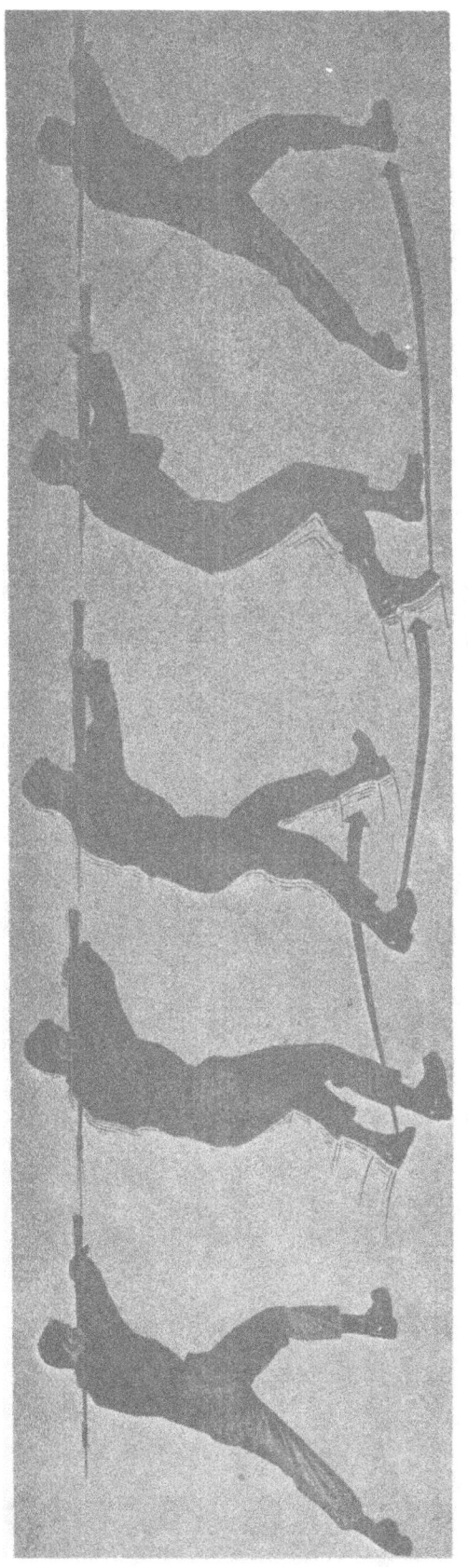

Figure 16. Smash (step two).

Figure 17. Slash (step three).

24

1 Parry right
Figure 18. Parries.

2 Parry right recovery and withdrawal
Figure 18—Continued.

1 Parry left
Figure 19. Parries.

2 Parry left recovery and withdrawal
Figure 19—Continued.

The momentum of the parry carries you into a thrust or butt stroke. The position of your opponent's weapon will determine in what direction you will parry. It is best, however, to make the parry in the direction that will give you an opening, so that you can instantly execute a thrust or butt stroke.

(2) *Parry right* (1, fig. 18).

(a) To parry right from the guard position, lunge forward as in a long thrust and step slightly to the right oblique.

(b) At the same time, thrust your rifle diagonally forward and to the right by straightening your left arm in the direction of the parry. Keep the rifle at the same angle as in the guard position. The comb of the stock is pressed firmly against the underside and inside surface of your right forearm. Your diagonal movement is stopped as soon as you force your opponent's blade clear of your body.

(c) The parry is continued into a long thrust during the same forward step. Your opponent's blade will be forced clear of your body as your bayonet strikes it. At the instant your bayonet glances off the opponent's weapon, drive your blade into him in the same continuous movement.

(d) The recovery from the parry right is the same as in the long thrust series (2, fig. 18).

(e) The withdrawal from the parry right is the same as in the long thrust series (2, fig. 18).

(f) To parry right using a short thrust, execute the same movement as when you use a long thrust. Make the parry as you lunge forward with your leading foot.

(3) *Parry left* (1, fig. 19).

(a) To parry left from the high port position, lunge forward as in the short thrust and step slightly to the left oblique.

(b) At the same time, thrust the rifle forward and to the left so that the butt is approximately in front of your left groin and beside your left knee, deflecting the opponent's bayonet clear of your body.

(c) The parry left is continued into a short thrust during the same forward step. However, if your bayonet point is not on line with your opponent so a thrust can be used effectively, a butt stroke can be used to continue the attack.

(d) The recovery and withdrawal from the parry left is the same as in the short thrust series (2, fig. 19).

i. Common Errors.

(1) Failing to use enough force and speed. This is caused by using your arms alone without the weight and power of your entire body.

(2) Making a wide sweeping movement and slapping your opponent's bayonet out of the way. A forward movement of your rifle is the only movement you can use to insure maximum penetration.

(3) Taking your eyes off your opponent's weapon.

Section IV. ASSAULT COURSE

9. General

The Bayonet Assault Course may be used as a qualification course to test the degree of proficiency of a bayonet fighter. Primarily, the Bayonet Assault Course, used in a course of bayonet training, accomplishes the following:

a. It provides bayonet fighting under conditions approximating combat.

b. It aids in developing speed, strength, endurance, and coordination.

c. It offers a challenge to the determination and willpower which are so essential in combat.

d. It provides a means for establishing good habits in group action and teamwork.

e. It measures skill in bayonet fighting.

f. It provides a means for maintaining skill by continued training and practice after hours.

10. Targets

Different types of targets should be constructed as an aid to training. There are four basic targets that must be used on all qualification courses. These are the thrust, the parry thrust, the parry vertical butt stroke, and the parry horizontal butt stroke targets. Frames and dimensions of these targets and various obstacles are shown in appendix II.

11. Qualification Course

a. Purpose. The qualification course gives the unit commander a means to measure the proficiency of his troops in the technique of bayonet fighting, and it increases esprit de corps within a unit by creating a competitive attitude and by offering special recognition to the men who qualify. It also makes demands on the soldier's speed, accuracy, strength, and endurance that approach the demands made on him in actual bayonet combat.

b. Description.
  (1) Assault courses should be laid out on rough terrain, preferably wooded. The length of the course may vary but should be 300 meters. Natural obstacles, such as streams, ravines, ridges, and thick woods, should be included. Artificial obstacles, such as dirt mounds, craters, wire entanglements, fences, log walls, hurdles, and horizontal ladders, should be added.
  (2) The qualification course consists of the Bayonet Assault Course containing a minimum of eight fixed targets, two each of the four basic targets, and eight obstacles of the type described in appendix II. The course should have sufficient lanes to permit a minimum of one-half of a squad to run the course under the squad, assistant squad, or other designated leader. A sample 10-lane course, showing the placement of targets and obstacles covering 300 meters, is shown in figure 20.

c. Running the Course.
  (1) During the training program, troops should first run the course at a moderate pace and increase their speed as their technique and physical condition develop. The instructor insures that discipline and organized control are maintained. He designates one man in each assaulting group as the leader. The group operates as a team under this leader. The instructor and his assistants will be stationed along the course to observe the methods of attack and to make corrections, when necessary.
  (2) For qualification the soldier takes the prone position back of the starting point. At the command UP, he springs to his feet and, with his weapon at high port, runs toward the first target. He negotiates each obstacle and attacks the targets in turn, insuring as he attacks from the high port that his weapon is deliberately moved through the guard position.

d. Supervisory Personnel. To insure impartial scoring and to maintain high standards for qualification, men who are not members of the company running the course are detailed to act as scorers. The scorers should be detailed well in advance to give the officer in charge time to refresh himself on the subject and, if necessary, to train the scorers. The officer detailed to administer the course should be experienced in bayonet training. His primary duty is to assign a scorer to each target and to insure that the scorer is qualified to grade the men on the execution of the movements for that target. He has overall supervisory responsibility for the scoring. He provides each scorer with scoresheets and totals each man's score for the entire course.

e. Scoring. Since assault courses at different installations may vary as to length and number of targets, it is not practical to prescribe a standard time limit or an invariable number of points for qualification. As a guide, 30 seconds for each 50 meters of a course can be used to establish a time limit. However, the total distance covered should be 300 meters and on short courses you may have to run portions of the course over to cover the required distance and

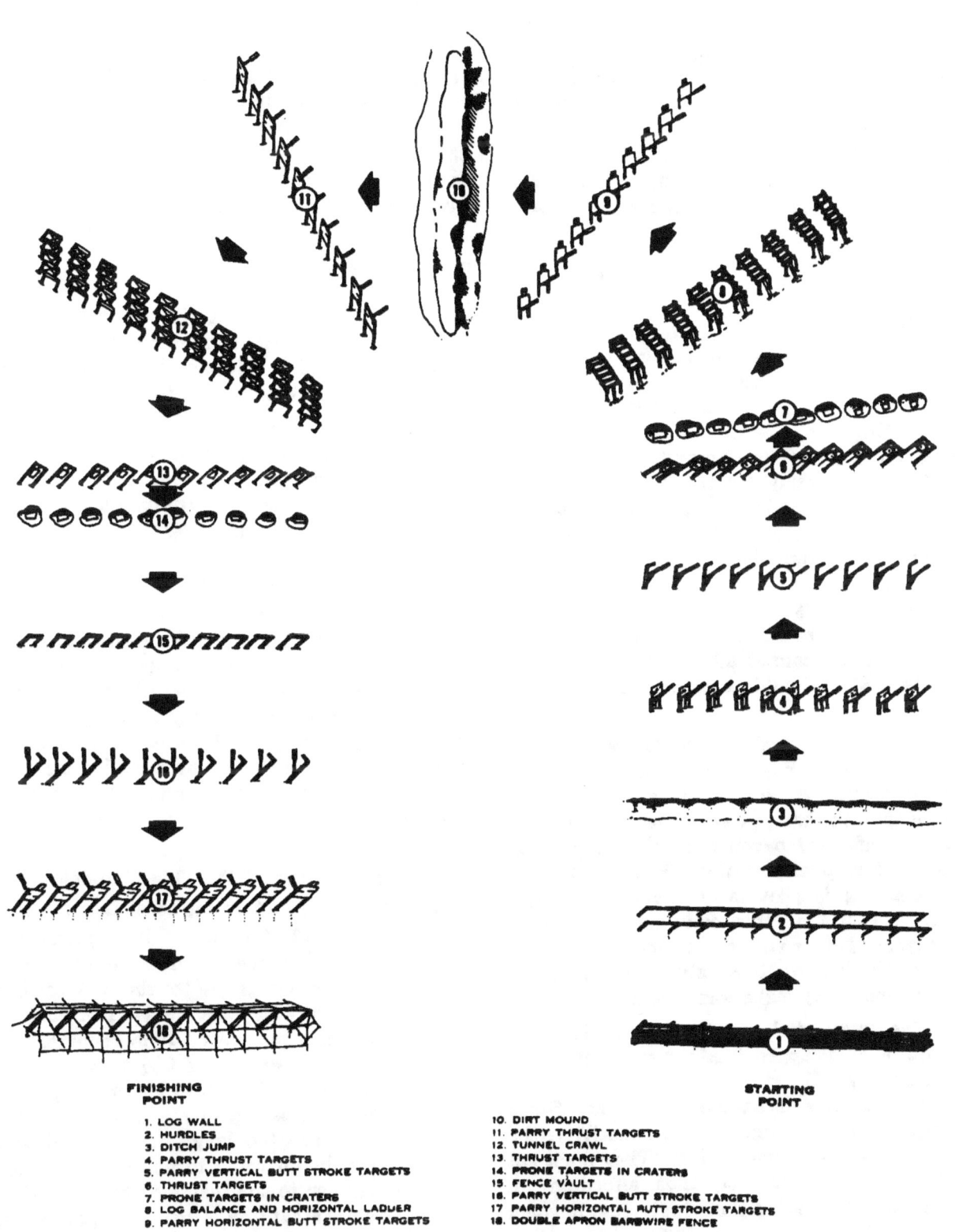

Figure 20. Sample of a 10-lane, 300 meter, Bayonet Assault Course.

attack the desired eight targets. The scoresheet (DA Form 1770-R, "Bayonet Qualification Course Scoresheet") insures a standard scoring system for each fixed target on any assault course. DA Form 1770-R may be reproduced locally on 8- by 5¼-inch paper. To qualify, the soldier must score at least 75 percent of the total possible points and must negotiate the course within the specified time limit. The officer in charge should thoroughly orient each man on all requirements for the qualification course, including the maximum time allowed and the minimum number of points needed to qualify. Sample scoresheets for both qualification scores and Expert Infantry Badge bayonet testing are shown in appendix II.

f. Award. A basic qualification badge with the bayonet bar to indicate expert qualification is awarded to participants who attain the qualifying score of 75 percent.

Section V. PUGIL TRAINING

12. Introduction

a. Until recently bayonet training has lacked realism. The instruction consisted of basic positions and movements, the fundamentals of bayonet fighting, and a practical examination conducted on the Bayonet Assault Course. This training is essential for the combat soldier; however, he has not experienced the realism of an actual bayonet fight. The targets used in training cannot fight back or take evasive action. The only true test of the soldier's skill with the bayonet is vicious, close combat against an armed opponent. Experience is a hard teacher and we cannot afford to learn on the battlefield what should be taught during training.

b. Pugil training is a means of teaching the soldier to use the bayonet with confidence and aggressiveness. After the soldier has become proficient in the basic positions and movements with the rifle and bayonet, he should then be introduced to pugil training. Realism in bayonet training is provided by using the pugil stick. The use of this equipment furnishes the bayonet fighter with an opponent, or target, who can think, move, be evasive, fight back, and (most important) make corrections.

c. The pugil stick, for maximum training benefit, should approximate the length and weight of the M14 rifle with bayonet attached because the stick is handled as a rifle. Since pugil training is a rugged contact activity, the participants must remain alert. They must act and react from instinct, thus affording an opportunity to develop their individual bayonet fighting style. Little or no effort is required on the part of the instructor to motivate the participants; the stick is the motivating force. Much physical benefit is derived from pugil training, as well as developing the aggressive mental spirit so essential if the bayonet fighter is to be successful in combat.

d. Several factors must be considered to gain maximum effectiveness from pugil training. They include protective equipment, training, control, supervision, and safety.

13. Protective Equipment

Protective equipment should allow the soldier to participate without either incurring or fearing injury. Being able to participate without the fear of injury will help the soldier to develop an individual style of fighting and improve his ability to fight with the bayonet. The areas which must be protected include the head and face, groin, and hands. The equipment described below is designed to prevent injuries (fig. 21).

a. Headgear (fig. 22). This includes a football helmet with a stainless steel face mask.

   (1) *Football helmet.* When purchasing these helmets, due consideration should be given to the variation in head size of individuals. For each 100 helmets purchased it is recommended that 10 percent be 6½ to 6¾ in size, 80 percent be 6⅞ to 7⅛ in size, and 10 percent be 7¼ to 7½ in size. Helmets that are too large for an individual can be adjusted to fit by adding foam rubber to the inside of the helmet. A chin strap made of vinyl plastic and foam rubber is used to secure the helmet to the head.

(2) *Face mask.* It is made of ¼-inch round stainless steel rods that are welded together by an electric arc welder. It is attached to the helmet by three leather anchor straps with two flathead copper rivets with washers (fig. 23). The leather anchor straps also serve as shock absorbers, taking some of the shock from a facial blow that would otherwise be absorbed by the back of the neck. A foam rubber mask pad (6½ inches long by 1¾ inches wide, and ¾ of an inch thick) is attached to the lower portion of the mask with two canvas straps that contain metal snaps. This pad serves to absorb shock received in the lower portion of the mask.

b. *Groin Equipment* (fig. 24). The groin is protected by a canvas apron which contains a protective cup of the variety used in athletic competition. It is worn over the outer clothing so that it can be put on and taken off quickly on the training field. Cloth, cotton duck (stock No. 8305-184-2034) is recommended for use in making the apron. Material such as salvaged shelter halves and squad tents may be used provided that the fabric is still durable.

c. *Hand Equipment* (fig. 25). Lacrosse gloves are recommended for use in pugil training. These gloves provide maximum protection for the fingers and joints of the hands and wrists and aid in controlling the stick.

d. *Pugil Stick.*
  (1) *General.* Materials needed for the construction of the pugil stick are shown in figure 26. For further protection, and to provide additional weight to light sticks, the shaft of the pugil stick may be wrapped with sponge or rubber, such as vehicle inner tubes.
  (2) *Construction procedures.* Steps used in the construction of the pugil stick are listed below and shown in figure 27.

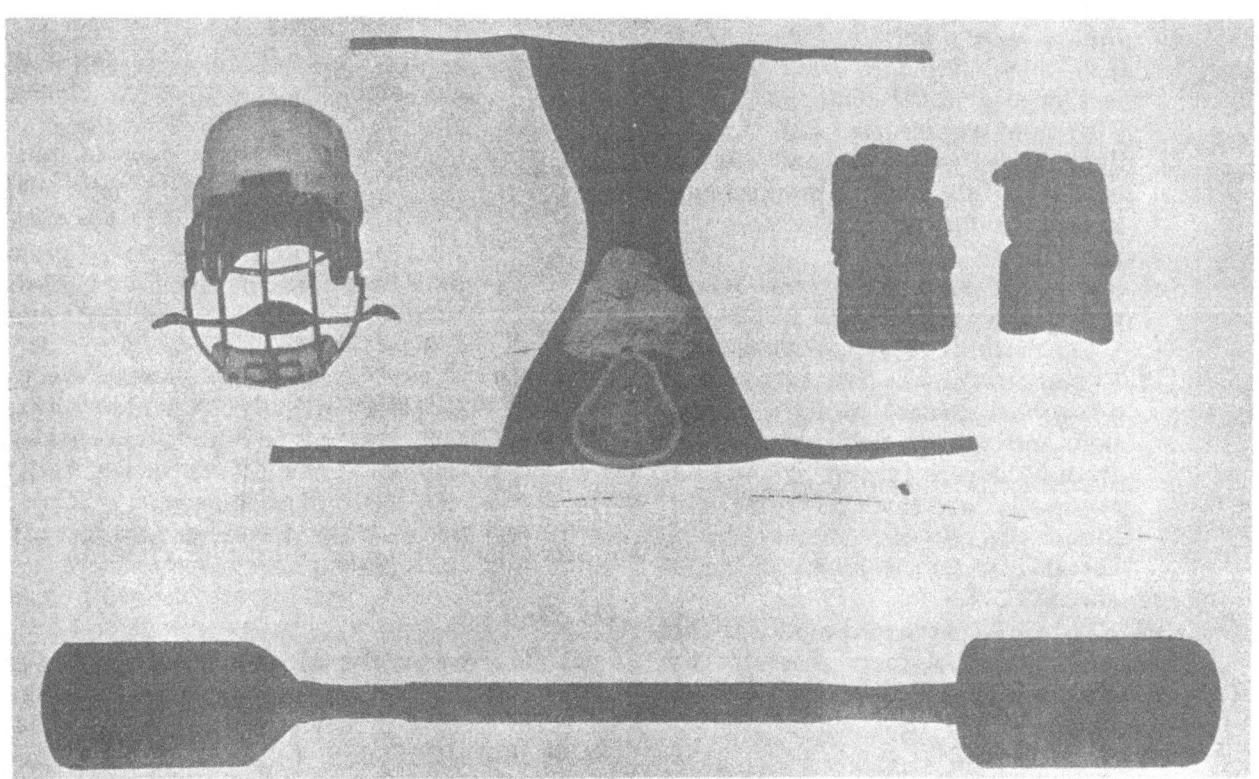

Figure 21. Pugil equipment.

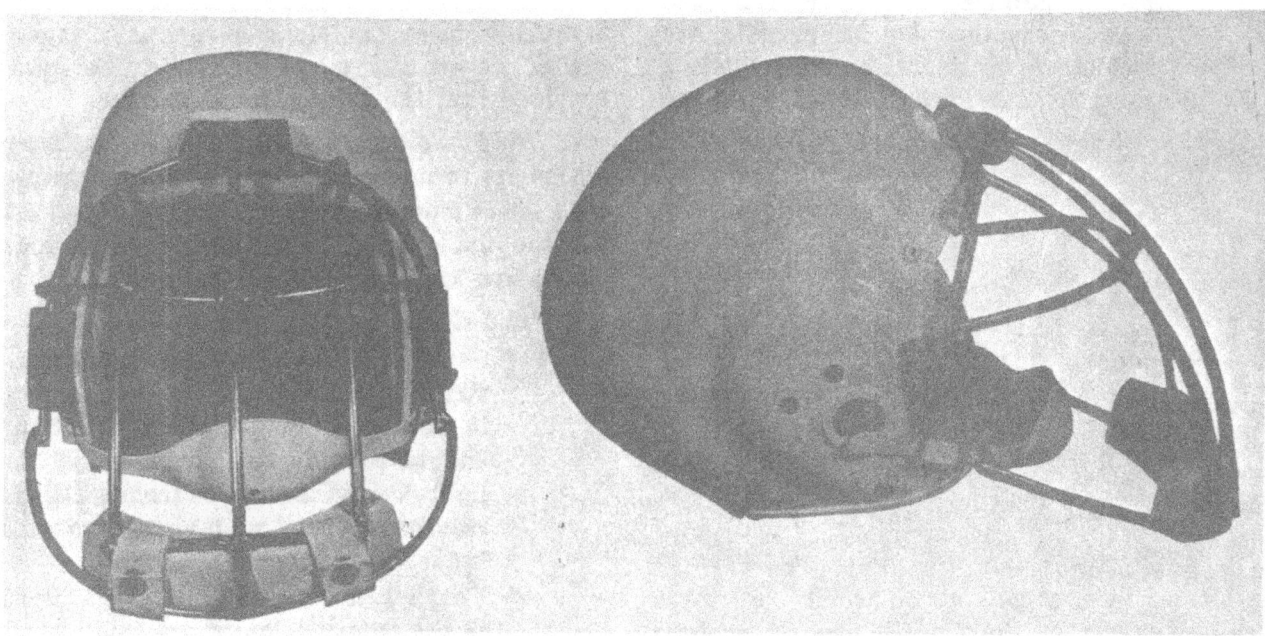

Figure 22. Pugil headgear.

(a) *Step 1.* Shape stick to required dimensions.
(b) *Step 2.* Lay a polyfoam sheet (½-inch thick, 5 inches wide, and 4 feet long) on a flat surface and roll it as tight as possible. Roll two of these pieces and place one roll at each end of the stick. Apply rubber cement to the binding surface as you roll it.
(c) *Step 3.* To prepare the blade end of the stick lay a thick polyfoam sheet (½-inch thick, 1½ feet wide, and 12 feet long), on a flat surface, apply rubber cement to the binding side, and roll as tight as possible around the core formed by the end of the stick and small polyfoam roll. Secure the roll with rubber bands. Let it dry for at least 24 hours (fig. 29).
(d) *Step 4.* To prepare the butt of the stick cut a polyfoam sheet to the tapered dimensions as indicated in figure 27 and then follow step 3c above (fig. 30).
(e) *Step 5.* Construct canvas bags 6 inches in diameter and 14 inches in length. Use the French stitch as shown in figure 27 for added strength in the seams.
(f) *Step 6.* Place the canvas bag over one end of an adjustable sleeve, such as No. 28 gauge sheet metal or stovepipe of the type used in military messhalls. On the opposite end, insert the polyfoam end of the stick (fig. 28). Apply the necessary pressure to the body of the sleeve; push the stick into the canvas bag; and remove the metal sleeve.
(g) *Step 7.* Secure the canvas bag to the stick wtih No. 4 screen tacks. Cut off excess canvas after assembly.
(h) *Step 8.* Cover No. 4 screen tacks with strip of cardboard.
(i) *Step 9.* Cover the strips (cardboard) with black plastic tape.

14. Training

a. The bayonet fighter should be taught the basic positions and movements, as well as the series of followup movements with the rifle, before beginning pugil training. The substitution of the pugil stick for the rifle provides an opportunity to improve skill and test the

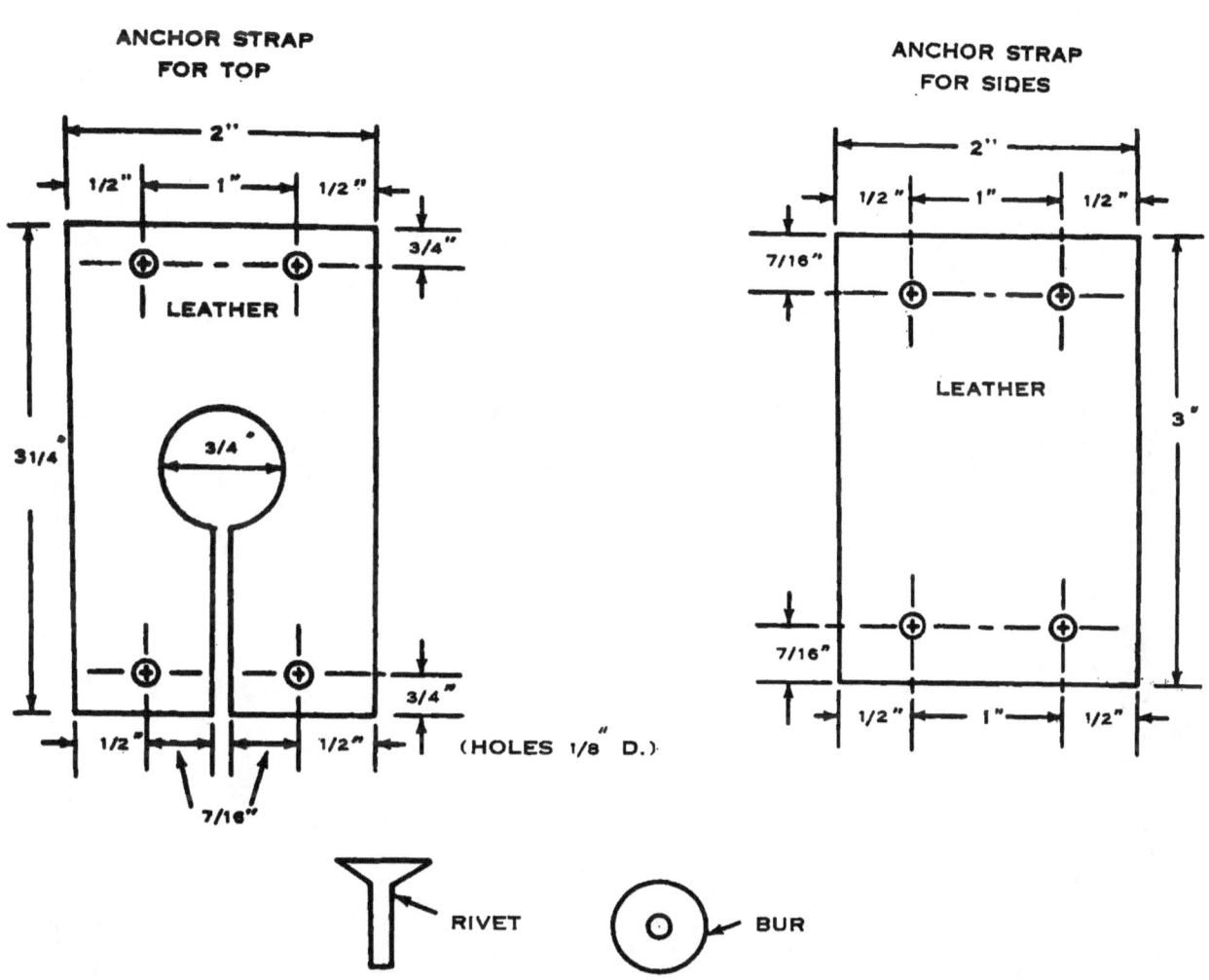

Figure 23. Leather anchor straps for face mask (construction diagram).

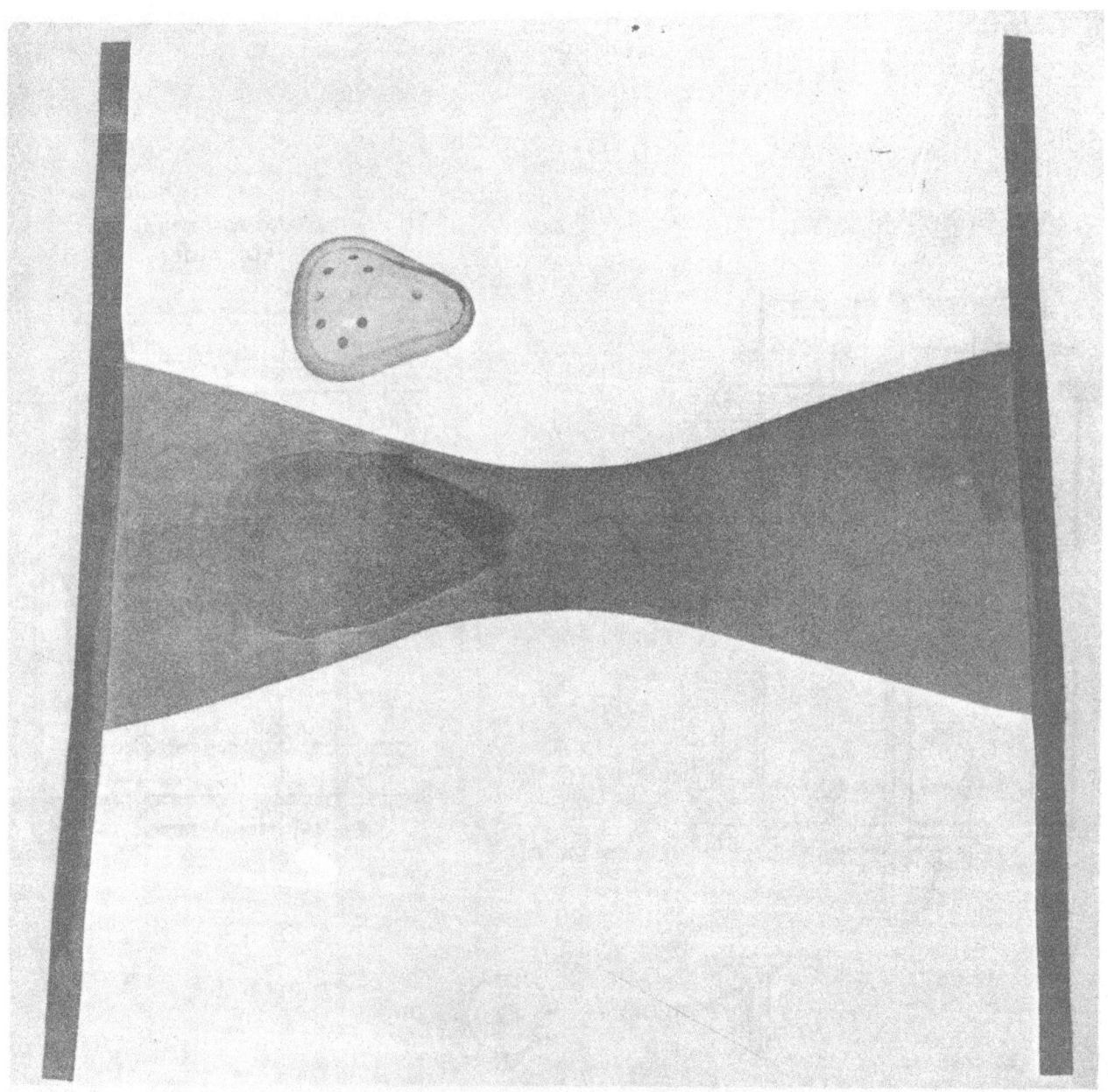

Figure 24. Canvas groin apron and protective cup.

individual's ability to perform against a realistic, evasive target. All positions and movements with the pugil stick are the same as with the rifle with bayonet attached (figs. 31–44).

b. In the early stages of pugil training, maximum benefit is gained by working with platoon-size groups (or smaller) in a circular formation. Two fighters engage in a bout in the center of the circle. Critiques are conducted so that all may learn from observed mistakes. All members of the group should participate in as many bouts as necessary to gain proficiency prior to going on to more advanced training. The platoon forms a circle at double-arm interval. Two contestants and one instructor are in the center. The contestants assume the high port position 12 steps from each other and in the first bout are allowed to move in and "mix it up." This is to show them that the equipment will provide ample protection from a hard blow. After the

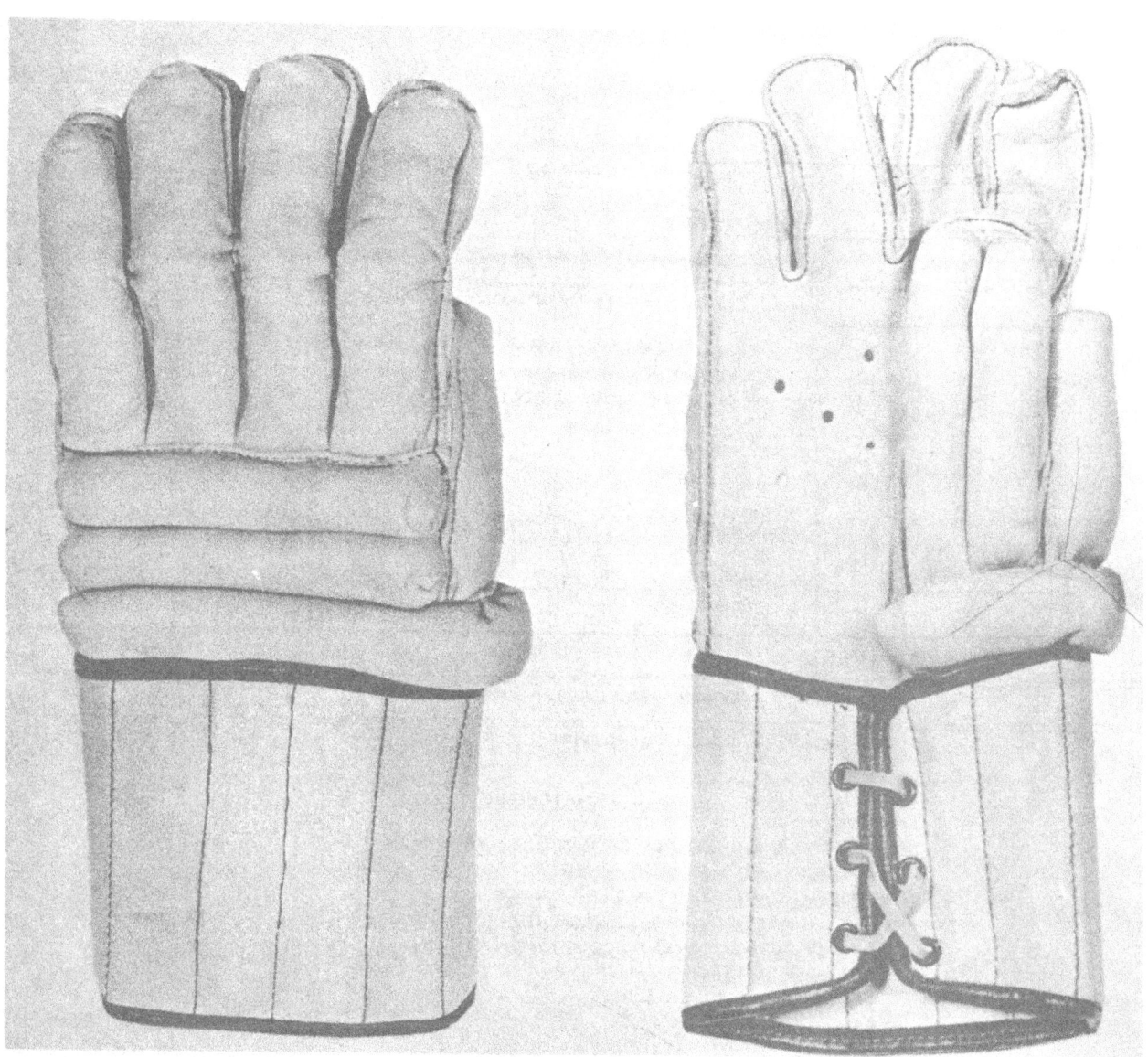

Figure 25. Lacrosse gloves.

initial bouts the instructor conducts graded bouts.

c. During the graded bouts the participants face each other 12 steps apart and each draws a line. The lines serve two purposes. They outline the area in which the bout is to be conducted, and force the nonaggressive contestant to stand and fight rather than withdraw over the boundary and lose the bout. The bout consists of three rounds. The instructor should be in a position where he can best control the bout. To score a point or win a round, a contestant must score a solid blow with either end of the pugil stick to a vulnerable point; e.g., the head, throat, chest, stomach, or groin region. To start the round the instructor blows a whistle and the contestants move toward one another in the attack. A point is awarded to the man striking the first killing blow. The whistle is used to stop the round. The contestants move back to their respective lines and assume the high port position and wait for the signal to start the next round. The contestant that wins two of the three rounds wins the bout.

15. Control, Supervision, and Safety

a. The instructor maintains control of the bout at all times. He is alert to prevent wild swinging with the sticks. Contestants use only the movements that have been taught in bayonet fighting. The instructor constantly observes to detect any loose or broken equipment worn by the contestants during the bout. Immediately upon detection of insecure equipment,

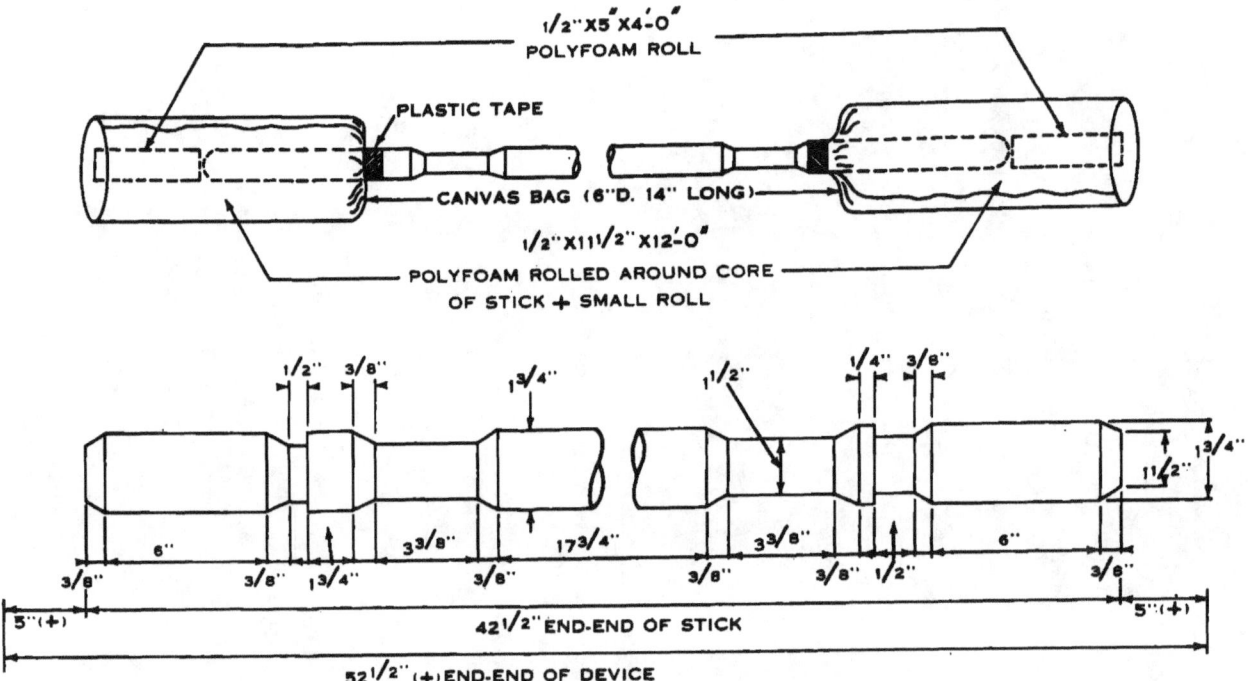

Figure 26. Materials needed for pugil stick construction.

he stops the bout to prevent possible injuries. After the deficiencies have been corrected the round is resumed.

b. The instructor insists that the contestants growl during the bouts; this adds to their aggressiveness and keeps the mouth open, thus lessening the possibility of chipped teeth by blows to the head. A contestant should be encouraged to move in aggressively and attack violently, using either a short or long thrust. If he misses, or his opponent sidesteps, he should follow up with a butt stroke, smash, slash, or another thrust until he has landed a killing blow.

c. Motivation is no problem in pugil training. The soldier who is hesitant to strike his opponent soon tires of being knocked around and will aggressively try to overcome his opponent in the shortest possible time.

d. The bayonet fighter soon learns that if he tries to defend he will always be one step behind his opponent. With the pugil stick, as with the bayonet, the fighter must always take the offensive.

e. One instructor is necessary for each bout. Additional assistance is necessary to supervise the fitting and exchange of equipment. The stick *must* be held in the same manner, and blows delivered, as with the rifle. Do not permit wild swinging of the stick. Insure that the fighters keep their eyes on one another. The instructor must control all bouts at all times;

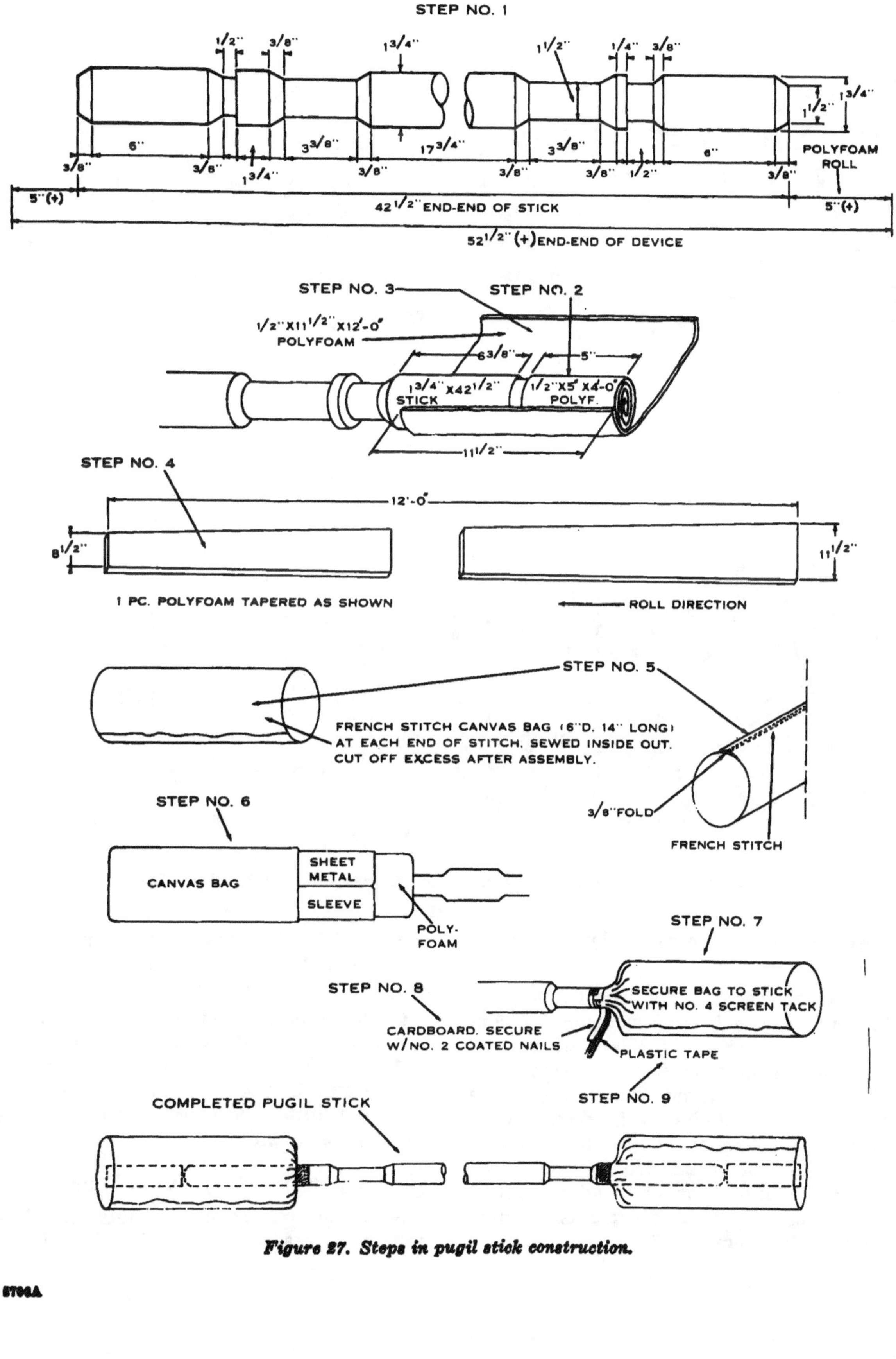

Figure 27. Steps in pugil stick construction.

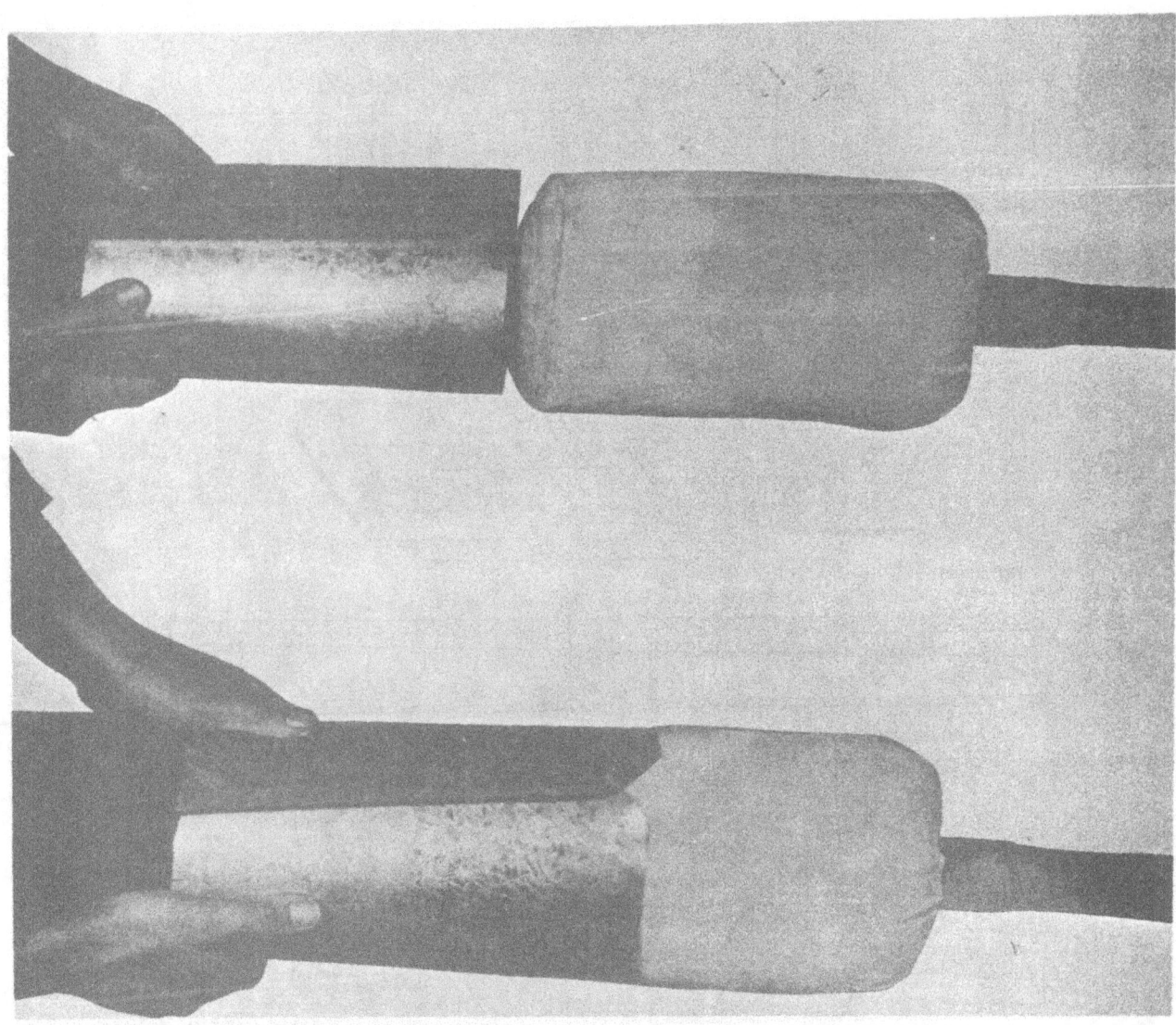

Figure 28. Using metal sleeve to insert polyfoam-covered stick end into bag.

his best method of control is by blowing a whistle.

f. Individuals who have had hernias, frequent headaches, previous brain concussions, recent teeth extractions, or current lacerations containing stitches must be excluded from pugil training for safety reasons. Therefore, before conducting pugil training it is necessary to screen individual medical records to determine if anyone will not be allowed to participate. Insure that your equipment is adequate and properly fitted. Instructors supervising pugil training must understand its values and limitations. Finally, always be alert for the unexpected and if in doubt stop the bout immediately to prevent injury.

g. Competition in pugil training is keen. Due to the nature of the two-man bouts, a squad, platoon, and finally a company champion may be selected. Competition should be encouraged by instructors whenever possible throughout the bayonet training program.

16. Human Thrusting Target Course

After several two-man bouts, the bayonet fighter is ready for the Human Thrusting

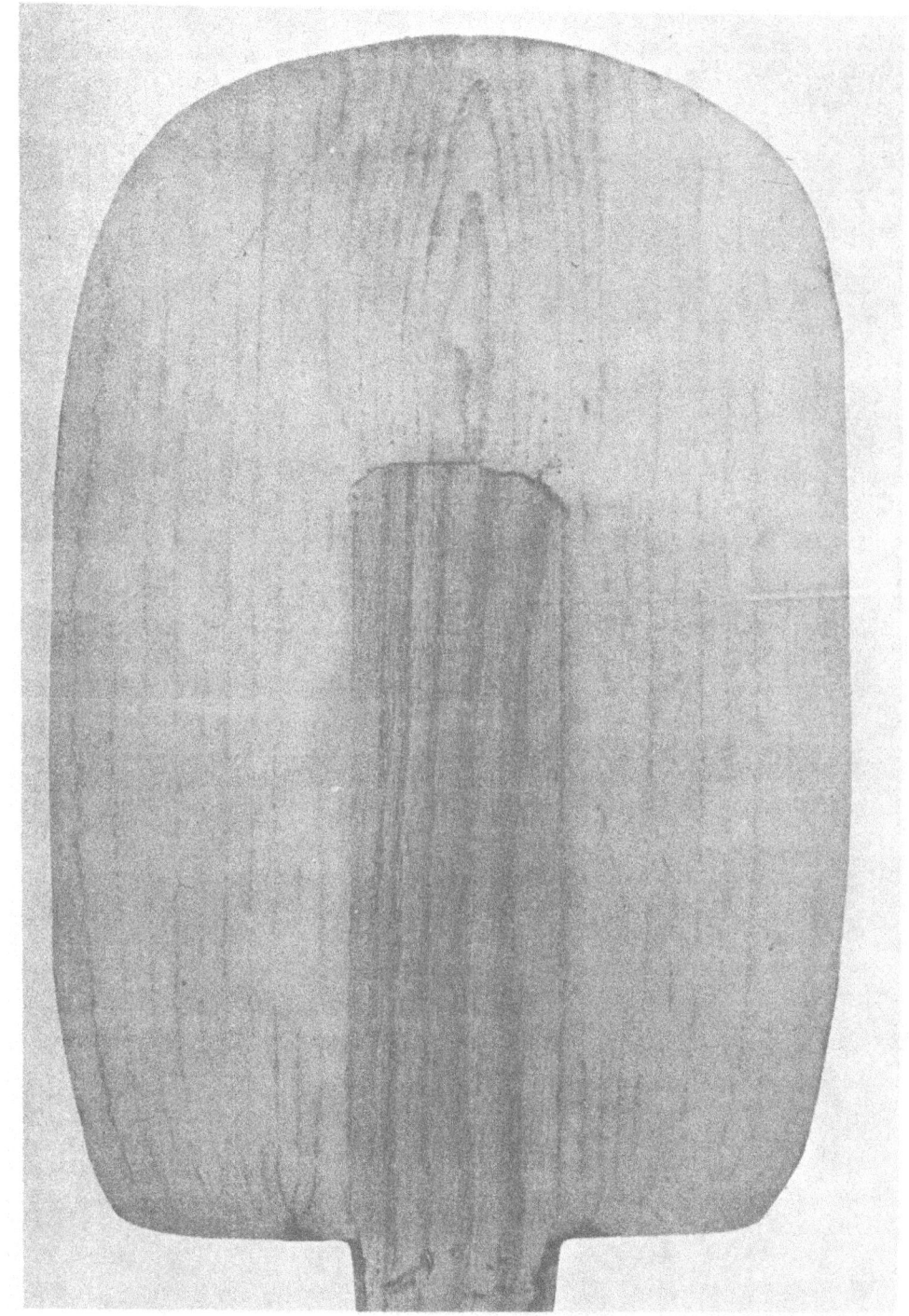

Figure 29. Cross section view of blade end of stick.

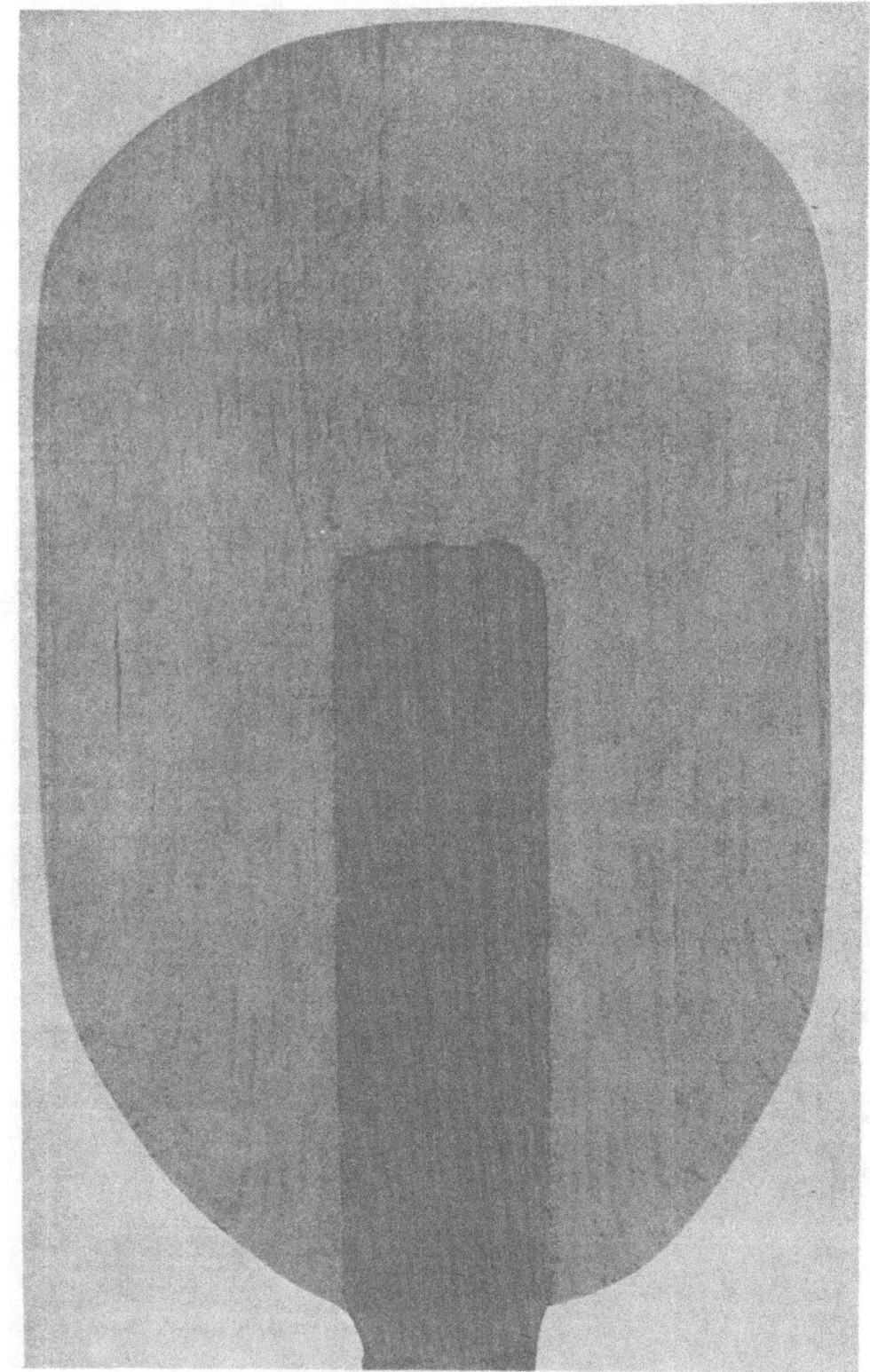

Figure 30. Cross section view of the stick butt.

Figure 31. Positions and movements with pugil stick are the same as with the rifle.

Figure 32. Guard, right side.

Figure 33. Guard, left side.

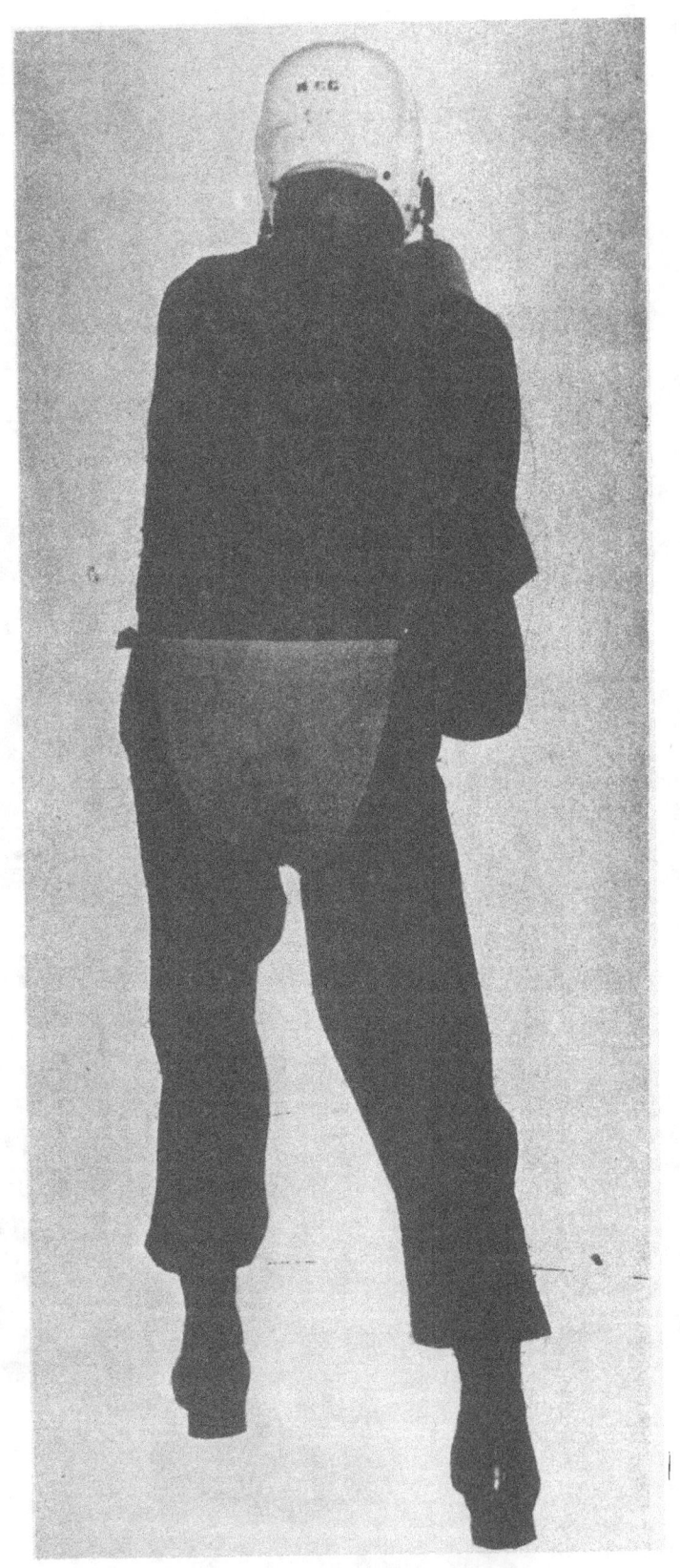

Figure 34. Guard, rear.

Figure 35. Short guard, right side.

Figure 36. High port, front.

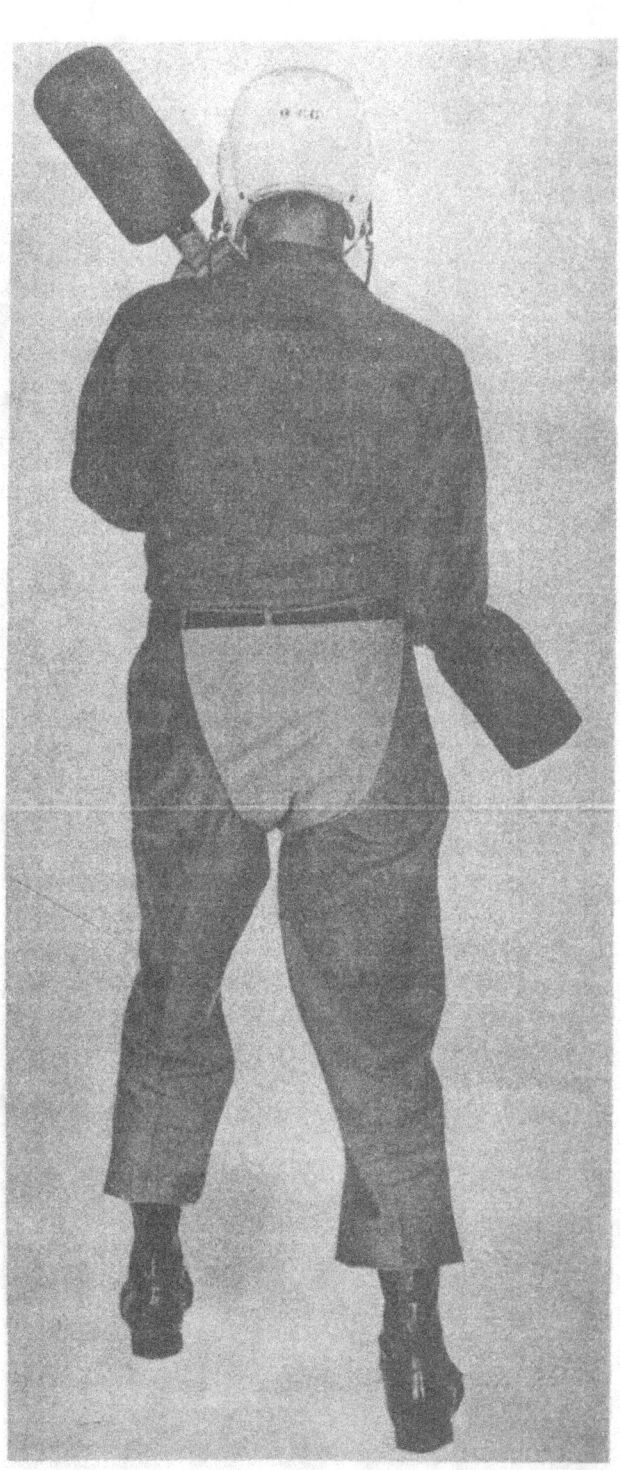

Figure 37. High port, rear.

Figure 38. High port, right side.

Figure 39. At ease.

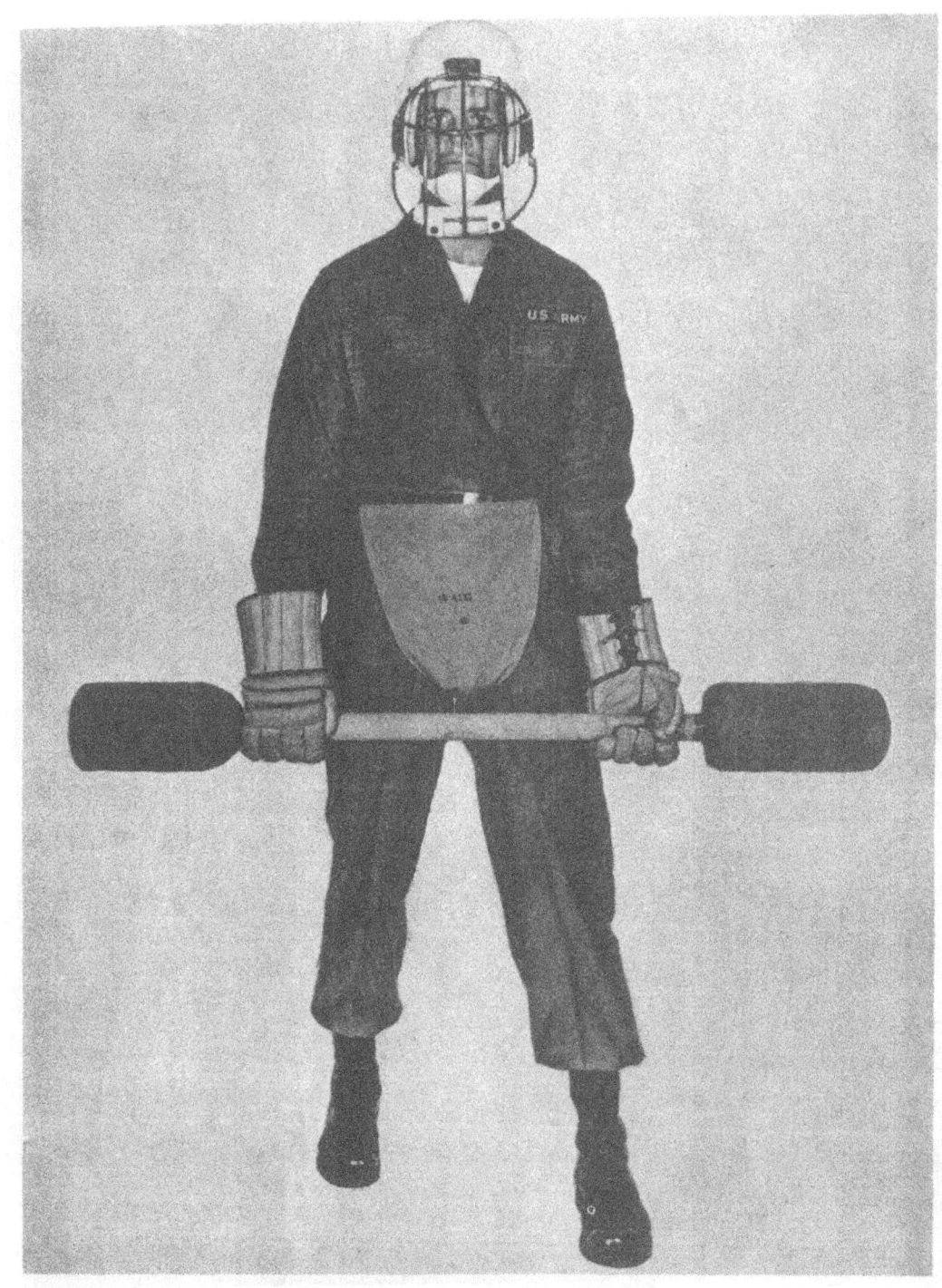

Figure 40. Relax.

Figure 41. Long thrust, right side.

Target Course. Eight to ten men in pugil equipment are lined up in file 12 steps apart. They are designated by the instructor to act as a specific target. The bayonet fighter, also in pugil gear, walks to each human target, moving with the pugil stick at high port. As the bayonet fighter approaches a "target" the "target" shouts the movement the bayonet fighter is to execute; e.g., slash, vertical butt stroke, or short thrust. After the movement the bayonet fighter pauses long enough for the "target" to make corrections, then he moves on to the next "target." The number of "walk-throughs" is dependent on the student's ability to execute the movements correctly. Next he runs the course at full speed, growling and executing the named movements with maximum force against his opponents, the human thrusting targets. Duties are rotated so that all individuals act as fighters and human targets.

17. Human Bayonet Assault Course

A qualification course can be conducted to measure the proficiency of the pugil stick fighter. This course should approximate the Bayonet Assault Course in length, number of targets, obstacles, and terrain. In laying out the course take advantage of natural obstacles such as streams, ditches, hills, and thick woods. Organization and conduct of the Human Bayonet Assault Course is the same as that for the Bayonet Assault Course with soldiers (clad in protective equipment) substituted for the bayonet targets. If a Bayonet Assault Course is available, it can be used by stationing soldiers (clad protectively) in front or to the side of the regular bayonet targets.

Figure 42. Long thrust, left side.

Figure 43. Short thrust, right side.

Figure 44. Short thrust, left side.

Section VI. GROUP ASSAULT TACTICS

18. General

a. When you engage in a bayonet fight you are acting as an individual. Remember, however, that while you are fighting for yourself, teamwork with your teammates may be essential for victory. When you and your teammates assault a position you will not know how many opponents will appear until you get within bayonet range. You will not know whether you will suddenly be attacked by several opponents at the same time, or whether you and your teammates will attack a single opponent. Bayonet fighters who have *teamwork, skill,* and *presence of mind* take quick advantage of any situation to gain numerical superiority. *There is strength in numbers.*

b. If two soldiers who suddenly confront one opponent are able to put him out of action in a few seconds they can quickly turn on another opponent. If you are able to do this in the first critical seconds of an engagement, you may be able to reduce an opposing unit's initial strength by many men. When you gain the numerical advantage, you can usually destroy any opposition in a matter of seconds. If your unit does not have training in team attack, a single opponent can hold off a pair of bayonet fighters for a few seconds. This will give another op-

Figure 45. Approach, two against one.

ponent time to rush in and aid his comrade, thus ending your two-to-one advantage.

c. To be effective, group assault tactics must be simple and flexible. It is impossible to know what the exact situation will be until you and an opponent are within a few paces of one another. Movements must be fast and automatic. You cannot take time in close combat to tell your teammate how to attack.

19. Group Assault Tactics

a. Two Against One. In a coordinated attack the teammate who makes the kill is usually the one who is not closely engaged with the opponent's bayonet. The entire operation is carried out in a few seconds. *The approach, attack, and contact are one continuous assault.*

(1) *Approach* (fig. 45). Let's say that your unit assaults a position and you and a teammate confront a single opponent. You do not know what the man is going to do so you cannot plan a coordinated attack at this time. Therefore, you advance straight forward at a run, but neither you nor your teammate converge on the enemy.

Figure 46. Contact, two against one.

Figure 47. Alternate, two against one.

Figure 12. Approach, three against two.

Figure 49. Contact, three against two.

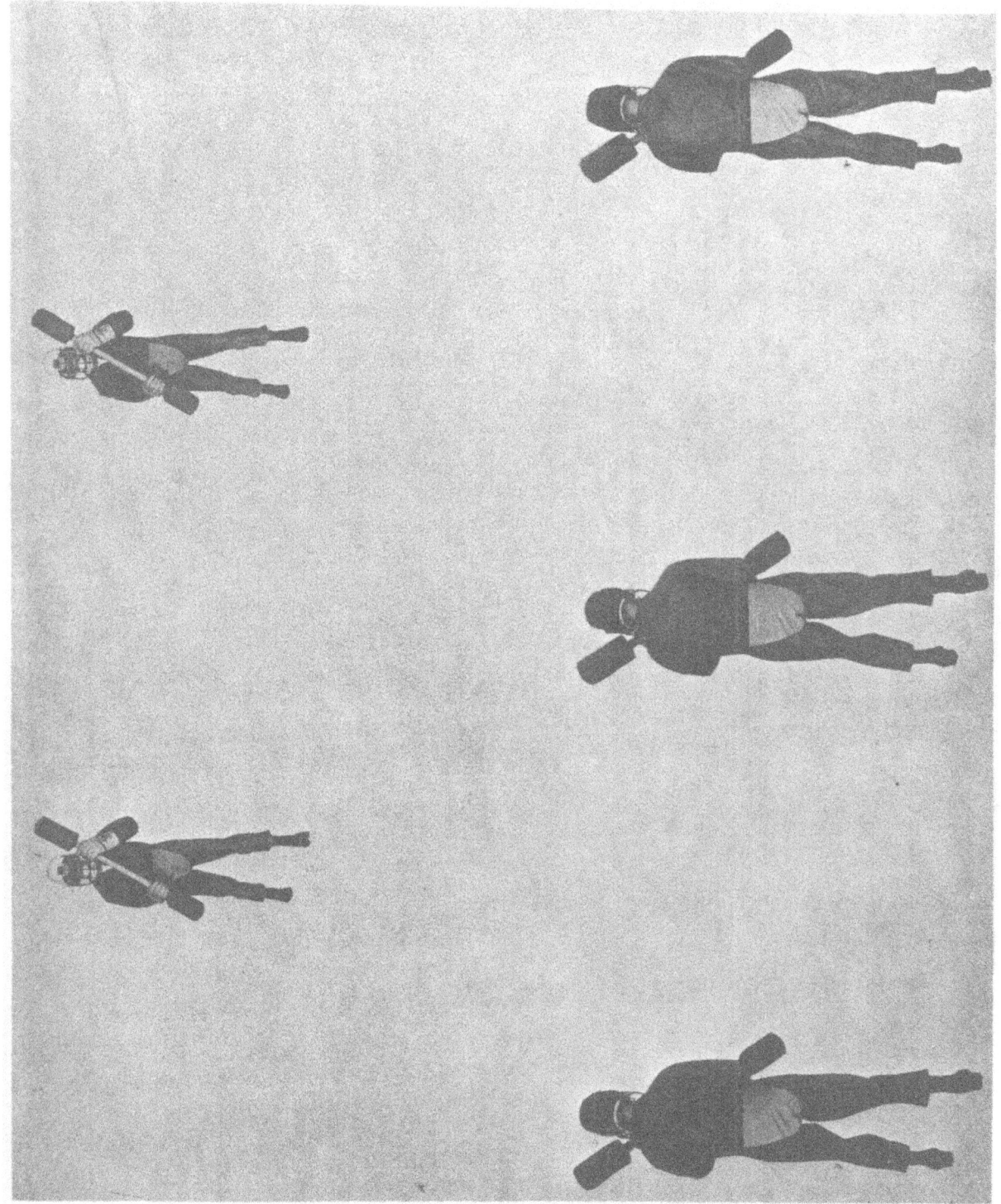

Figure 50. Approach, two against three.

Figure 51. Contact, two against three.

Figure 52. Approach, one against two.

(2) *Contact* (fig. 46). As you and your teammate move forward, you do so by moving slightly to each flank as you approach bayonet range. One of you will be attacked by the opponent. The opponent will advance in a frontal attack; maybe he will engage you. Then your teammate moves quickly until he is opposite the opponent's flank and rapidly strikes the opponent's exposed flank or rear.

(3) *Alternate attack* (fig. 47). If the opponent suddenly turns toward your teammate, he exposes himself to you and you strike instantly.

b. *Three Against Two.*

(1) *Approach* (fig. 48). When three teammates approach two opponents, the

Figure 53. Contact, one against two.

trio does not know which one will be engaged first by the opponents. Therefore, the three teammates move straight forward at a run.

(2) *Contact* (fig. 49). As they get within bayonet range, two of the teammates normally will be engaged by the two opponents. For the moment, one teammate is left free. He continues forward until he is opposite the flank of the nearest opponent. He turns suddenly toward that opponent and strikes him in the exposed side, as in the two-against-one maneuver. The other two teammates maintain their frontal attacks.

(3) *Alternate attack.* When one of the two opponents is killed, the other opponent is stuck in the flank by the first free teammate who can reach him. If either opponent whose flank is being attacked turns to defend himself, he leaves himself open to the teammate making the frontal assault.

c. Two Against Three. When the situation is reversed and you and your teammate are confronted by three opponents, each of you attack a man on the flank, leaving one opponent in the middle (fig. 50). He is attacked immediately after you or your teammate have killed your opponents (fig. 51).

d. One Against Two. When two opponents confront you, dart to the flank of one opponent (fig. 52). Do not permit yourself to be caught between your opponents. By moving quickly to one side or the other, you keep the opponent nearest you between yourself and the opponent farthest from you. Then concentrate on killing one opponent at a time (fig. 53).

CHAPTER 2
HAND-TO-HAND COMBAT

Section I. INTRODUCTION

20. Purpose and Scope

This chapter teaches you hand-to-hand combat. It describes the various blows, throws, holds, takedowns, counters, footwork, armwork, and other maneuvers used to disable or kill an opponent in hand-to-hand fighting. It also explains how to use available objects as weapons. Hand-to-hand combat stresses simple, aggressive tactics. You can subdue an opponent only through offensive measures.

21. Necessity for Training

The average soldier, if trained only in the use of his basic weapon, loses his effectiveness if his weapon fails to fire or if he should lose or break it. With a knowledge of hand-to-hand combat and the confidence and aggressiveness to fight hand-to-hand, the soldier is able to attack and dispose of his opponent. Training in hand-to-hand combat is advantageous for several reasons. It is an excellent physical conditioner and body toughener. It builds a spirit of aggressiveness in the individual soldier and instills the will to fight. It instills confidence in your ability and that of your fellow soldiers. Hand-to-hand combat teaches you the techniques of fighting or defending yourself when unarmed and confronted with an armed opponent. It is valuable for night patrols and other occasions when silence is required. This type fighting is taught to soldiers in rear areas, as well as those in frontline units, because of the threat of infiltration, airborne attacks, and guerrilla warfare.

Section II. FUNDAMENTALS

22. General

Five fundamentals are used as a guide in learning hand-to-hand combat. The fundamentals are: making full use of any available weapon; attacking aggressively by using your maximum strength against your enemy's weakest point; maintaining your balance while knocking your opponent off balance; using an

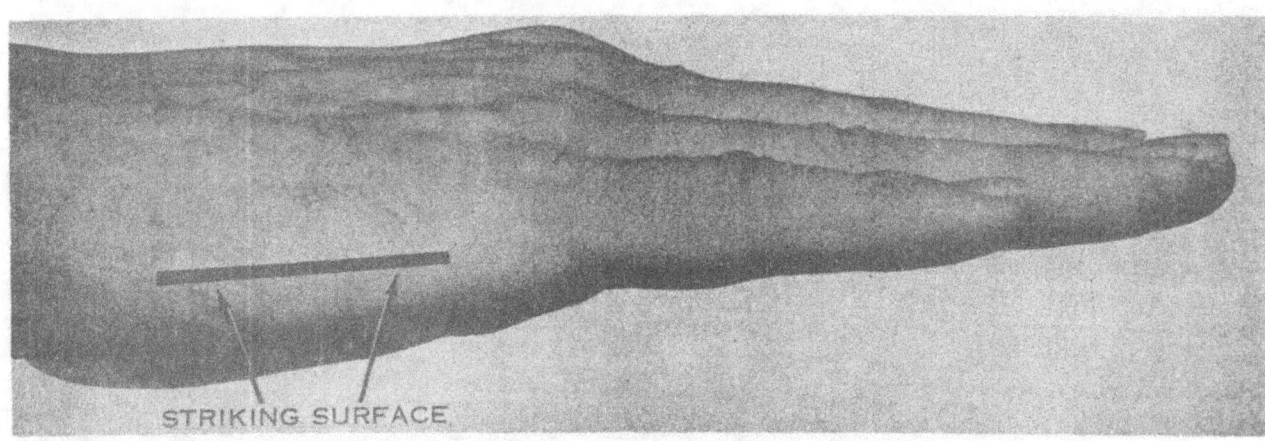

Figure 54. Knife edge of the hand.

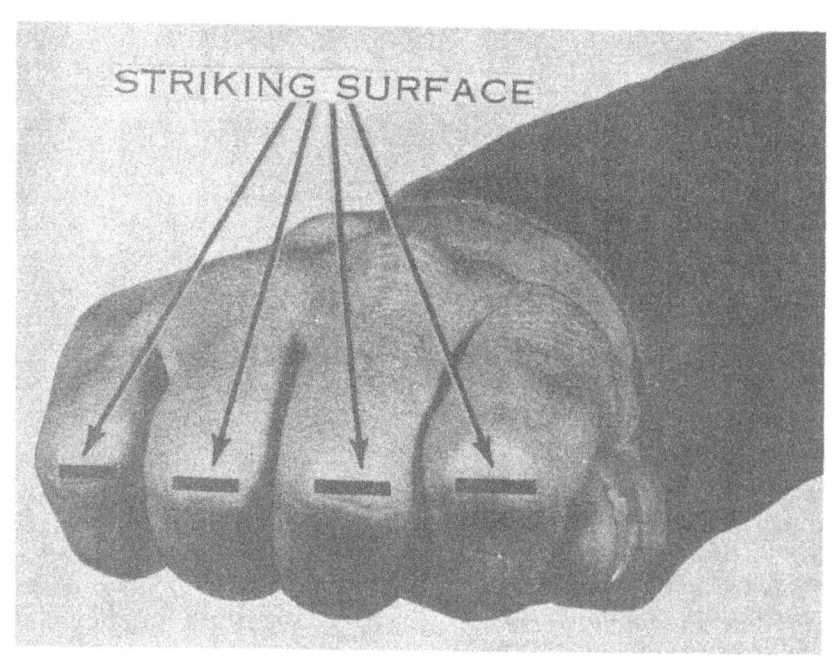

Figure 55. Small fist.

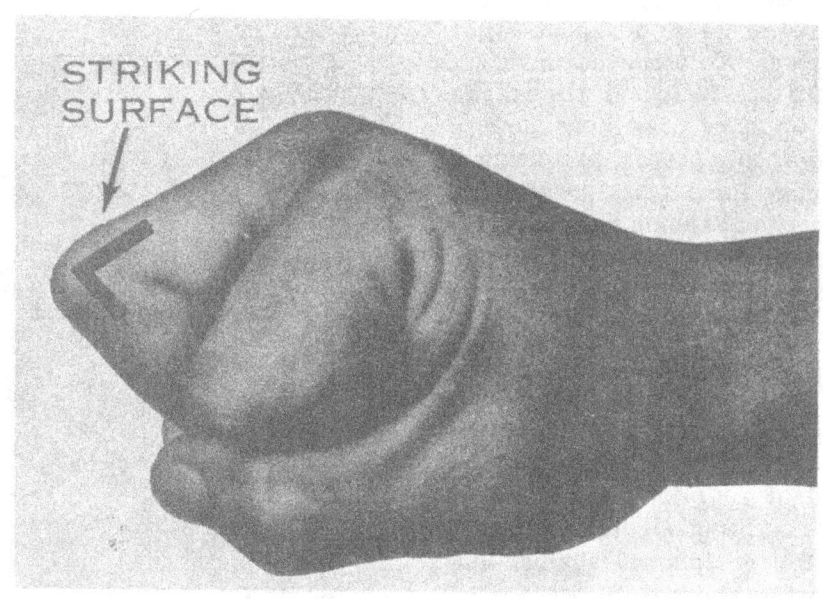

Figure 56. Pointed fist.

opponent's momentum to your advantage; and learning each phase of all the movements precisely and accurately and then attaining speed through constant practice.

23. Using Available Weapons

a. When fighting hand-to-hand, your life is always at stake; therefore, you use any available object as a weapon to help subdue your opponent. You can make your opponent duck or turn aside by throwing sand or dirt in his face or by striking at him with an entrenching tool, a steel helmet, or a web belt. When no object is available, just the pretense of throwing something may cause an opponent to flinch and cover up. When he does this, you must take advantage of his distraction to attack aggressively with one purpose in mind—to kill.

b. If no objects are available to use as a weapon, you must use your natural weapons. These are—

(1) *The knife edge of your hand* (fig. 54). Extend your fingers rigidly so the little-finger edge of your hand is as hard as possible. Keep your thumb alongside your forefinger. Using your hand in this fashion allows you to strike disabling and fatal blows.

(2) *The small fist* (fig. 55). The average fist covers an area of about eight square inches. To form the small fist the fingers are folded at the second knuckles to make a striking surface about two inches square, producing a sharper edge for a more penetrating blow. Keep your thumb pressed tightly against the forefinger to stiffen your hand and keep your wrist straight.

(3) *The pointed fist* (fig. 56). Fold the middle finger at the second knuckle and wedge the second knuckle of the two adjacent fingers into its sides. Keep the end of the thumb over the fingernail of your middle finger and keep your wrist straight. The raised knuckle can be rammed against vulnerable points about the body.

(4) *The padded fist* (fig. 57). When using the little-finger edge of your fist as a weapon, strike blows in the same motion as when using an ice pick. Blows to the temple in this manner can kill an opponent.

(5) *The heel of your hand* (fig. 58). Keep the fingers slightly curled and force the back of your hand toward the wrist to make the heel of your hand as solid as possible. You can deliver a more damaging blow with the heel of your hand than with your fist. The curled fingers can be used effectively to gouge an opponent's eyes or attack other parts of his face.

(6) *Boot kick* (fig. 59). For most kicks, use the outside or inside edge of your boot rather than the toe. This provides a larger striking surface with which to attack small, exposed bony areas. A toe kick may glance off small areas.

(7) *Other.* In addition to natural weapons already mentioned, you can use your knees, elbows, shoulders, head, and teeth to disable an opponent.

Figure 57. Padded fist.

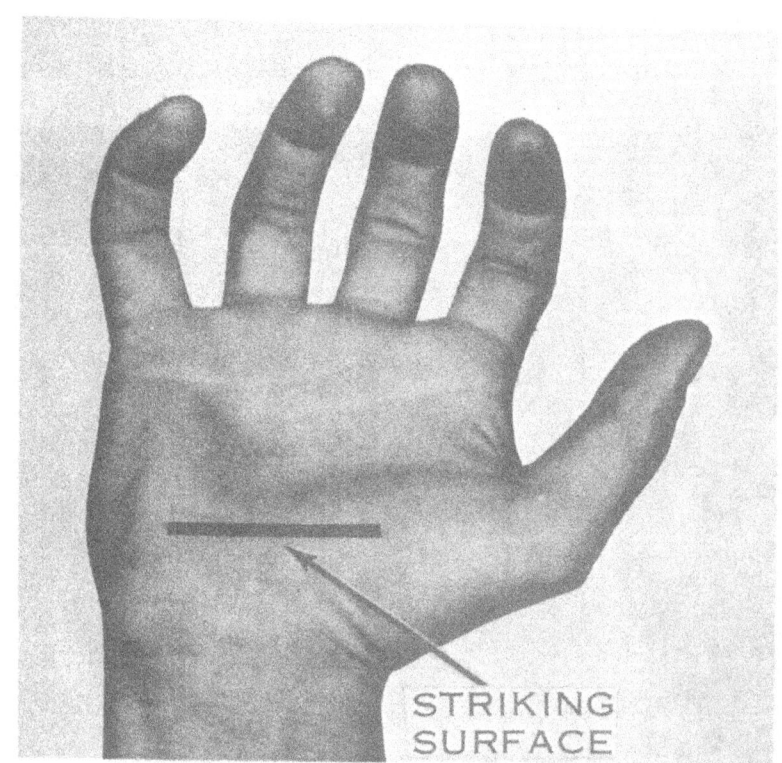

Figure 58. Heel of the hand.

Figure 59. The boot.

Figure 60. The guard position.

24. Maximum Strength Against Weakest Point

Using maximum strength against your opponent's weakest point is an axiom of war that equally applies to combat between individuals. In every situation, some vulnerable area of your opponent is open to attack. By aggressively assaulting these vulnerable areas, using the maximum strength offered by your position, you can gain a quick victory. Attacking rather than defending is the keynote of hand-to-hand combat because only through the use of offensive tactics can you dispose of your opponent.

25. Balance

a. Keeping your balance, while causing your opponent to lose his, is an important essential of successful fighting. Assume the guard position for all-round protection when engaging your opponent (fig. 60). This position is similar to a boxer's crouch and enables you to react rapidly and move in any direction. Spread your feet about shoulder width apart, with your left heel generally on line with your right toe. If you are left handed, reverse this position and bring your left foot behind your right foot. Bend your body forward at the waist and bend the knees slightly. Hold the hands approximately six inches in front of the face with the fingertips at eye level. Use the knife edge of your hands with the palms facing inward. Face your opponent. The guard position is the best balanced position you can obtain before closing with your opponent. You will improve your sense of balance and learn to knock your opponent off balance by practicing the maneuvers presented in this manual.

b. When fighting, keep your feet spread laterally to maintain balance. Try to disrupt your opponent's mental balance by growling and yelling as you strike at him.

26. Momentum

Using your opponent's momentum to your own advantage is another fundamental. Always assume that your opponent is stronger than you and never oppose him directly in a test of strength. Instead, utilize his momentum and strength to overcome him. Examples of using your opponent's momentum include tripping him, stepping aside as he rushes you, or ducking his blow.

27. Accuracy and Speed

You will have little time to stop and think when engaging in hand-to-hand combat; therefore, your actions must be automatic. At the beginning, learn each phase of each movement accurately, stressing precision. As you progress, work for speed through constant practice. Speed is essential to the successful employment of most of the maneuvers outlined in this manual.

Section III. VULNERABLE POINTS

28. General

a. Vulnerable points are areas of the body that are particularly susceptible to blows or pressure. Knowledge of these points and how to attack them, plus aggressiveness and confidence, will enable you to attack and quickly disable or kill an opponent in hand-to-hand combat.

b. When you are attacking an opponent your first reaction normally is to strike him on the jaw with your fist. This is one of the poorest ways to fight. A better attack is to strike your opponent on one of the vulnerable parts of his body. These actions must be performed without hesitation and aggressively.

29. Body Regions

The body is divided into three regions: the head and neck, the trunk, and the limbs. The major vulnerable points (fig. 61) of each region are listed below.

Head and Neck	*Trunk*	*Limbs*
Ears	Collarbone	Fingers
Temple	Armpit	Wrist
Eyes	Solar plexus	Elbow
Nose	Stomach	Shoulder
Upper lip	Groin	Knee
Chin	Floating ribs	Ankle
Adam's apple	Kidney	Instep
Base of throat	Spine	
Side of neck		
Nape of neck		

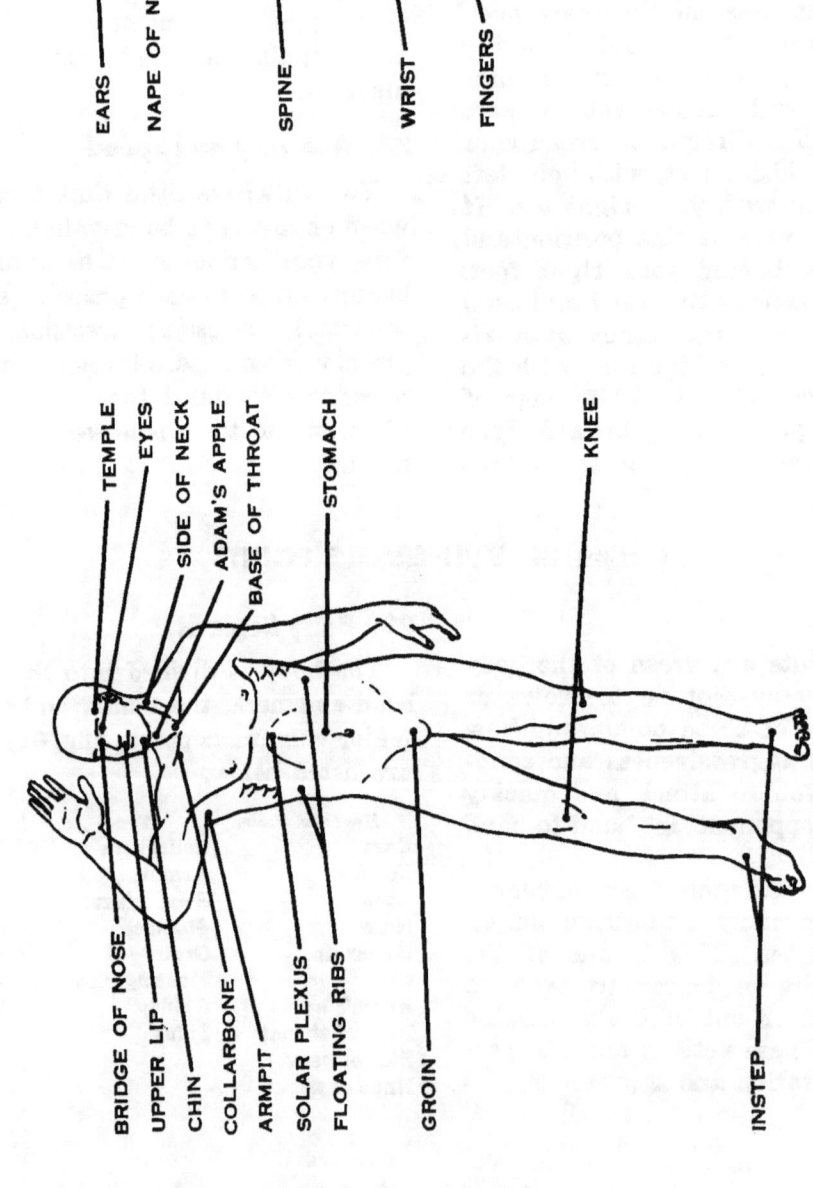

Figure 61. Vulnerable parts of the body.

30. Caution

Only a small amount of pressure or a light blow is needed to injure or kill a man when attacking some of the vulnerable points. It is important, therefore, to strike very light blows in training when learning how to attack these points. When thoroughly trained, you may add a little more force to your blows; but remember the vulnerability of the area being attacked in order not to injure your training partner.

31. Attacking the Head and Neck Region

a. Ears. Cup your hands and clap them simultaneously over your opponent's ears (fig. 62). This is a dangerous blow and may burst his eardrums, cause nerve shock, or result in possible internal bleeding. A sharp enough blow can cause a brain concussion or death.

Figure 62. Clapping cupped hands over an opponent's ears.

b. *Temple.* A blow to the temple can kill or cause a concussion (fig. 63). The bone structure at this spot is weak and an artery and a large nerve lie close to the skin. Attack the temple with the knife edge of your hand or with the padded fist. A jab with the point of your elbow can also be used. If you succeed in knocking your opponent down, kick him on the temple with the toe of your boot.

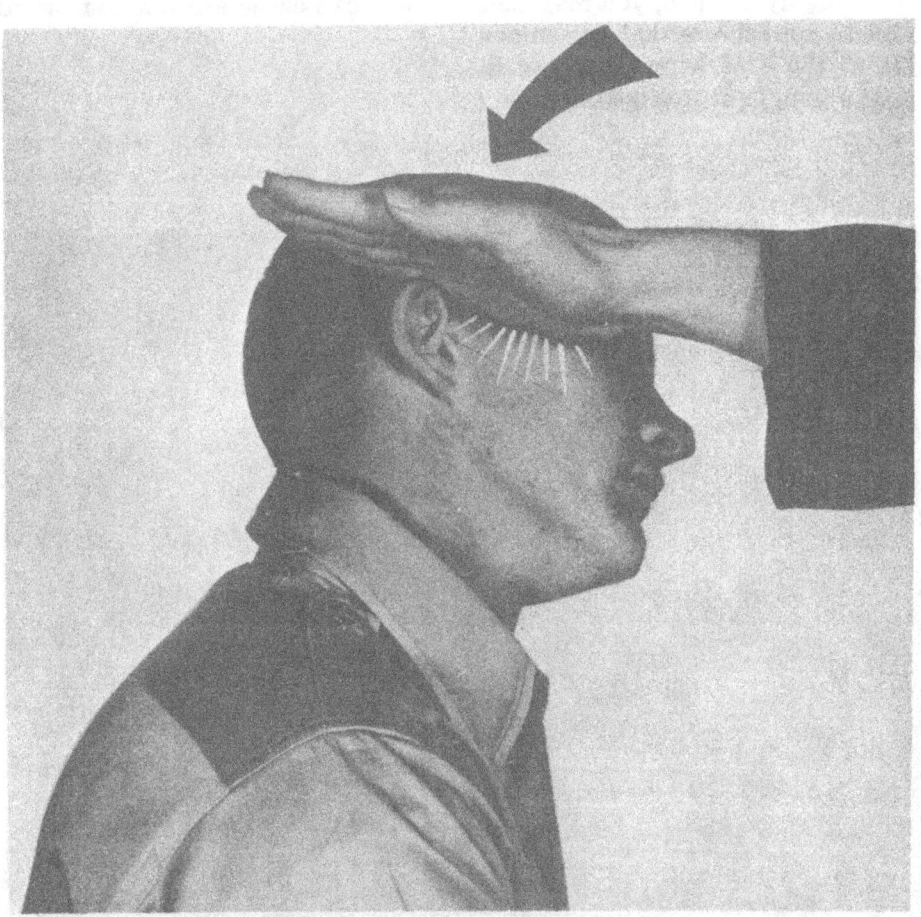

Figure 63. The temple is a weak point.

c. Eyes. There are various ways to blind an opponent. One is to form your index and middle fingers into a V and drive them into your opponent's eyes (fig. 64). Keep your fingers stiff and your wrist stiff. You can also use the knuckles (second row) of two adjacent fingers in a sharp thrust at the eyes. The eyes can be gouged out by using your thumbs or fingers.

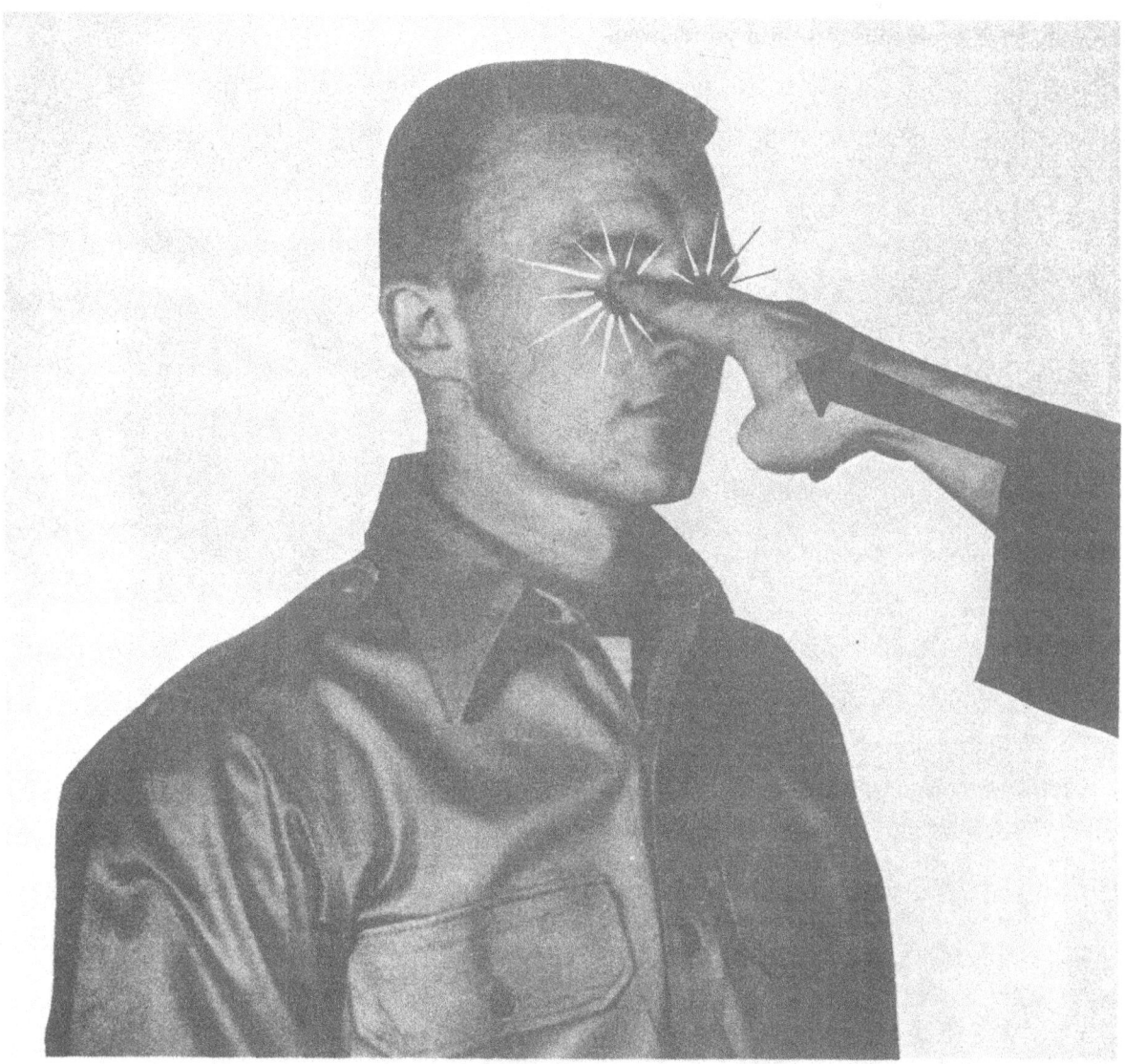

Figure 64. Fingertips forcefully driven into an opponent's eyes can blind him.

d. Nose. When attacking the nose, strike a forceful blow with the knife edge of your hand across the bridge (fig. 65). This blow can break the thin bone, causing your opponent extreme pain and temporary blindness. A very sharp blow could drive bone splinters into your opponent's brain and kill him instantly. You can also use the outside edge of your closed fist. When fighting at close quarters, attack the nose by hitting the bottom of it an upward blow with the heel of your hand.

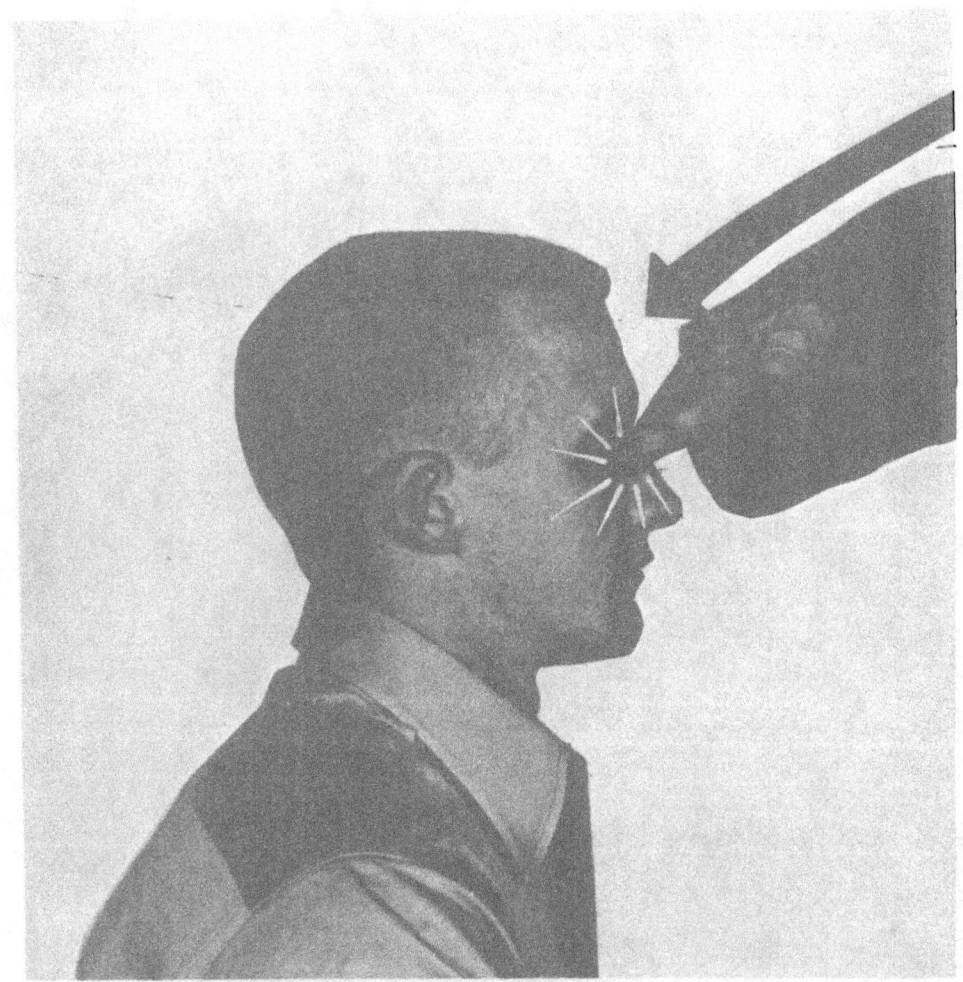

Figure 65. A hard blow on the bridge of an opponent's nose can disable him.

e. Upper Lip. A vulnerable part of the face is the upper lip where the nose cartilage joins the bone. The nerves here are close to the skin. This area can be attacked by delivering a sharp blow with the knife edge of your hand at a slightly upward angle (fig. 66). A very sharp blow can cause unconsciousness. A lesser blow causes extreme pain. A jab with the small fist can also be used.

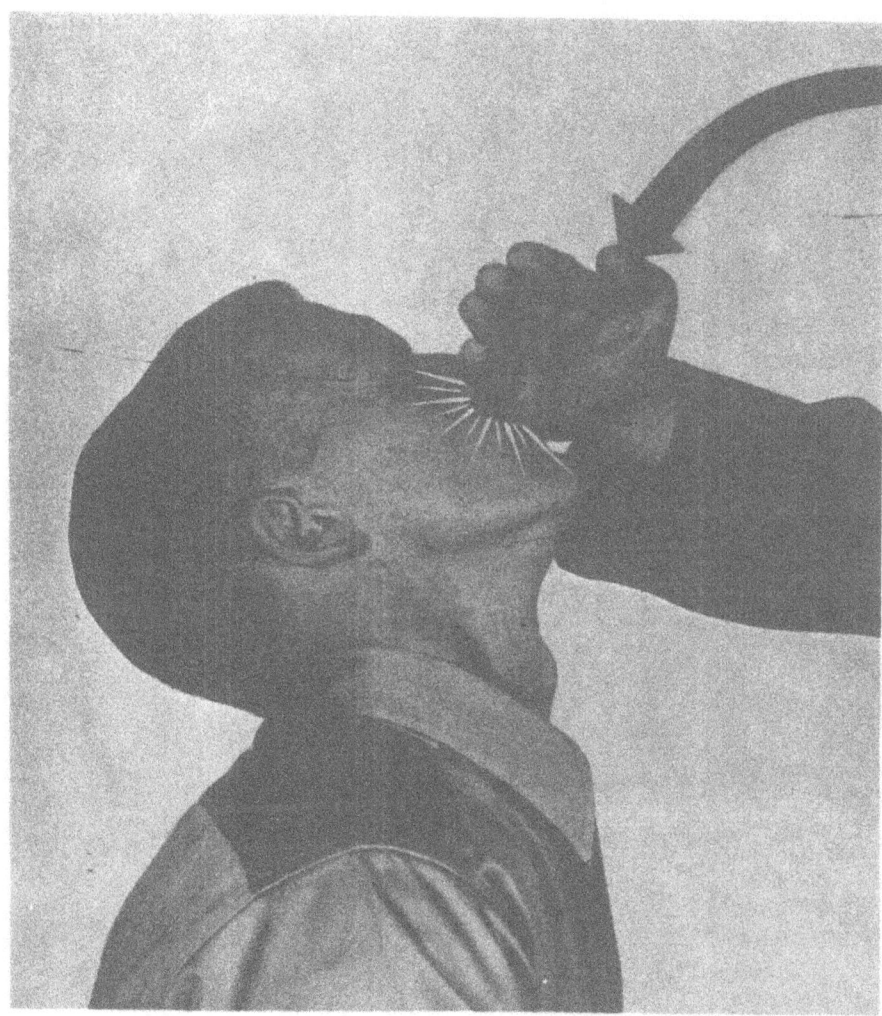

Figure 66. The upper lip is a sensitive area.

f. Chin. An effective blow can be delivered to your opponent's chin with the heel of your hand (fig. 67), which is better than the fist. You may break a bone in your hand by using your fist.

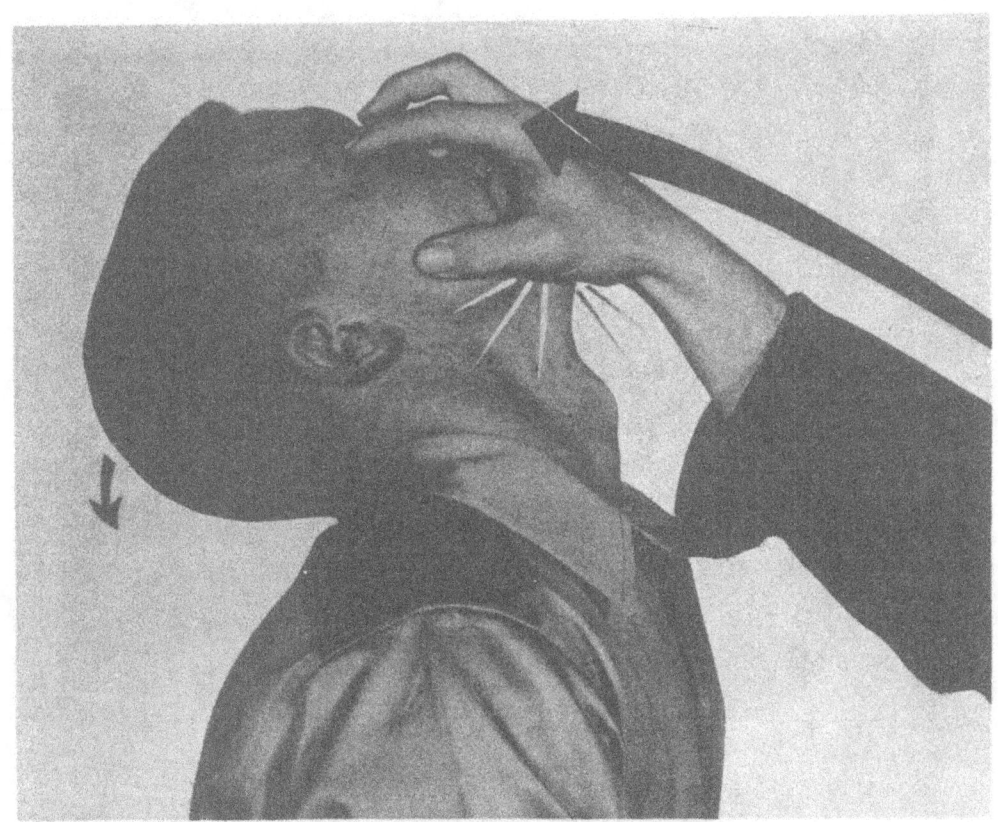

Figure 67. Attacking the chin with the heel of the hand.

g. Adam's Apple. Attack the Adam's apple with the knife edge of your hand (fig. 68). A severe blow can result in death by severing the windpipe. A lesser blow is painful and causes your opponent to gag. The Adam's apple is also vulnerable to attack with the fist, toe, or knee, depending upon your opponent's position. Squeezing it or pulling it outward with the fingers and thumb is another effective method of attack.

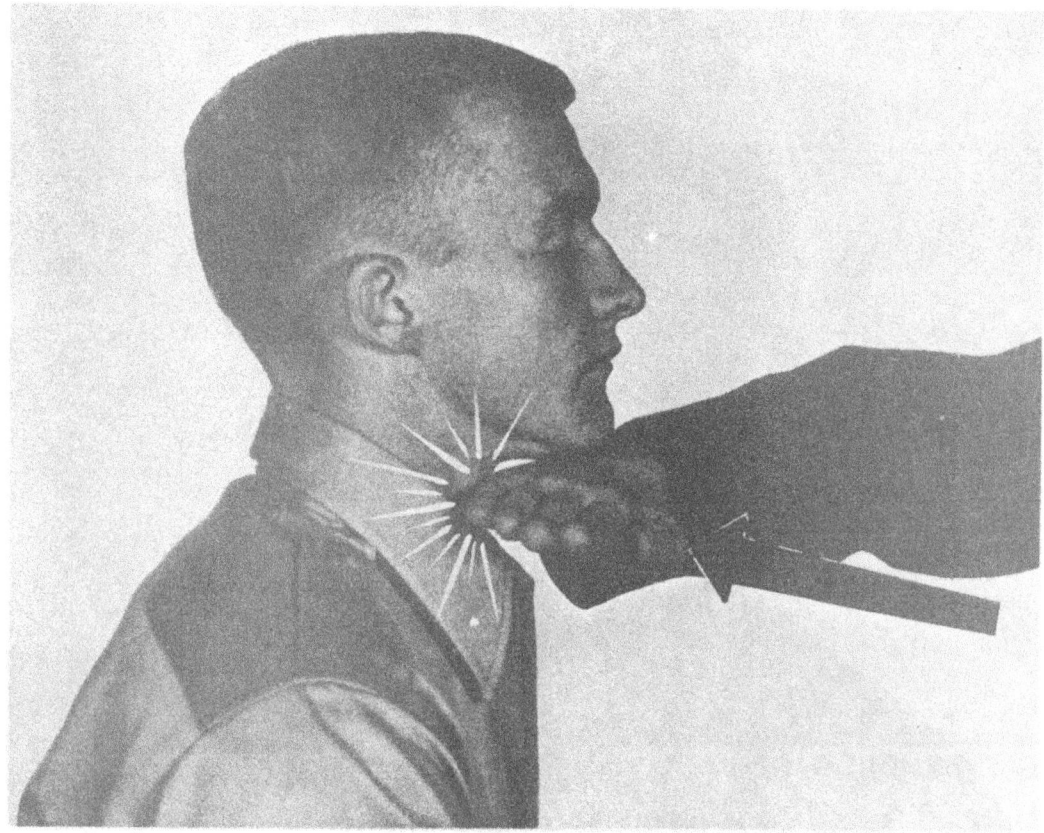

Figure 68. Attacking the Adam's apple.

h. Base of the Throat. One way to break an opponent's hold on you is to quickly thrust one or two extended fingers into the small indentation at the base of his throat (fig. 69). The blow is painful and causes him to gag and cough. Severe injury could result if the thin layer of skin at this point is pierced.

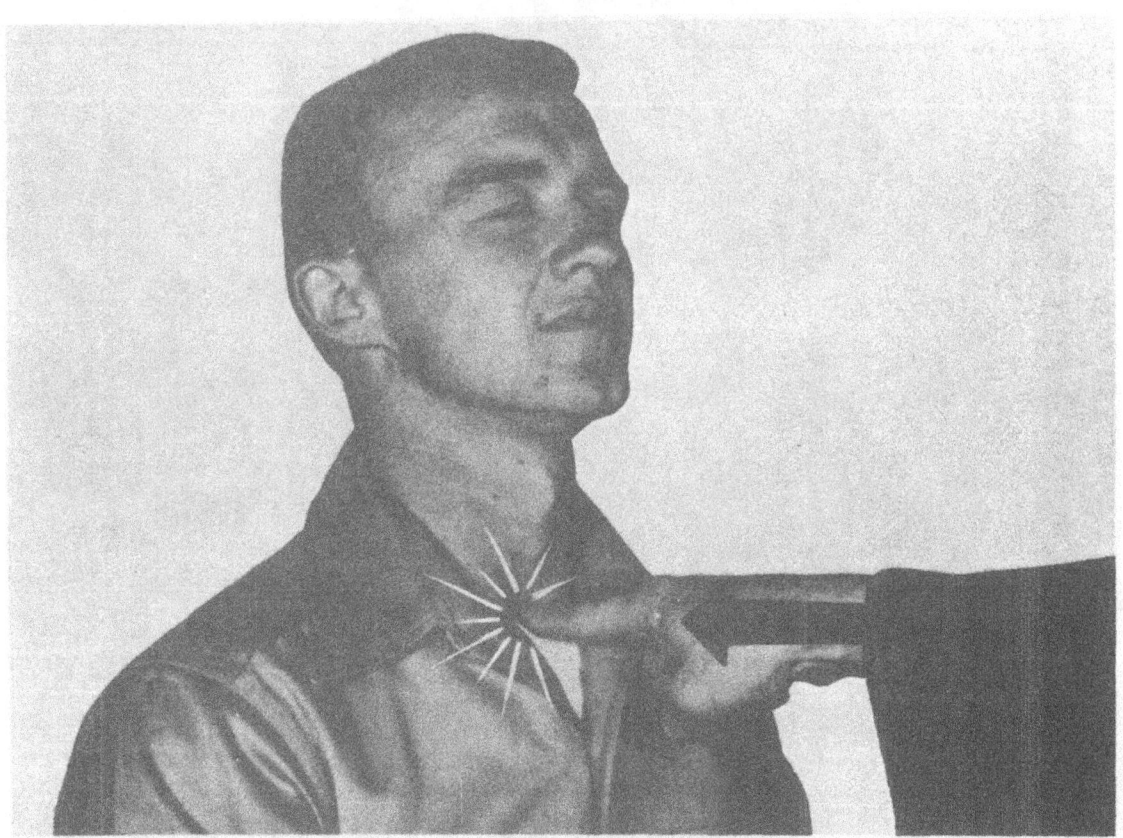

Figure 69. Attacking the base of the throat.

i. Side of the Neck. One way to knock your opponent unconscious is to deliver a sharp blow with the knife edge of your hand to the side of the neck, below and slightly to the front of the ear (fig. 70). You can deliver the blow in two ways: a backhand delivery with the palm down; or a forward slash with the palm up. This type blow causes unconsciousness by shock produced when the jugular vein, the carotid artery, and vagus nerve are struck. It is not particularly dangerous.

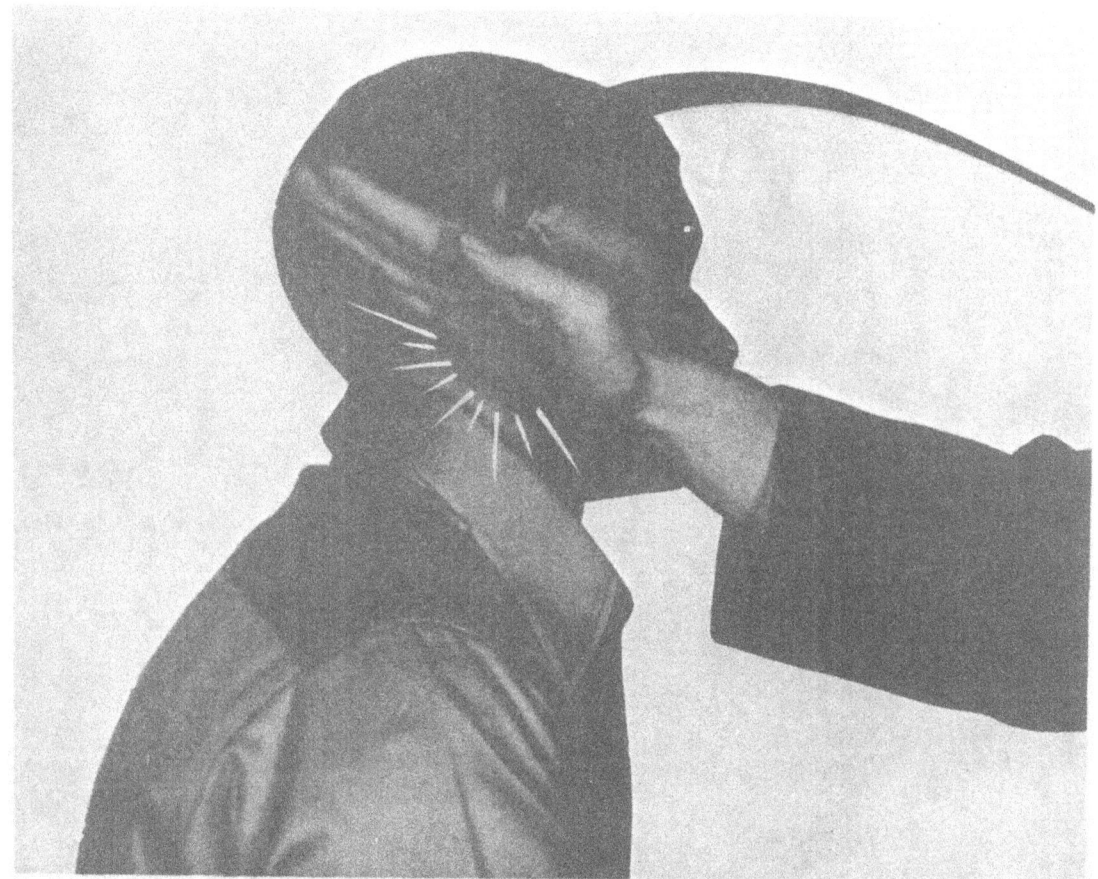

Figure 70. Attacking the side of the neck.

j. Nape of the Neck. A blow with the knife edge of your hand to your opponent's nape (rabbit punch) could kill him by breaking his neck (fig. 71). The outside edge of your fist can also be used. Use this blow if your opponent charges low and his hands are not guarding the upper regions of his body. If you succeed in knocking your opponent down kick his nape with the toe of your boot, stomp it with your boot heel, or strike it with the knife edge of your hand.

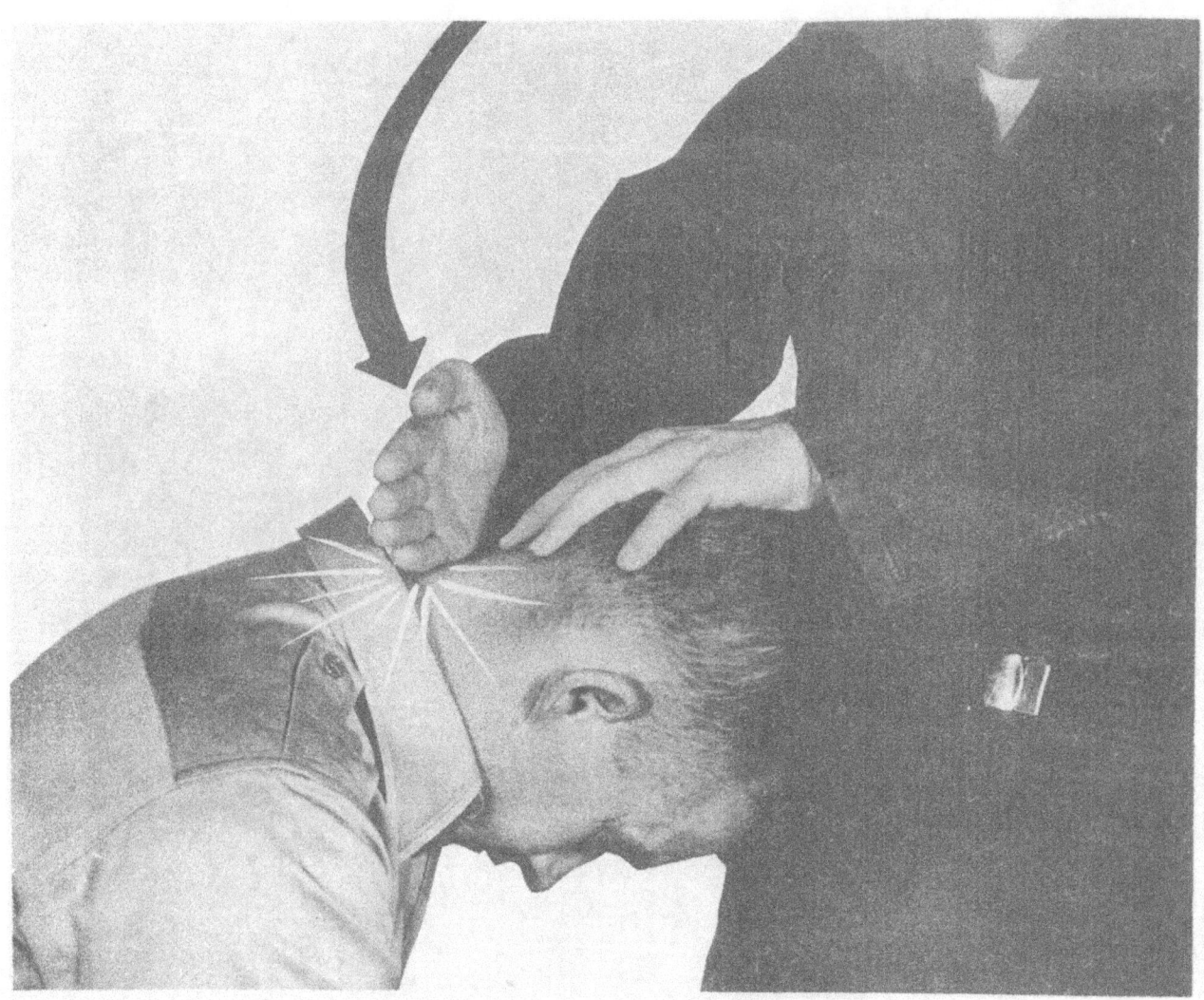

Figure 71. Rabbit punch to the nape of the neck.

32. Attacking the Trunk Region

a. Collarbone. A forceful blow delivered straight down on the collarbone at the side of the neck with the knife edge of your hand can fracture the bone and cause your opponent to drop to his knees (fig. 72). Another way of attacking this point, and a particularly good way if your opponent is shorter than you, is to drive your elbow down into the collarbone.

b. Armpit. A large nerve is close to the skin in each armpit. A blow to this area causes severe pain and temporary, partial paralysis. If you succeed in knocking your opponent down, attack the armpit with a toe kick (fig. 73).

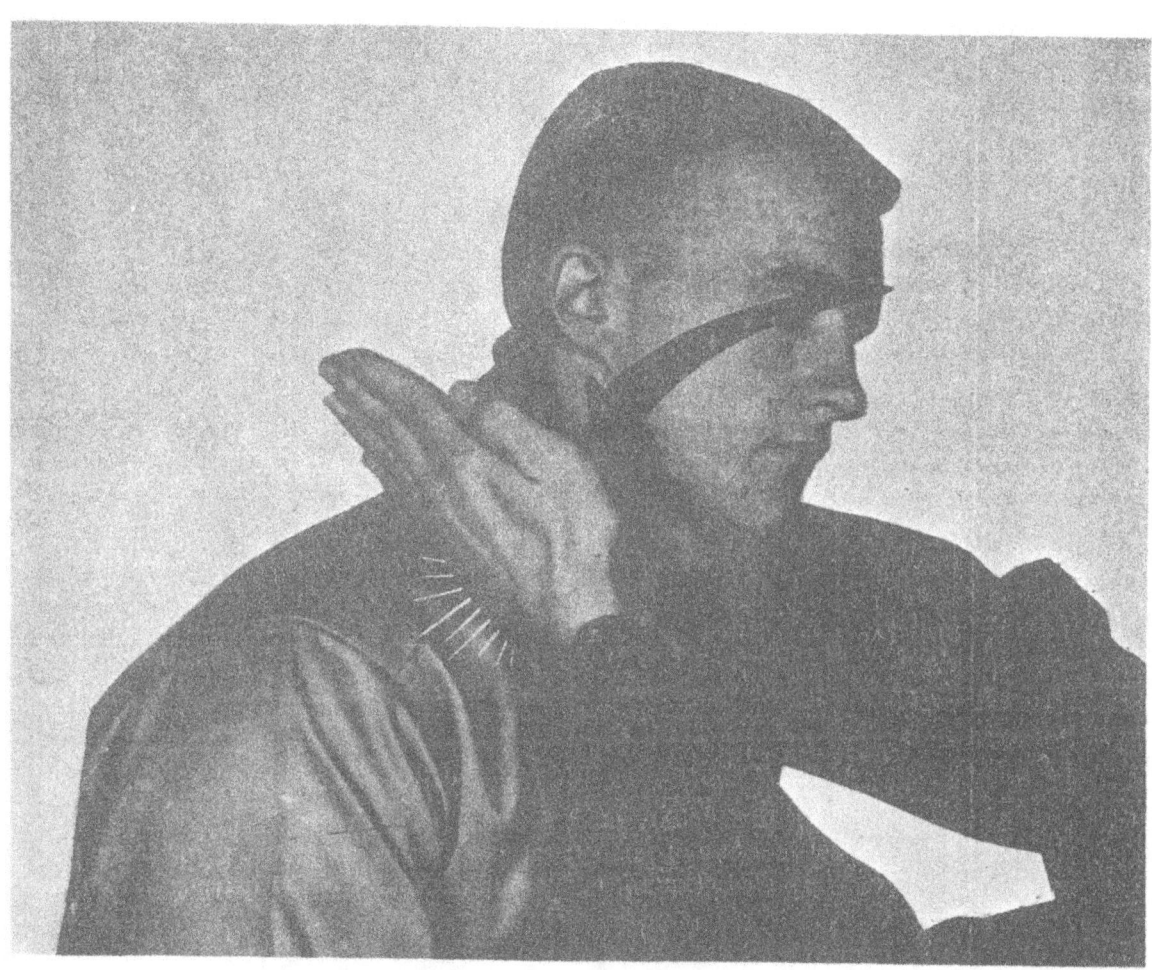

Figure 72. Attacking the collarbone.

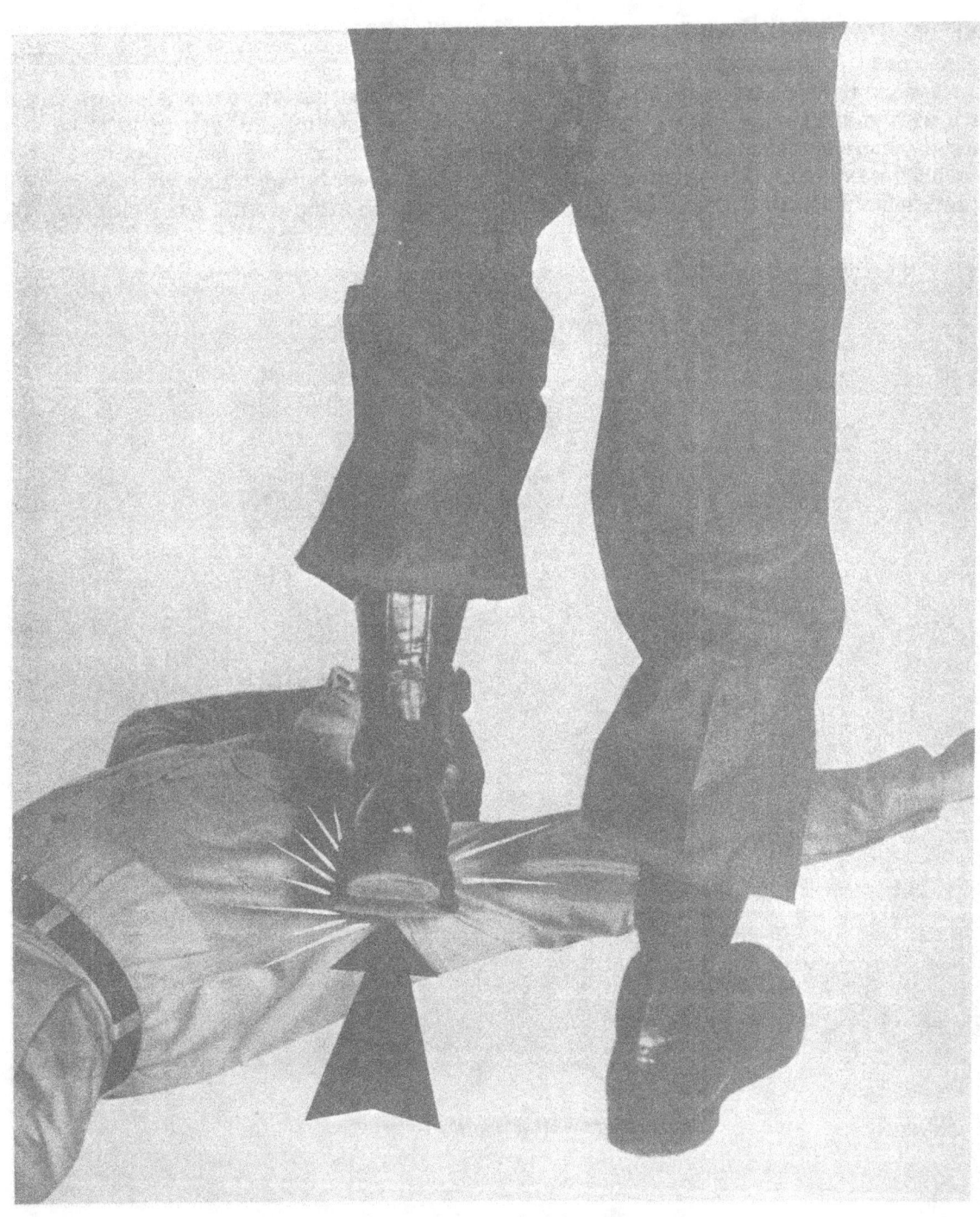

Figure 73. Attacking the armpit.

c. *Solar Plexus.* The solar plexus is at the bottom of the rib cage, just beneath the breastbone. To attack this area, thrust sharply with the pointed fist (fig. 74). This method permits deep penetration and is, therefore, more effective than striking this small target with the fist or the knife edge of your hand. Any penetrating blow to the solar plexus causes extreme pain and may either bend your opponent forward or drop him to his knees. Death may result from a severe blow.

Figure 74. Attacking the solar plexus.

d. Stomach. A blow to your opponent's stomach with the small fist causes him to loosen his hold on you (fig. 75). If he bends forward, strike him in the face with your knee or deliver a rabbit punch to his nape. The knuckle blow gives deeper penetration than a blow with the elbow or fist. A toe kick or a knee lift can also be used and could cause serious injury.

e. Groin. When closing with an opponent, keep in mind that one of the best points to attack is the groin. Use the knee lift attack by kicking up forcefully with your knee (fig. 76). You can also use your closed fist, the knife edge of your hand, a toe kick, a heel stomp, or a violent handgrasp to subdue an opponent.

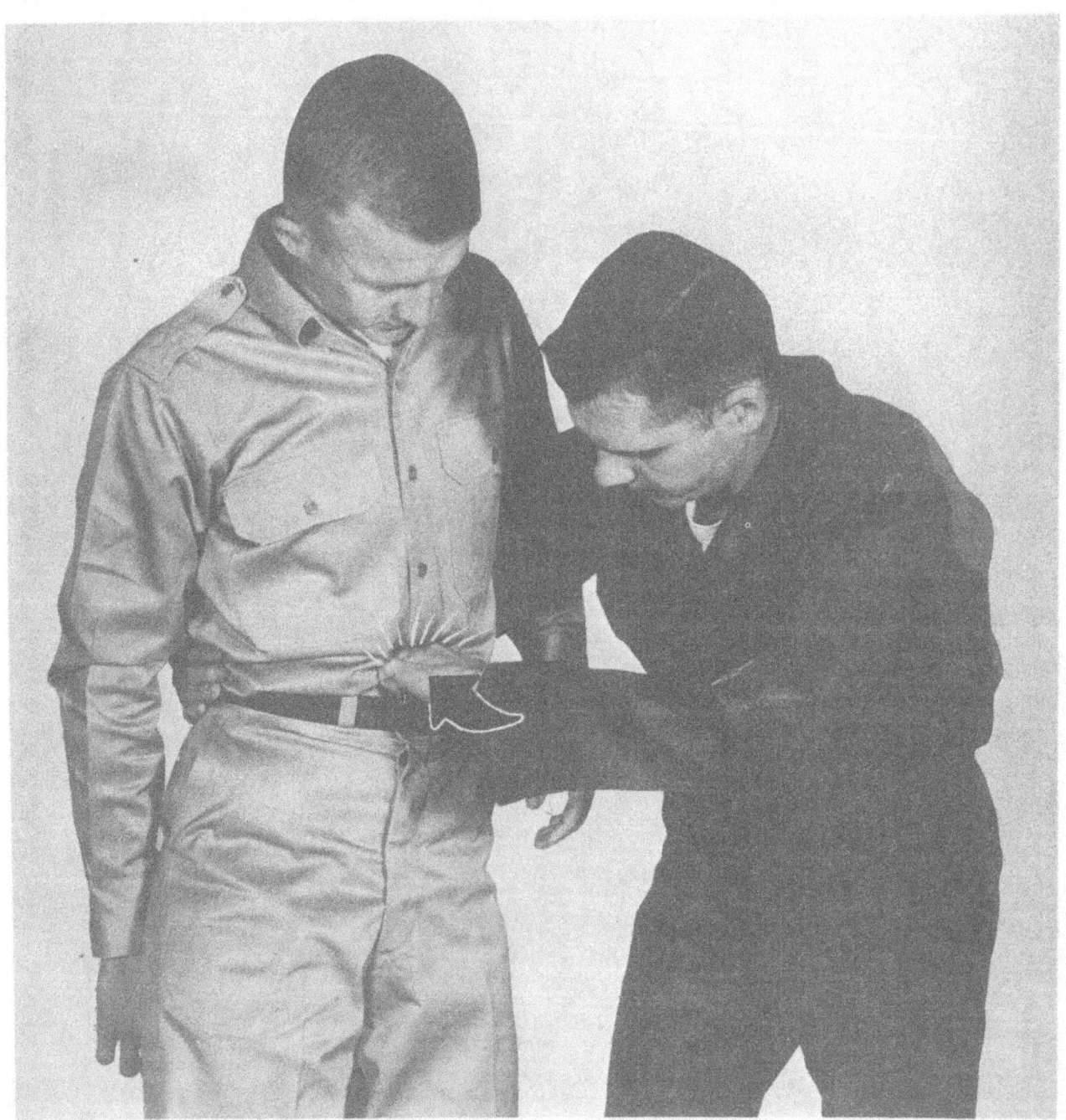

Figure 75. Attacking the stomach.

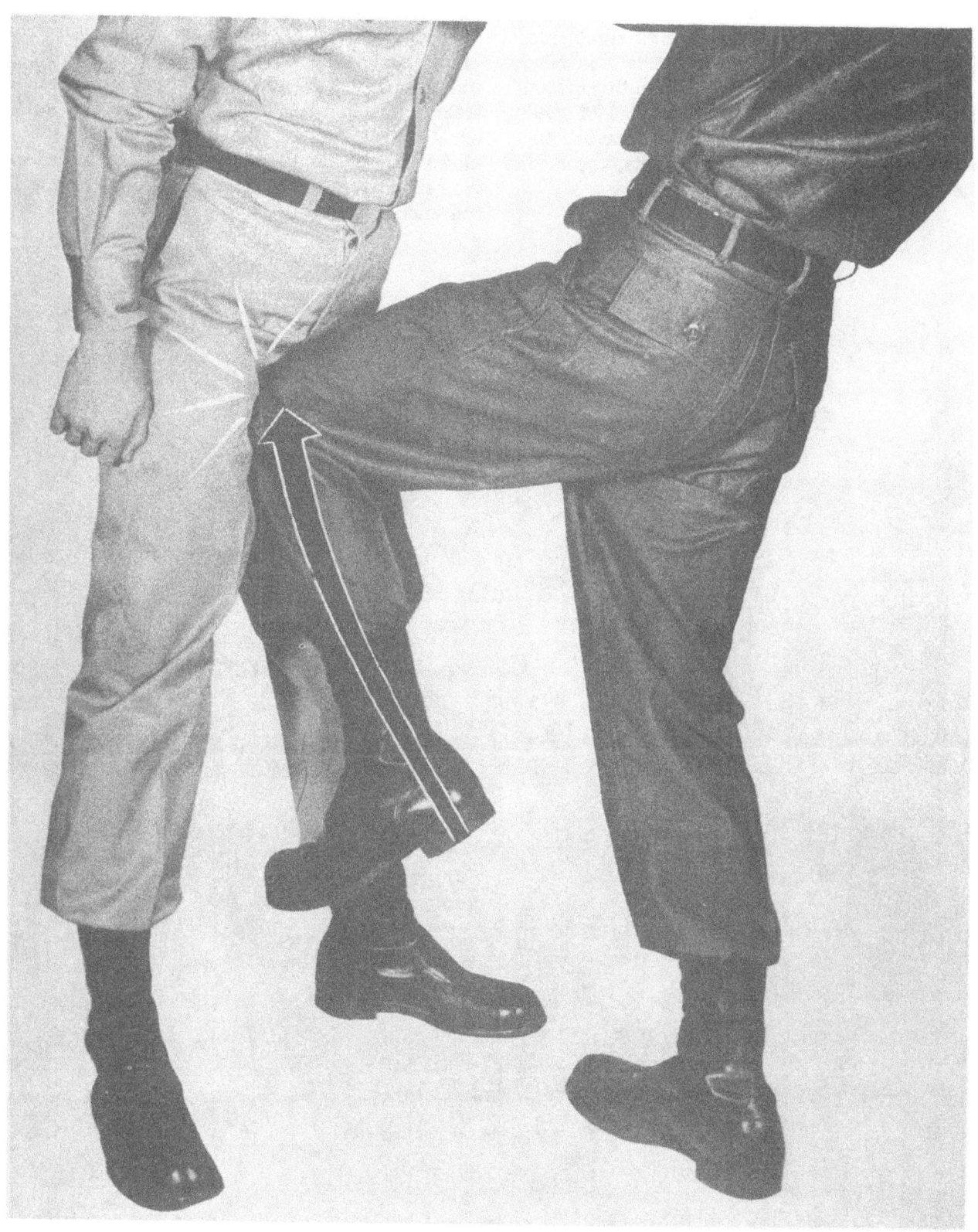

Figure 76. Attacking the groin.

f. Floating Ribs. Attack the floating ribs from either the front or rear, but if possible, strike the blow to your opponent's right side. The liver is located here just below the ribs, and the blow causes terrific shock to this organ. Attack this area with the knife edge of your hand (fig. 77), the outside edge of your fist, the knuckles folded at the second joints, the heel, the toe, or the knee.

g. Kidney. Certain large nerves, branching from the spine, are close to the skin surface over the kidneys. A blow here can rupture the kidney and cause severe nervous shock or death unless the victim receives immediate medical attention. To attack this area, use the knife edge of your hand (fig. 78). Other effective blows can be delivered with fingers folded at the second joints, the outside edge of your fist, the knee, or a toe kick.

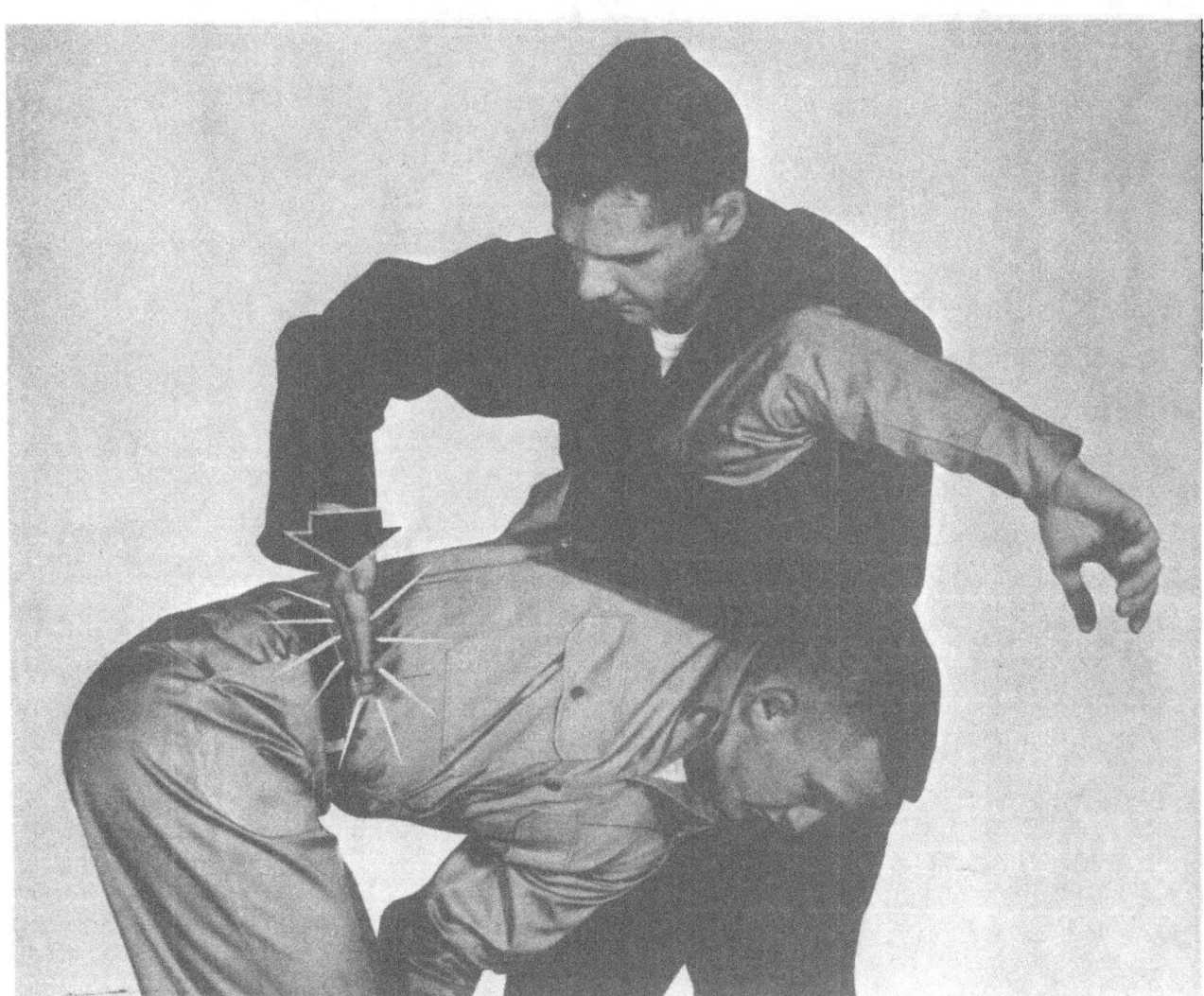

Figure 77. Attacking the floating ribs.

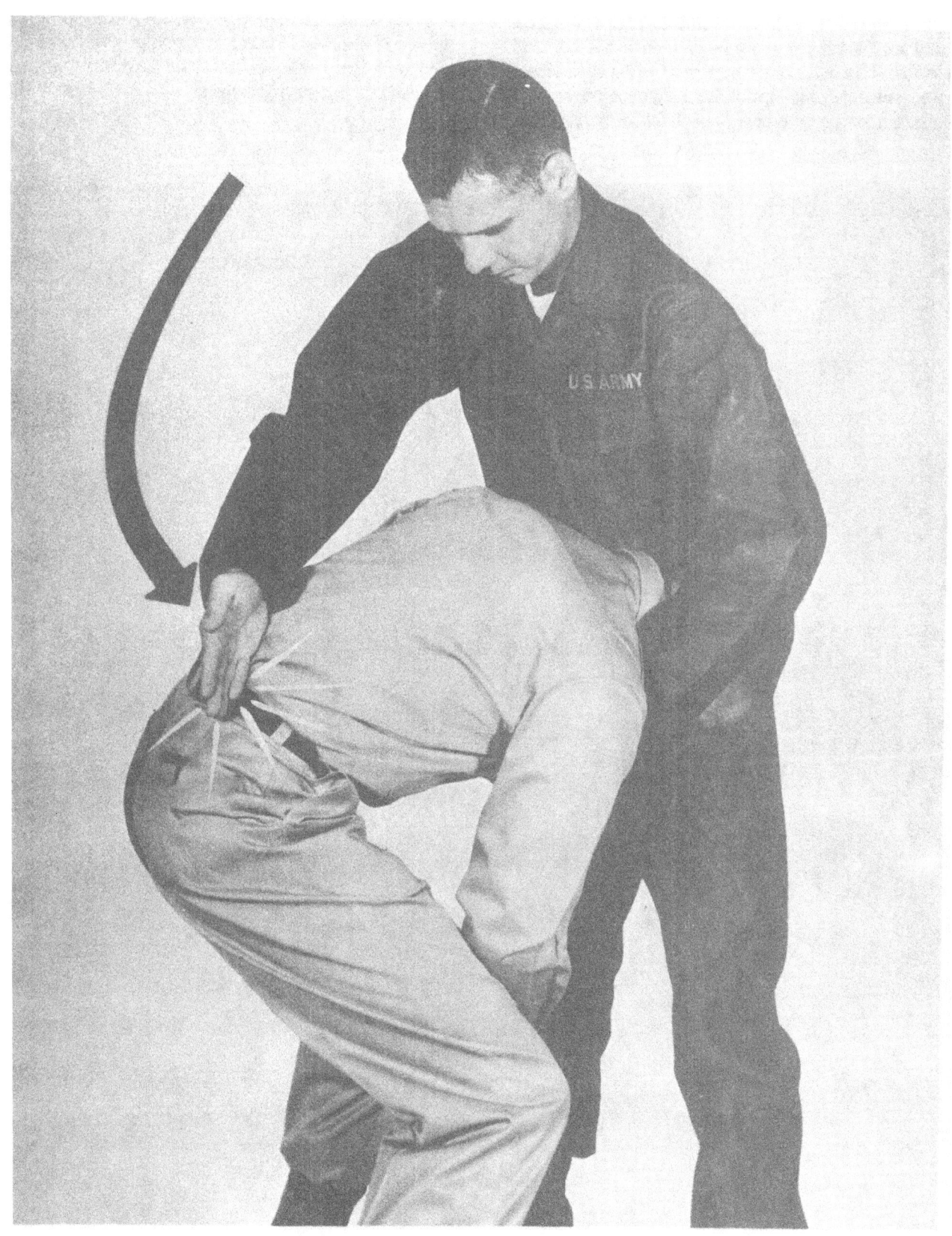

Figure 78. Attacking the kidney.

h. Spine. The spinal column houses the spinal cord and a blow here can dislocate the column, resulting in paralysis or death. If you succeed in knocking your opponent down, a blow with your knee, your elbow, the heel of your boot, or a toe kick can kill or seriously injure him (fig. 79). The best place to strike this blow is three or four inches above the belt line where the spine is least protected.

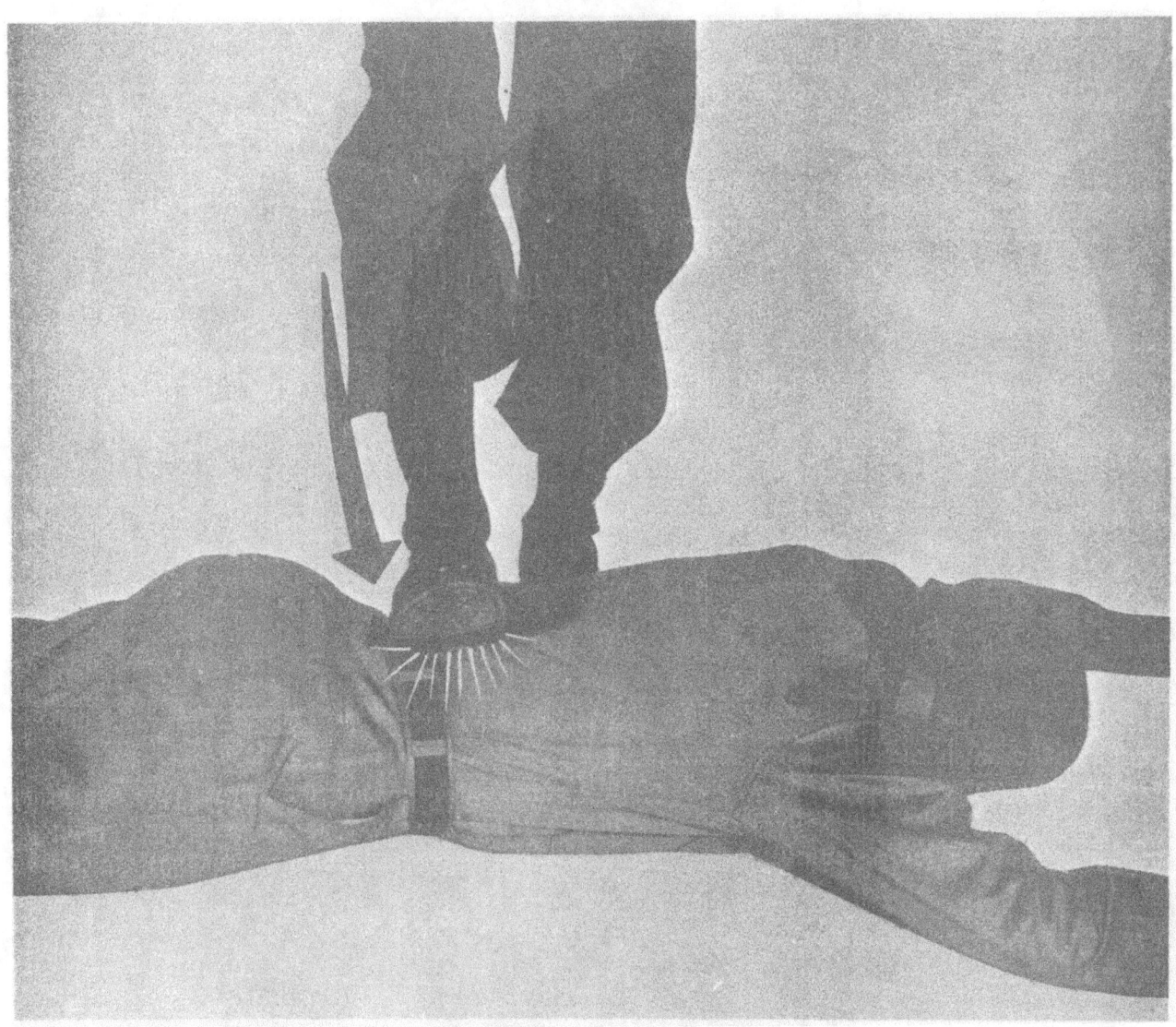

Figure 79. Attacking the spine.

33. Attacking the Limb Region

a. Fingers. To break a rear underarm hold around your waist, grab any one of your opponent's fingers with one hand while securing his wrist with your other hand (fig. 80). Push down on his wrist and, at the same time, bend his finger back toward his wrist. This will break his finger.

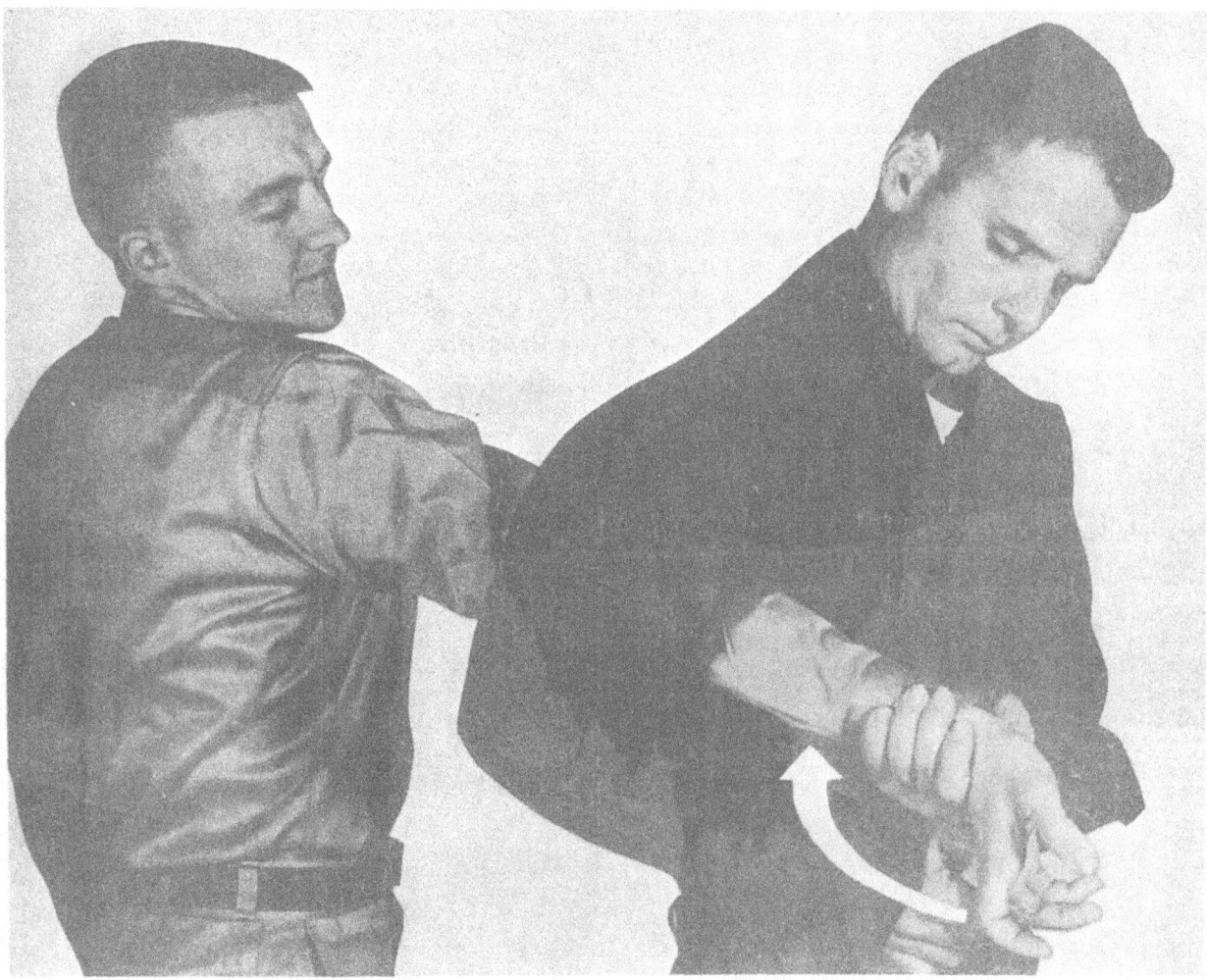

Figure 80. Breaking the fingers.

b. Wrist. Bending the wrist excessively in any direction causes extreme pain. Use a wristlock when attacking this area. Place both your thumbs on the back of your opponent's hand. Bend his wrist at a right angle to his forearm (fig. 81). You can control your opponent when you get him in this position.

Figure 81. Using a wristlock.

c. *Elbow.* The elbow joint is a comparatively weak part of the body and a forceful blow can dislocate it. Grab your opponent's wrist or forearm and pull it behind him, stiffening his arm (fig. 82). As you do this, give his elbow a sharp blow with the heel of your hand. The knife edge of your hand or your knee can also be used.

d. *Shoulder.* After you knock your opponent down you can dislocate his shoulder with a knee drop. You do this by twisting his arm behind his back and dropping on his shoulder with one knee (fig. 83). When you are in position to do this you also can fall on your opponent's spine, causing paralysis or immediate death.

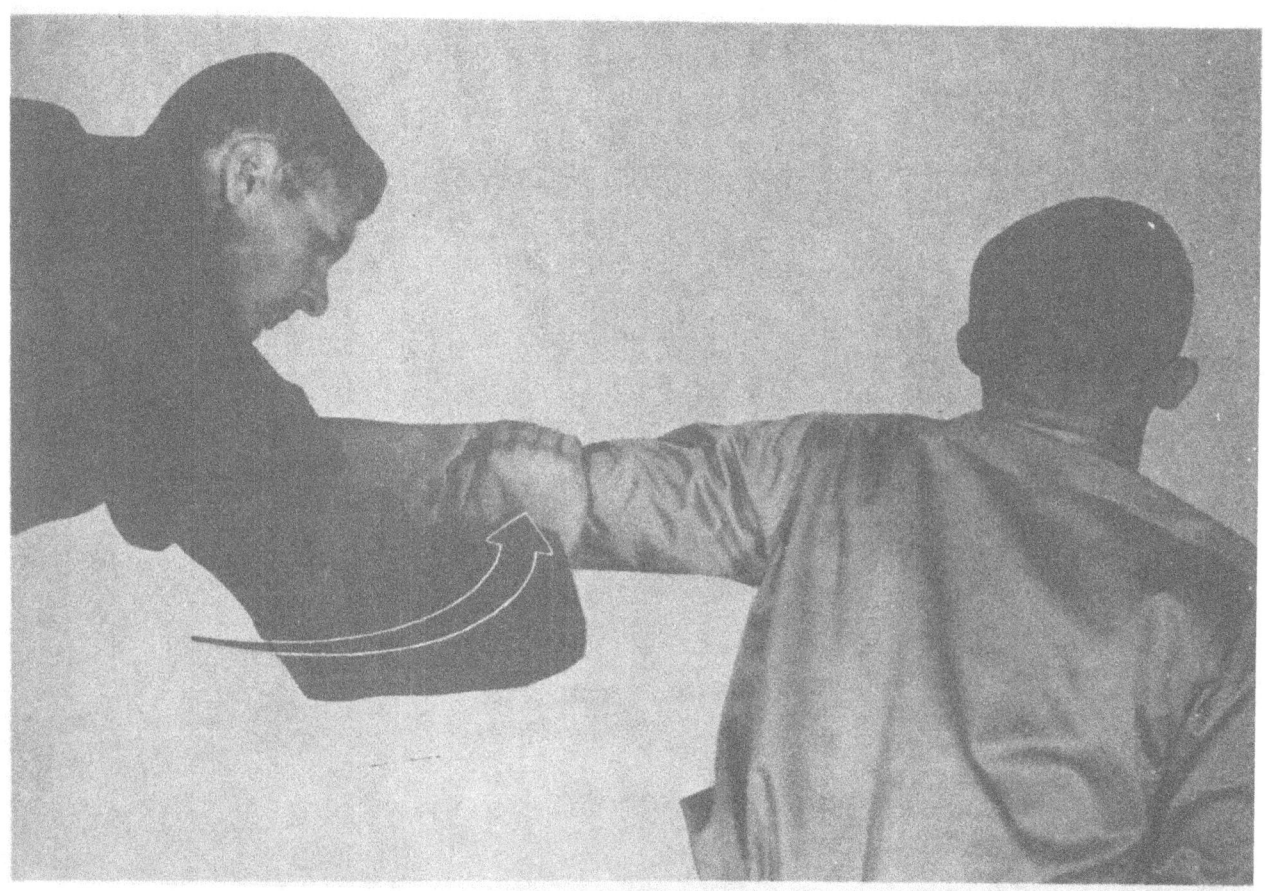

Figure 82. Attacking the elbow.

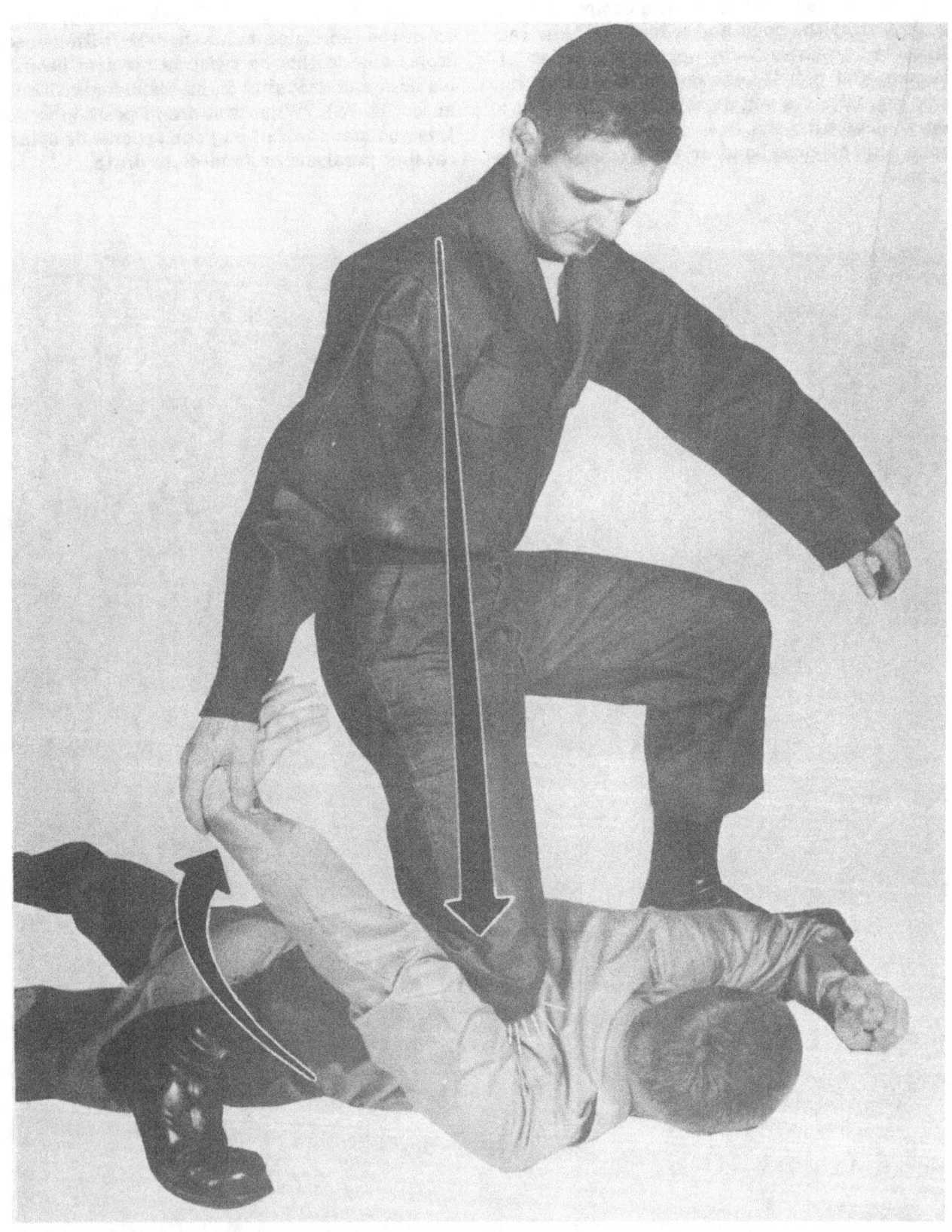

Figure 83. Attacking the shoulder.

e. Knee. Kick your opponent's knee or kneecap with the edge of your boot (fig. 84). The blow will tear ligaments and cartilage, causing him extreme pain and affecting his mobility. If you succeed in getting behind your opponent, a direct toe kick to the back of his knee could penetrate his flesh and injure the nerves.

f. Ankle. Kick your opponent squarely on the outside of his ankle with the outside edge of your boot. Do not use a toe kick because it may slip off your opponent's ankle without doing any damage.

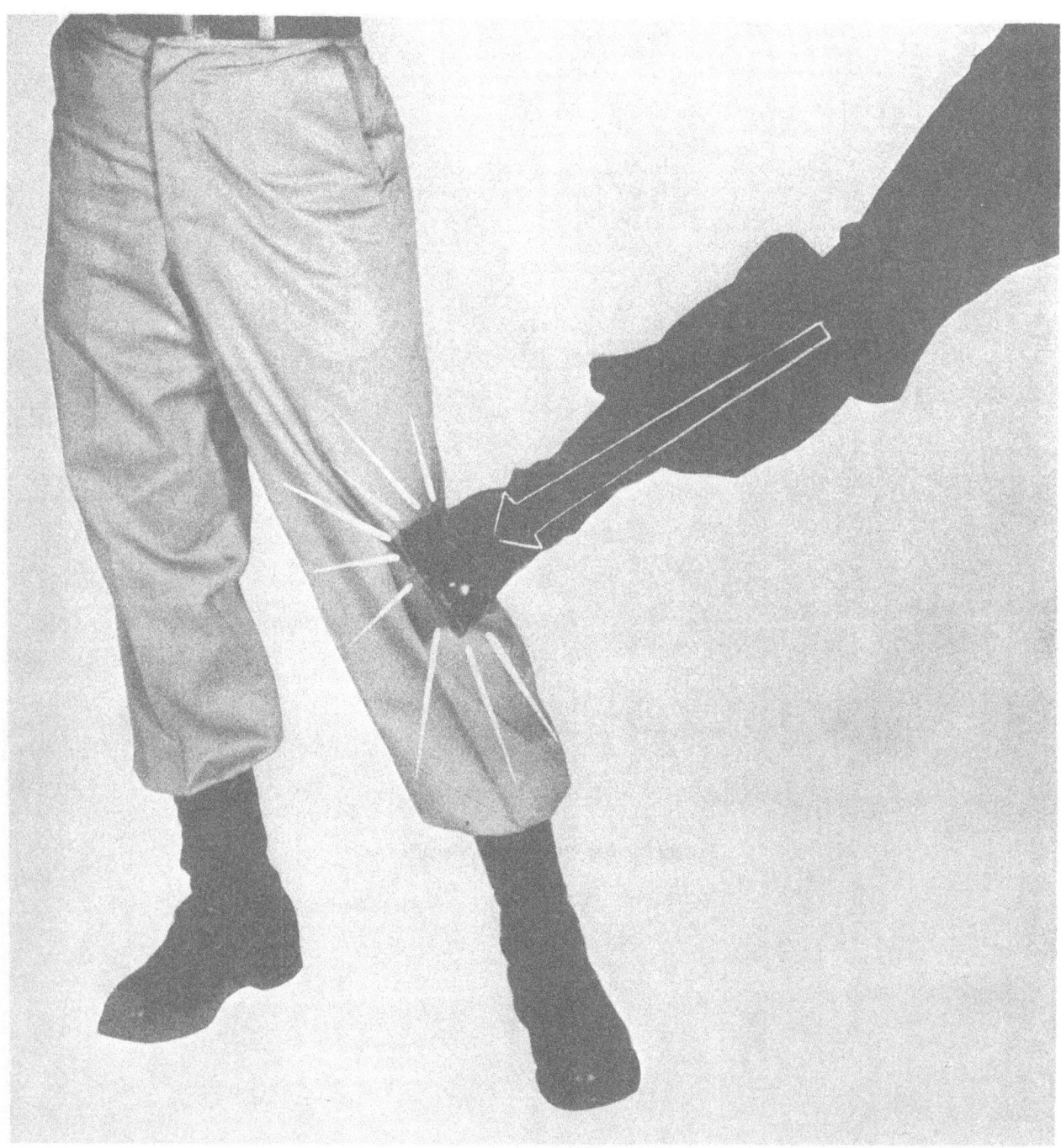

Figure 84. Attacking the knee.

g. Instep. The small bones of the foot's instep can be broken with a foot stomp, causing severe pain to your opponent as well as hindering his movement. When facing your opponent, deliver a foot stomp with the edge of your left boot to his left instep (fig. 85), or with the edge of your right boot to his right instep. This type delivery protects your groin area as you turn. Follow the blow to the instep with a blow to the ankle.

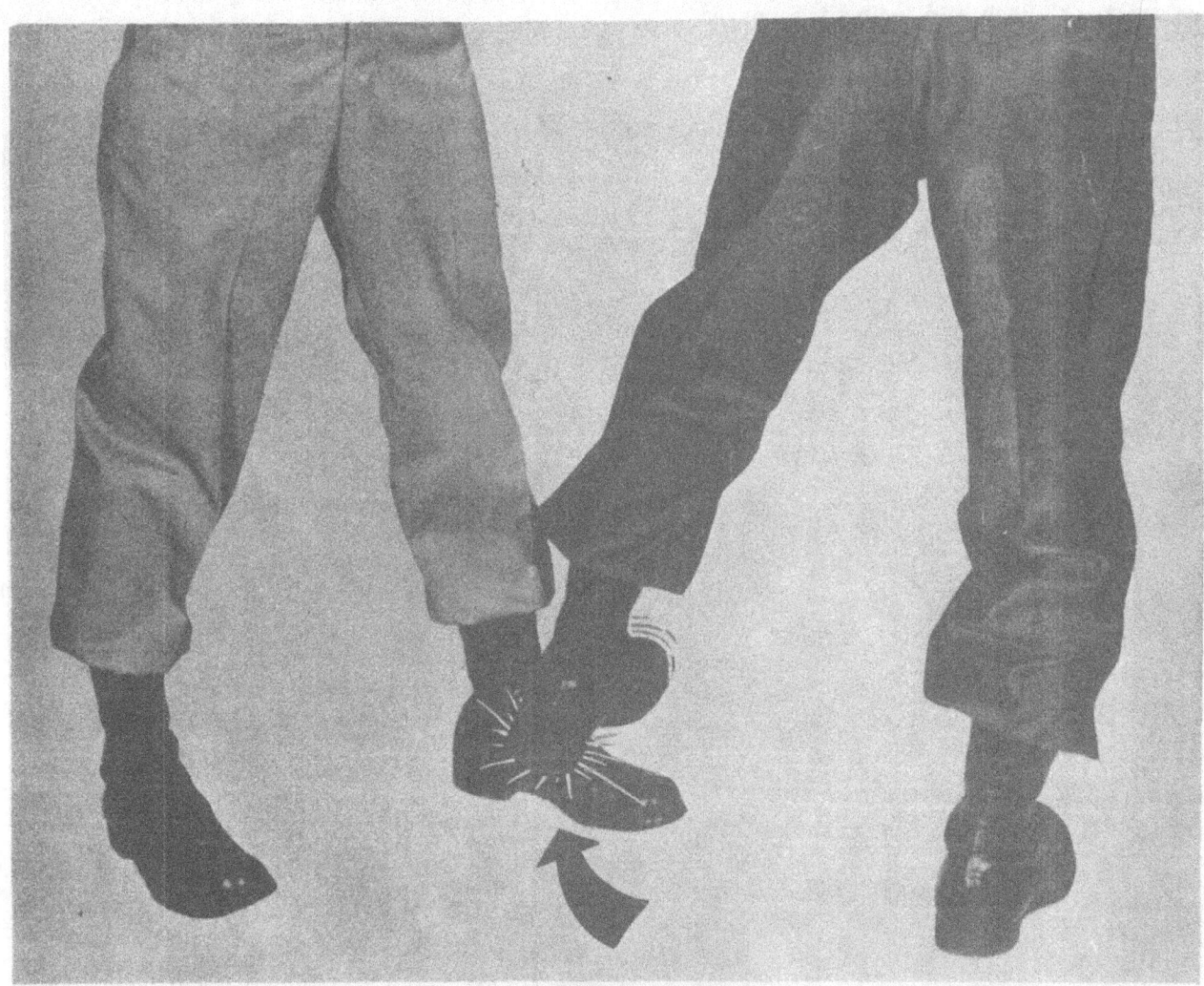

Figure 85. Stomping an opponent's foot.

34. Attacking the Vulnerable Points with Available Weapons

You can attack many of the vulnerable points more effectively by using objects as weapons.

a. Bayonet Hilt. Grasp the bayonet so the hilt protrudes from the little-finger edge of your hand (fig. 86). This provides a blunt instrument that can be used to subdue an opponent by hitting him about the head.

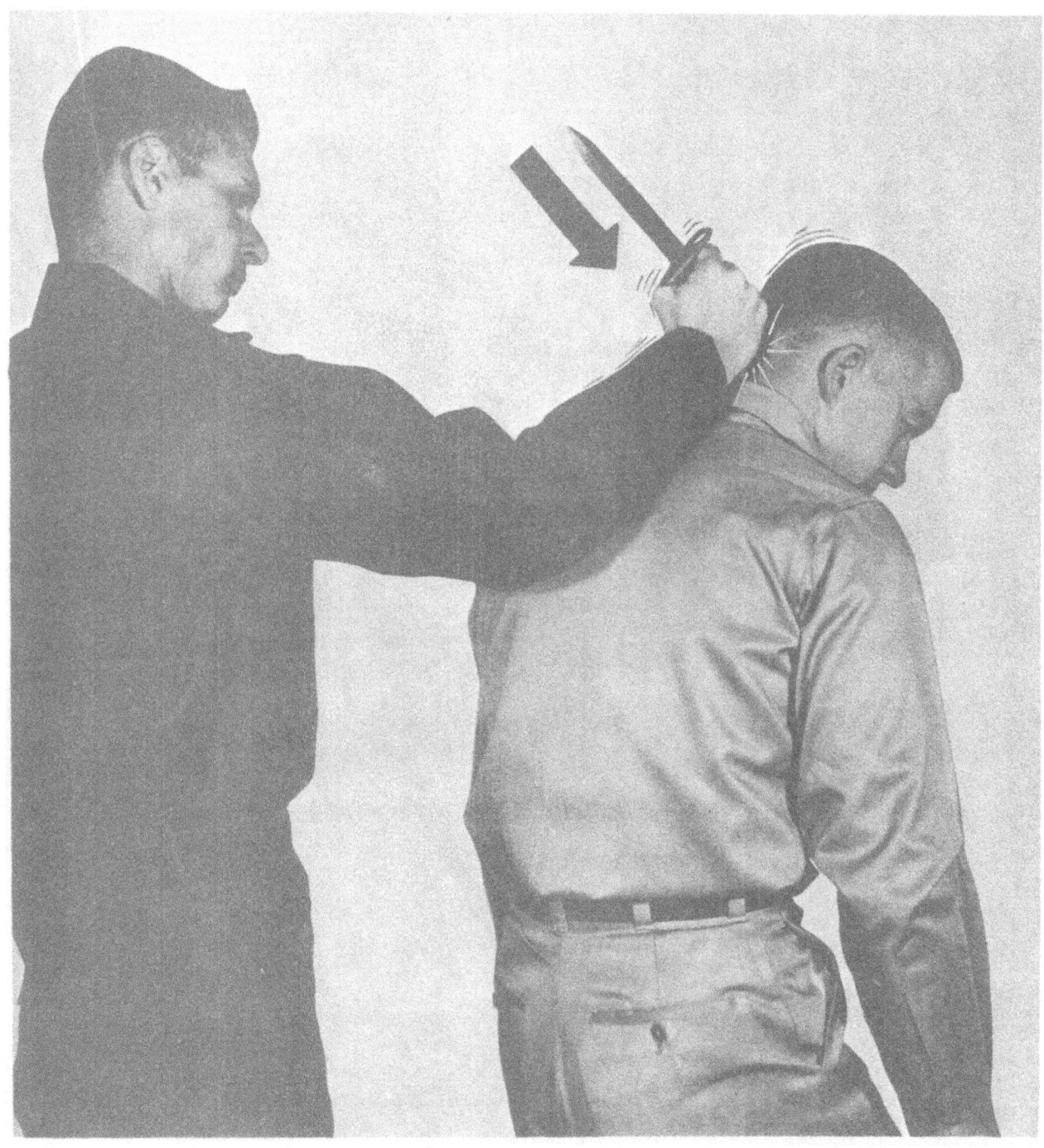

Figure 86. Attacking with the bayonet hilt.

b. Homemade Blackjack. You can make a blackjack by placing wet sand or a bar of soap in a sock. Tie a knot in the sock just above the sand or soap. When attacking an opponent, strike him on the back of his head (fig. 87).

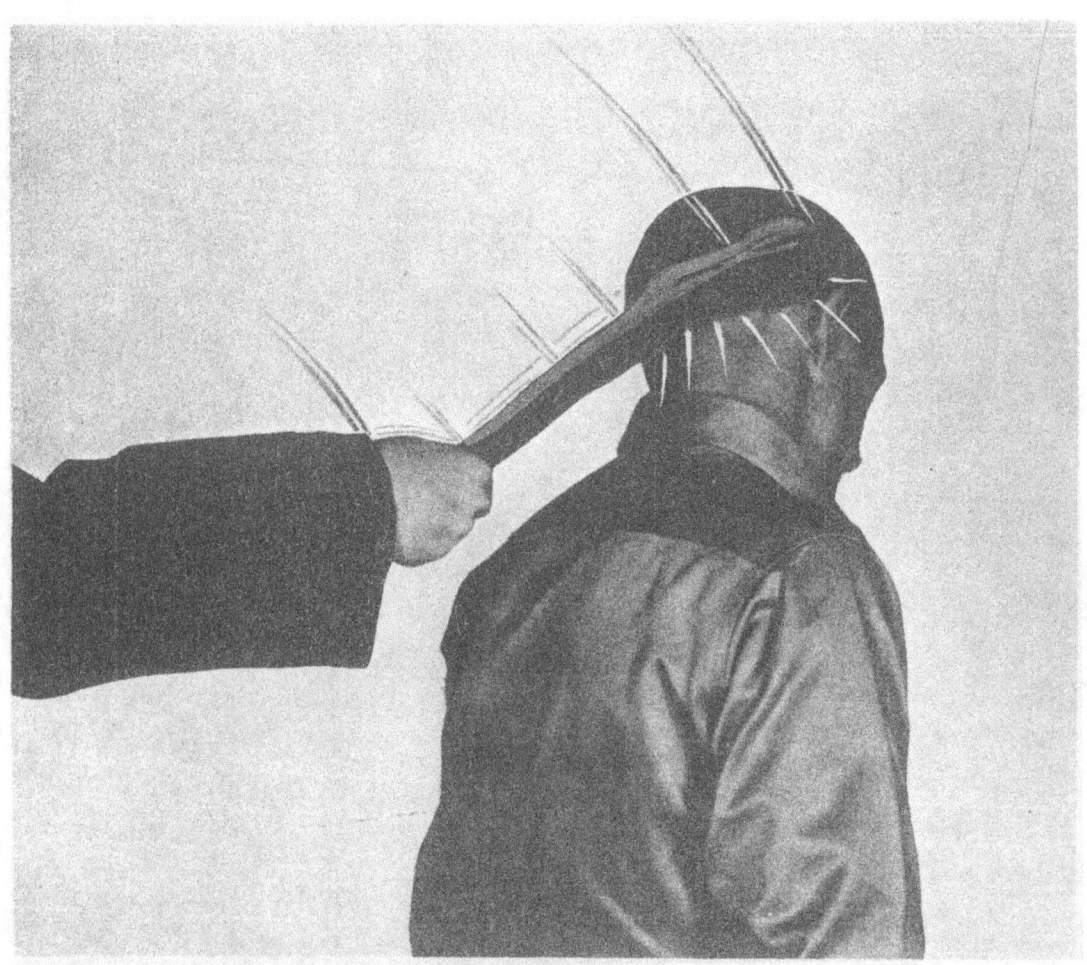

Figure 87. Attacking with a homemade blackjack.

c. Blunt Objects. By striking your opponent between the shoulder blades on his spine with a blunt object you can knock him out noiselessly. You can use the blunt end of a hand axe or the butt of a rifle (fig. 88). A blow with the toe of the rifle or the edge of the axe will kill him.

d. Miscellaneous. When you find yourself unarmed you can, on most occasions, find a piece of equipment like an entrenching tool, or a rock, stick, or club to use as a weapon. By using these and attacking viciously, concentrating on your opponent's vulnerable points, you can disable or kill him.

Figure 88. Attacking with the rifle butt.

Section IV. FALL POSITIONS

35. General

You must learn various fall positions before you attempt the throws that are taught in hand-to-hand combat. Constant practice in these positions will enable you to be thrown without being injured.

36. Right Side Fall Position

The points to check for the right side fall position (fig. 89) are as follows:

a. Your left foot is driven to the ground, taking up the initial shock of the fall. It strikes the ground behind your right leg at the knee. The sole of your foot is flat on the ground.

b. Your right arm is the "beating" arm and takes up additional shock. It is extended along the ground, palm down with fingers extended and joined, at an angle of 45° to the body. This arm makes contact with the ground at the same time as your left foot.

c. Your chin is tucked into your chest, keeping your head off the ground. Your neck remains tense to prevent your head from striking the ground and being injured.

d. Your left arm is held across the face. This prevents injury to your left elbow and offers some protection to the head and throat from the blows of your opponent.

e. The entire right side of your body makes solid contact with the ground. To prevent your right leg from being injured relax it by bending it slightly at the knee.

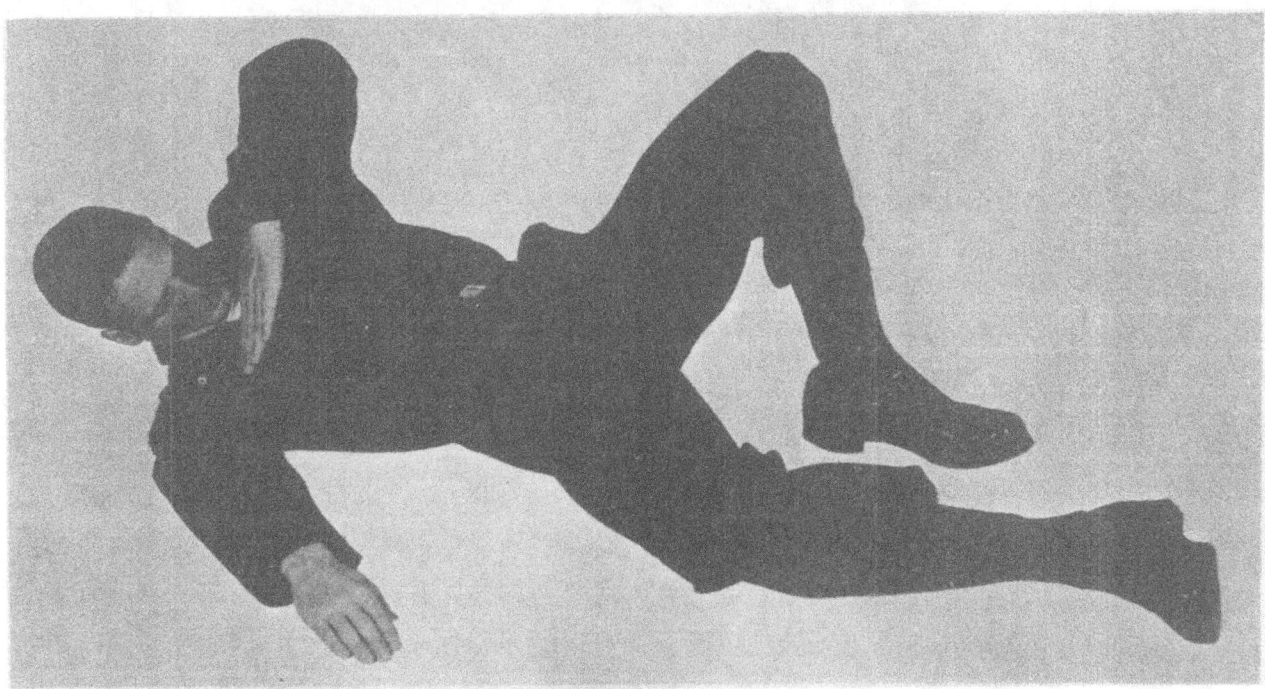

Figure 89. Right side fall position.

37. Left Side Fall Position

The points to check for the left side fall position are the same as those for the right side fall position. Simply substitute the words "left" for "right" and "right" for "left" (fig. 90).

38. Practicing the Right Fall

a. Starting Position (fig. 91). First, you lie on your back, then raise your body off the ground supporting your weight on your left hand and left foot. The right arm is held across the face and the right leg is extended parallel with the ground or slightly higher.

b. Execution. Bend the left arm and left leg slightly, canting your entire body to the left. Watch the ground over your right shoulder. Simultaneously swing the right arm forcefully to the right, and thrust your body into the air in a rolling motion to the right by extending your left arm and left leg vigorously. Your right hand and left foot strike the ground first, taking the initial shock of the fall. Keep your chin tucked tightly into your chest to prevent your head from striking the ground. The completed fall should be the same as in figure 89.

39. Practicing the Left Side Fall

The starting position (fig. 92) and execution (fig. 90), to practice the left side fall, are the same as those for the right side, just substitute the words "left" for "right" and "right" for "left."

Figure 90. Left side fall position.

Figure 91. Starting position to practice right side falls; (top) right side view; (bottom) left side view.

Figure 92. Starting position to practice left side falls; (top) left side view; (bottom) right side view.

40. Rear Fall Position

The points to check for the rear fall position (fig. 93) are as follows:

a. The soles of your feet are driven to the ground about shoulder width apart, keeping your lower legs at a 90° angle to the ground. This takes up the initial shock of the fall.

b. Both hands strike the ground in a slapping motion at the same time as your feet. The arms are fully extended, forming a 45° angle to your body, and the palms of your hands are down. This slapping motion gives you contact with the ground along both arms and across the shoulders, taking up additional shock of the fall.

c. Keep your stomach muscles tightened so your buttocks will not strike the ground when you land. This prevents injury to your spine.

d. Your chin is tucked into your chest so that your head does not strike the ground.

41. Practicing the Rear Fall Position

a. Starting Position (fig. 94). Assume the squatting position and place your hands between your knees, with the palms flat on the ground and fingers pointing toward each other. Arch your back and tuck your chin into your chest to keep your head from striking the ground.

b. Execution. Roll forward in a somersault. At the peak of the forwarded roll, drive the soles of the feet to the ground about shoulder width apart and simultaneously slap both hands to the ground. The arms are fully extended with the hands palm down, forming a 45° angle to your body. The chin remains tucked tightly into the chest to prevent the head from hitting the ground. The completed fall should be the same as in figure 93.

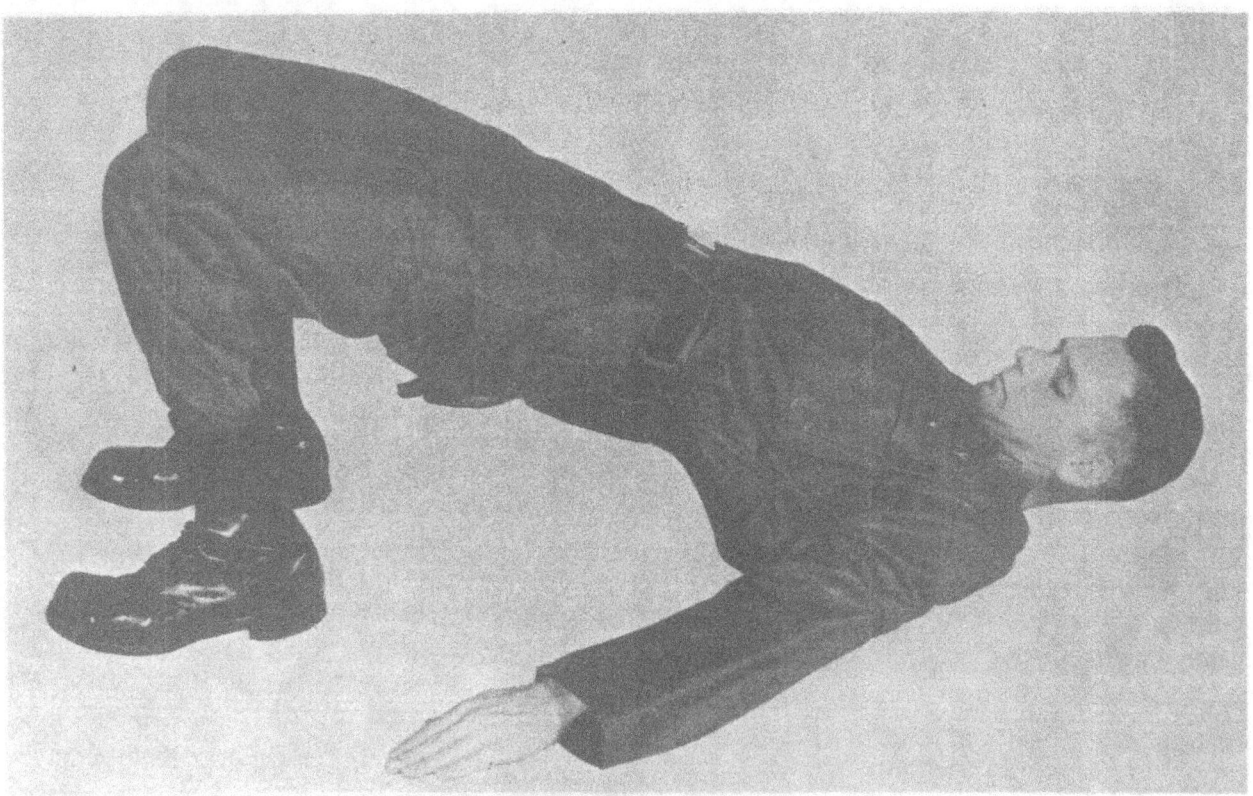

Figure 93. Rear fall position.

Figure 94. Starting position to practice rear fall.

42. Advance Falling Practice

a. Right Side Fall. Start from the standing position and raise your left arm over your head with the palm of your hand facing to the left. Take several steps forward to build up momentum. When your left foot strikes the ground swing your raised left arm down in an arc through your legs so that you go into a forward somersault. Keep your chin tucked into your chest. At the peak of your forward roll thrust your flexed legs so that your body is propelled into the air feet first and parallel to the ground in an extended position. The sole of your left foot and the palm of the right hand are driven to the ground and make the initial contact to absorb most of the shock. The completed fall position should be the same as in figure 89.

b. Left Side Fall. The left side fall position can be practiced in a similar manner, substituting the words "left" for "right" and "right" for "left."

c. Rear Fall Position. Start from the standing position and take a few steps forward to buildup momentum. Then execute the fall as described in paragraph 41.

Section V. BASIC THROWS AND TAKEDOWNS

43. General

Sometimes in hand-to-hand combat, you have to throw your opponent to the ground before you can attack a vulnerable part of his body. The basic throws and takedowns used are the hip throw, the reverse hip throw, the overshoulder throw, the overhead throw, the crosshock takedown, and the rear takedown. Variations of the throws and takedowns can be used and new ones taught after you have learned the basic ones.

a. Speed is the primary factor in throwing an opponent in combat. In training, however, strive for precision and accuracy. Do each phase of a throw or takedown with deliberate action. Once you have thoroughly learned the movements, speed will come through constant practice.

b. In the beginning, your partner should offer no resistance. He should cooperate and permit you to execute the throw or takedown while he concentrates on assuming a good fall position.

c. The throws and takedowns described may be executed from either side simply by substituting the words "right" for "left" and "left" for "right."

44. Hip Throw (Right or Left)

a. Start the right hip throw from the guard position (facing your opponent). Place your left foot in front and slightly inside of your opponent's left foot. At the same time, strike your opponent vigorously on his right shoulder with the heel of your left hand and grab his clothing at the shoulder (1, fig. 95). This blow knocks him off balance.

b. Pivot to your left 180° on the ball of your left foot. During the pivot place your right arm around your opponent's waist and jerk him forward forcefully with both arms, driving his midsection into your buttocks. This maneuver bends your opponent over your right hip at his waist and leaves him partially suspended in this position. At the completion of this manuever your knees are bent (2, fig. 95).

①
Figure 95. Right hip throw.

②
Figure 95—Continued.

c. Straighten your legs quickly, thrusting your buttocks forcefully into your opponent's midsection. At the same time, bend forward at the waist and pull forward and downward with both arms, driving your opponent to the ground (3, fig. 95). Use your hip as a fulcrum, throwing the man over your right hip and not over the outside of your leg. At the completion of the throw your opponent lands in the left side fall position. You are poised to deliver a blow to a vulnerable part of his body.

45. Reverse Hip Throw

a. Start the reverse hip throw from the guard position (facing your opponent). Stand slightly closer to him than in the hip throw maneuver. Take a long step forward with your left foot and place it slightly outside of and a few inches beyond your opponent's right foot. Most of your weight is supported on your left foot. At the same time, strike your opponent forcefully on his right upper arm with your left hand and grab his arm at this point (1, fig. 96). This blow causes him to lose his balance to the rear.

b. Step around your opponent with your right foot and place it directly behind him. At the same time, encircle his waist with your right arm. Thrust your hips to your right as far as possible to gain buttock-to-buttock contact, pulling your opponent into position on your right hip and suspending him in midair. Now lock your opponent's right arm to your side with your left elbow (2, fig. 96).

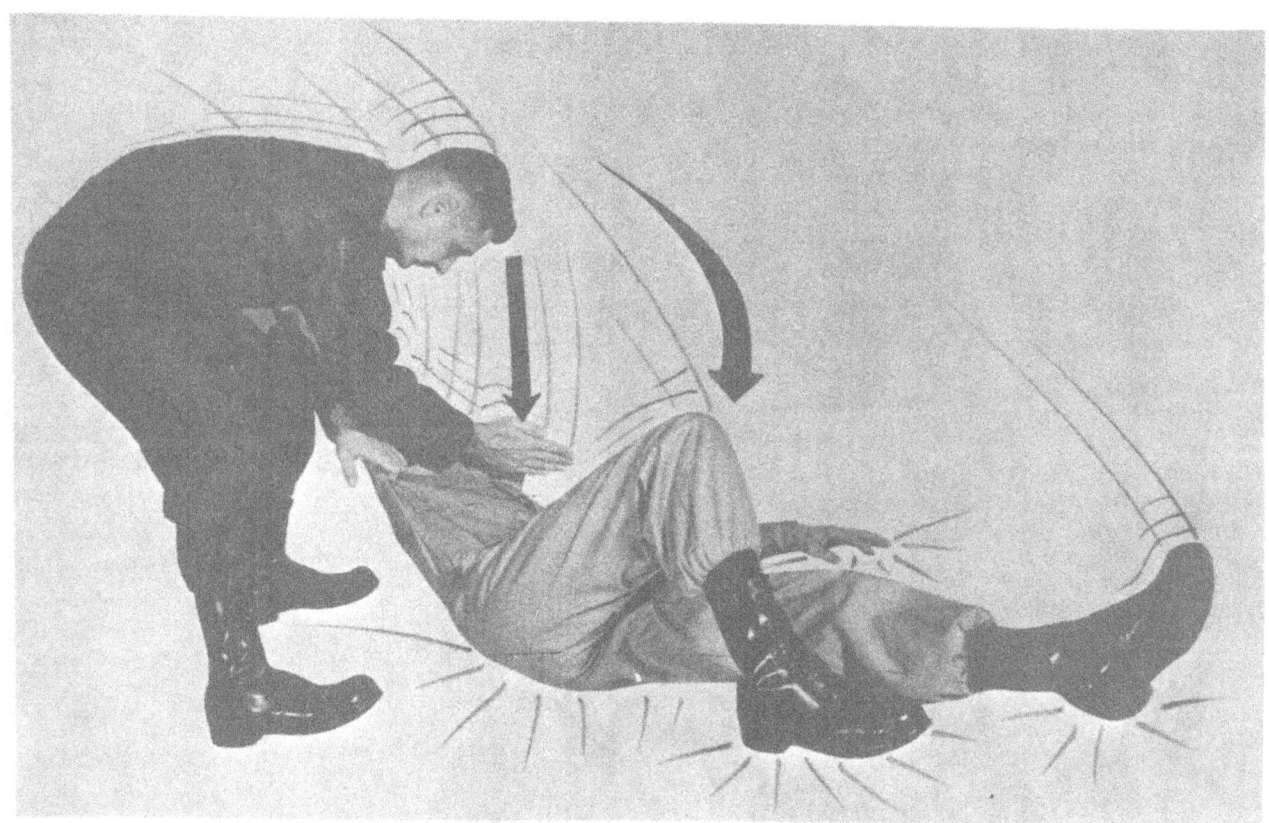

③

Figure 95—Continued.

①
Figure 96. Reverse hip throw.

②
Figure 96—Continued.

c. Straighten your legs, use your right hip as a fulcrum, and slam your opponent to the ground (3, fig. 96). Be sure to throw him over your hip, not over the side of your right leg. You retain the armlock on your opponent's right arm. Your opponent assumes the left side fall position. In combat this fall may knock your opponent unconscious and always leaves him open to a vulnerable blow.

46. Overshoulder Throw

a. Start the overshoulder throw from the guard position (facing your opponent). The first phase of this throw is identical to the first phase of the right hip throw and the footwork is identical throughout to that used in right hip throw. Place your left foot in front and slightly inside of your opponent's left foot. At the same time, strike him vigorously on his right shoulder with the heel of your left hand and grab his clothing (1, fig. 97).

b. Pivot to your left 180° on the ball of your left foot. Keep your right arm in position to protect your head and neck region until you near the completion of the pivot. Reach up and grab your opponent's clothing at his right shoulder with your right hand, and then grip him at this point with a double-hand hold. As you complete the pivot, pull your opponent forward and drive his midsection into your buttocks (2, fig. 97). Your buttocks are directly in front of your opponent's hips, your right foot is in front and slightly outside of your opponent's right foot, your elbows are as close to your body as possible, and your knees are bent.

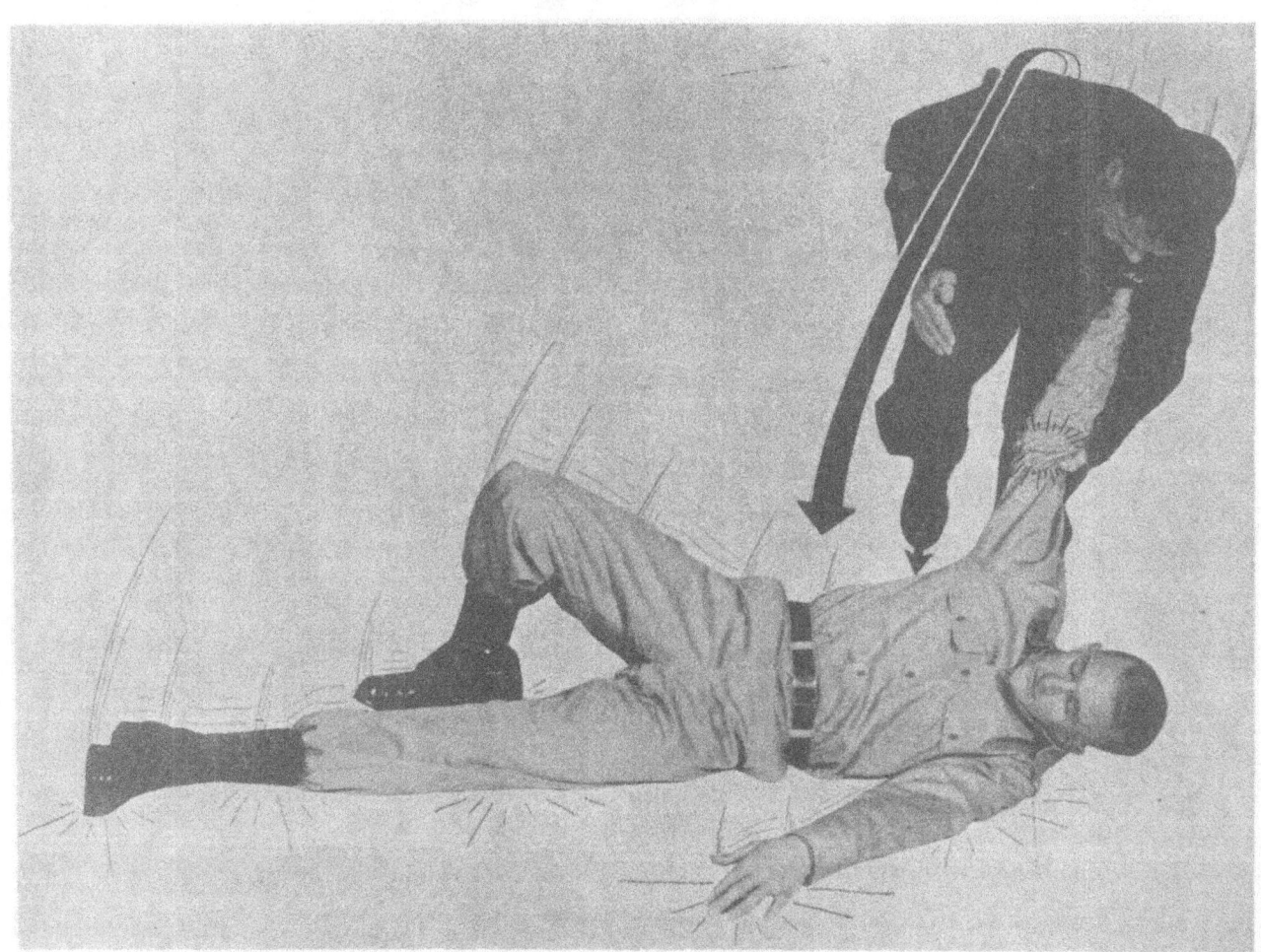

③

Figure 96—Continued.

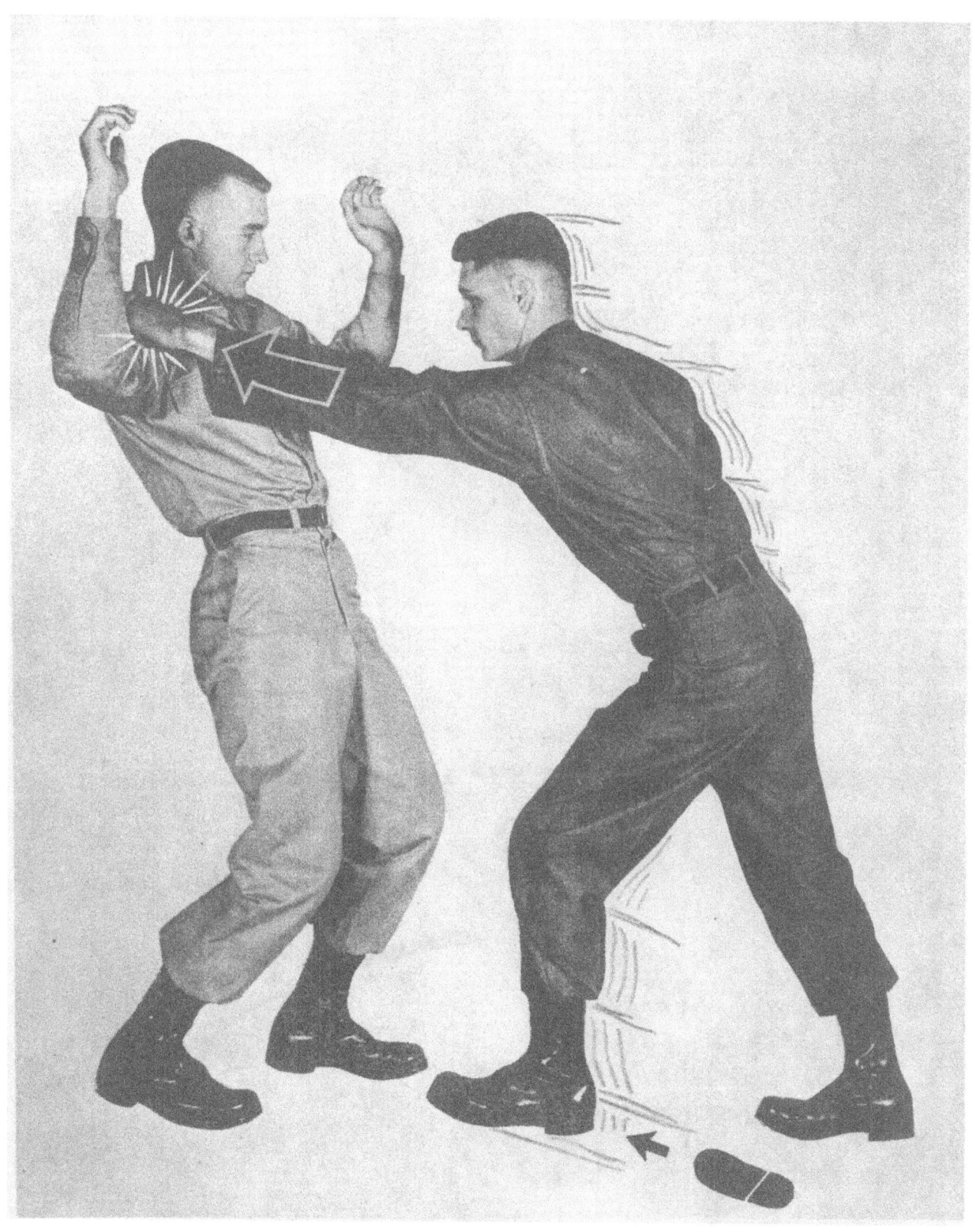

①
Figure 97. Overshoulder throw.

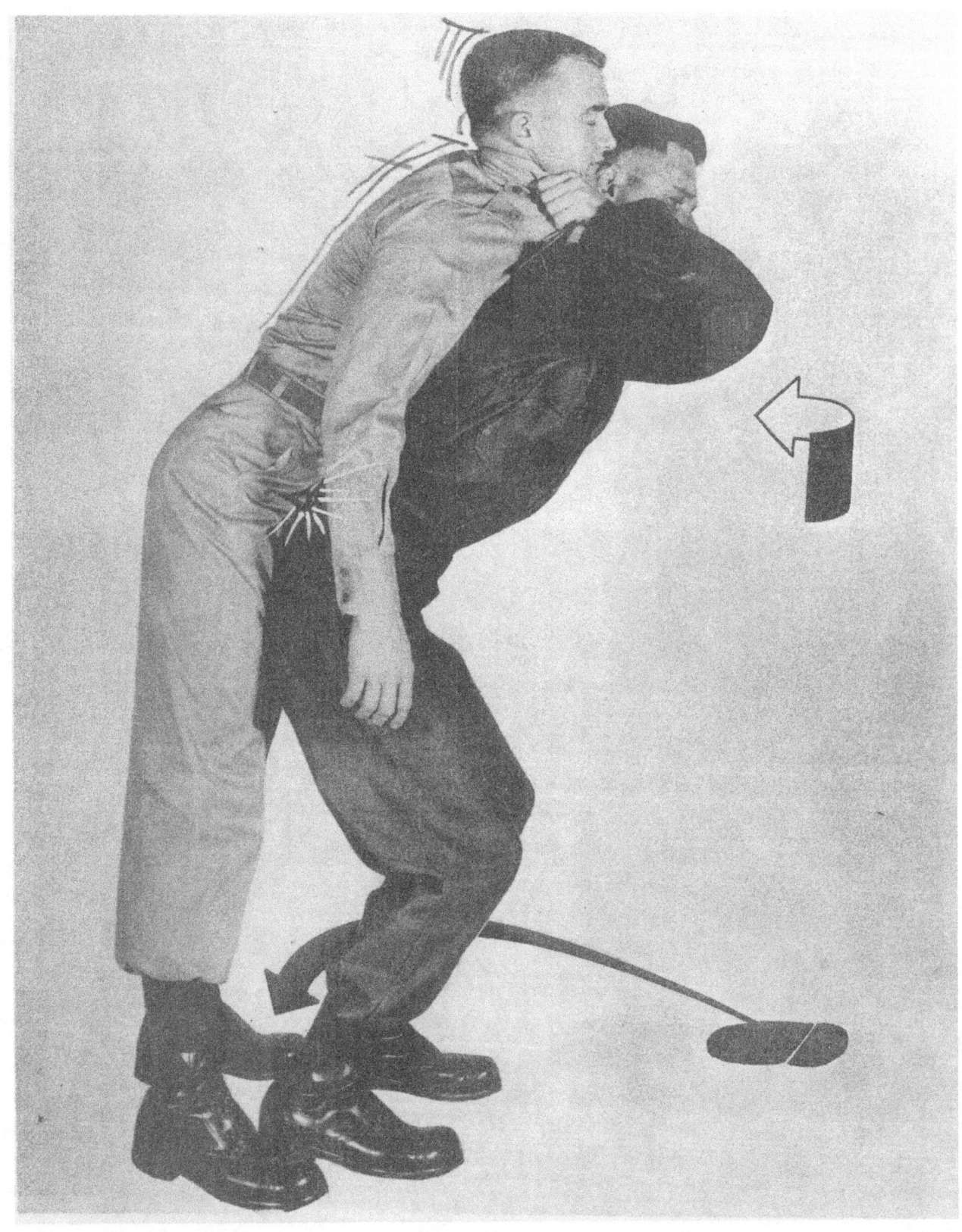

Figure 97—Continued.

c. Straighten your legs, bend at the waist, and pull downward with both hands. This action will catapult your opponent over your shoulder (3, fig. 97). He assumes the rear fall position as he strikes the ground.

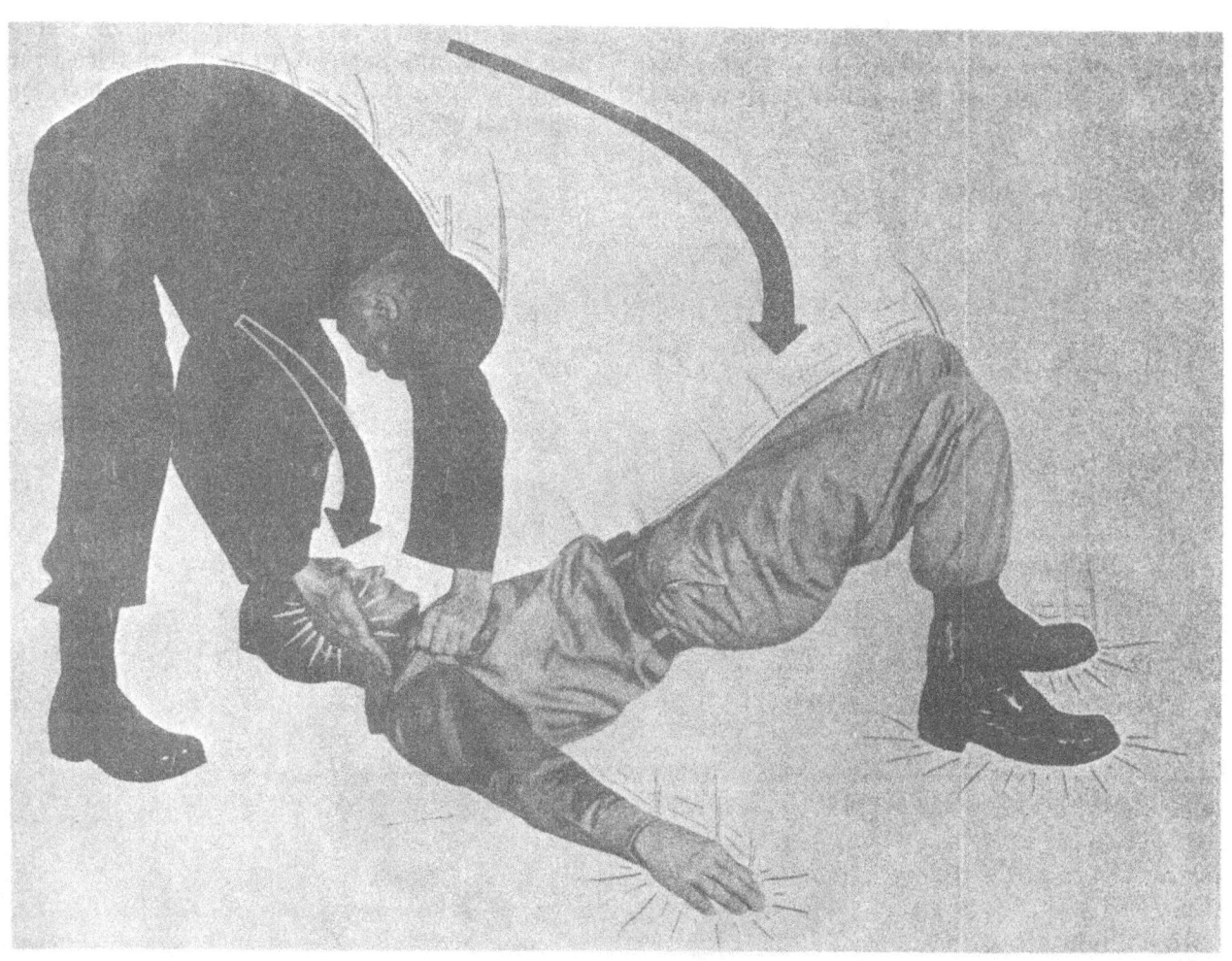

③
Figure 97—Continued.

47. Overhead Throw

a. You take full advantage of your opponent's momentum when using this throw. You start this throw from the guard position, facing your opponent who is about five to six steps away. As your opponent rushes forward you grab his lapels with both hands. Simultaneously you raise either your left or right leg and place the sole of your foot solidly against his stomach (1, fig. 98).

b. Still maintaining the hold on your opponent's lapels, and with your foot against his stomach, drop back until your buttocks strike the ground and you are in a sitting position. Continue moving backward until your back and shoulders touch the ground, keeping your opponent pulled firmly against your foot. Using your opponent's momentum, pull him with your hands until he is suspended over your body on your foot (2, fig. 98).

①
Figure 98. Overhead throw.

②
Figure 98—Continued.

c. Catapult your opponent into the air by maintaining a tight handhold and thrusting your leg vigorously into his stomach and arching your back so that you rock back onto your shoulders. Your opponent assumes the rear fall position (3, fig. 98).

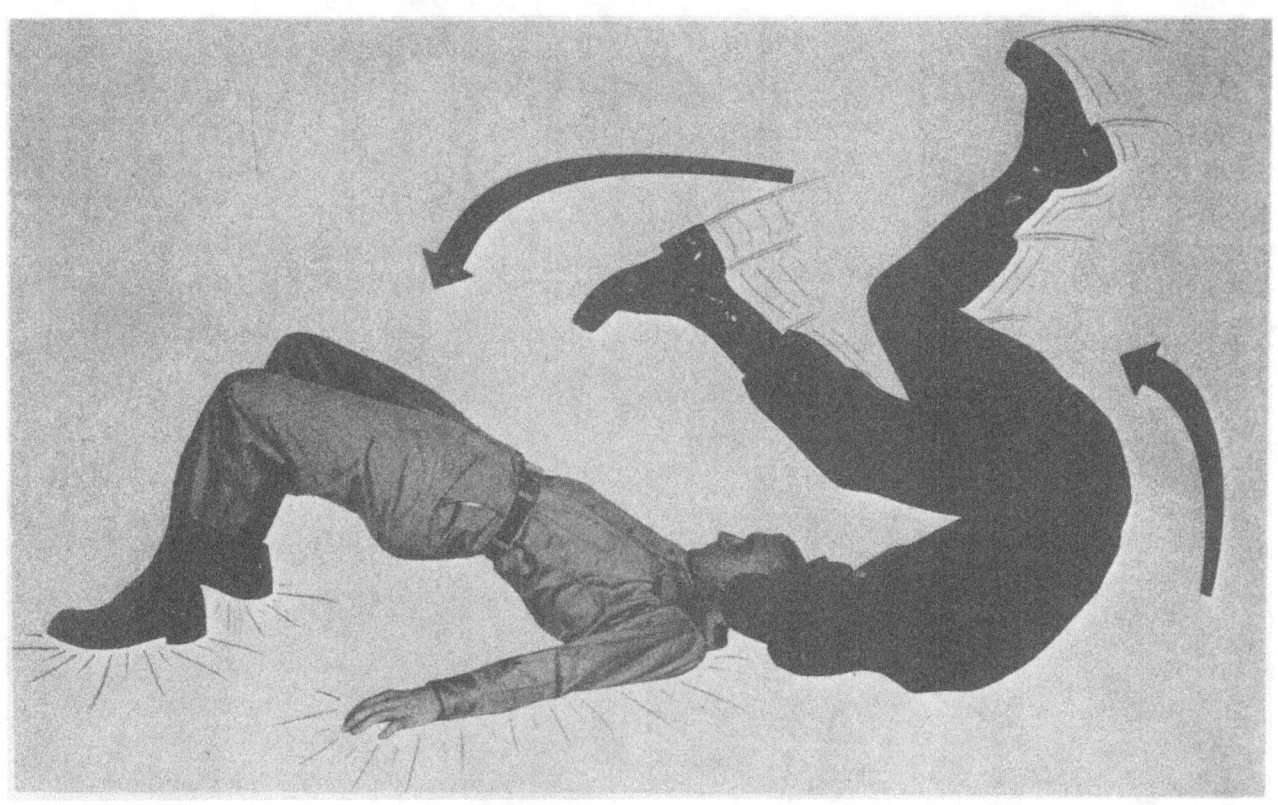

③
Figure 98—Continued.

d. By maintaining a firm grip with your hands on his lapels you will be pulled over your shoulders completing a rear somersault landing astride your opponent's chest (4, fig. 98).

48. Cross-Hock Takedown

a. Start the cross-hock takedown from the guard position (facing your opponent). Step in with your left foot placing it slightly outside of your opponent's right foot. Simultaneously strike your opponent vigorously on both shoulders with the heel of your hands and grab his clothing. This blow knocks him off balance to the rear (1, fig. 99).

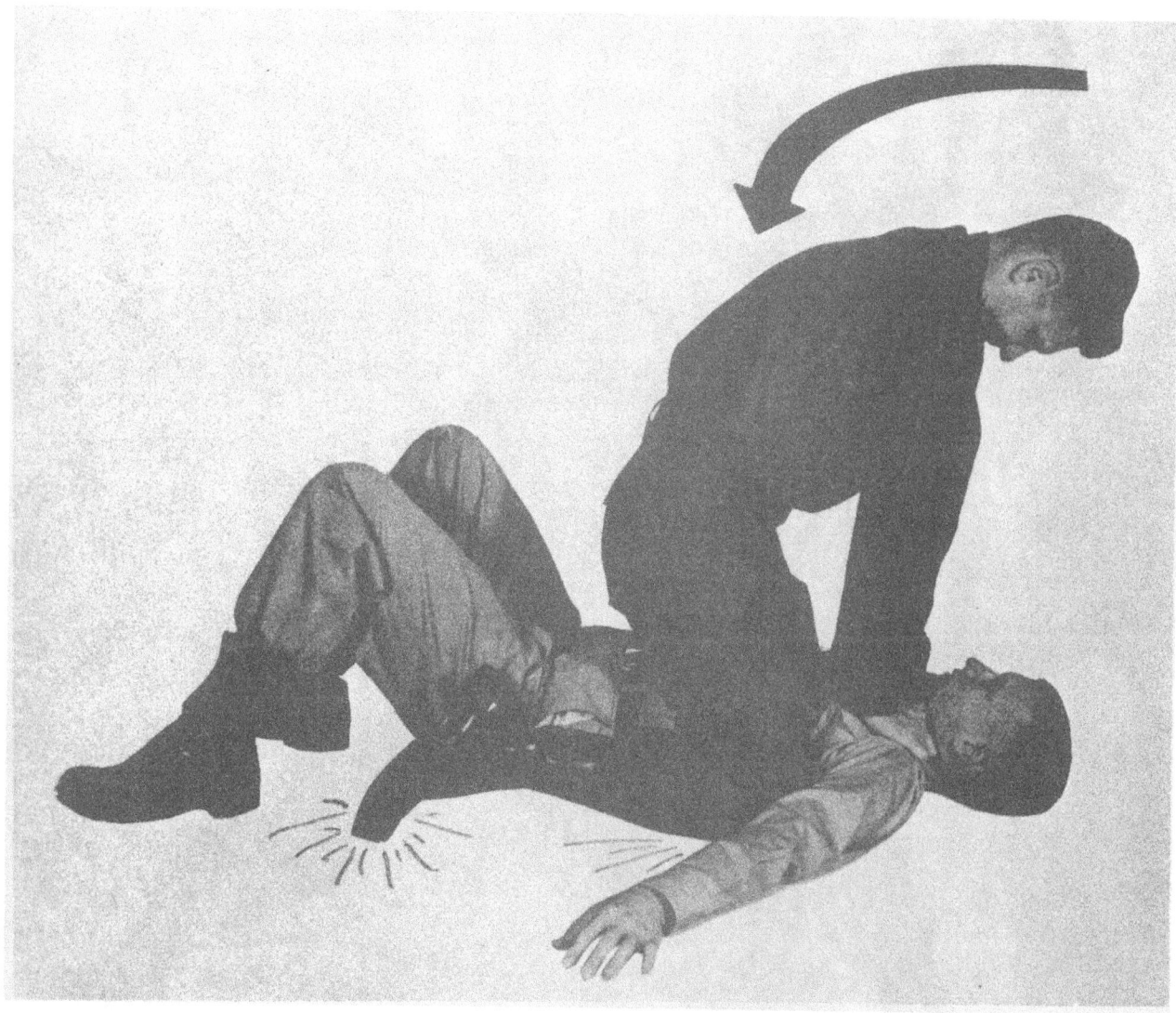

④
Figure 98—Continued.

b. Move forward shifting your weight to your left foot, maintaining your hold on his shoulders. As you shift your weight, swing your right leg forward in an arc between your left leg and your opponent's right leg until it reaches a point parallel with the ground (2, fig. 99).

c. Swing your raised right leg downward, forcefully striking your opponent's right leg and making calf-to-calf contact. As you kick his right leg, drive his shoulders viciously into the ground (3, fig. 99). Follow with a blow to a vulnerable point.

①

Figure 99. Cross-hock takedown.

②
Figure 99—Continued.

③
Figure 99—Continued.

49. Rear Takedown

a. Start the rear takedown from the guard position, standing directly behind your opponent, facing his back. Step in with your left foot placing it to the left and slightly to the rear of your opponent's left foot. Simultaneously raise your hands with the palms down directly above his shoulders (1, fig. 100). This movement is executed swiftly, in one motion.

b. Drive your right foot into the rear of your opponent's trailing knee and at the same time forcefully strike downward on your opponent's shoulders, pulling to your right rear with both hands, throwing him to the rear (2, fig. 100). Knocking your opponent off balance to the rear and driving him to the ground must be one continuous motion. To knock your opponent unconscious, drive your knee to the base of his skull as he goes down.

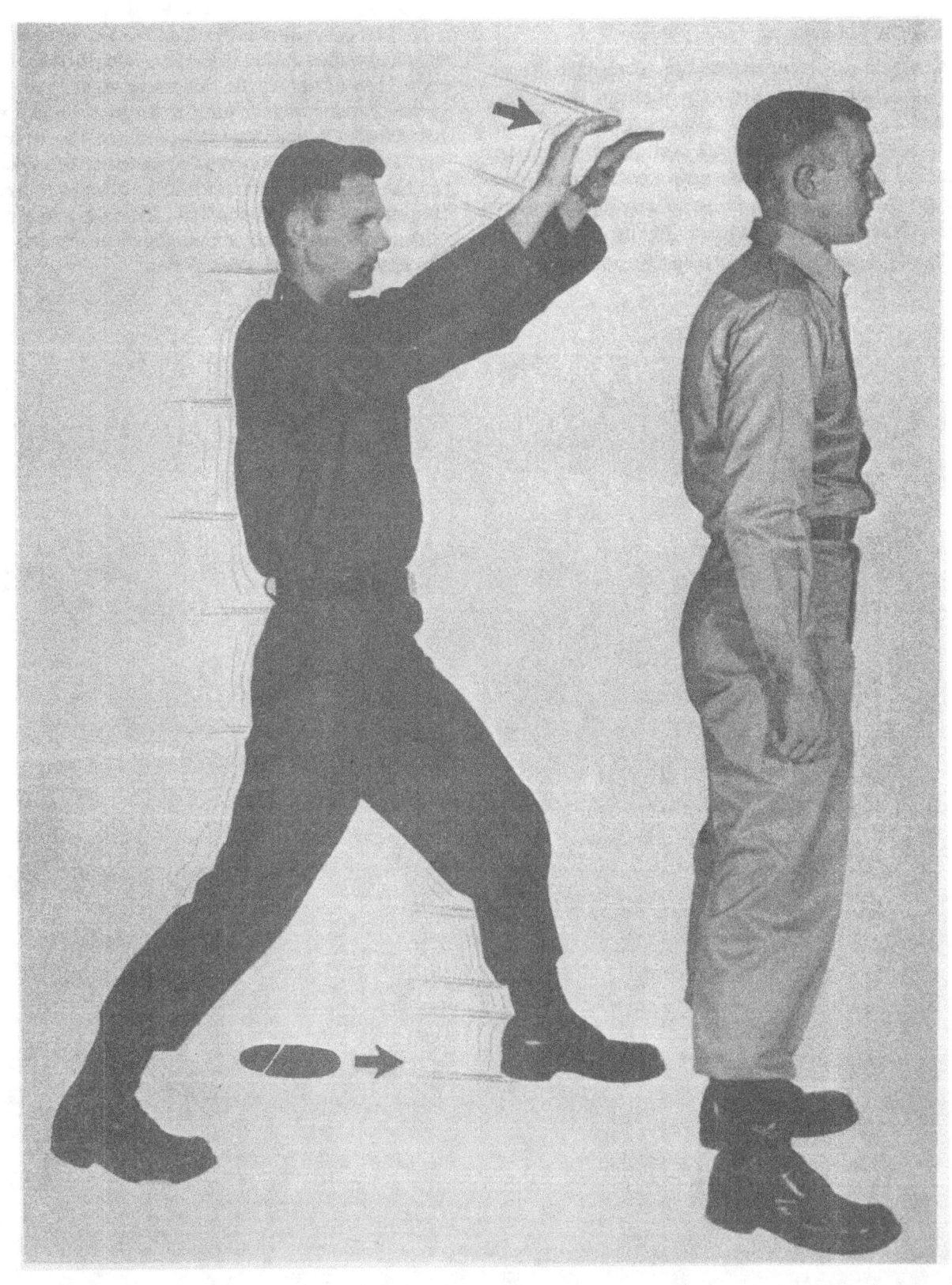

①
Figure 100. Rear takedown.

③
Figure 100—Continued.

Section VI. VARIATIONS OF BASIC THROWS AND TAKEDOWNS

50. Variations of the Hip Throw

  a. Both of your opponent's arms are securely pinned, his right arm with a single elbow lock and his left arm clasped at the elbow (fig. 101).

Figure 101. Variation of the hip throw.

b. You grab your opponent's right arm with both hands and use your hip as a fulcrum (fig. 102).

c. Place your right arm around your opponent's neck as you pivot, rather than around his waist. Your left hand locks your right arm (fig. 103).

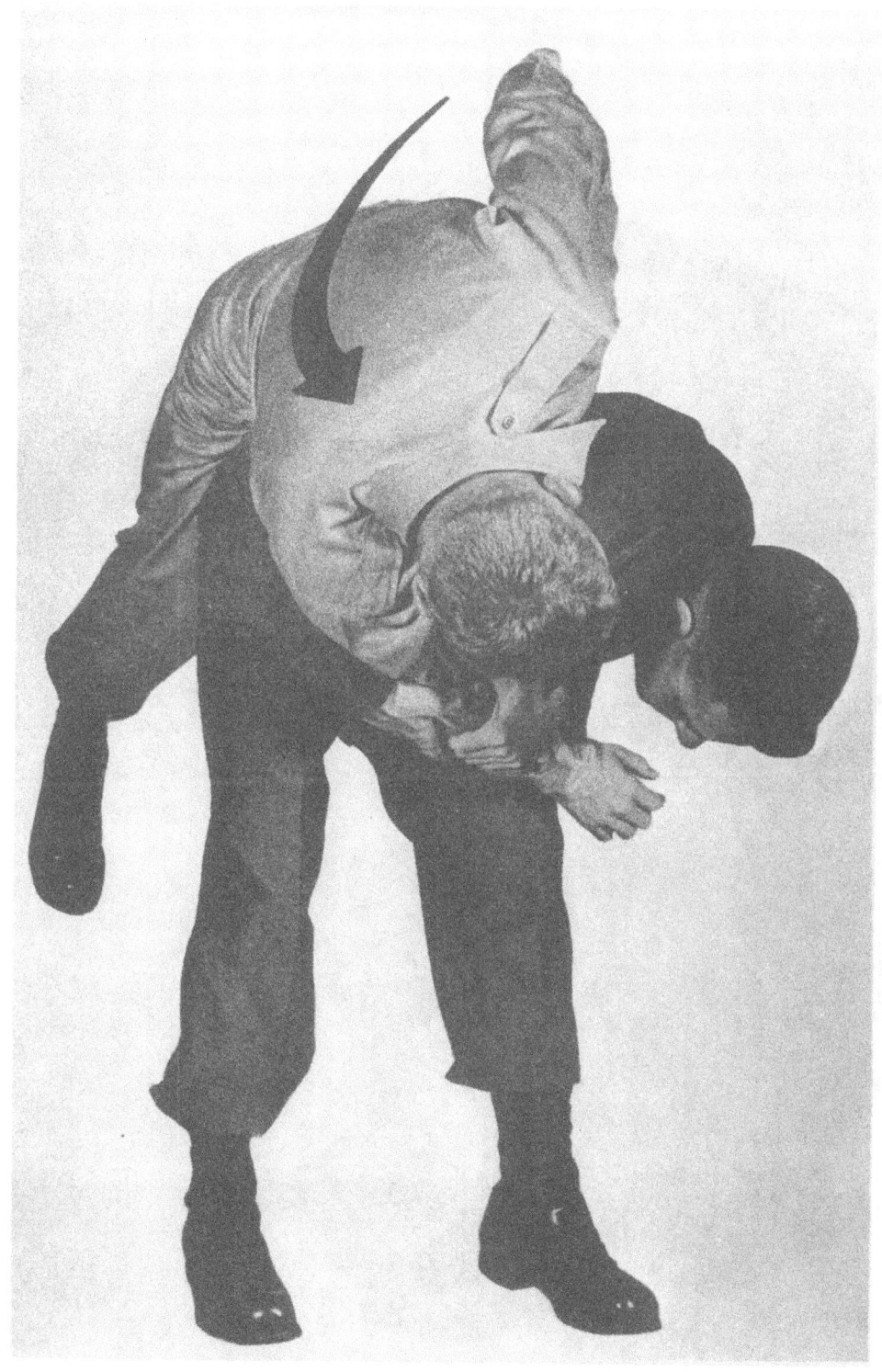

Figure 102. Variation of the hip throw.

51. Variations of the Reverse Hip Throw

a. Instead of placing your right arm around your opponent's waist, get a strangle hold around his throat (fig. 104).

b. Grab the hand of your arm which you placed around your opponent's throat as described in *a* above. This gives you a better strangle hold (fig. 105).

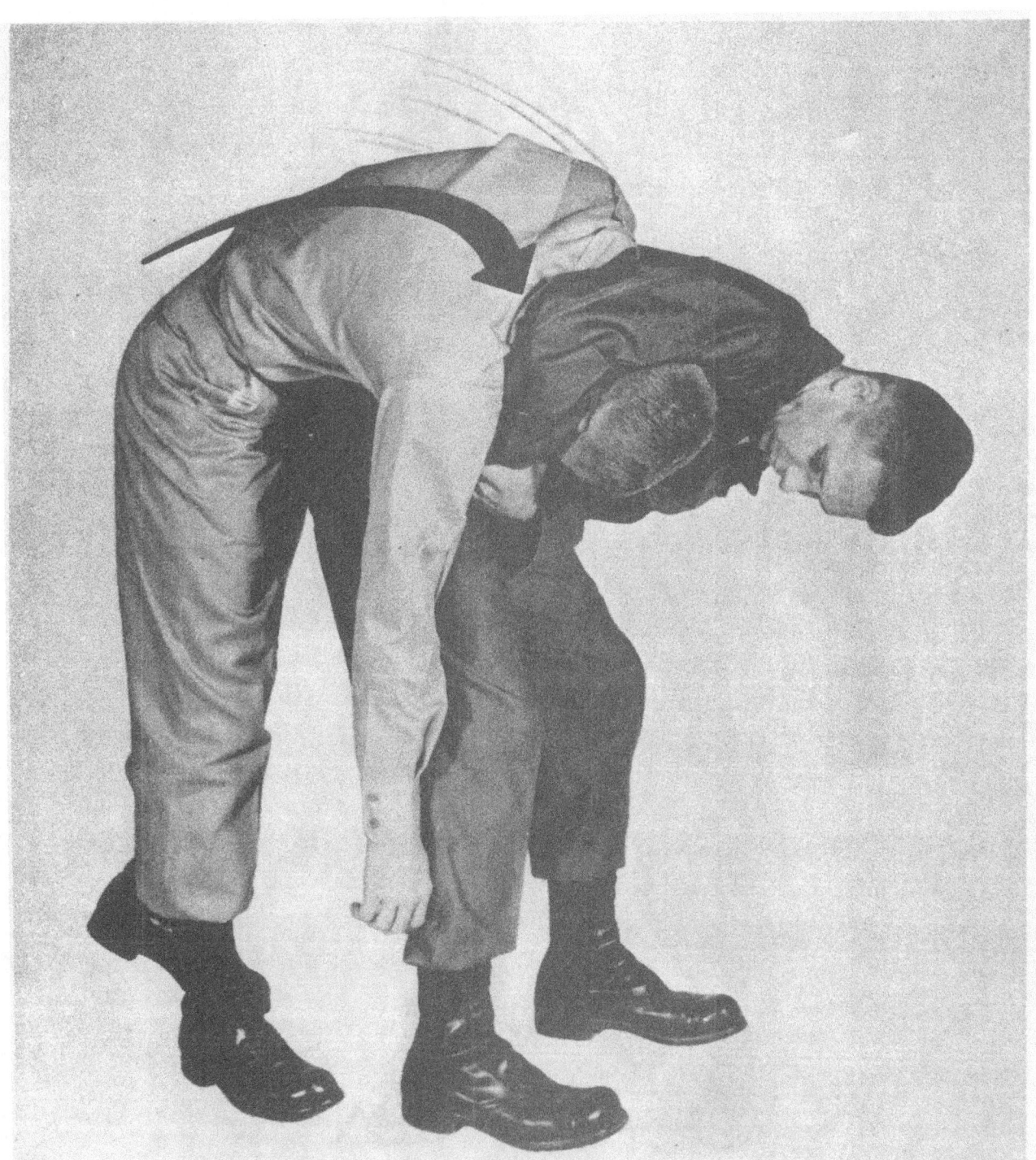

Figure 103. Variation of the hip throw.

Figure 104. Variation of the reverse hip throw.

Figure 105. Variation of the reverse hip throw.

52. Variations of the Overshoulder Throw

a. While facing your opponent grab his right wrist with your left hand. This is done when countering against an overhead blow delivered by your opponent. Then pivot to your left 180°, pulling him forward as you turn. Grab his right upper arm with your right hand and throw him over your right shoulder (fig. 106).

b. From a position facing your opponent grab his left lapel with your right hand. Maintain this hold and pivot 180° to the left, placing your right forearm under his right armpit as you complete the pivot. Grab his right arm at the elbow as you are executing the pivot. Throw him over your right shoulder (fig. 107).

Figure 106. Variation of the overshoulder throw, using opponent's arm.

Figure 107. Variation of the overshoulder throw, using your opponent's clothing.

53. Rear Strangle Takedown

a. Start from the guard position, standing directly behind and facing the same direction as your opponent. Step in with your right foot placing it directly behind your opponent. Simultaneously thrust your right arm, palm down, around your opponent's neck, striking him viciously on the Adam's apple with the large bone of your forearm. With your left fist strike your opponent a vigorous blow in the kidney region to break his balance to the rear (1, fig. 108).

①

Figure 108. Rear strangle takedown.

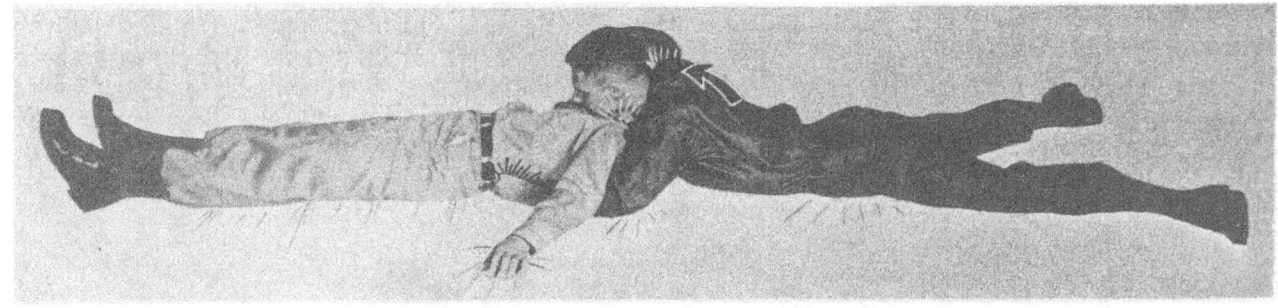
Figure 108—Continued.

b. Maintaining a firm hold with the right arm and keeping your opponent off balance with your left fist and your head along the left side of his head, walk backwards pulling him to the ground. Now you should be lying on the ground, stomach down, with your opponent on his back with his body in direct line with yours. Your legs should be spread apart to prevent your opponent from rolling you over (2, fig. 108).

c. Pull your right arm tight into your opponent's throat and place your chin over the back your right hand, locking your opponent's head into the hold. By pulling in with the right arm and rolling your right shoulder up behind your opponent's head, you can apply enough pressure to strangle him or break his neck.

d. In combat you would lunge at your opponent from his rear, applying the takedown hold described in a through c above. This lunge movement IS NOT to be used in training since the opponent's neck can be broken upon impact from the fall.

Section VII. HOLDS

54. General

The two main purposes of a hold are—

a. To kill your opponent immediately by applying enough pressure to certain parts of his body.

b. To hold your opponent until you can follow through with a blow to a vulnerable part of his body.

55. Front Strangle Hold

a. The front strangle hold is particularly good against a low frontal attack. As your opponent charges, strike his right shoulder with your left hand to slow his momentum and slip your right forearm under his throat and clamp his head under your right arm. Clasp your left wrist with your right hand. Apply pressure by leaning backward and lifting with your right forearm. You can choke your opponent in this position (fig. 109).

b. Another method of executing this hold, and one which acts more swiftly, is to grab the knife edge of your right hand with the fingers of your left hand (fig. 110). Pull forcefully toward your chest and, at the same time, lean backward. Properly executed, any strangle hold can cause unconsciousness in approximately 10 seconds. Continued pressure will kill a man in less than one minute. When applying this hold to keep the bony, inside edge of your forearm across your opponent's Adam's apple for maximum effectiveness.

56. Side Collar Strangle Hold

Grip your opponent well back on his collar with both hands, palms down (fig. 111). Use the back of collar for leverage and roll the second knuckles of your forefingers into the carotid arteries at the sides of his neck. Place both your thumbs below his Adam's apple, applying continuous pressure inward and upward.

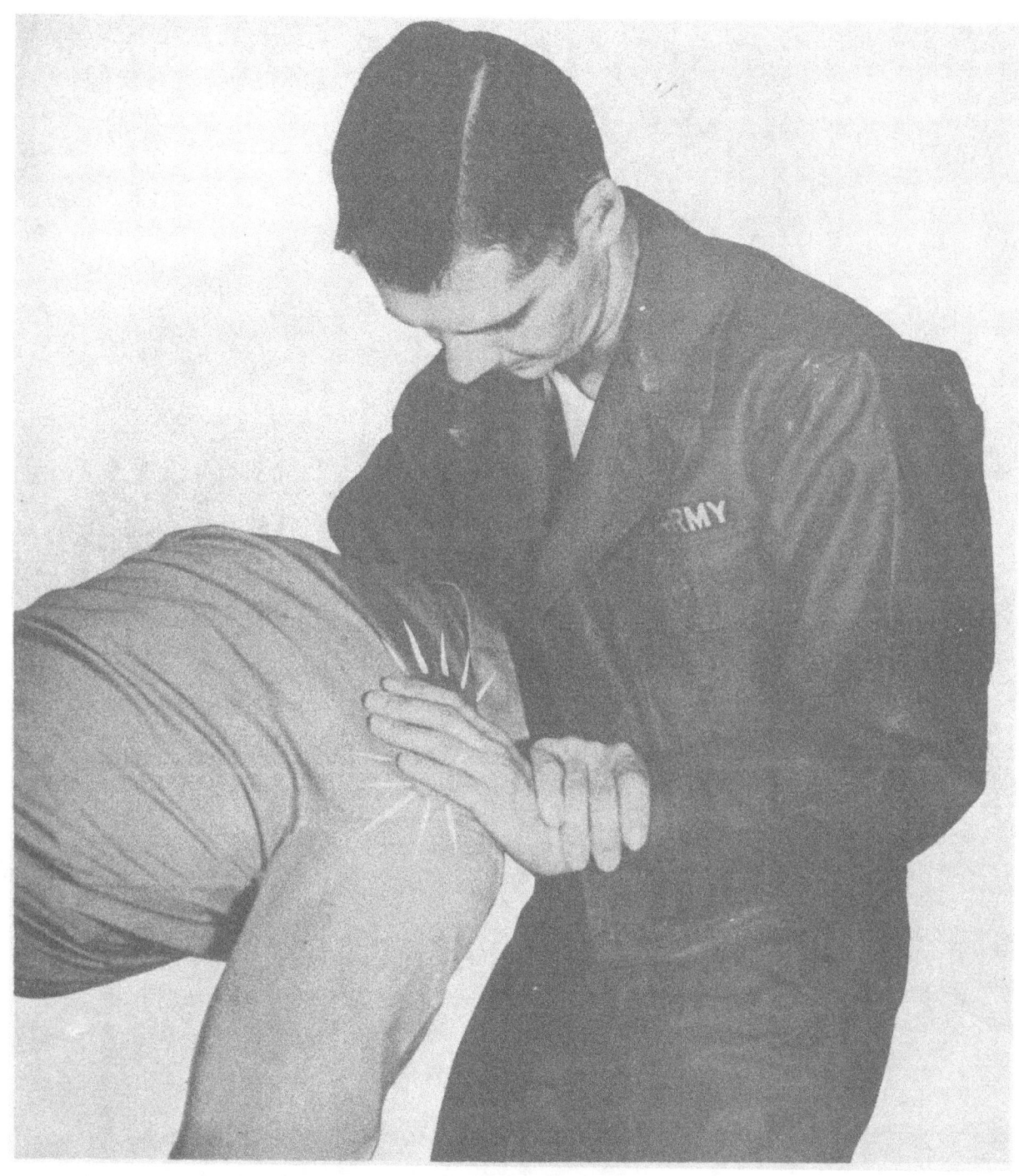

Figure 109. Front strangle hold.

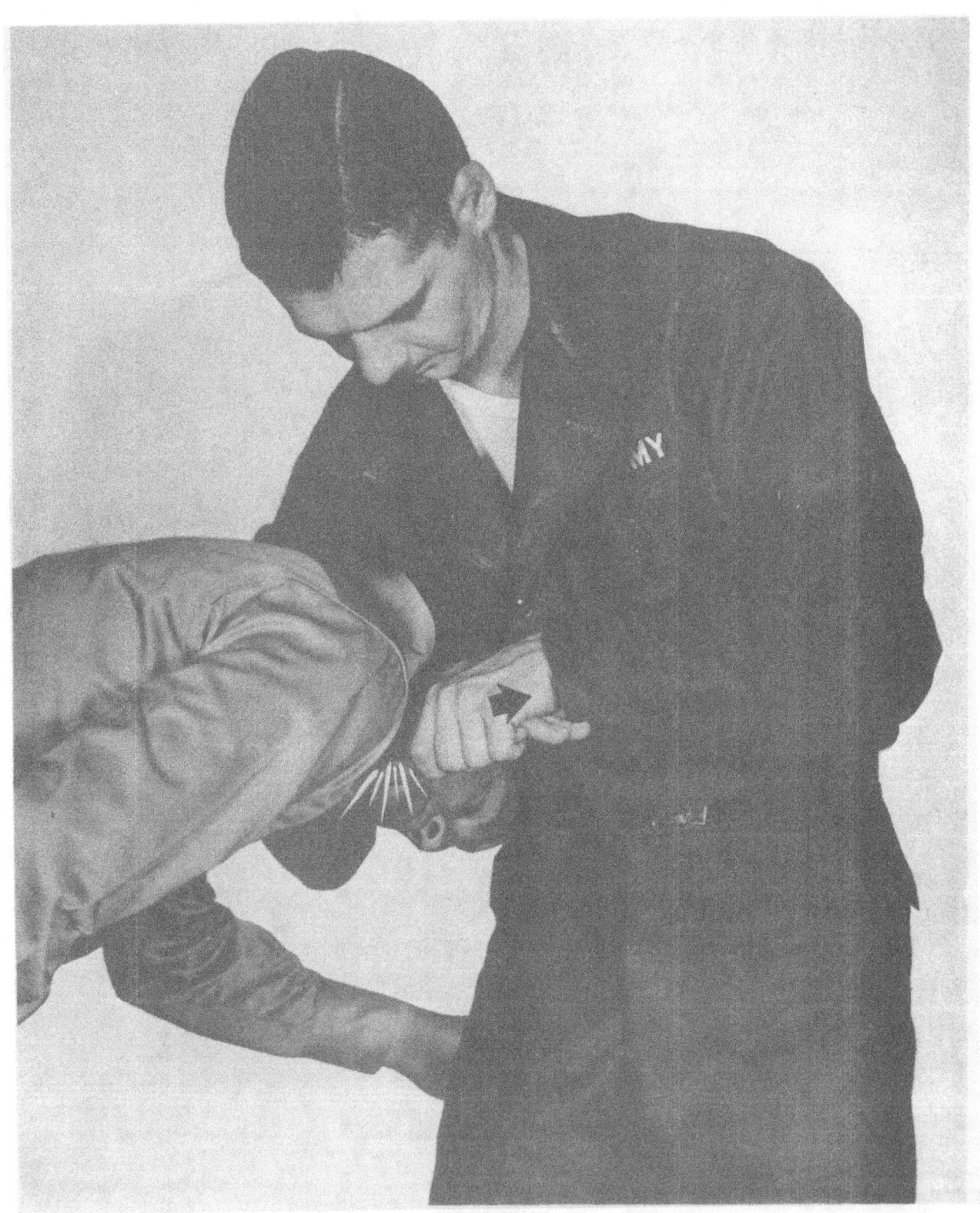

Figure 110. Variation of the front strangle hold.

This hold is best used when your opponent is on the ground and unable to attack your groin. It causes unconsciousness and eventual death by stopping the flow of blood to the brain.

57. Cross Collar Strangle Hold

To be effective, this hold must be executed on an opponent who is wearing an open collar or who has open lapels on his coat or jacket. Cross your hands at the wrists and grab the collar openings with your fingers on the inside and your thumbs on the outside (fig. 112). Pull with your fingers and scissor your hands against your opponent's throat. He will drop to the ground unconscious if the hold is properly executed. This strangle hold can also be executed from the rear. Cross your arms in front of your opponent's throat, seize his clothing at the neck, and press your hands into his throat by pulling back.

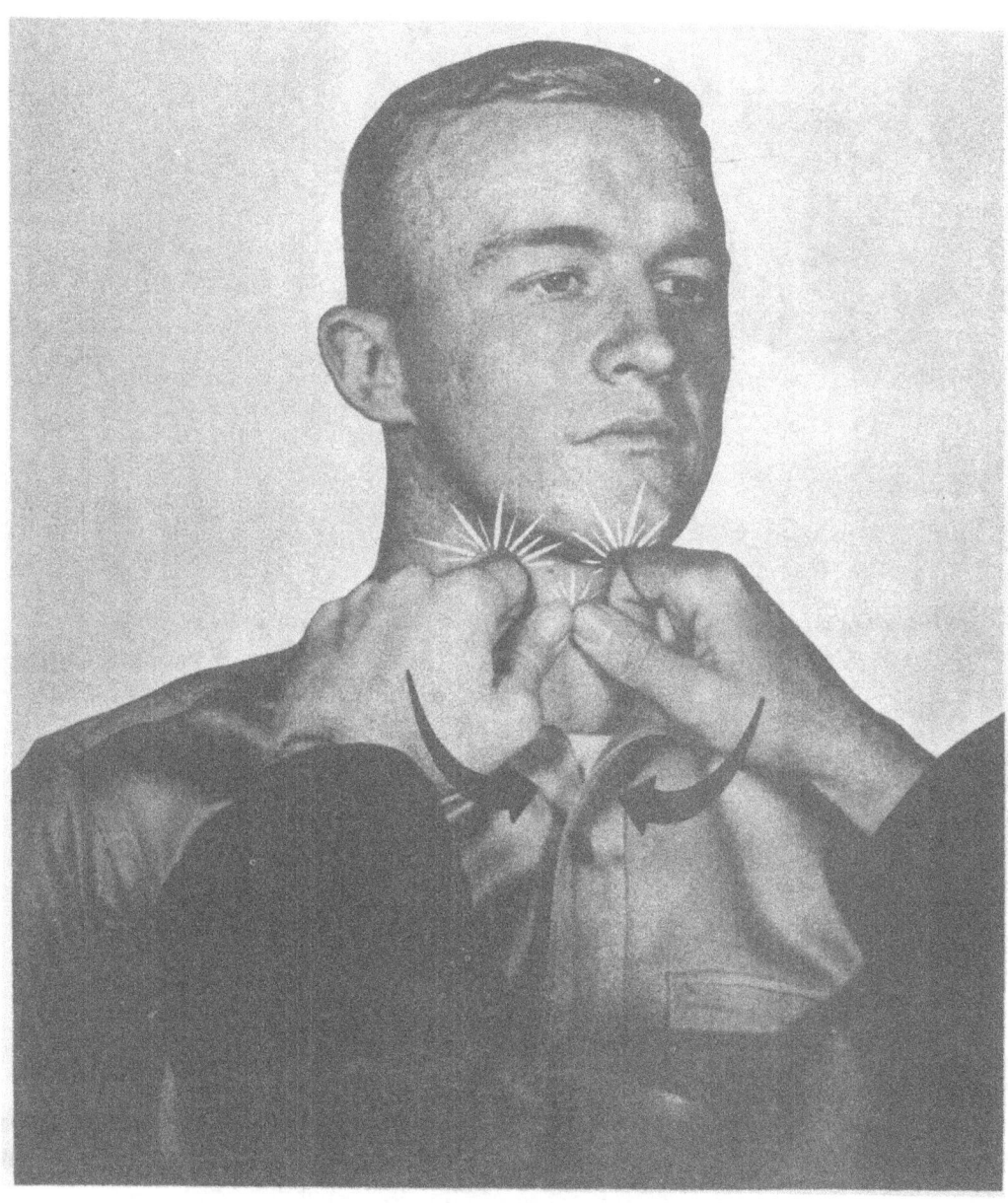

Figure 111. Side collar strangle hold.

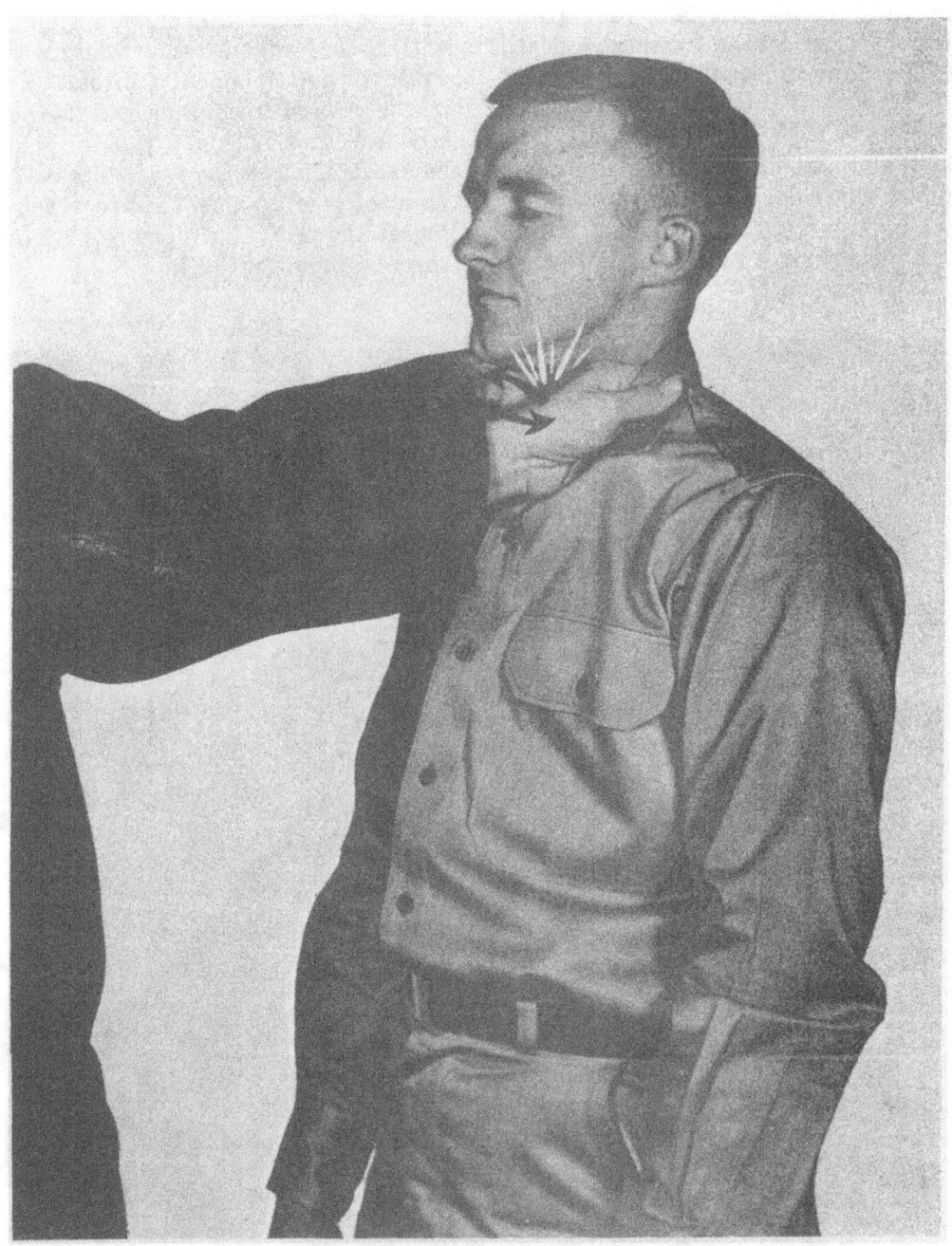

Figure 112. Cross collar strangle hold.

58. Full Nelson

a. Execute this hold from the rear. Place both arms well up into your opponent's armpits and place your hands on the back of his head. Interlock your fingers (1, fig. 113).

b. Apply downward pressure on **his head and** upward pressure under his arms (2, fig. 113). This should subdue him.

①
Figure 113. Full nelson.

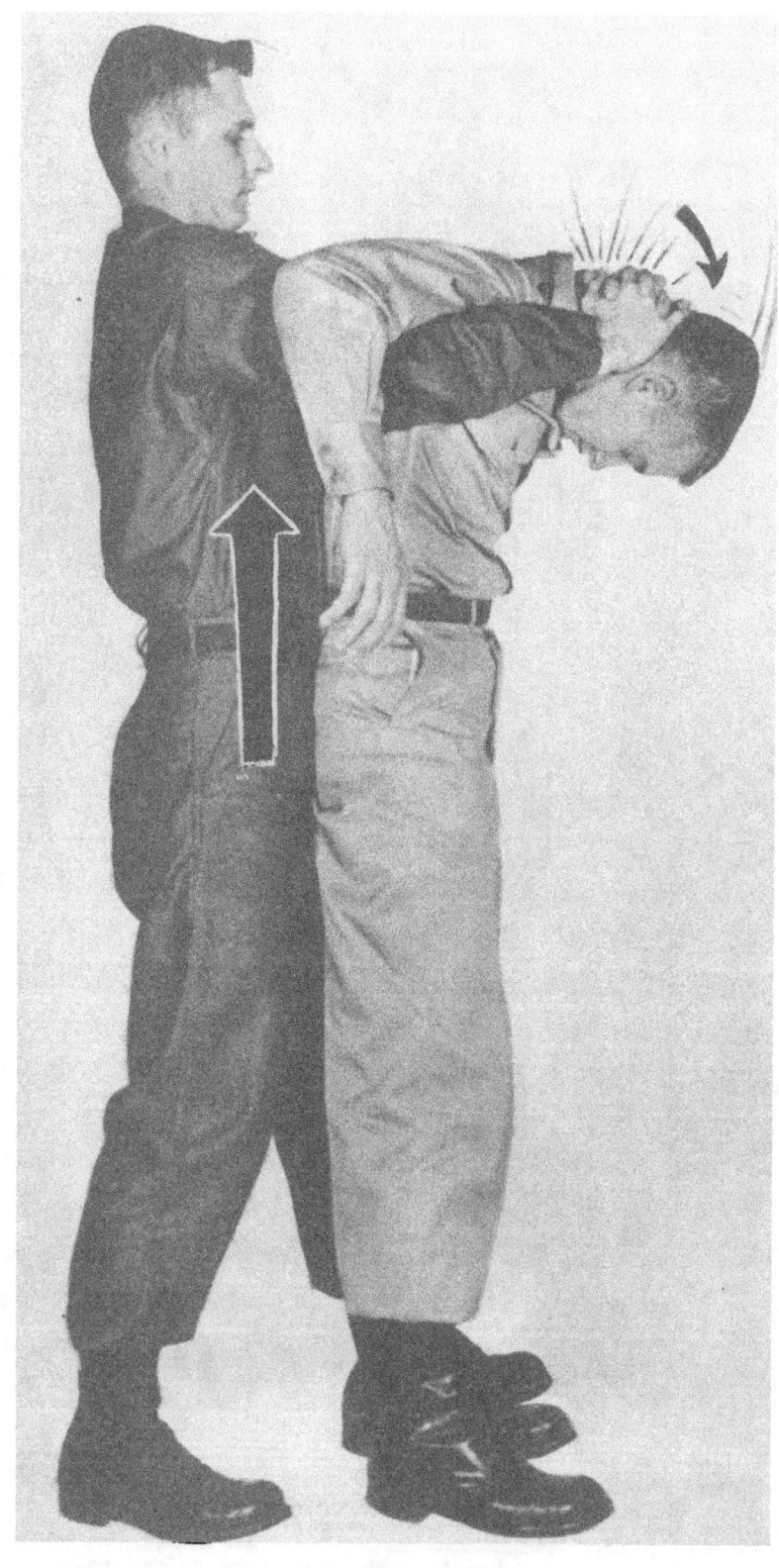

②

Figure 113—Continued.

59. Hammerlock

a. To execute the hammerlock from the rear, grab your opponent's hand or wrist and pull backward. Then force his forearm up toward his head. By keeping your right hand at his right elbow and continuing to force his arm up, you can dislocate his shoulder (fig. 114).

b. To execute the hammerlock when facing your opponent, grab his right wrist with both hands. Pivot to your left 180°. During the pivot, raise your opponent's arm above your head and step beneath it and behind him at the completion of your turn.

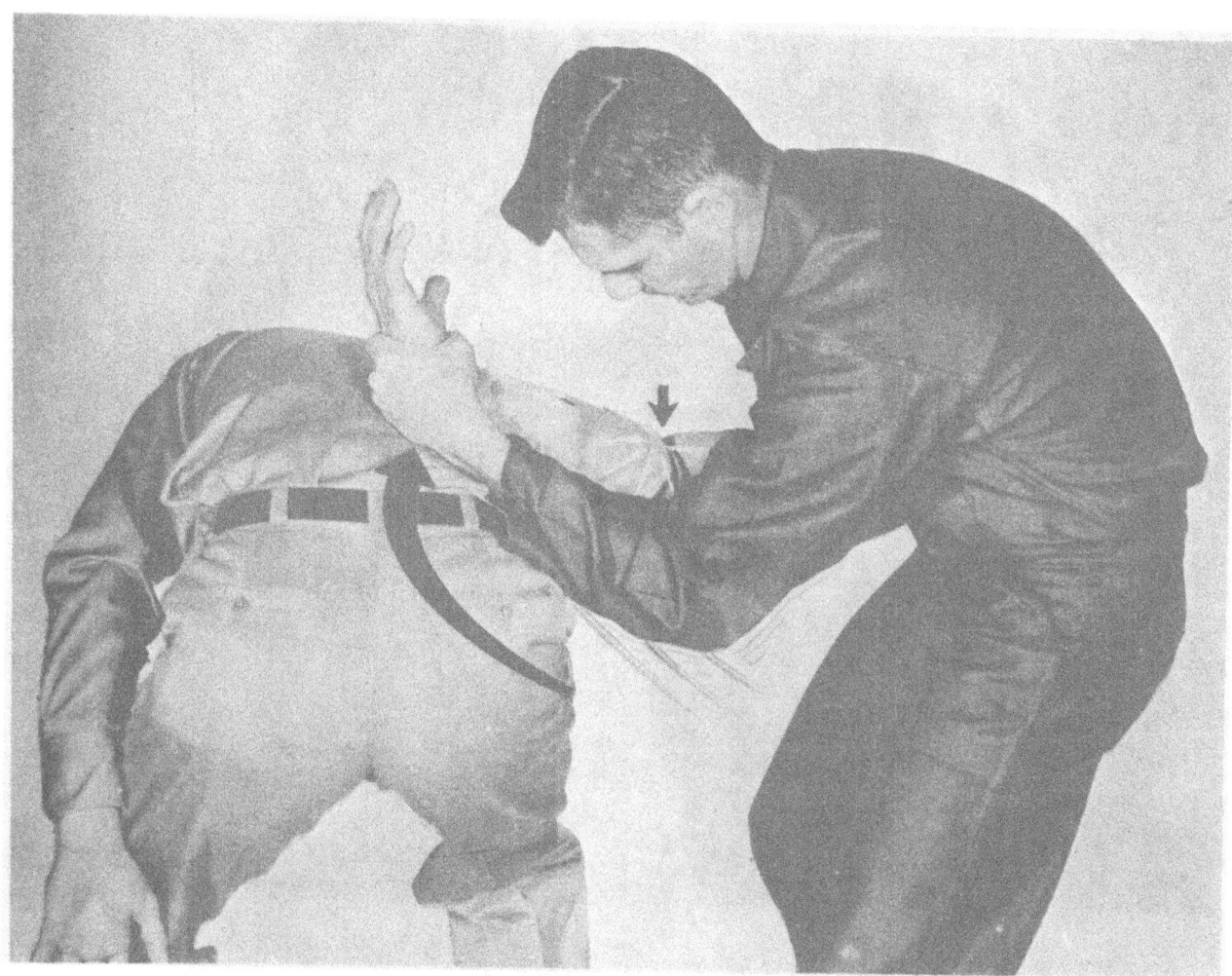

Figure 114. Hammerlock.

60. Rear Strangle Hold

a. Use the rear strangle hold when approaching your opponent from his rear. Place your left hand on the back of his head and, at the same time, cross your right forearm under his neck from the right (1, fig. 115). Striking your opponent's Adam's apple as you go into this hold will stun him temporarily.

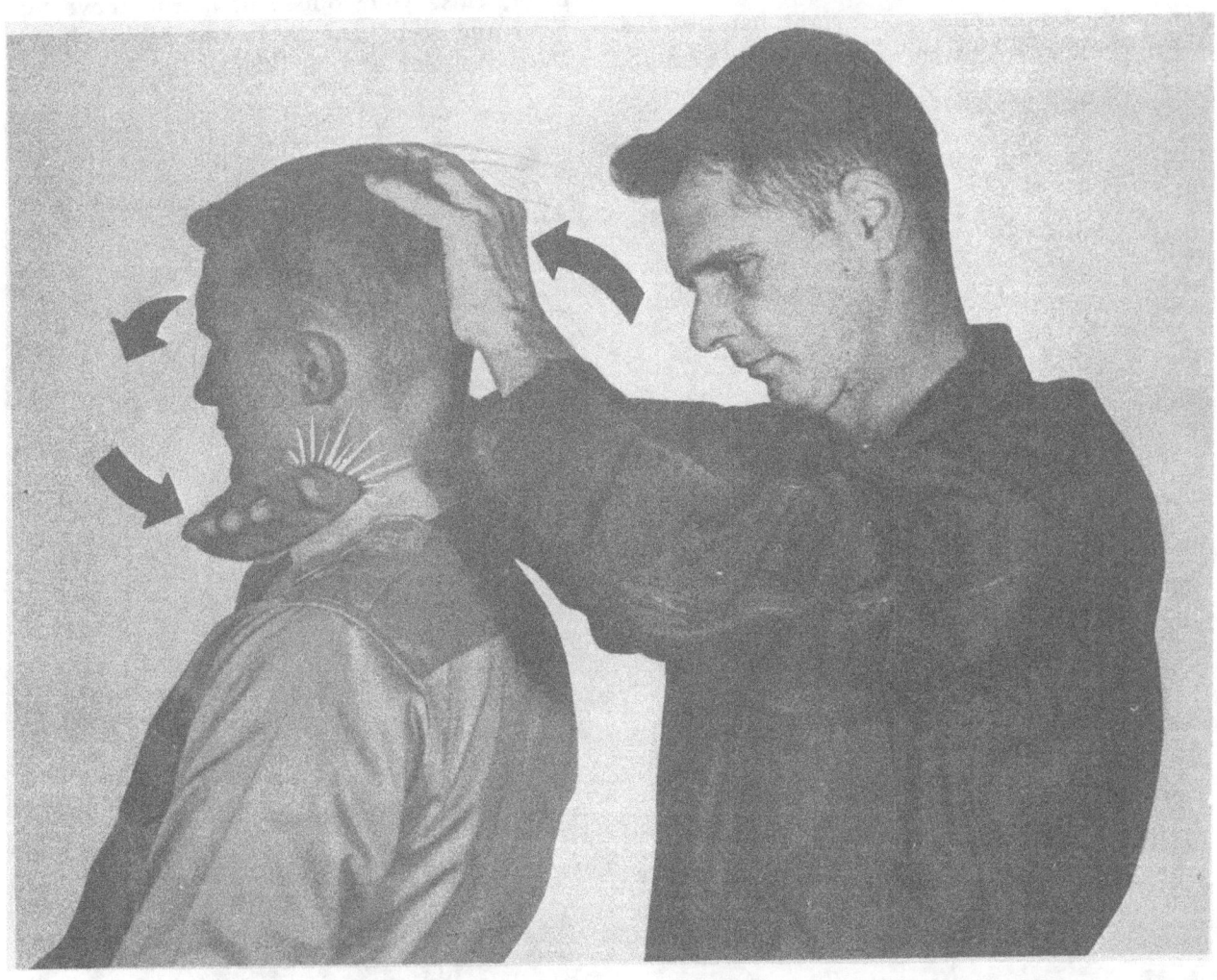

①
Figure 115. Rear strangle hold.

b. Place your left elbow over your opponent's left shoulder and lock it in place with your right hand (2, fig. 115). In this position, push with your left hand on the back of his head and lean forward; enough pressure can break his neck. Keep the inside, bony edge of your right forearm against his Adam's apple.

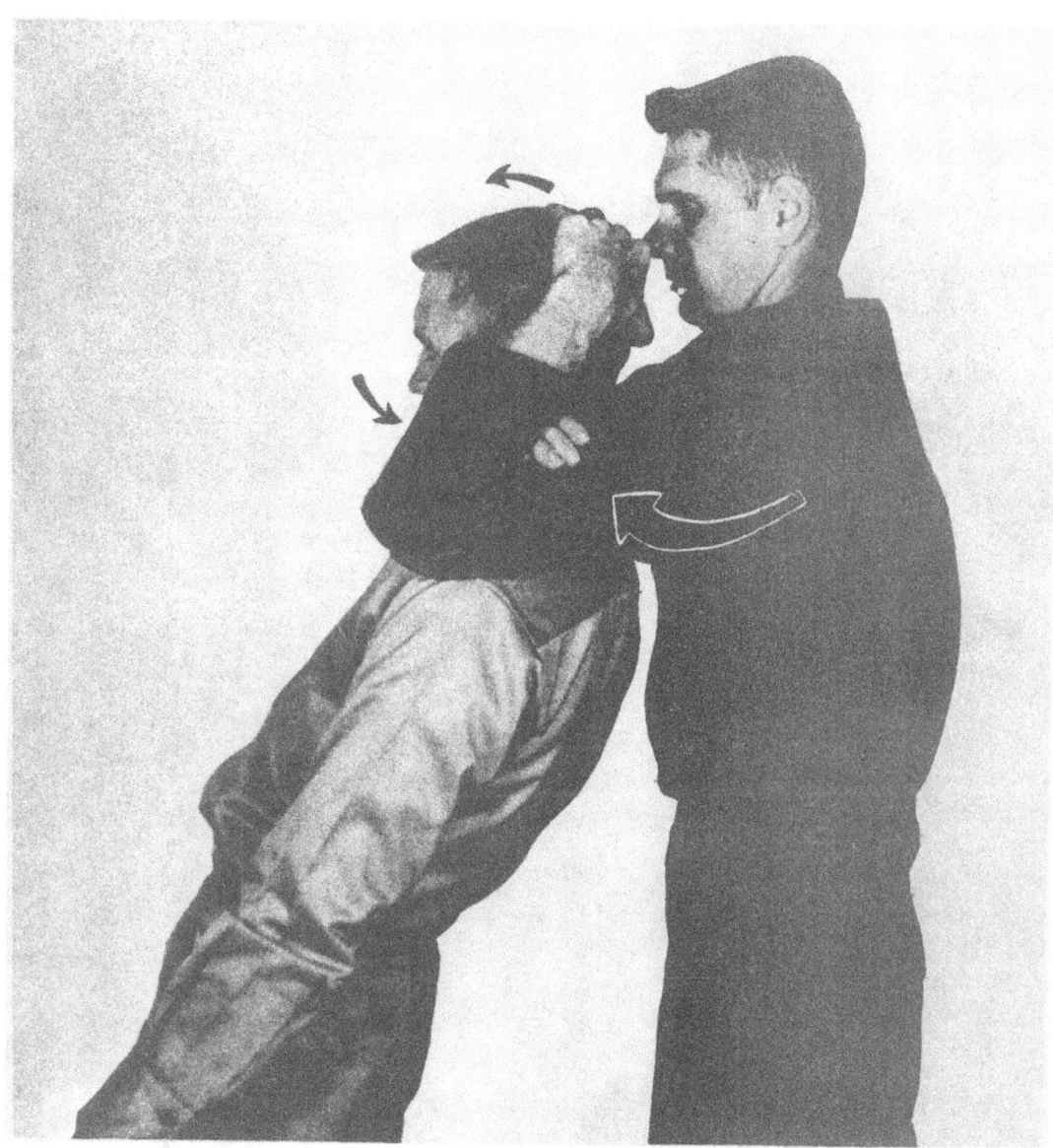

Figure 115—Continued.

61. Double Wristlock

a. To execute a double wristlock, grab your opponent's right wrist with your left hand. Pass your right hand and arm over his right upper arm, under his bent elbow, and clasp your left wrist, completing the double wristlock (fig. 116).

Figure 116. Double wristlock.

b. You can continue into a twisting hammerlock by jerking his arm up and back (fig. 117).

c. Figure 118 illustrates a variation of the double wristlock.

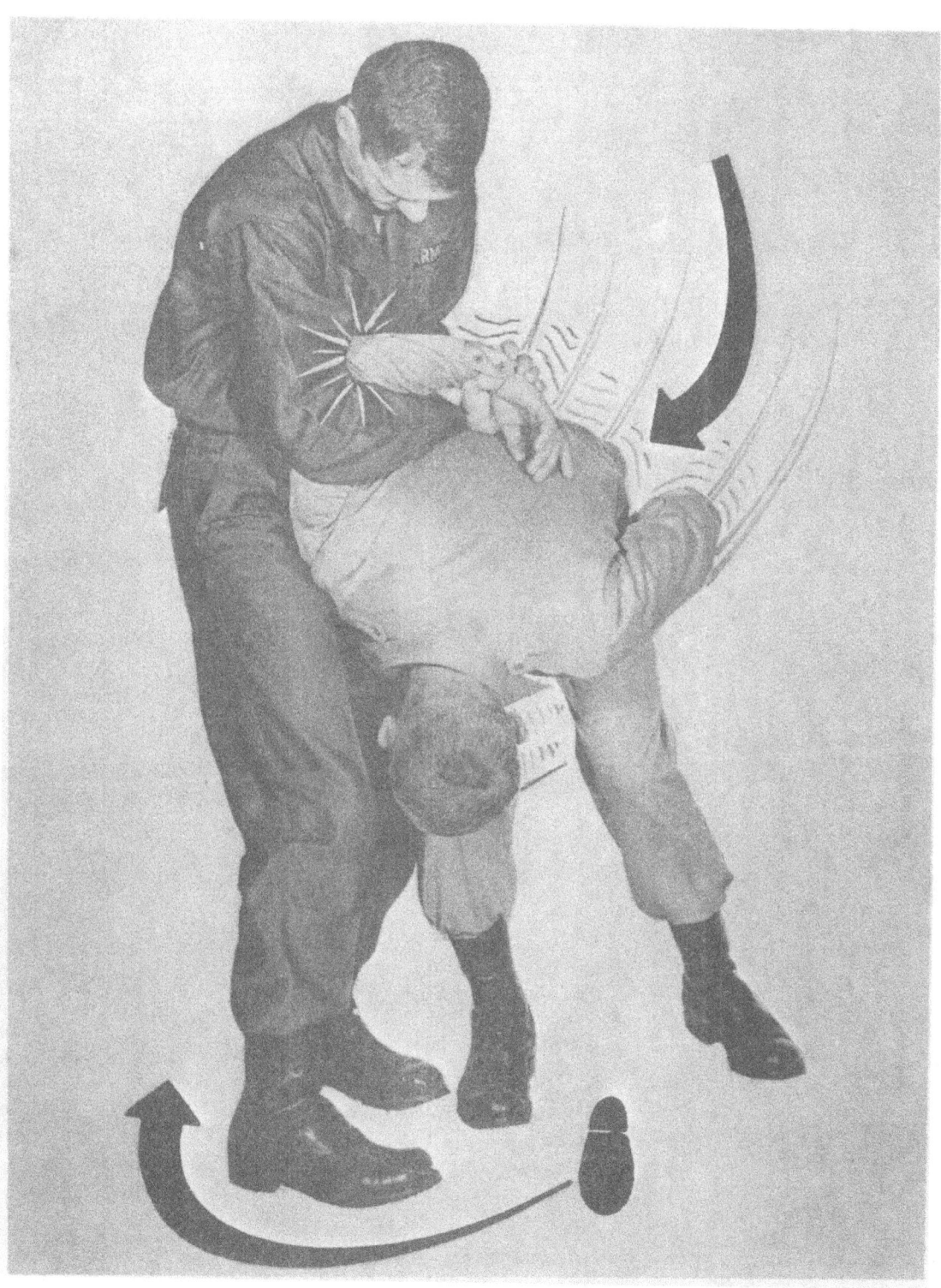

Figure 117. Double wristlock to hammerlock.

Figure 118. Double wristlock variation.

Section VIII. ESCAPE FROM HOLDS

62. General

If your opponent succeeds in getting a hold on you, you must break the hold before or immediately after he completes it. Bite, kick, or hit him at vulnerable points to help loosen or break the hold before he can apply pressure. By

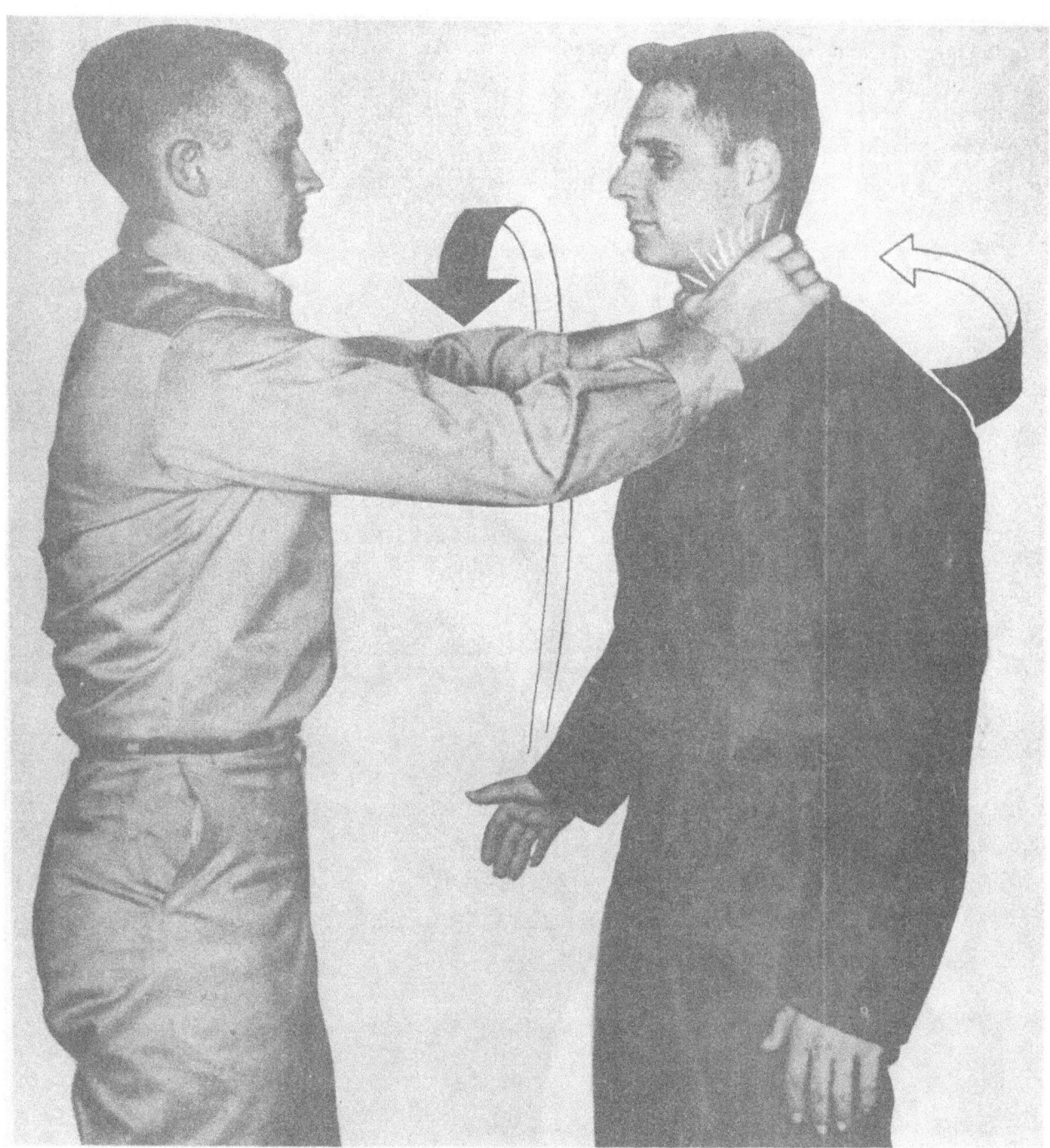

①
Figure 119. Breaking a choke hold.

escaping from your opponent's grasp immediately, you can take the offensive and attack him.

63. Escape from Choke Hold

a. When your opponent attempts to choke you, use a roundhouse arm swing to break his hold (1, fig. 119).

b. Swing your arm over his arms in a forceful roundhouse blow. As you do this, pivot in the direction of your swing to get as much of your body weight as possible behind your arm swing (2, fig. 119). This causes your opponent to loosen his hold. Be prepared to strike him about the face or neck with a backward, knife edge blow of your hand before he recovers.

c. This escape can also be used against a choke hold from the rear. Swing your arm and pivot around facing your opponent as you swing.

64. Another Escape from a Choke Hold

a. As your opponent gains the choke hold, clasp your hands together (1, fig. 120). Grip the knife edge of your left hand with the fingers of your right hand and tightly wrap the left thumb around the right thumb. Do not interlock your fingers.

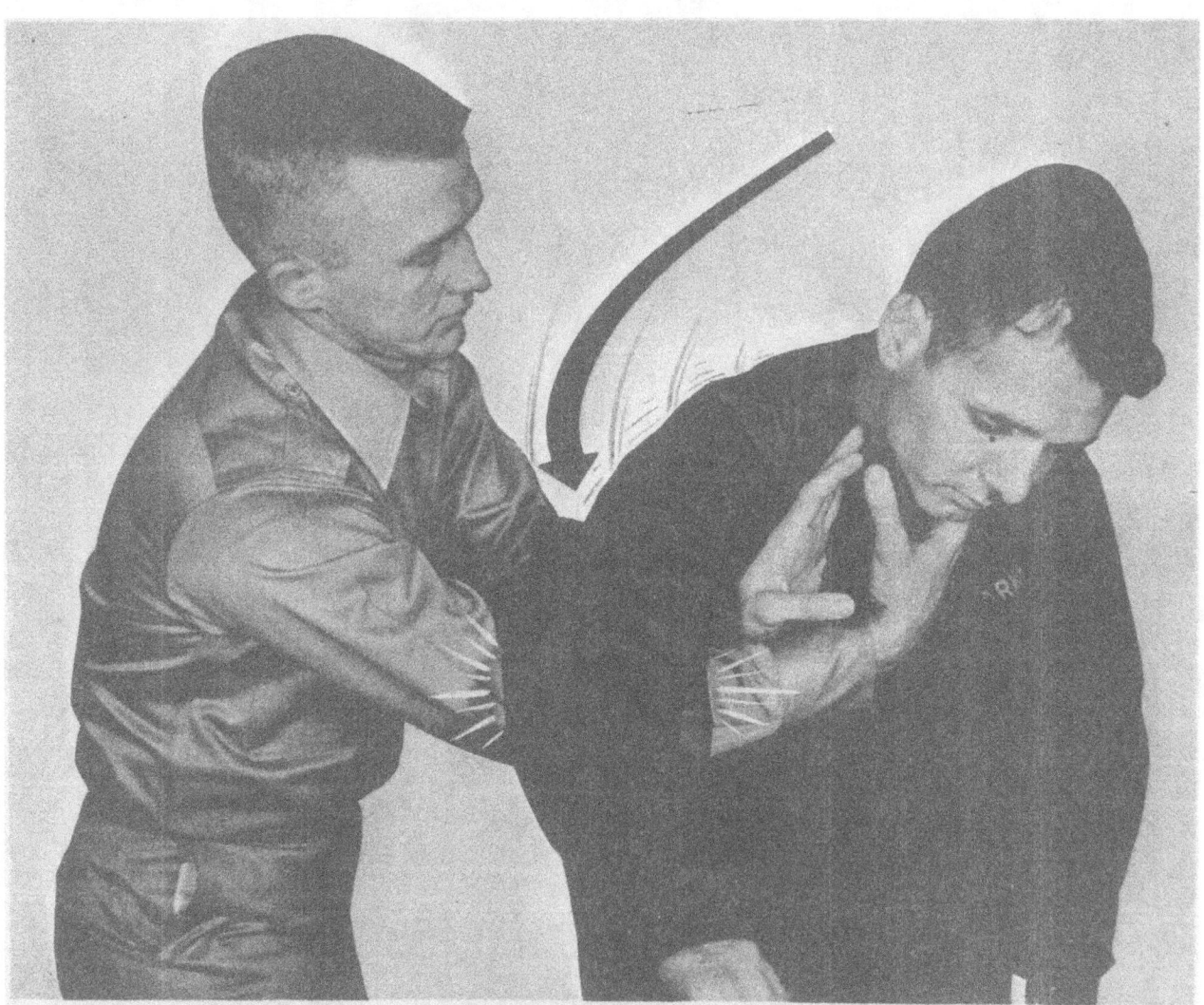

Figure 119—Continued.

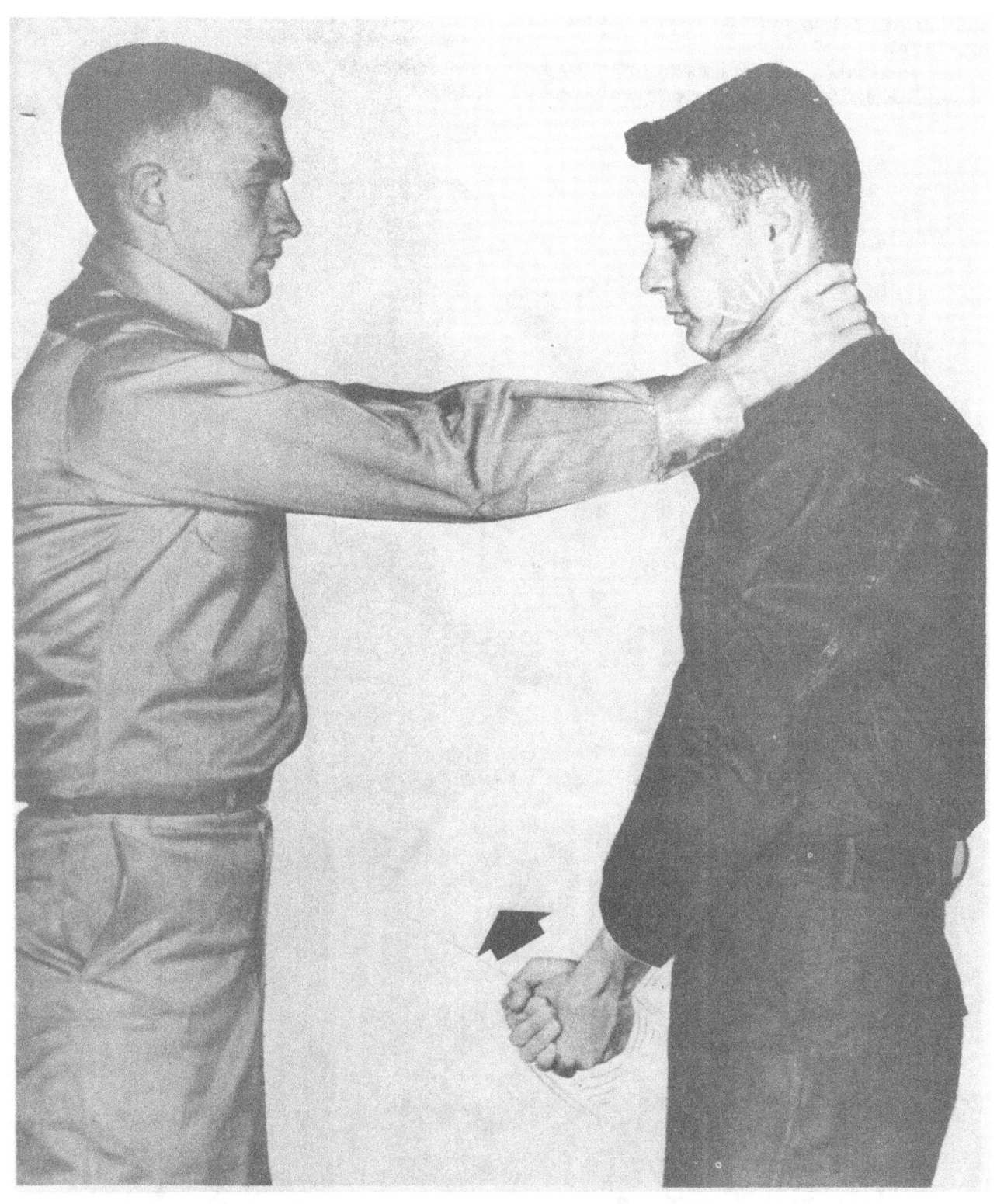

①
Figure 120. Another escape from a choke hold.

b. Drive your hands up between your opponent's arms forcing him to loosen his hold (2, fig. 120).

c. From this position, smash your clasped hands on the bridge of his nose or grab the back of his head and pull it down, meeting it with a knee lift (3, fig. 120). You can also separate your hands after breaking the hold and strike his collarbone with the knife edge of your hands.

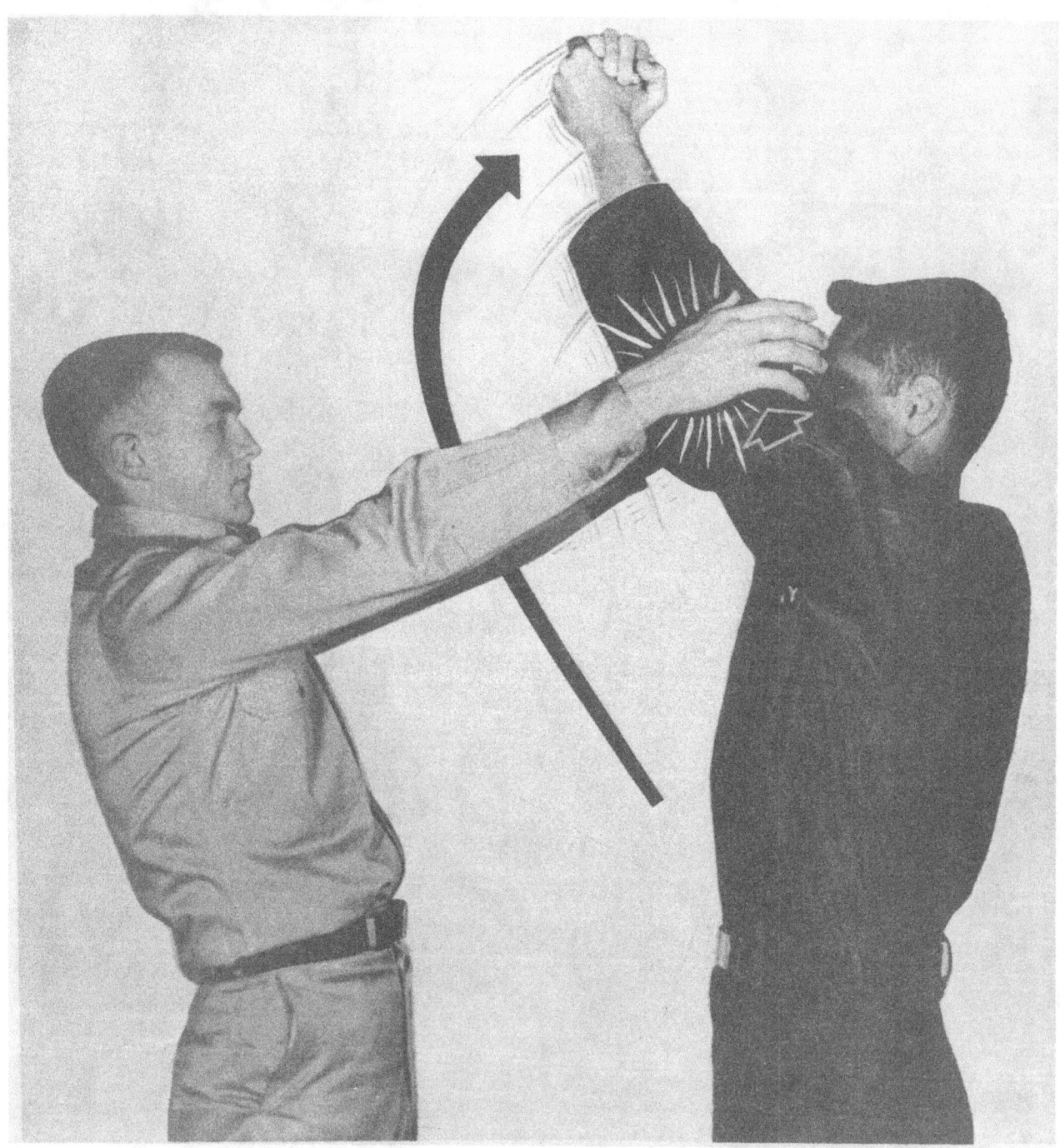

Figure 120—Continued.

③
Figure 120—Continued.

65. Escaping a Two-Hand Front Strangle Hold When Pinned Against a Wall

a. Ordinarily, an opponent attempting to strangle you while your back is to a wall extends his arms, squeezes his fingers, and pushes you against a wall (1, fig. 121).

b. To escape this hold you place the heel of your right hand on his left elbow and the heel of your left hand on his right elbow. Apply pressure inward and away from yourself (2, fig. 121). This prevents your opponent from using the power of his fingers and he cannot choke you. To force him back, drive your knee or toe into his groin.

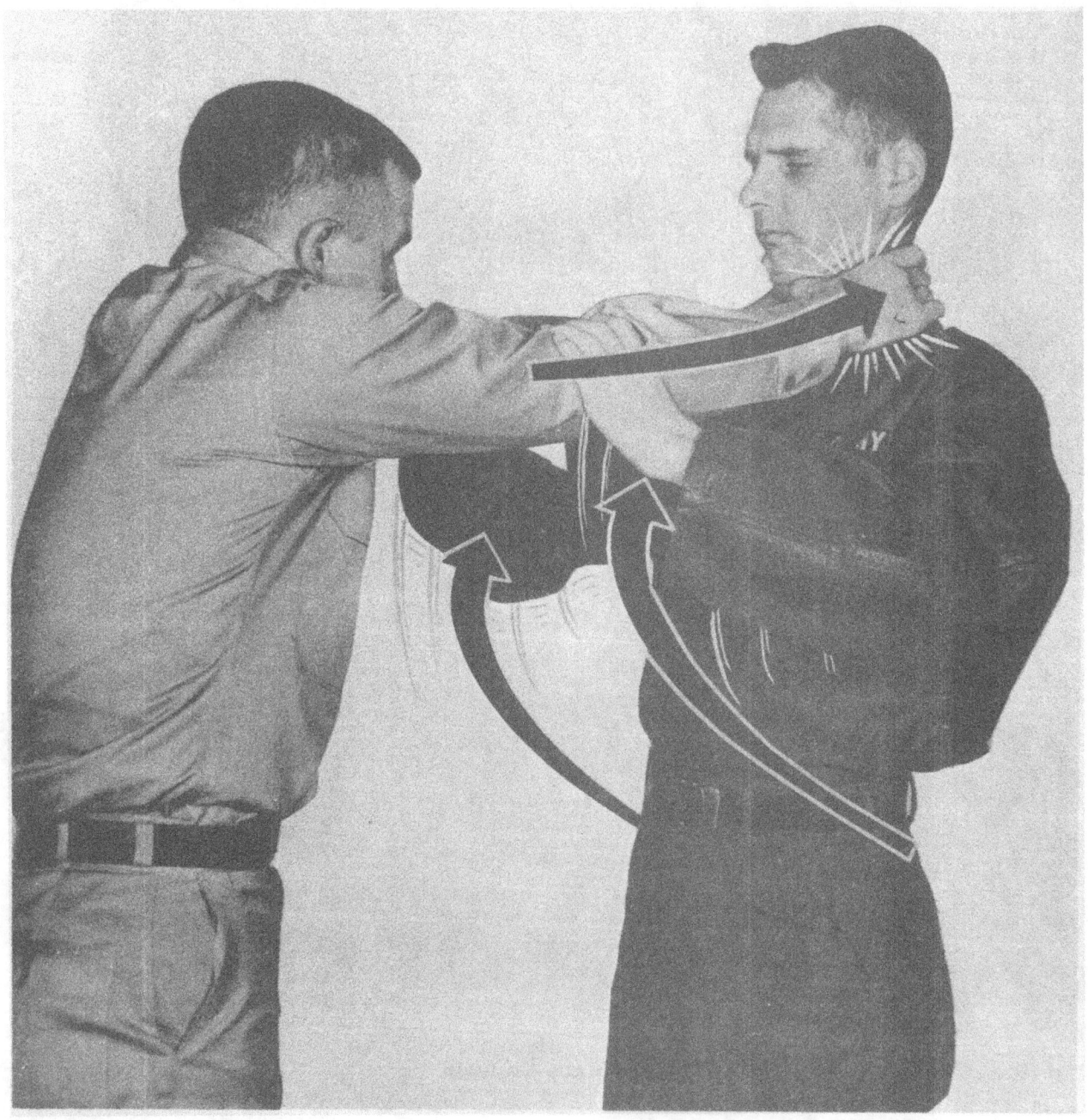

①

Figure 121. Escaping a two-hand front strangle hold.

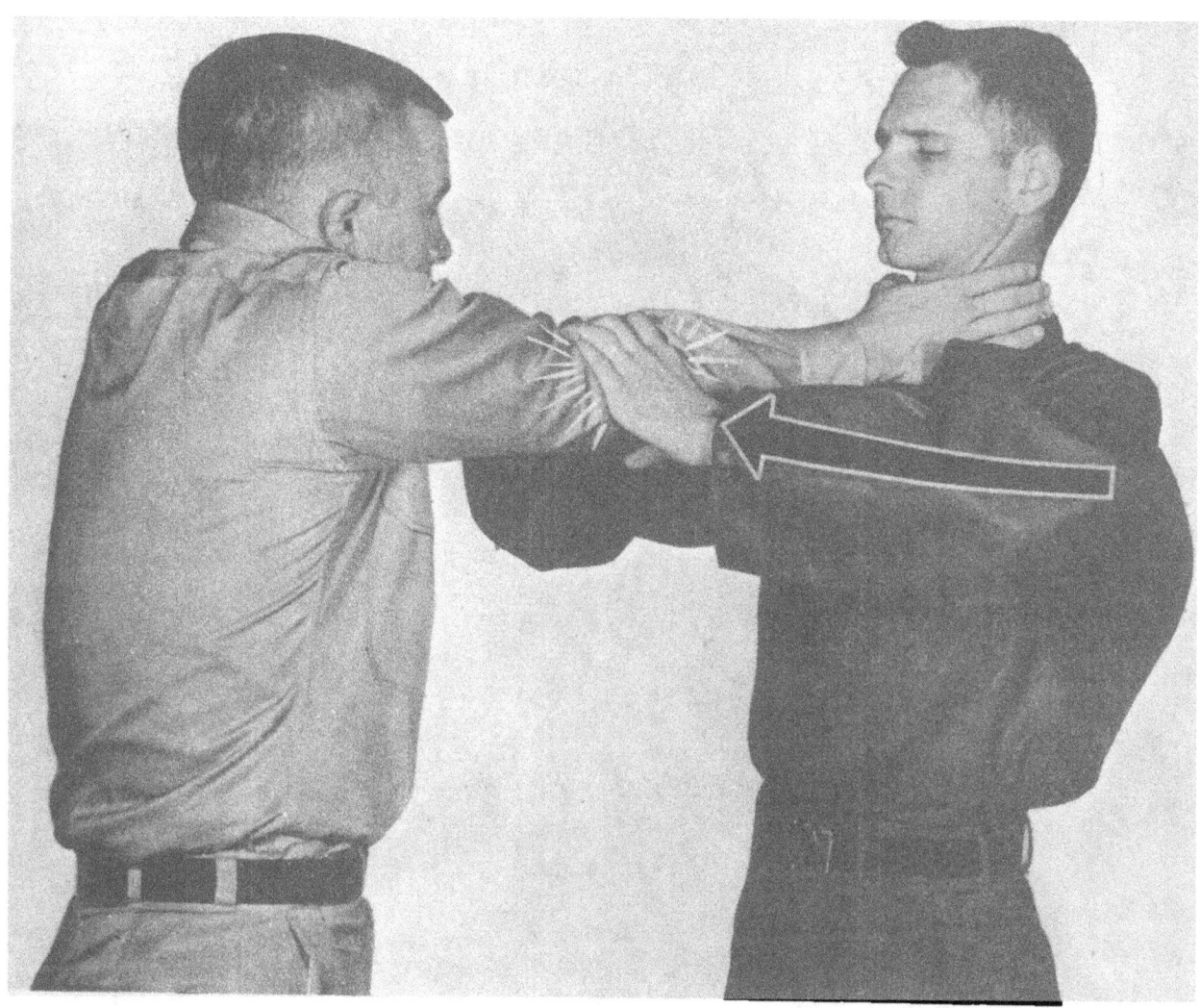

①
Figure 121—Continued.

66. Escaping a Front Overarm Bear Hug

a. To escape an opponent who has grabbed you around the body and pinned your arms in a front overarm bear hug (1, fig. 122), bring your thumbs into his groin forcing his hips backward and leaving a space between your bodies (2, fig. 122).

b. Pivoting on your left foot, place your right foot outside of your opponent's right foot. Slip your right arm under his left armpit and grab him across the back. With your left hand grab his right upper arm, pulling it forcefully. Drive your buttocks into his midsection and at the same time twist to your left. Lift with your right arm and pull with your left hand, throwing your opponent over your hip and to the ground (3, fig. 122). As your opponent strikes the ground followup with a blow to a vulnerable point.

1 Front overarm
Figure 122. Bear hug.

2 Escaping a front overarm bear hug
Figure 122—Continued.

3 Escaping a front overarm bear hug—Continued.
Figure 122—Continued.

67. Escape from Front Underarm Bear Hug

a. An opponent may lock his arms around your waist and attempt to bend you over backwards with a front underarm bear hug (1, fig. 123).

b. To escape this hold, place the thumb of your left hand under the base of your opponent's nose. Put your right arm around his waist. By pressing with your left thumb and pulling his waist toward you, he either loosens his grip or is forced backward (2, fig. 123).

1 Front underarm bear hug
Figure 123. Bear hug.

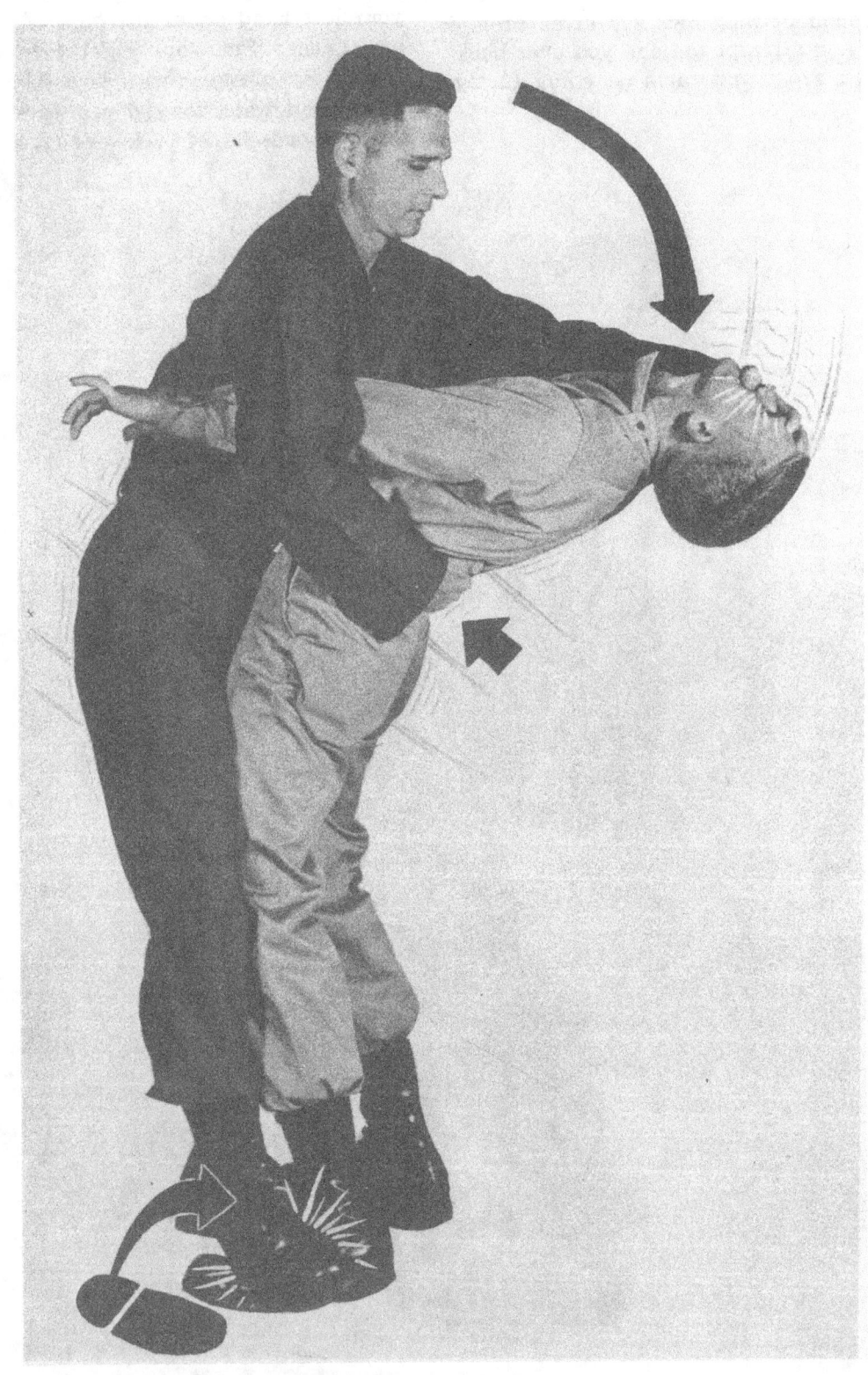

2 Escaping a front underarm bear hug
Figure 123—Continued.

68. Escaping a Two-Hand Grip on One Wrist

a. Your opponent may grab you with a two-hand grip on one wrist (1, fig. 124).

b. To escape, step forward with your right foot and bend both knees. Keeping the trunk of your body upright, bring your right elbow close to your stomach and reach across with your left hand and grab your right fist (2, fig. 124).

c. By straightening your legs and pulling back with the power of your body and arms, you bring pressure on your opponent's thumbs, forcing him to release his hold. At the com-

1 Two-hand grip on right wrist
Figure 124. Two-hand grip.

pletion of the escape you are in position to deliver a blow to your opponent's head or neck with the knife edge of your right hand (3 fig. 124).

69. Escaping an Overhand Grip on Both Wrists

a. Your opponent may grab you with an overhand grip on both wrists (1, fig. 125).

b. To escape, step forward with either foot and bend both knees. At the same time, bend your arms so the elbows are close to your lower abdomen. Pull your opponent forward and downward (2, fig. 125).

c. Execute the escape by straightening your legs, pulling back with your body, and pushing your arms upward in one motion. Speed is important if the escape movement is to be effective (3, fig. 125).

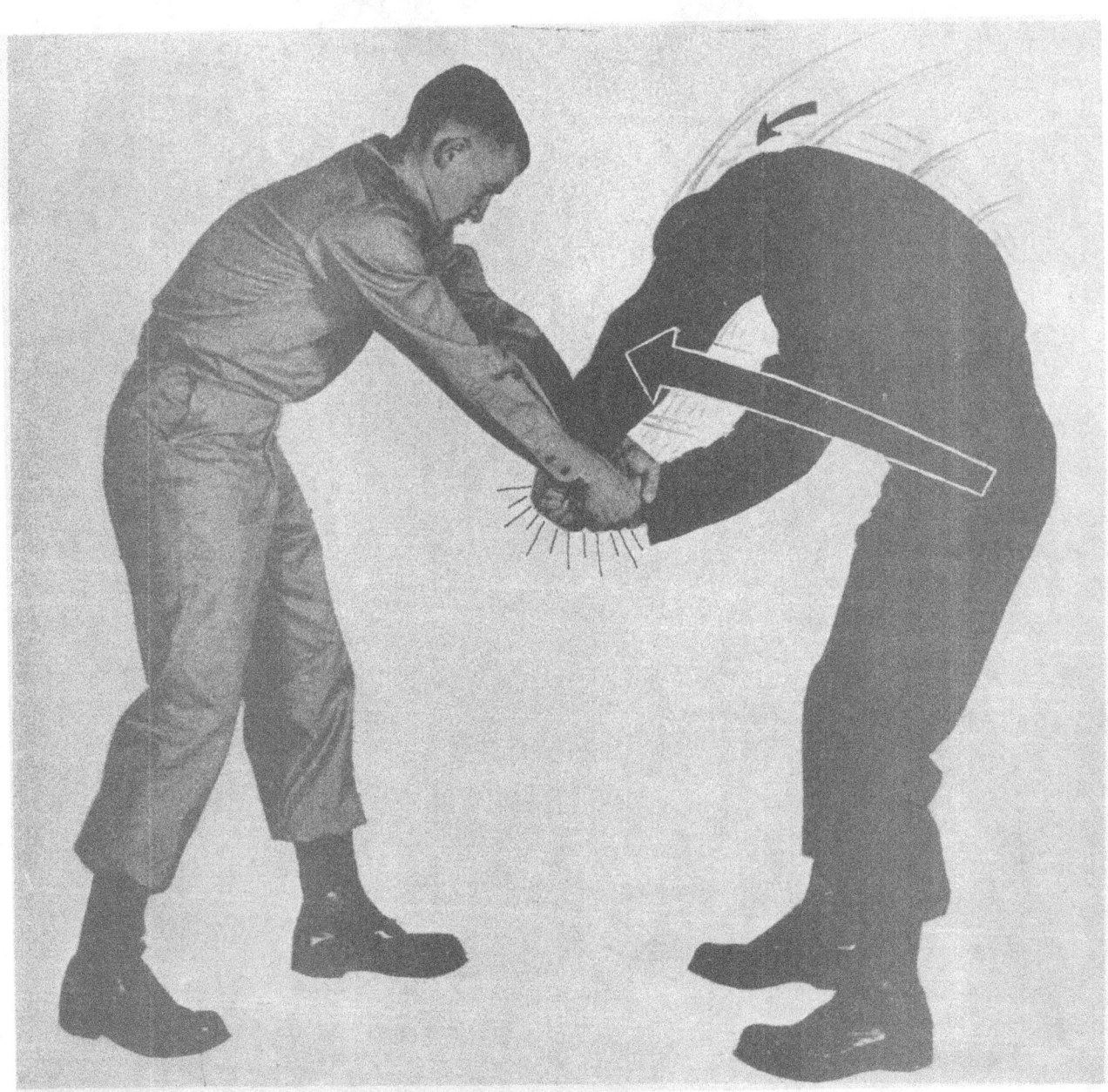

2 Escaping a two-hand grip on right wrist
Figure 124—Continued.

3 Escaping a two-hand grip on right wrist—Continued
Figure 124—Continued.

1 Overhand grip on both wrists
Figure 125. Overhand grip.

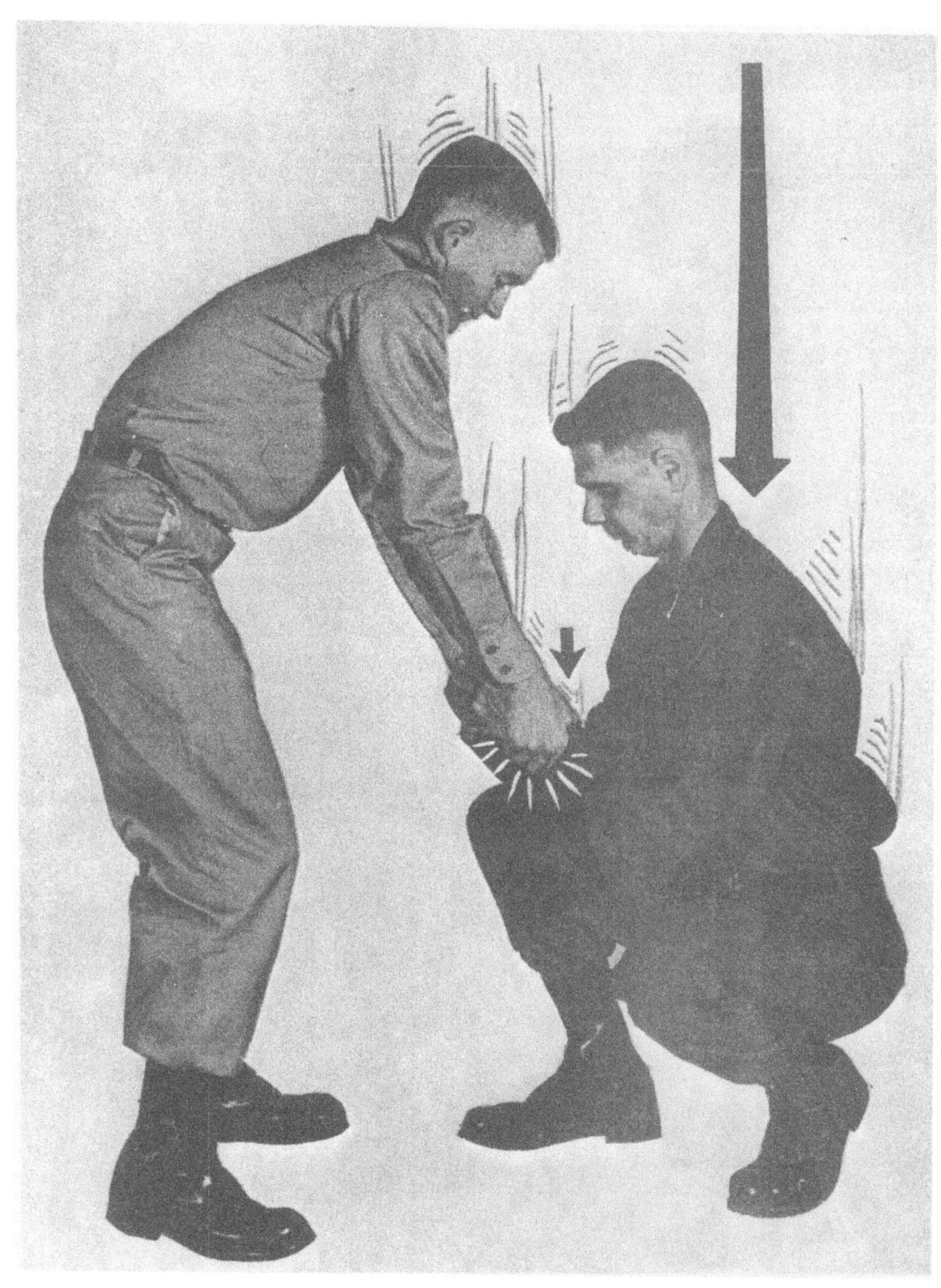

2 Escaping overhand grip on both wrists
Figure 125—Continued.

3 Escaping overhand grip on both wrists—Continued
Figure 125—Continued.

70. Escaping a One-Arm Strangle Hold from the Rear

a. An opponent may attack you from the rear with a one-arm strangle hold (1, fig. 126).

b. Reach up with your left hand and grab his right forearm. Pull down on his forearm.

1 One-arm rear strangle hold

Figure 126. Rear strangle hold.

and at the same time tuck your chin into your chest so he cannot choke you. Grab your opponent's right shoulder with your right hand (2, fig. 126).

c. Drive your buttocks against his midsection, retaining your hold on his forearm and shoulder with both hands. By bending from the waist and straightening your legs swiftly you can throw your opponent over your head and to the ground (3, fig. 126).

71. Escaping a Rear Overarm Body Hold

a. An opponent may grab you around the body and pin both your arms in a rear overarm body hold (1, fig. 127).

b. Loosen his grip by stomping on his instep or kicking him on the shin. Raise your elbows shoulder high and at the same time lower your body quickly by bending your knees (2, fig. 127).

2 Escaping a one-arm rear strangle hold
Figure 126—Continued.

c. Turning your body slightly to the right, drive your elbow forcefully into your opponent's side or midsection so he will release his grip (3, fig. 127).

d. Continue the movement by reaching up with your right hand and grabbing his right upper arm just above his elbow. Grip his right wrist with your left hand and throw him over your head (4, fig. 127). As your opponent hits the ground you strike at a vulnerable point.

3 Escaping a one-arm strangle hold—Continued
Figure 126—Continued.

1 Rear overarm body hold
Figure 127. Body hold.

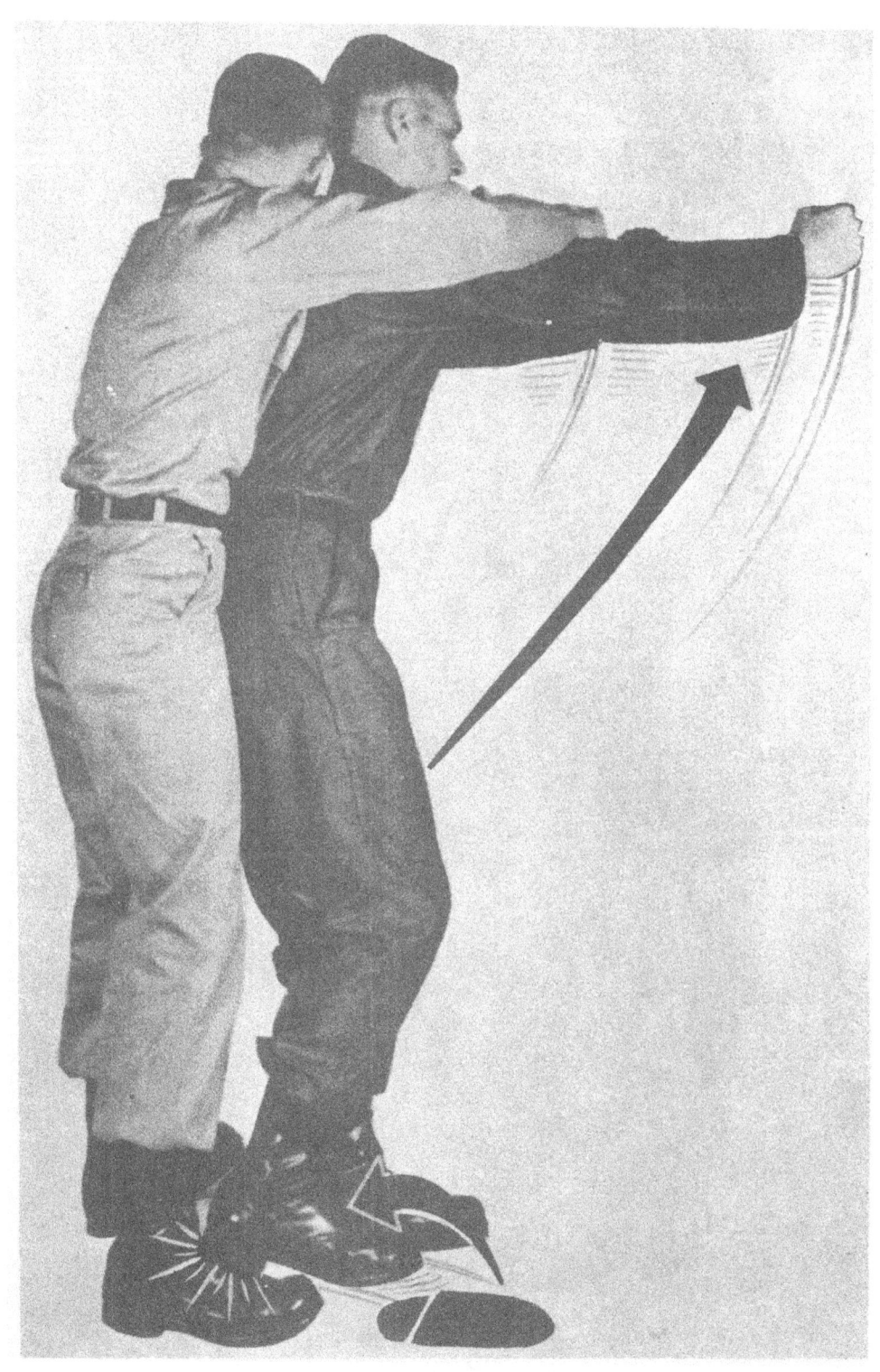

2 Escaping a rear overarm body hold
Figure 127—Continued.

3 Escaping a rear overarm body hold—Continued
Figure 127—Continued.

4 Escaping a rear overarm body hold—Continued
Figure 127—Continued.

72. Escape from Rear Underarm Body Hold

a. An opponent may grab you around the body in a rear underarm body hold (1, fig. 128).

b. Reach down with your left hand and place it just above his left knee. Press down on this spot with most of your weight (2, fig. 128).

1 Rear underarm body hold
Figure 128. Underarm body hold.

c. You now have a firm base on which to pivot. Lift both your feet from the ground and switch your left leg behind your opponent's right leg. As soon as your feet are firmly planted on the ground, bring your left hand under your opponent's left knee and your right hand under his right knee (3, fig. 128).

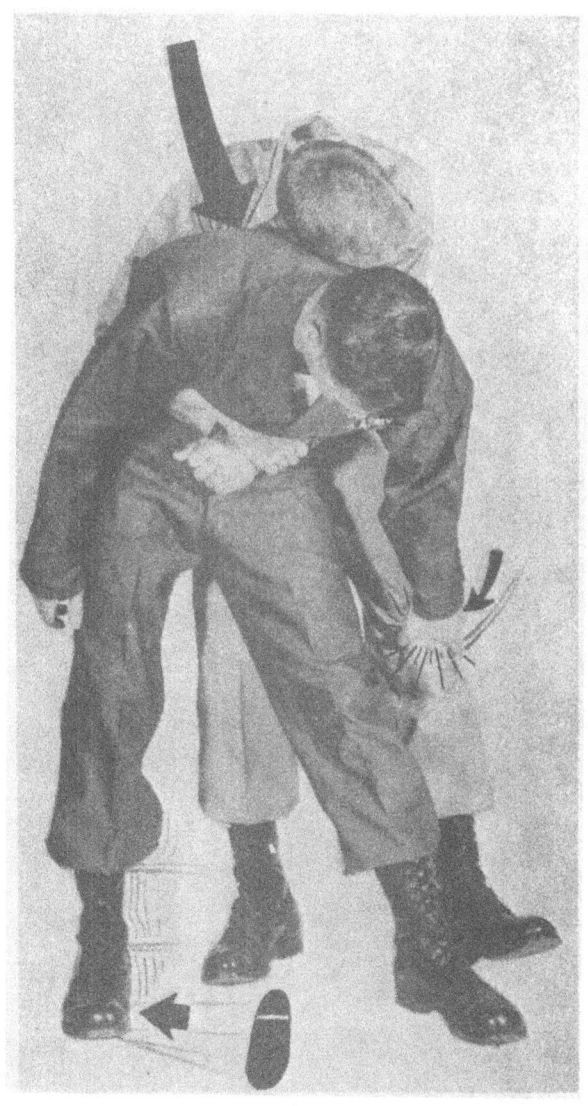

2 Escaping a rear underarm body hold
Figure 128—Continued.

d. Lift up and raise your opponent off the ground, lifting his feet as high as possible (4, fig. 128).

e. If your opponent releases his hold, you can drive his head to the ground. If he maintains his hold, fall on him and force his head to the ground.

3　Escaping a rear underarm body hold—Continued
Figure 128—Continued.

4 Escaping a rear underarm body hold—Continued
Figure 128—Continued.

73. Another Escape from a Rear Underarm Body Hold

a. Your opponent uses the same grasp around your waist as explained in paragraph 72, but this time he braces himself by placing one leg between your legs and putting his head behind your shoulder blade out of reach of your arms (1, fig. 129).

1 Another type rear underarm body hold

Figure 129. Underarm body hold.

b. To break this hold, bend swiftly from the waist and grab the ankle of the foot which he has placed between your legs (2, fig. 129).

c. Keep your hold on his ankle and straighten your body. This puts pressure on your opponent's knee, causing him to release his hold and drop on his back (3, fig. 129). If he keeps his hold, you should fall back on top of him so that your weight hits his midsection.

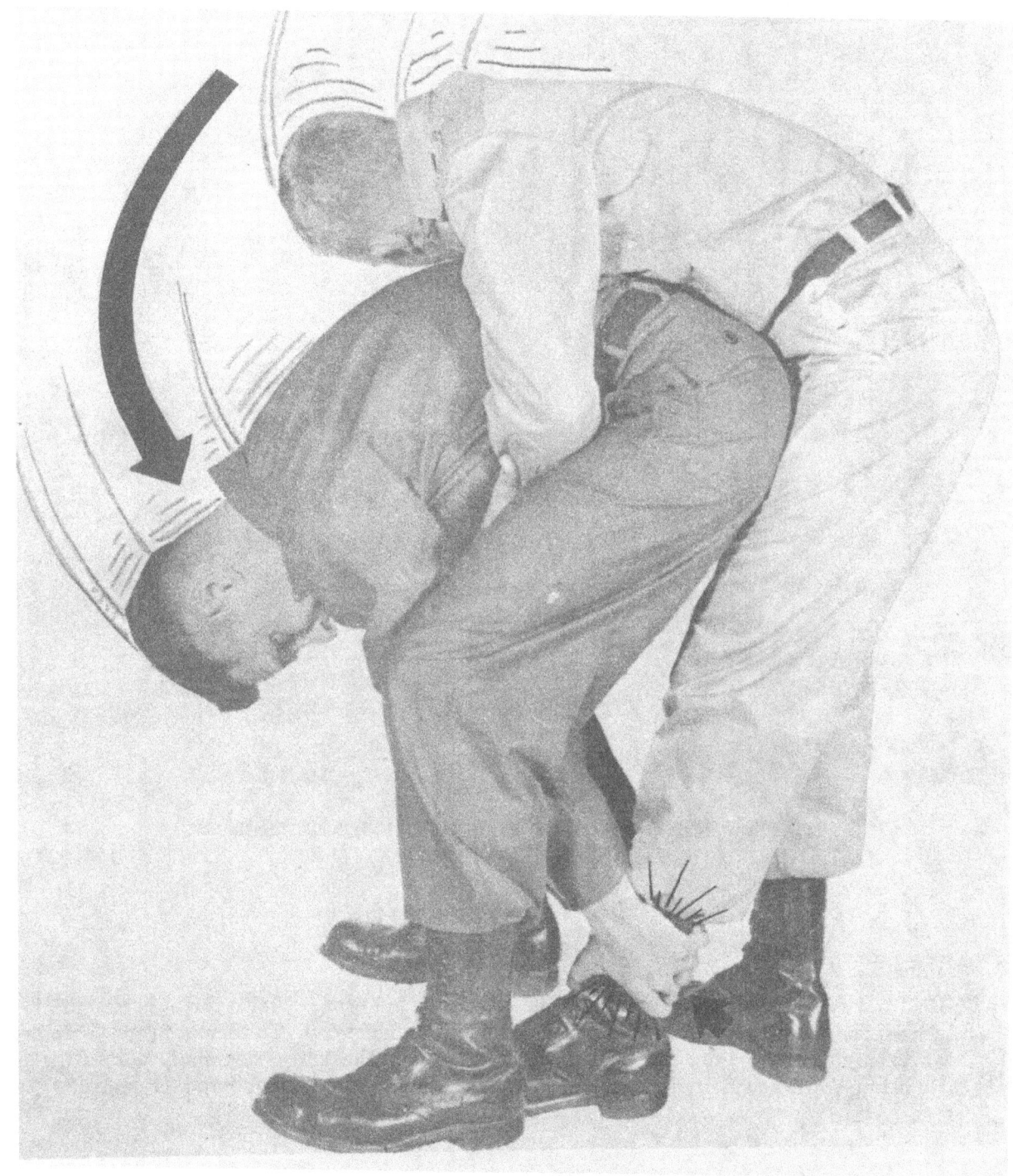

2 Escaping from another type rear underarm body hold

Figure 129—Continued.

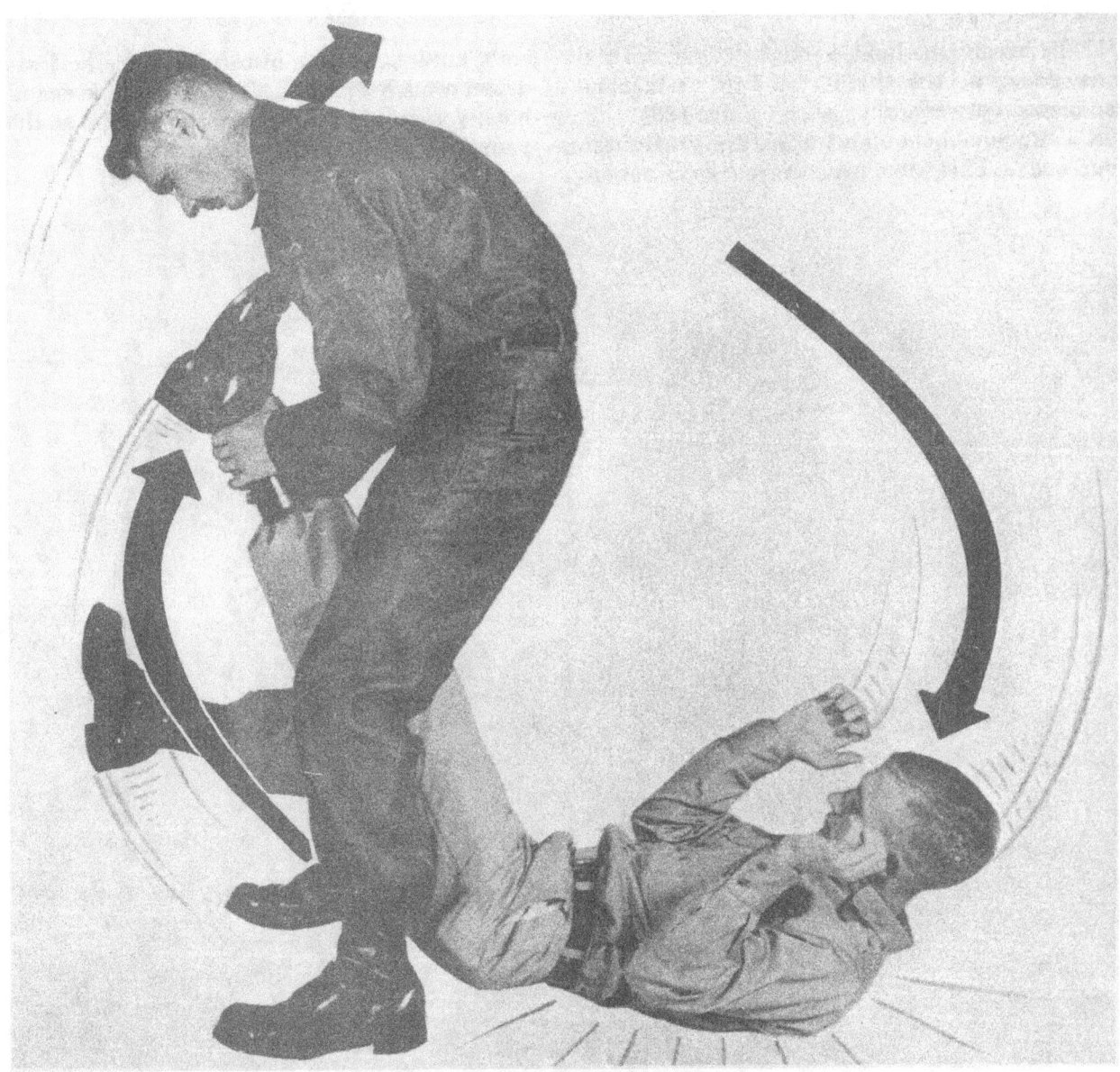

3 Escaping from another type rear underarm body hold—Continued
Figure 129—Continued.

Section IX. KNIFE ATTACK

74. General

A knife (or bayonet), properly employed, is a deadly weapon. You can use it on patrols to silence an enemy sentry or you can use it for close-in fighting when you do not have a rifle.

75. Grip

a. The proper knife grip is essential for maximum control. To form a proper grip begin by laying the knife diagonally across the outstretched palm of your hand (1, fig. 130).

b. Grasp the small part of the handle next to the cross guard with your thumb and forefinger. Your middle finger encircles the handle at its largest point (2, fig. 130).

c. When the knife is held in this manner it can be maneuvered in all directions. You can control the direction of the blade by a combination movement of the forefinger and middle finger and a turning of the wrist. When the palm is turned up and you are holding the knife in your right hand, you can slash to the right or left. When the palm is turned down, you can also slash in either direction. You can thrust when the palm is held either up or down. As the knife makes contact you hold it tightly with all fingers (3, fig. 130).

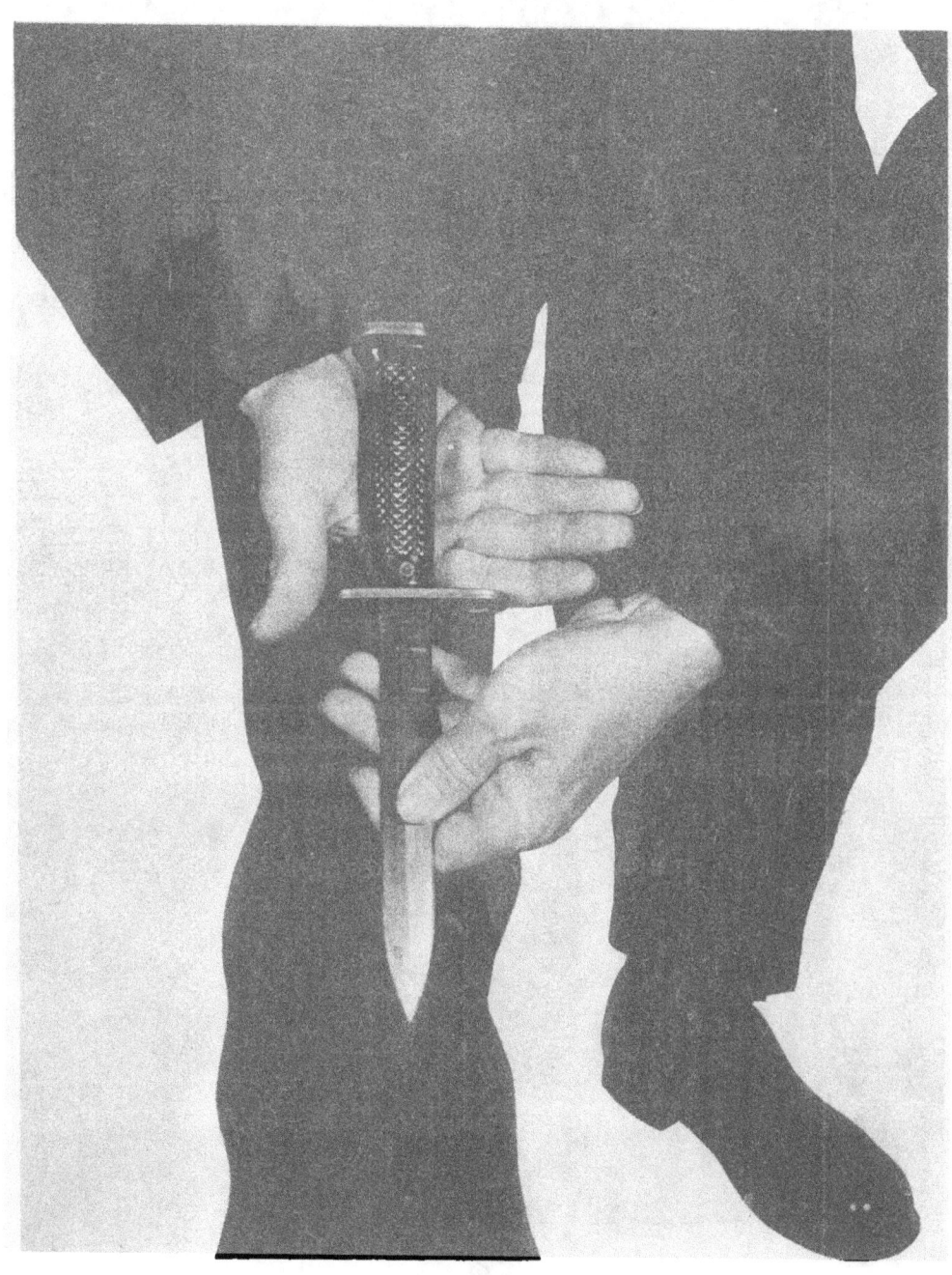

①

Figure 130. Gripping the knife.

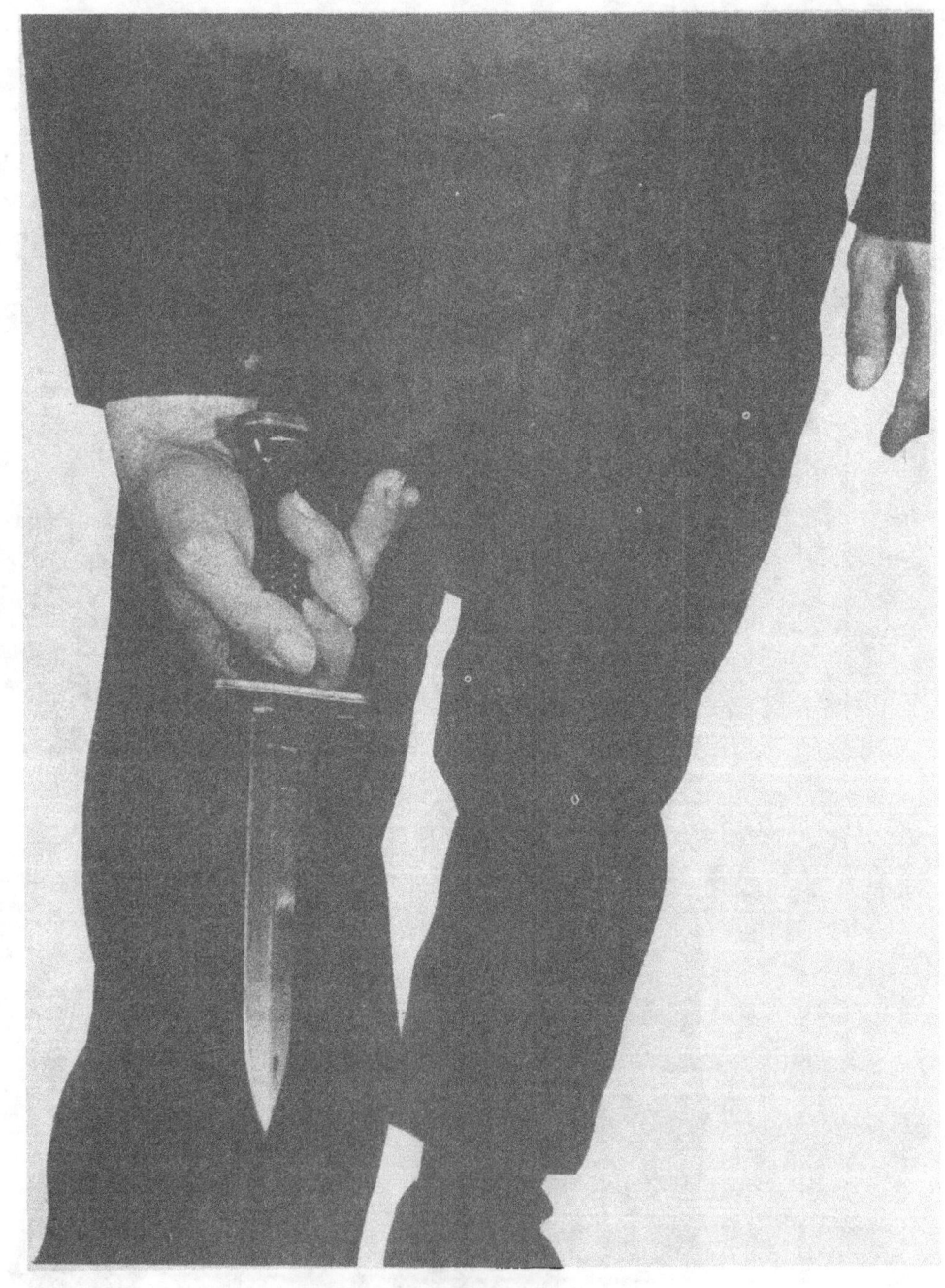

Figure 130—Continued.

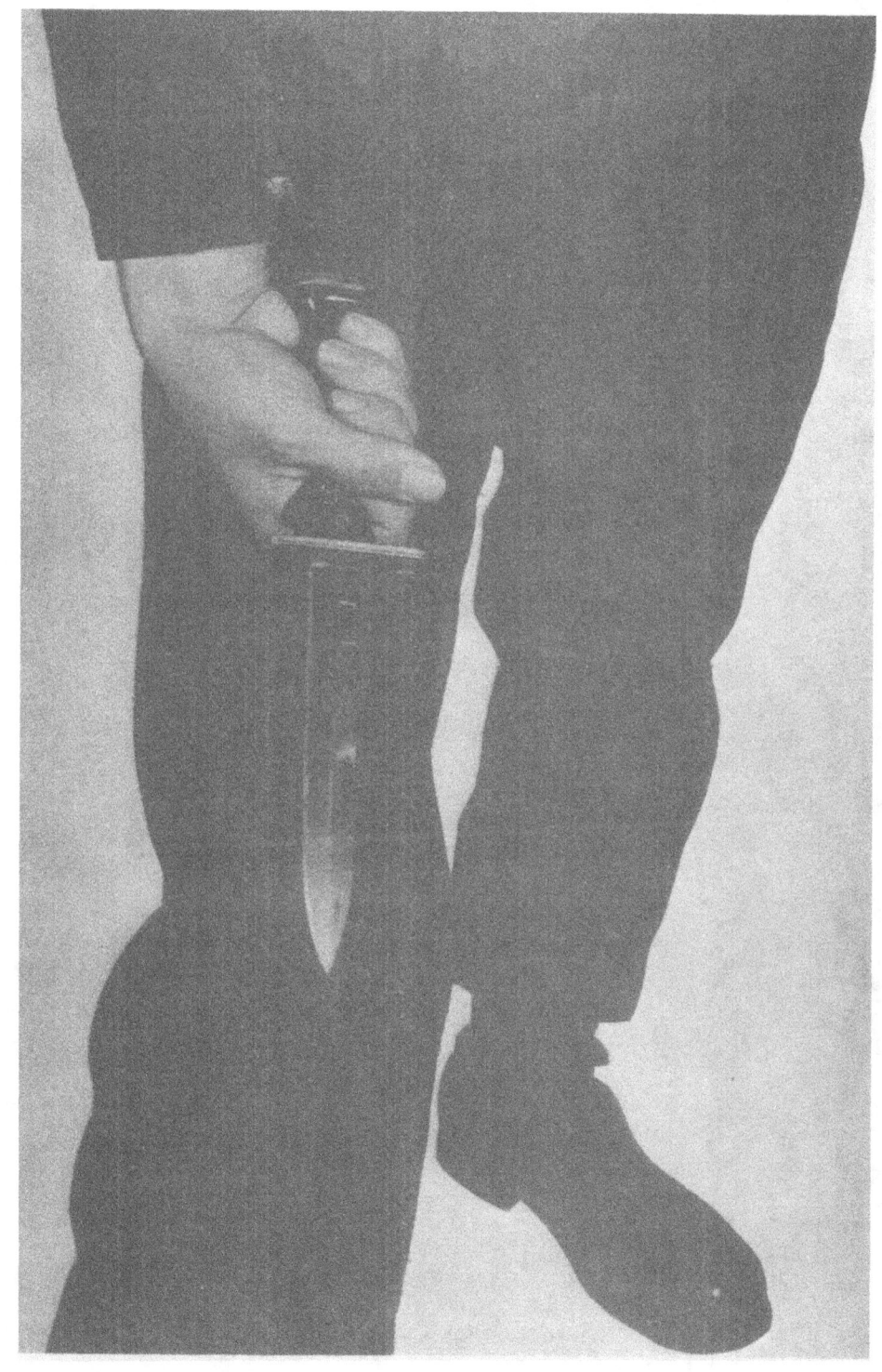

②
Figure 130—Continued.

76. Stance

When engaging in a knife attack your stance (fig. 131) is similar to the hand-to-hand guard position. The only difference is the position of your right arm. The knife is held down beside your right leg. Your left arm and hand acts as a guard or foil and helps create an opening for a slash or thrust. You may also use your left hand to distract your opponent's attention by waving it in his face, by throwing some-

Figure 131. Stance with knife.

thing, or by making sudden darting motions toward him. When you are in this stance your knees are bent to provide mobility and balance. In this stance you are also able to protect your midsection and throat area.

77. Modified Stance

In the modified stance (fig. 132) you conceal the knife until you thrust or slash with it. The knife is held behind the right leg.

Figure 132. Modified stance with knife.

78. Frontal Attack

When you attack an opponent from the front with a knife he instinctively tries to protect his stomach and throat. If he is wounded in one of these places his fear may be so great that he forgets to defend himself and you can kill him.

a. The Throat. You can attack the throat with either a thrust or a slash. The thrust is most effective if the knife is driven into the base of the throat just below the Adam's apple (fig. 133). This type blow cuts the jugular vein and results in instant death. A slash to either side of the neck cuts the carotid artery which carries blood to the brain. Your opponent will die within a few seconds from loss of blood.

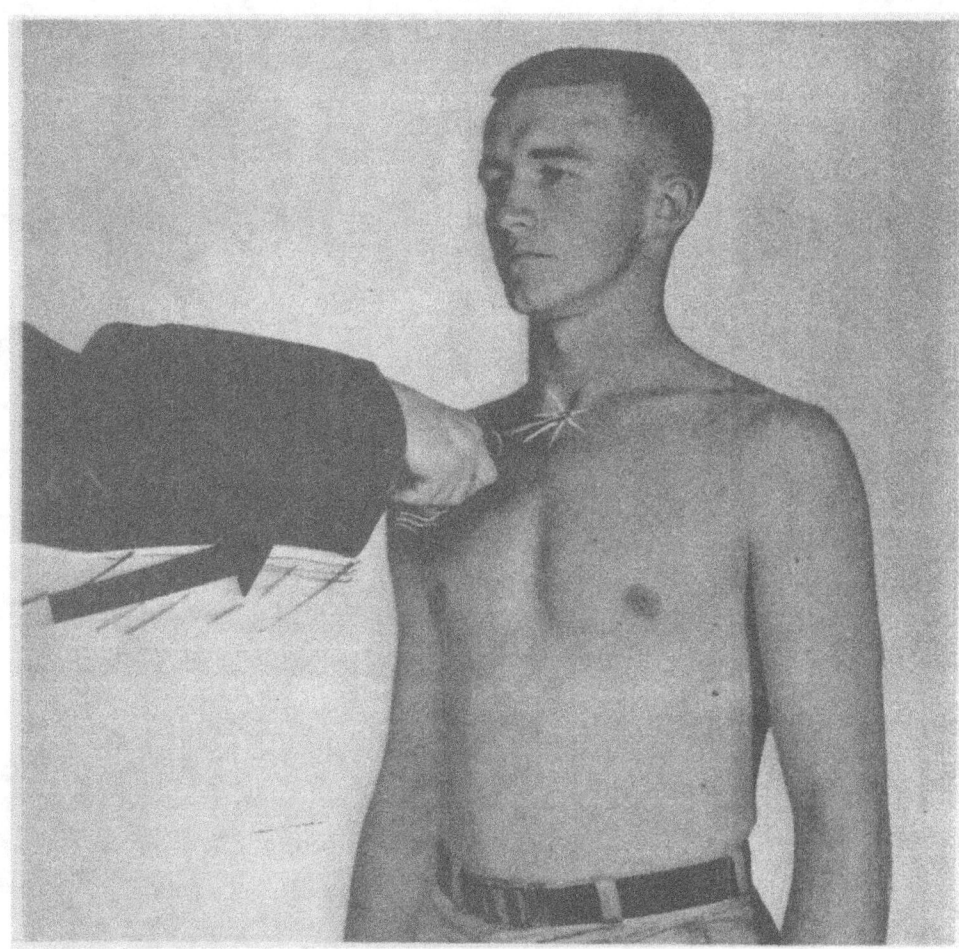

Figure 133. Knife attack at base of throat.

b. The Stomach. A thrust combined with a slash to the stomach produces great shock (fig. 134). Your opponent will be stunned and unable to defend himself. You can then deliver a killing blow. A deep wound in the stomach causes death if the wound is unattended.

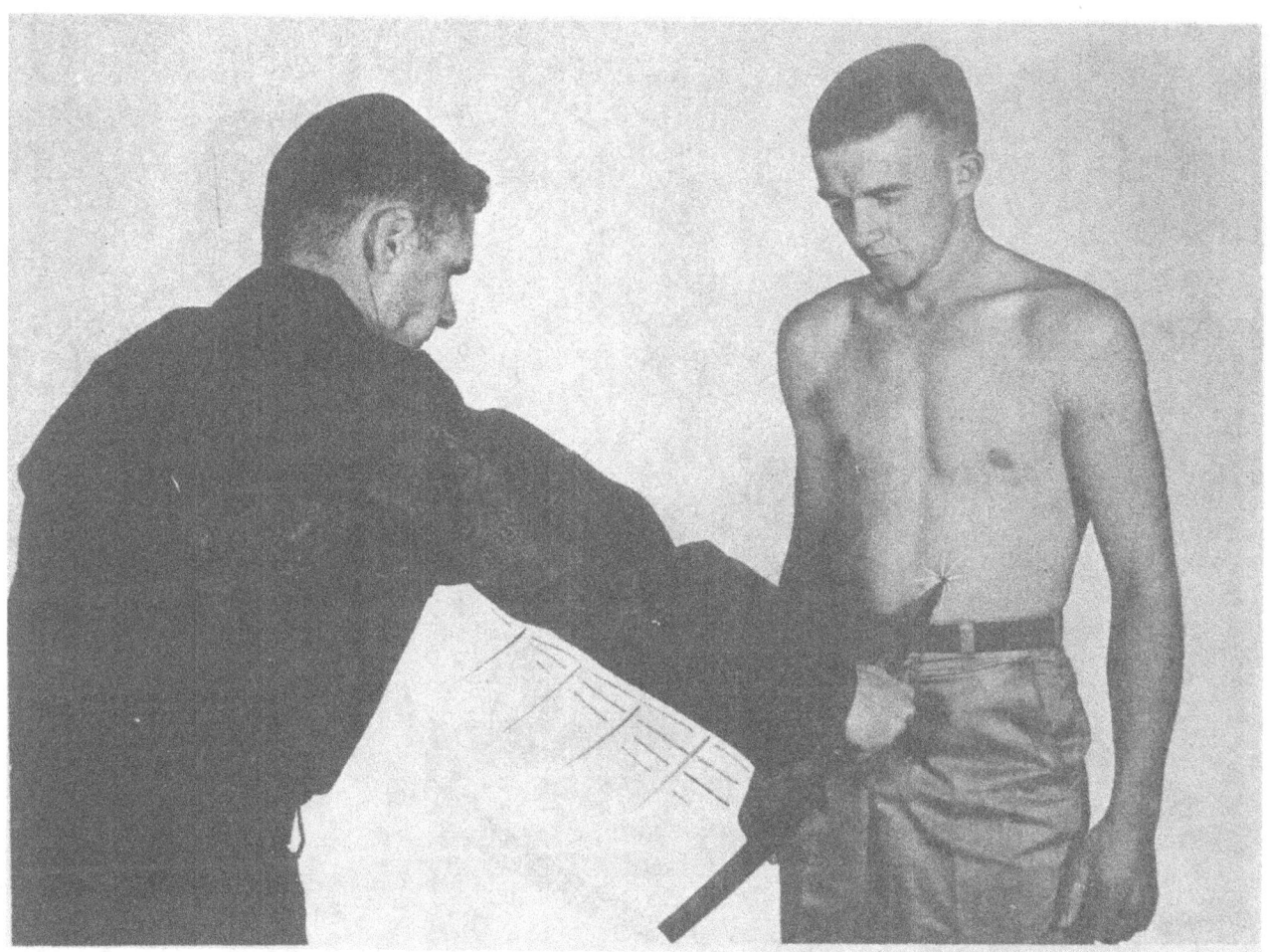

Figure 134. Knife attack to the stomach.

c. *The Heart.* A thrust into the heart causes instant death (fig. 135). This spot is difficult to hit because of the protecting ribs. A hard thrust usually will slip off the rib and penetrate the heart, however.

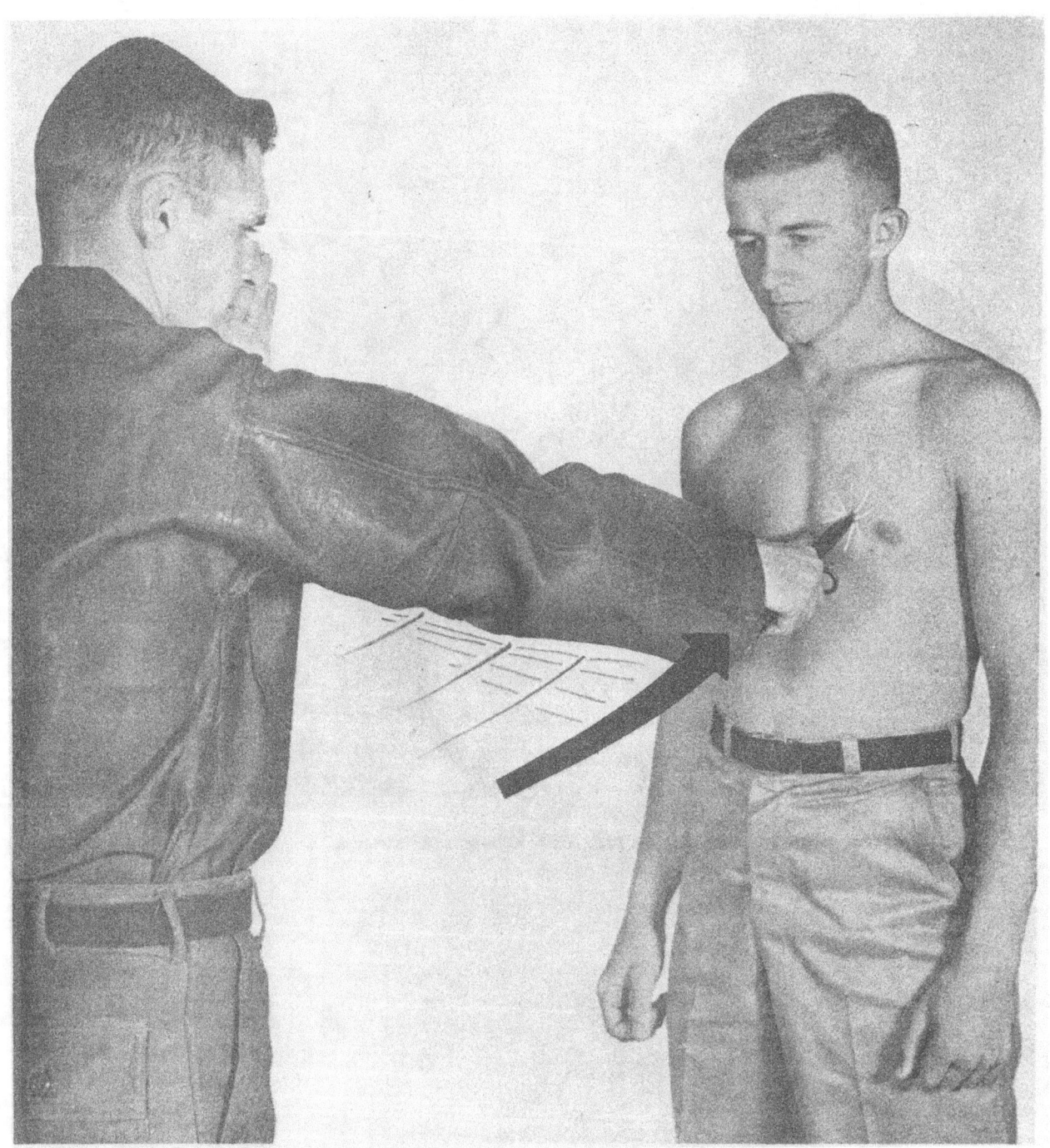

Figure 135. Knife attack to the heart.

d. The Wrist. A slash to the wrist will sever the radial artery, causing death within two minutes (fig. 136). This type attack is excellent if your opponent attempts to grab your clothing or arm. The radial artery is only one-quarter inch below the surface of the skin. Unconsciousness results in about 30 seconds.

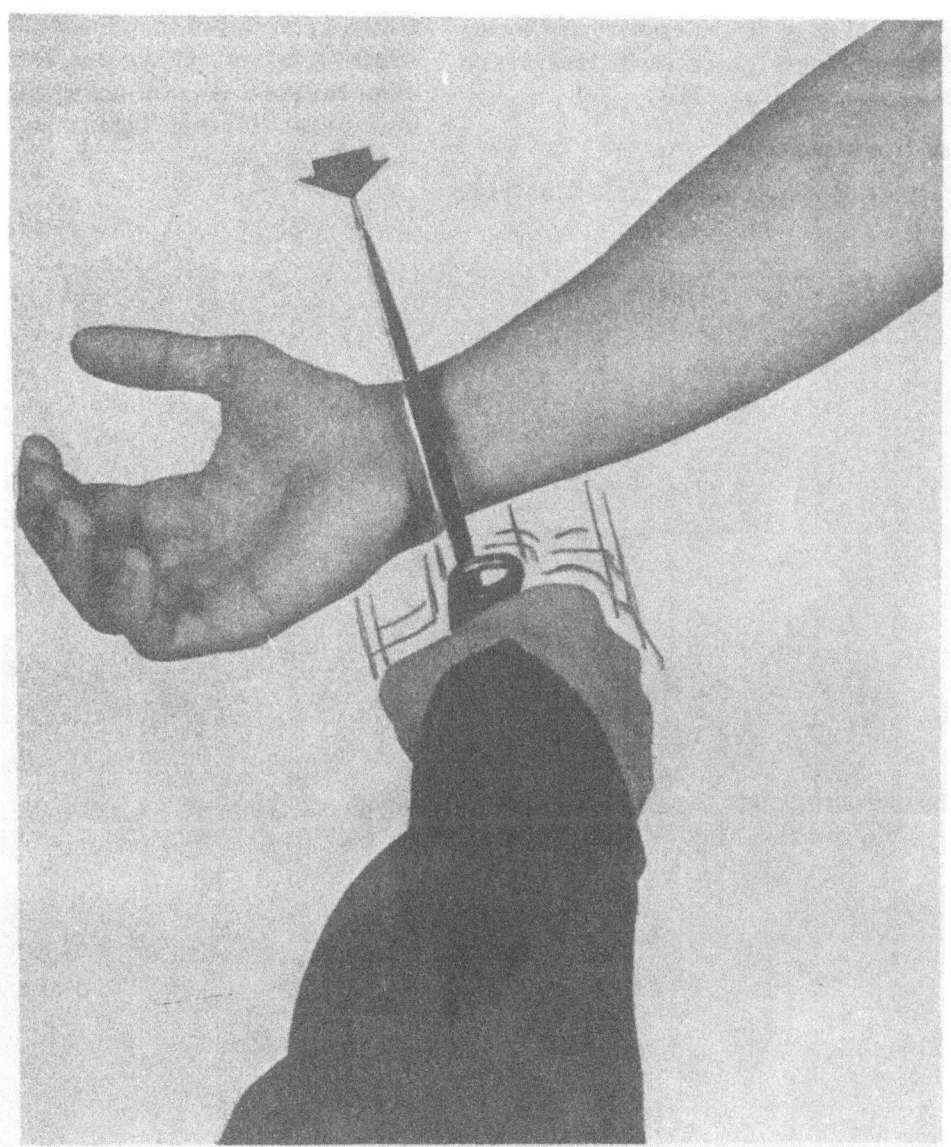

Figure 136. Knife attack on the wrist.

e. The Upper Arm. A slash to the upper arm just above the inside of the elbow cuts the brachial artery and causes death within two minutes (fig. 137). This artery is about one-half inch below the skin surface. Unconsciousness occurs in about 15 seconds.

f. The Leg. A slash to the inside of the leg near the groin severs the arteries there and makes the leg useless (fig. 138).

79. Attack from the Rear

When attacking an opponent from the rear you should launch your attack immediately upon reaching a position not less than five feet from him.

a. The Kidney. Thrust the knife into your opponent's kidney and simultaneously grab his mouth and nose with your other hand (fig. 139). After a short interval withdraw the blade, slashing as you do so, and then cut his throat. The thrust to the kidney produces great shock and causes internal hemorrhage and death.

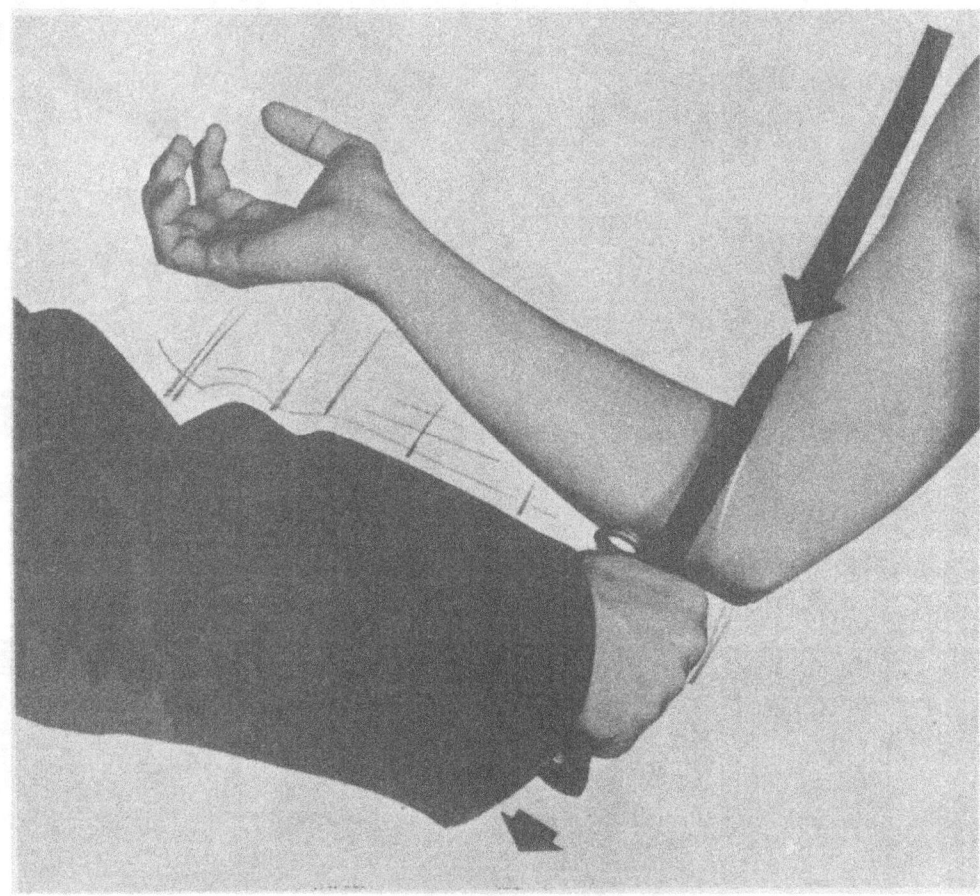

Figure 137. Knife attack to the upper arm.

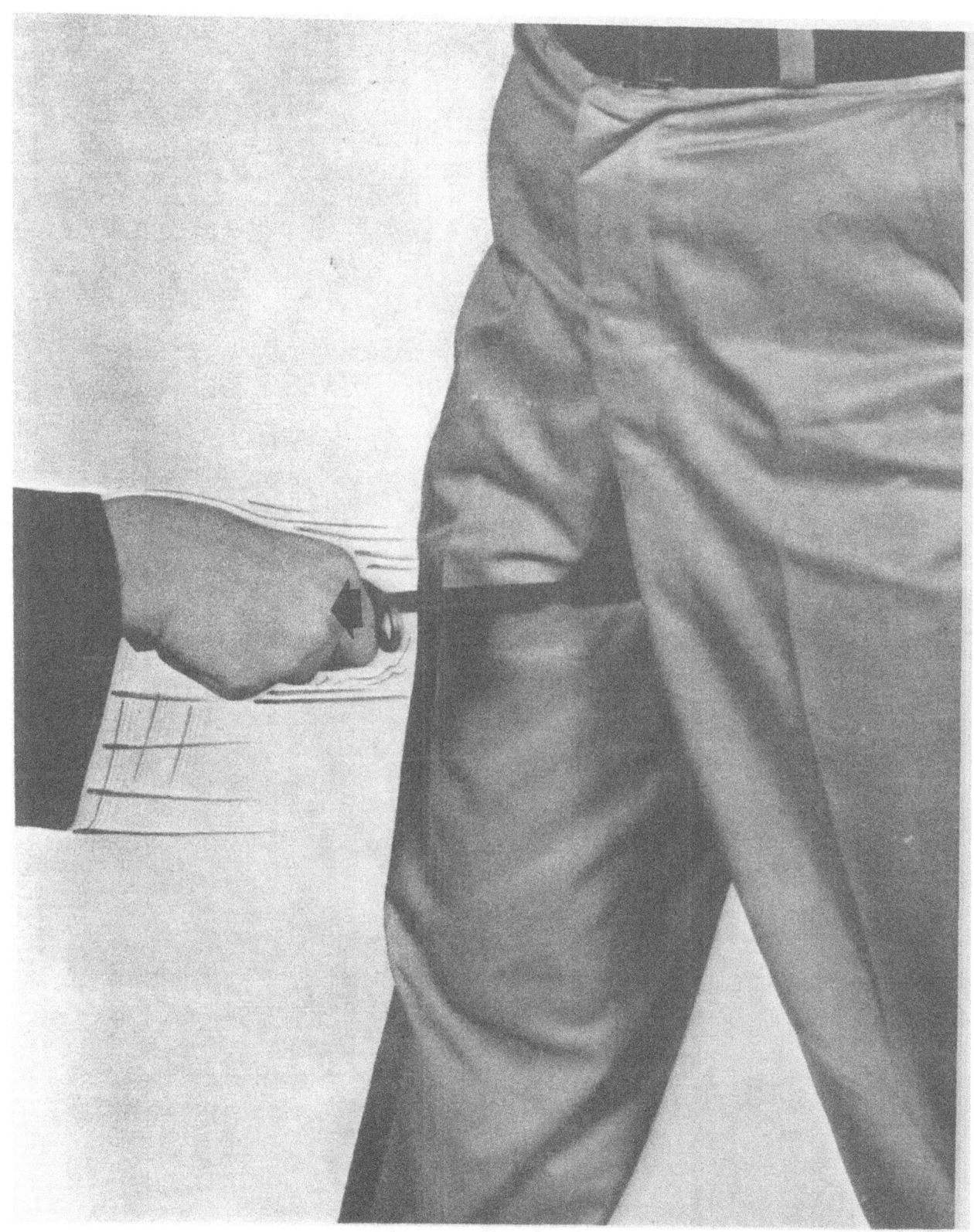

Figure 138. Knife attack to leg.

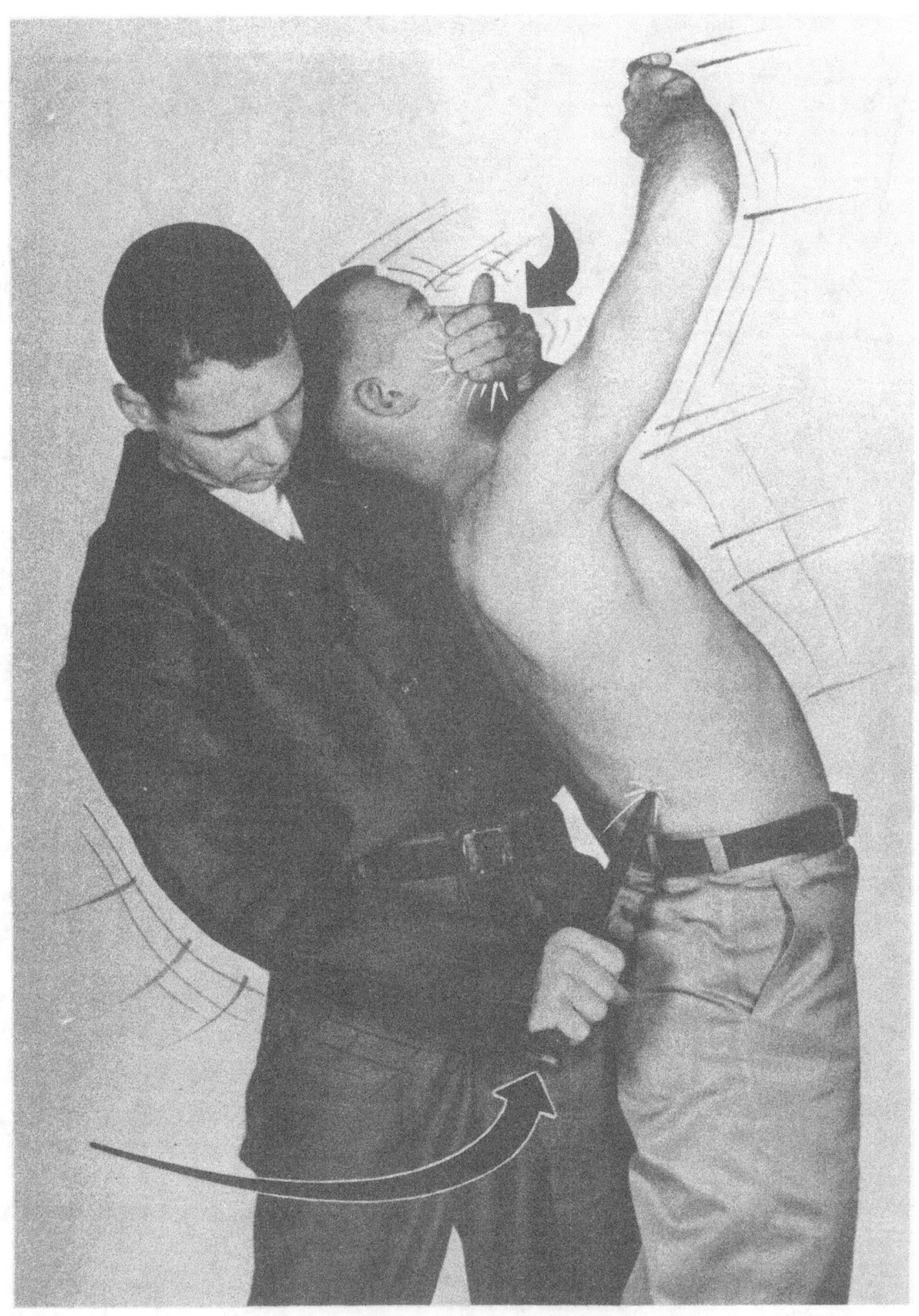
Figure 139. Knife attack from the rear to the kidney.

b. Side of The Neck. A thrust into the side of the neck is effective when you want to maintain silence (fig. 140).

c. The Throat. A slash across the throat from the rear severs the windpipe and jugular vein (fig. 141).

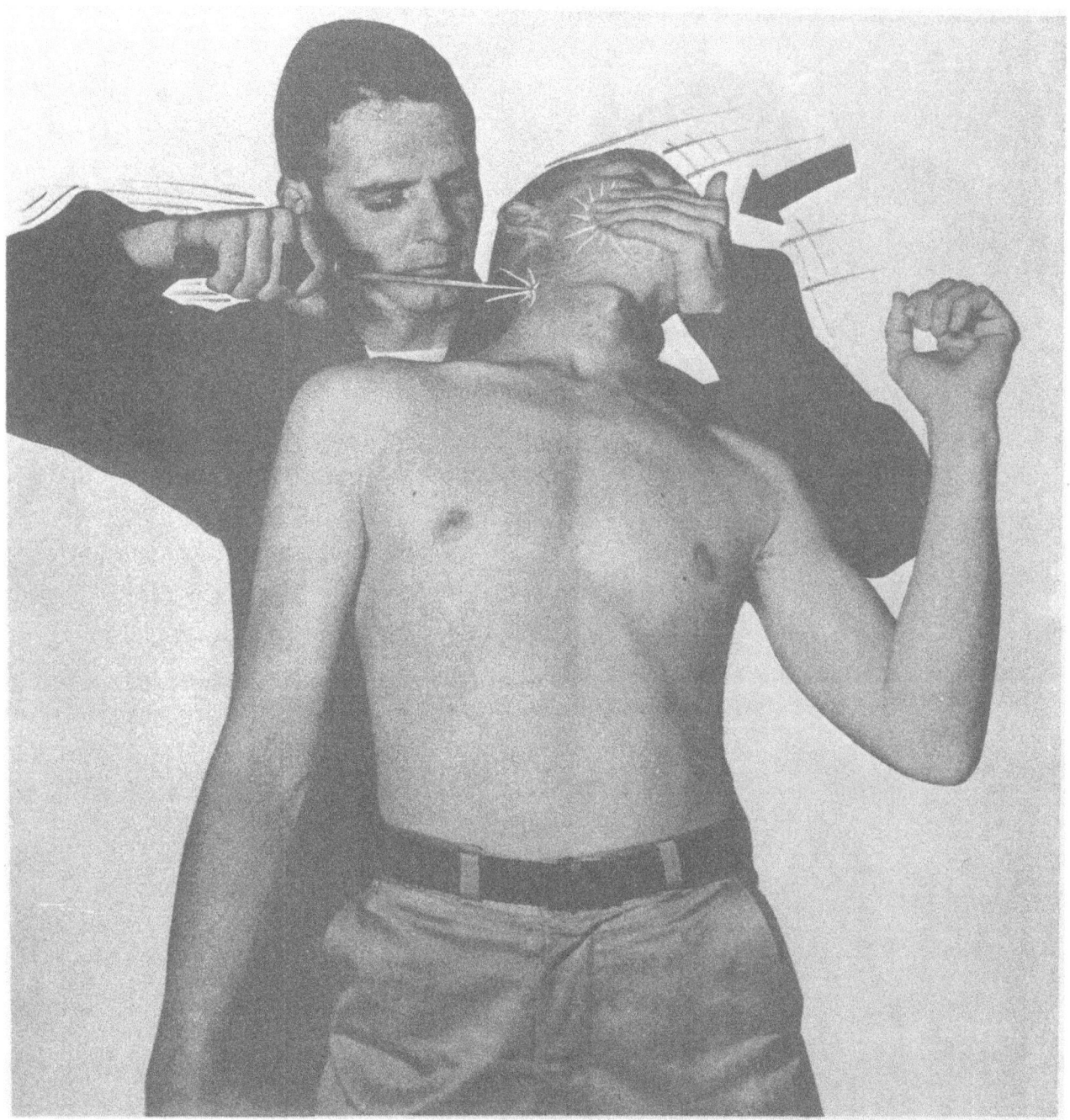

Figure 140. Knife attack from the rear to the side of the neck.

d. The Subclavian Artery. The subclavian artery is approximately two and one-half inches below the surface between the collarbone and the shoulder blade. Attack this spot with a thrust by gripping the knife as you would an ice pick (fig. 142). As you withdraw the knife, slash to make the wound as large as possible. This artery is difficult to hit; but once it is cut the bleeding cannot be stopped and your opponent will lose consciousness within seconds. Death will follow rapidly.

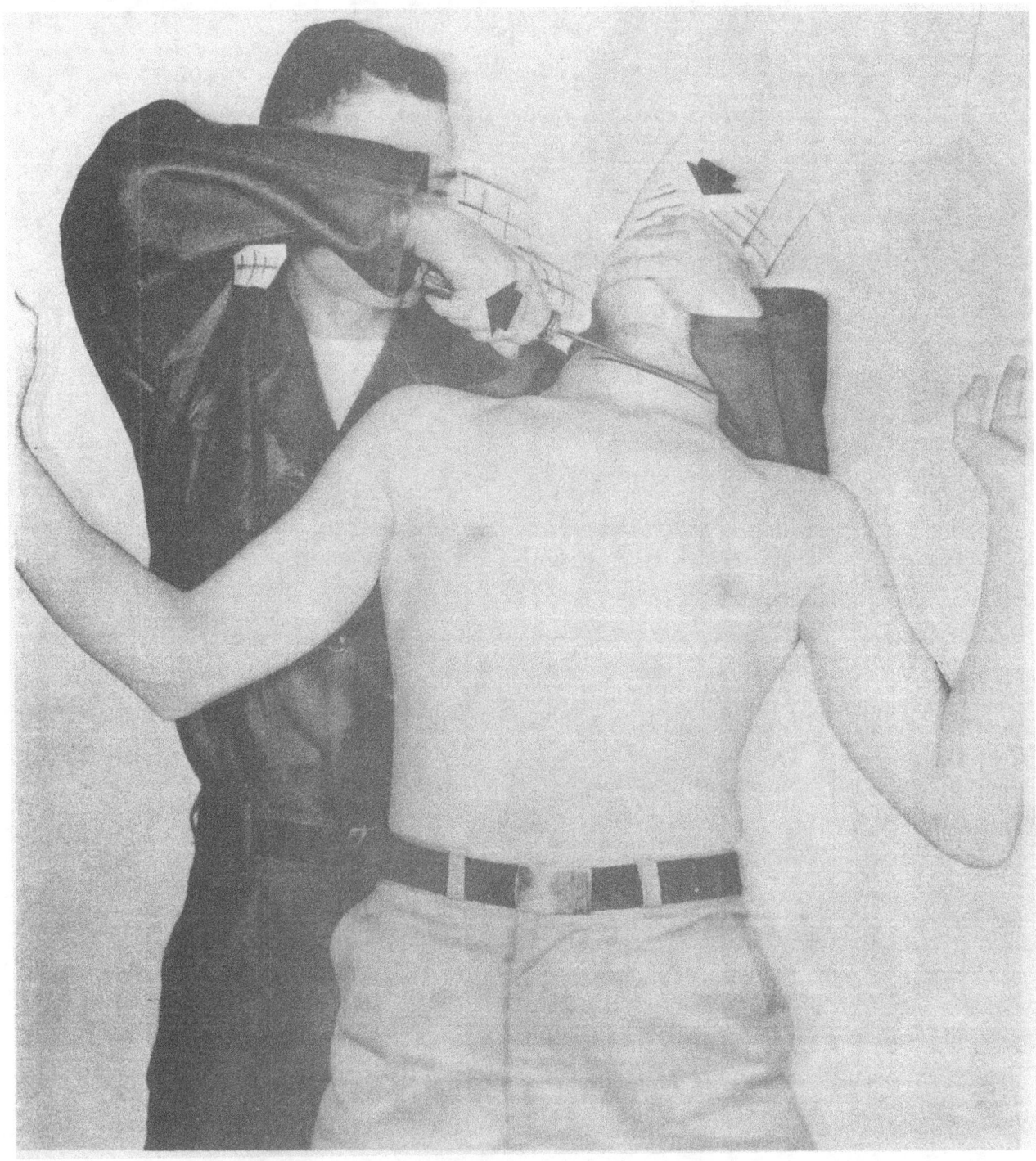

Figure 141. Knife attack from the rear to the throat.

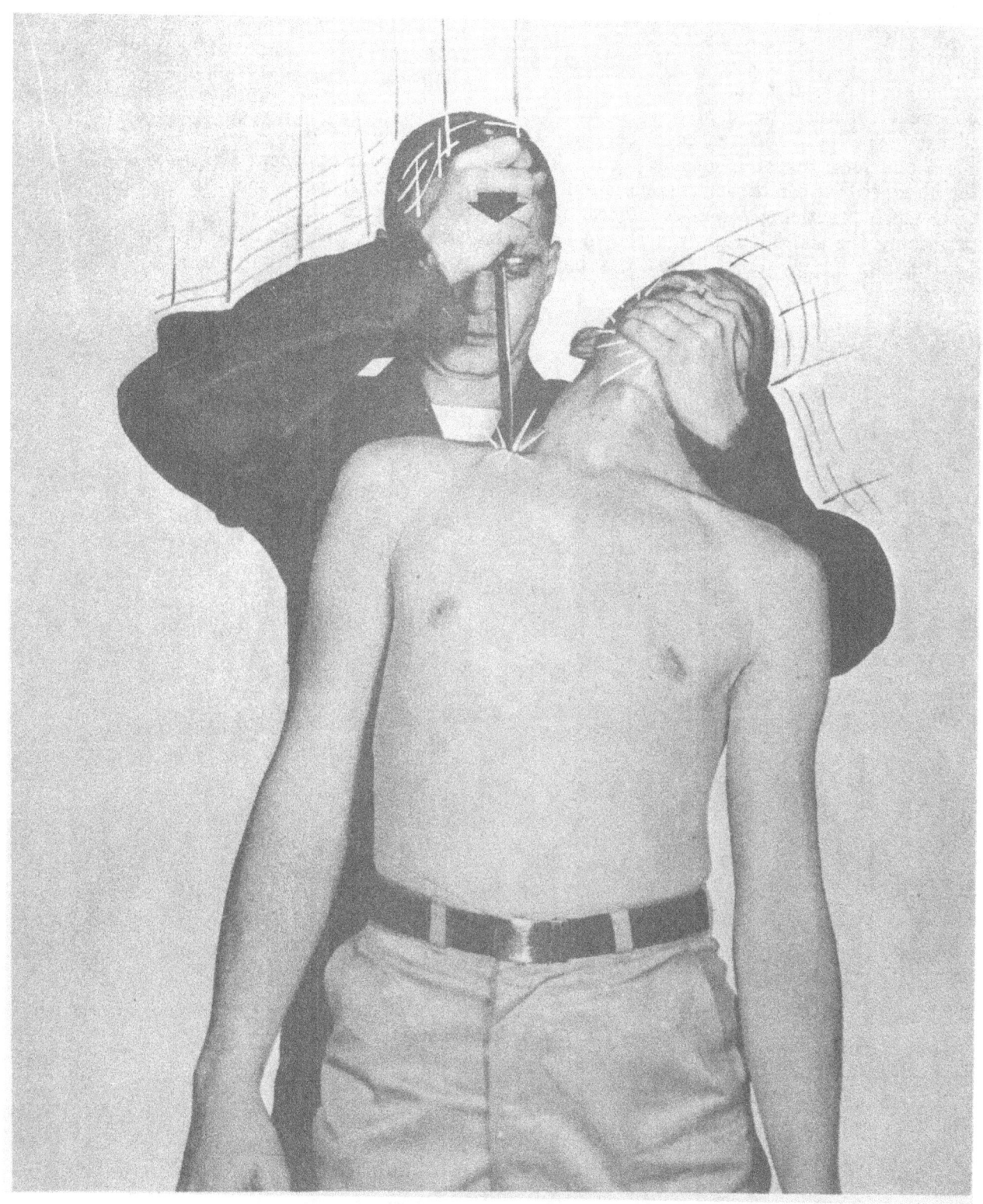

Figure 142. Knife attack from the rear to the subclavian artery.

Section X. BAYONET DISARMING

80. General

In training you are taught bayonet disarming methods for both long and short thrust attacks. In combat, however, any of the methods described in this section can be used to disarm an opponent whether he uses a long or short thrust. The text differentiates between the short and long thrust to enable you to judge the distance between the bayonet point and your body when practicing these techniques. When practicing the short thrust, you should be approximately arm's length from the bayonet point. When practicing the long thrust, the distance is increased by one foot. The unarmed soldier in training should wait until his armed opponent has committed himself before attempting a disarming maneuver.

81. Counter Against Short Thrust

a. If your opponent attacks you with a short thrust, twist your body to the left but keep your feet in place. At the same time, strike the bayonet with the palm of your right hand to deflect the blade from your body (1, fig. 143).

①

Figure 143. Counter against a short thrust.

b. As soon as the bayonet has passed your body, grab your opponent's left hand with your right hand. At the same time, take a long step with your left foot toward your opponent's right, reach under his rifle with your left hand, and press your left shoulder against the upper portion of the handguard. With your left hand, grab his right hand where it holds the top of the small of the stock (2, fig. 143).

c. Pull with your left hand and push with your right hand. Keep your weight on your left foot and kick your opponent so that the calf of your right leg makes calf-to-calf contact on his right leg (3, fig. 143).

d. Your opponent will fall to the ground and loosen his grip on his rifle (4, fig. 143). After taking your opponent's rifle kill him with a bayonet thrust.

③

Figure 143—Continued.

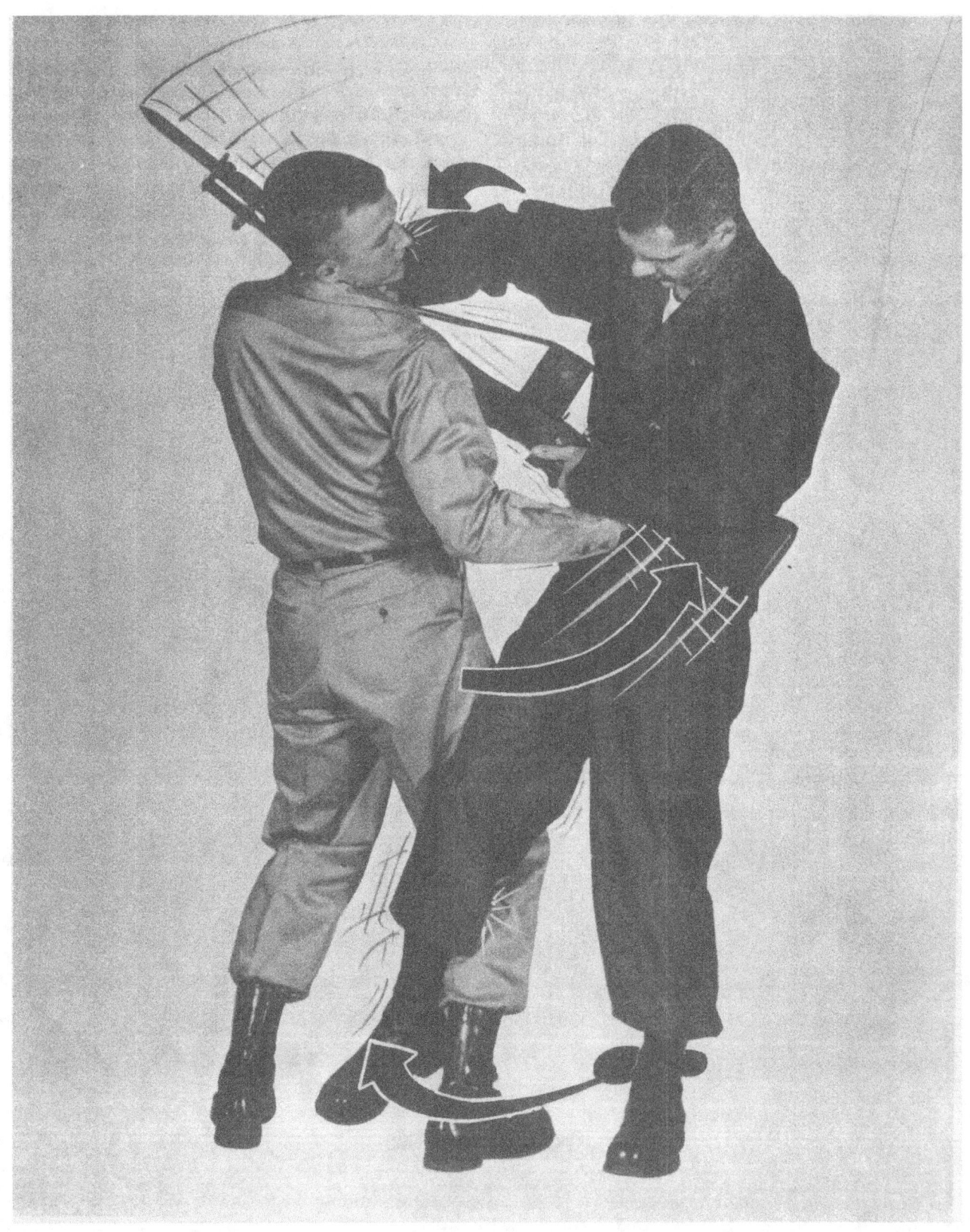

Figure 143—Continued.

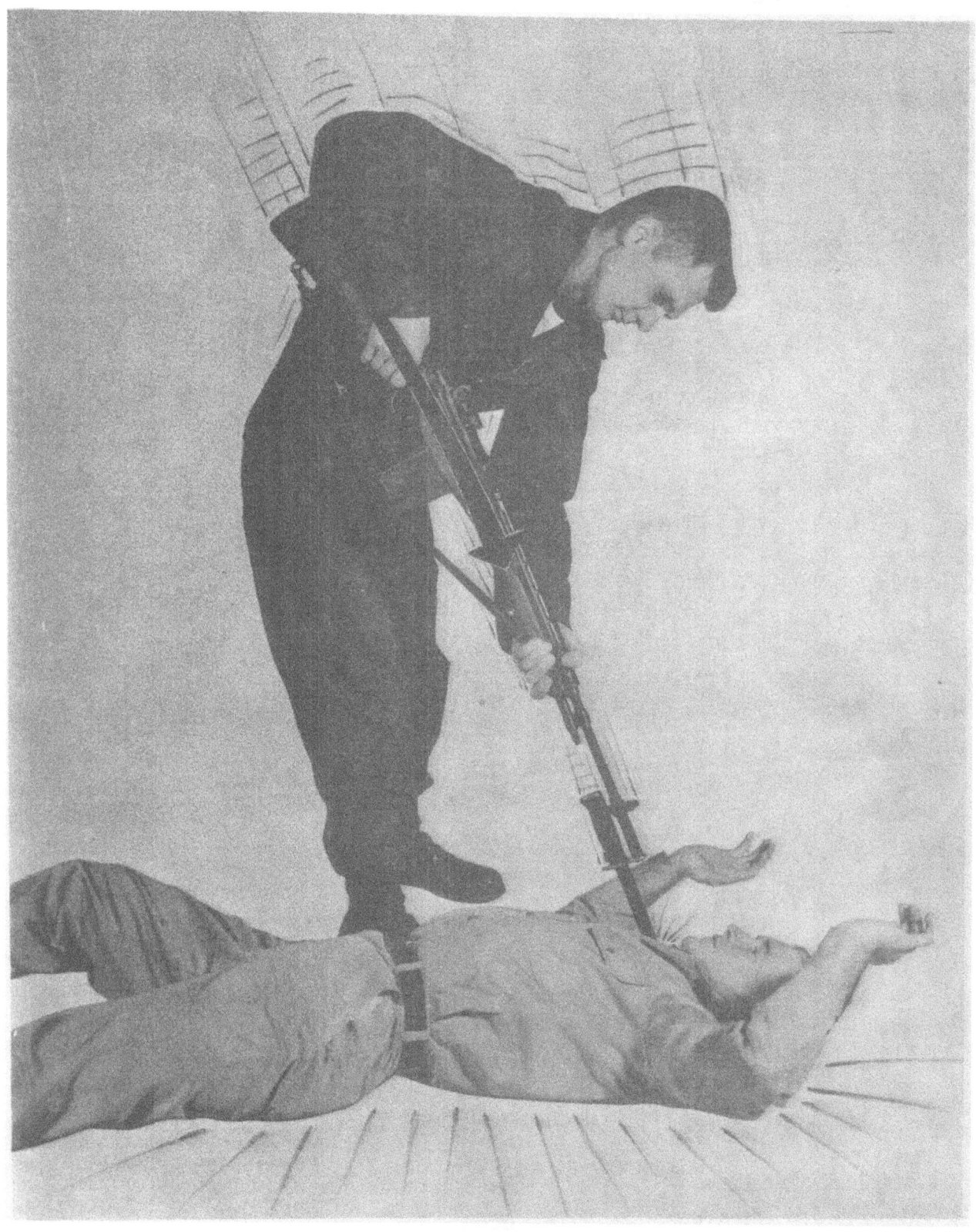

④
Figure 143—Continued.

82. Second Counter Against Short Thrust

a. As your opponent makes his thrust, use the palm of your right hand to parry his bayonet to your left and, at the same time, sidestep to your right oblique. You are now in a position facing his rifle from the side with your groin area protected by your right leg (1, fig. 144).

①
Figure 144. Second counter against a short thrust.

b. With your left hand, palm up, grab the upper portion of the rifle. At the same time, strike the inside of your opponent's left elbow sharply with the knife edge of your right hand (2, fig. 144).

c. Keep a firm hold on the rifle. Step through with your left foot, moving quickly past your opponent on his left, and jerk the rifle up and backward in an arc over his shoulder (3, fig. 144). If he keeps his hold on the rifle, kick him on a vulnerable point and yank the rifle away from him. Then whirl and attack him with the bayonet.

③
Figure 144—Continued.

③
Figure 144—Continued.

83. Third Counter Against Short Thrust

a. As your opponent makes his thrust, use the palm of your left hand to parry the bayonet to your right and sidestep to your left oblique. You are now in a position facing the side of his rifle with your groin area protected by your left leg (1, fig. 145).

①

Figure 145. Third counter against a short thrust.

b. With your right hand, palm up, grab the rifle anywhere on the upper part of the handguard and with your left hand, palm down, grab the rifle on top of the receiver (2, fig. 145).

Figure 145—Continued.

c. Keep a firm hold on the rifle with both hands and step through with your right foot, moving quickly past your opponent. Jerk the rifle up sharply and backward in an arc over your opponent's shoulder and twist it out of his hands (3, fig. 145). Now whirl and smash him with the rifle butt or attack him with the bayonet.

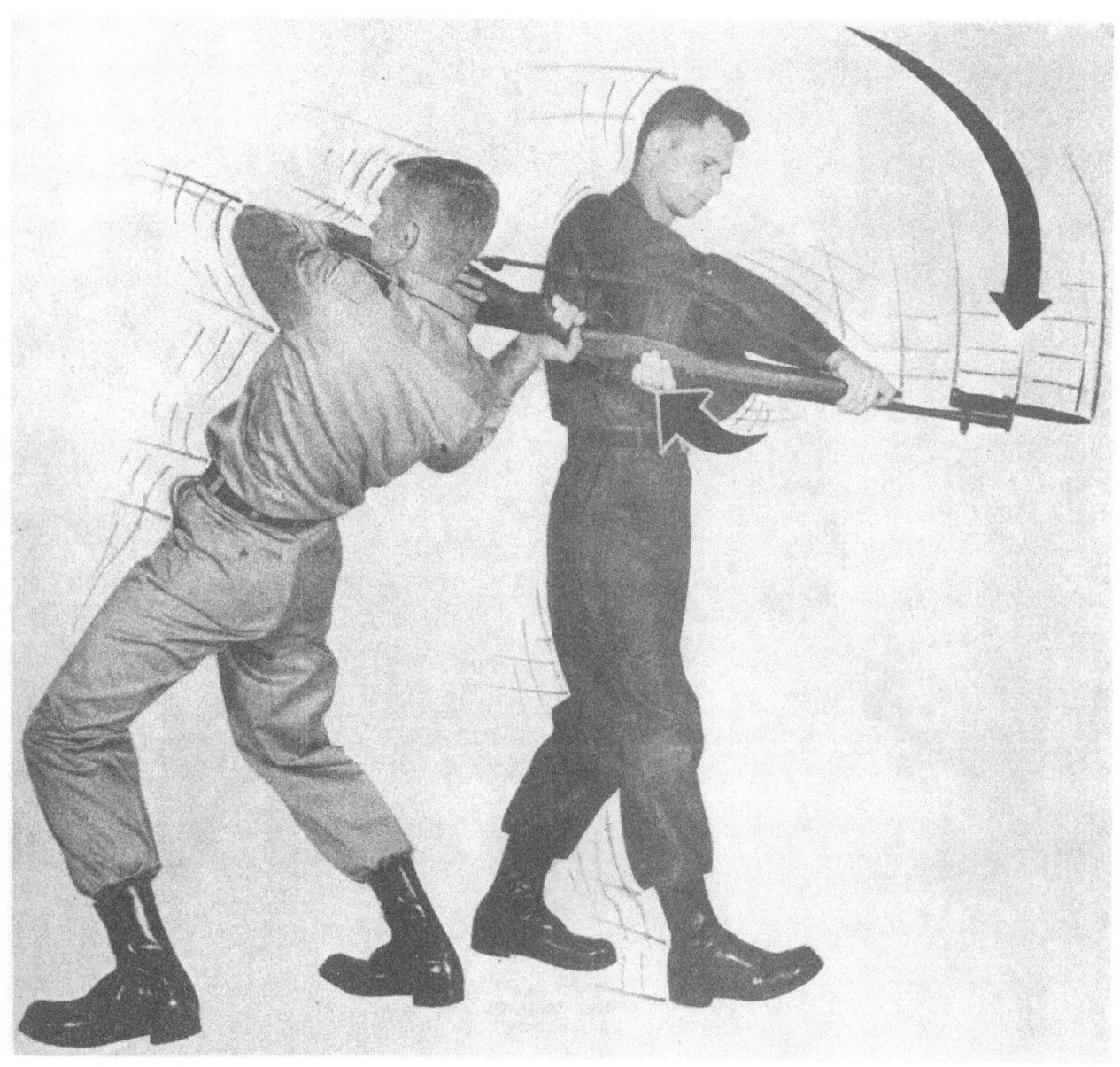

③
Figure 145—Continued.

84. Counter Against Long Thrust

a. As your opponent executes the long thrust, parry the bayonet to your left with the palm of your right hand and sidestep to the right oblique. You are now in a position facing the side of his rifle with your groin area protected by your right leg (1, fig. 146).

Figure 146. Counter against a long thrust.

b. With your left hand, palm up, grab your opponent's left hand and the rifle from underneath (2, fig. 146).

c. Twist your body to the left in front of your opponent and place your right leg in front of his body (3, fig. 146).

②

Figure 146—Continued.

③

Figure 146—Continued.

d. With the right hand, palm down, grab his rifle from above at the receiver. Twist the rifle and pull your opponent across your right leg. At the same time, exert pressure with the right elbow against the outside of his left arm and elbow (4, fig. 146). Sufficient downward pressure with your elbow, while twisting and pulling up on the rifle, can break your opponent's elbow.

e. Continue the twisting motion and pull your opponent across your leg, throwing him to the ground (5, fig. 146).

f. Grab the rifle again and follow through with your attack (6, fig. 146).

④

Figure 146—Continued.

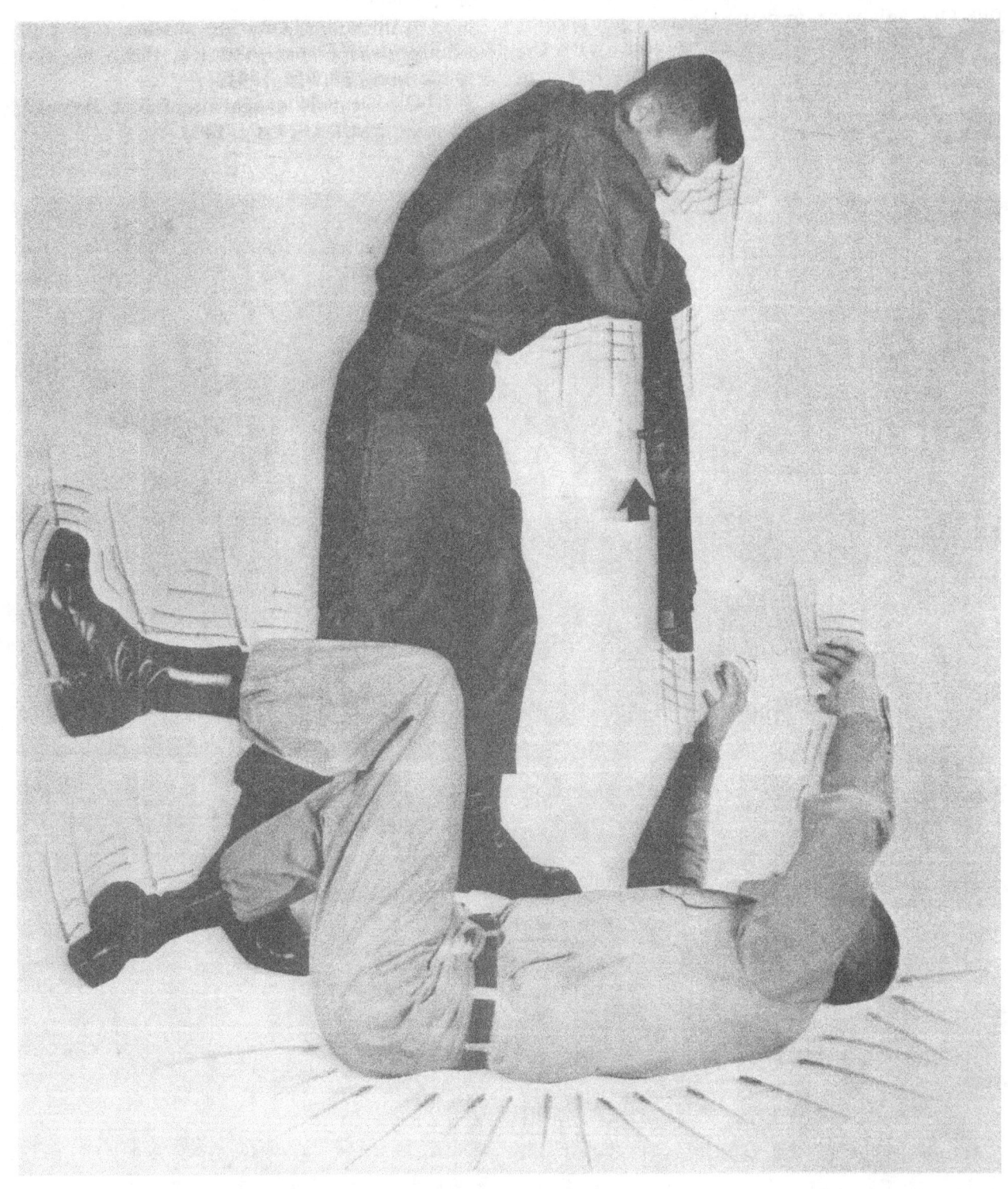

⑤

Figure 146—Continued.

Figure 146—Continued.

85. Second Counter Against Long Thrust

a. As your opponent executes the long thrust, parry his bayonet to your right with the palm of your left hand. As you parry with your left hand, move your body to the left oblique, stepping off to your left front with your left foot. You are now in a position facing his rifle from the side with your groin area protected by your left leg (1, fig. 147).

①

Figure 147. Second counter against a long thrust.

b. With the palms of your hands strike his rifle near the muzzle and drive the bayonet point into the ground (2, fig. 147). Do not follow the rifle all the way down. Allow your opponent's momentum to ram the bayonet into the ground.

②

Figure 147—Continued.

c. Grab the rifle butt with your left hand and with your right hand grab your opponent anywhere on his back or head (3, fig. 147).

d. To disarm your opponent you drive the stock of his rifle into his body and simultaneously pull him with your right hand, spinning him to the ground (4, fig. 147).

e. Now you should be in possession of your opponent's rifle and in a position to attack him (5, fig. 147).

③

Figure 147—Continued.

④
Figure 147—Continued.

⑤
Figure 147—Continued.

Section XI. RIFLE AND PISTOL DISARMING

86. Speed in Disarming

When disarming an opponent who has a rifle or pistol, make each movement quickly and without hesitation. Although your opponent has the weapon, you are in a good position because you know what you are going to do whereas he has to react to your movement. *Although his reaction may be quick, it may not be quick enough to counter your move.*

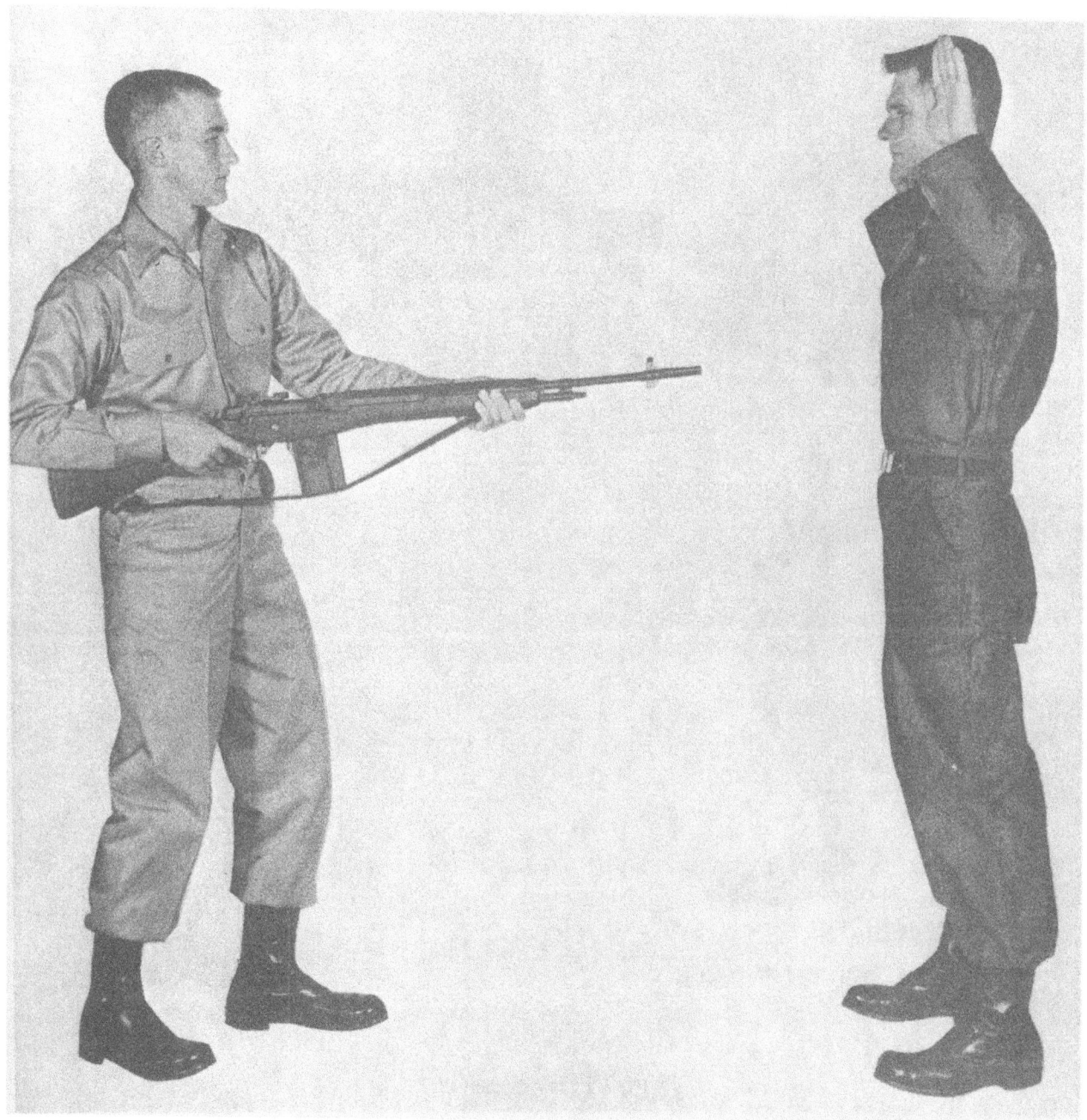

①

Figure 148. Counter against rifle in front.

87. Counter Against Rifle in Front

a. When your opponent orders "hands up," (1, fig. 148) bring your hands to shoulder level. Then, in one motion, twist your body to your right and strike his rifle muzzle away from your body with your left hand (2, fig. 148).

②
Figure 148—Continued.

b. As you strike the muzzle, step forward with your left foot and grab the upper part of the handguard with your right hand and the small of the stock with your left hand (3, fig. 148).

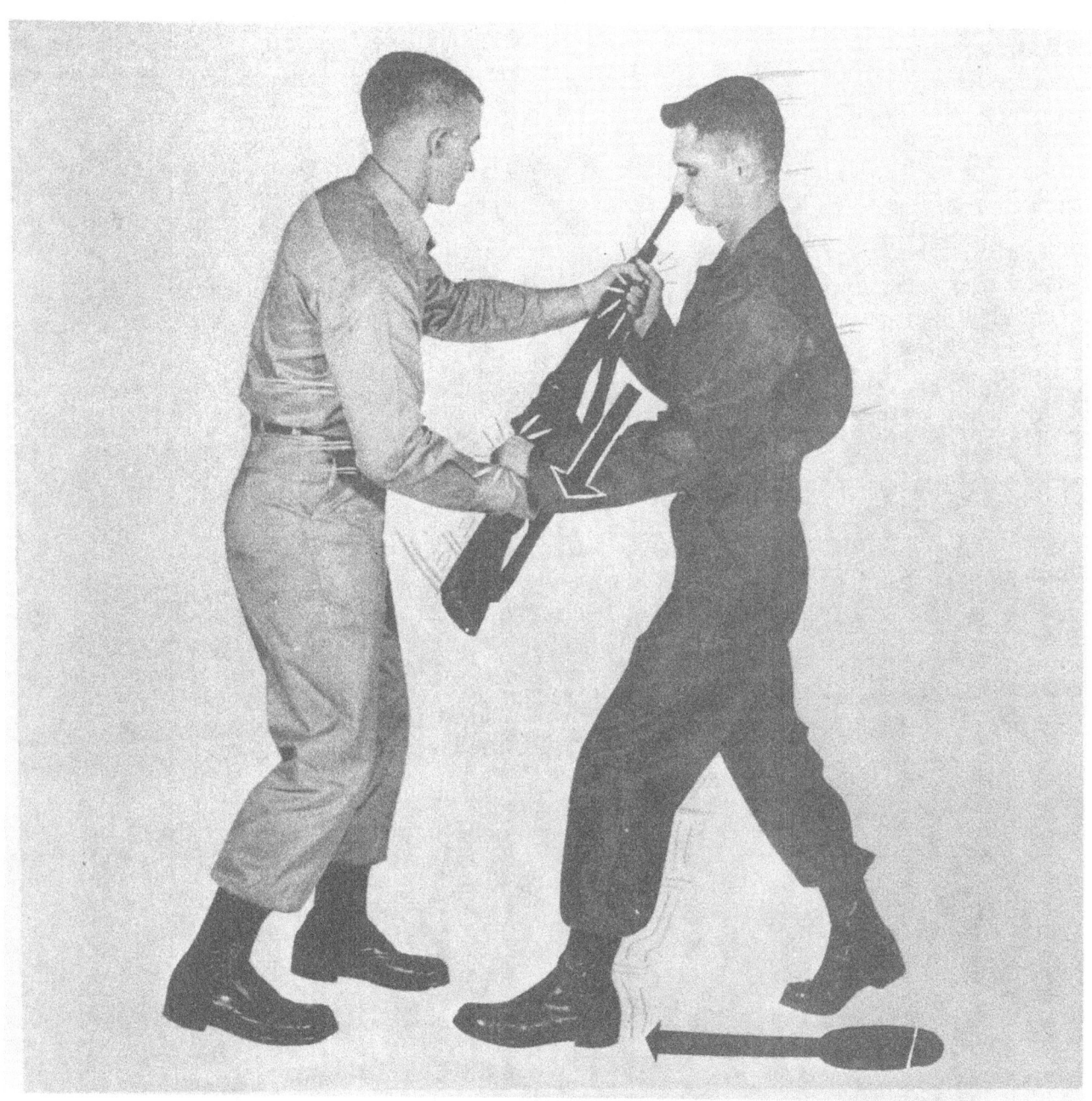

Figure 148—Continued.

c. Pull with your left hand and push with your right hand and step to your opponent's right with your right foot. This knocks him off balance and enables you to strike him on the head with the rifle muzzle or take the rifle from him by twisting it over his right shoulder (4, fig. 148).

88. Counter Against Rifle in Back

a. When your opponent has his rifle in your back as shown in 1, figure 149, start to raise your hands when ordered. When your hands reach shoulder height, twist from the hips to your right and bring your right elbow back, striking the rifle muzzle. This deflects the rifle away from your body. Do not move your feet (2, fig. 149).

④
Figure 148—Continued.

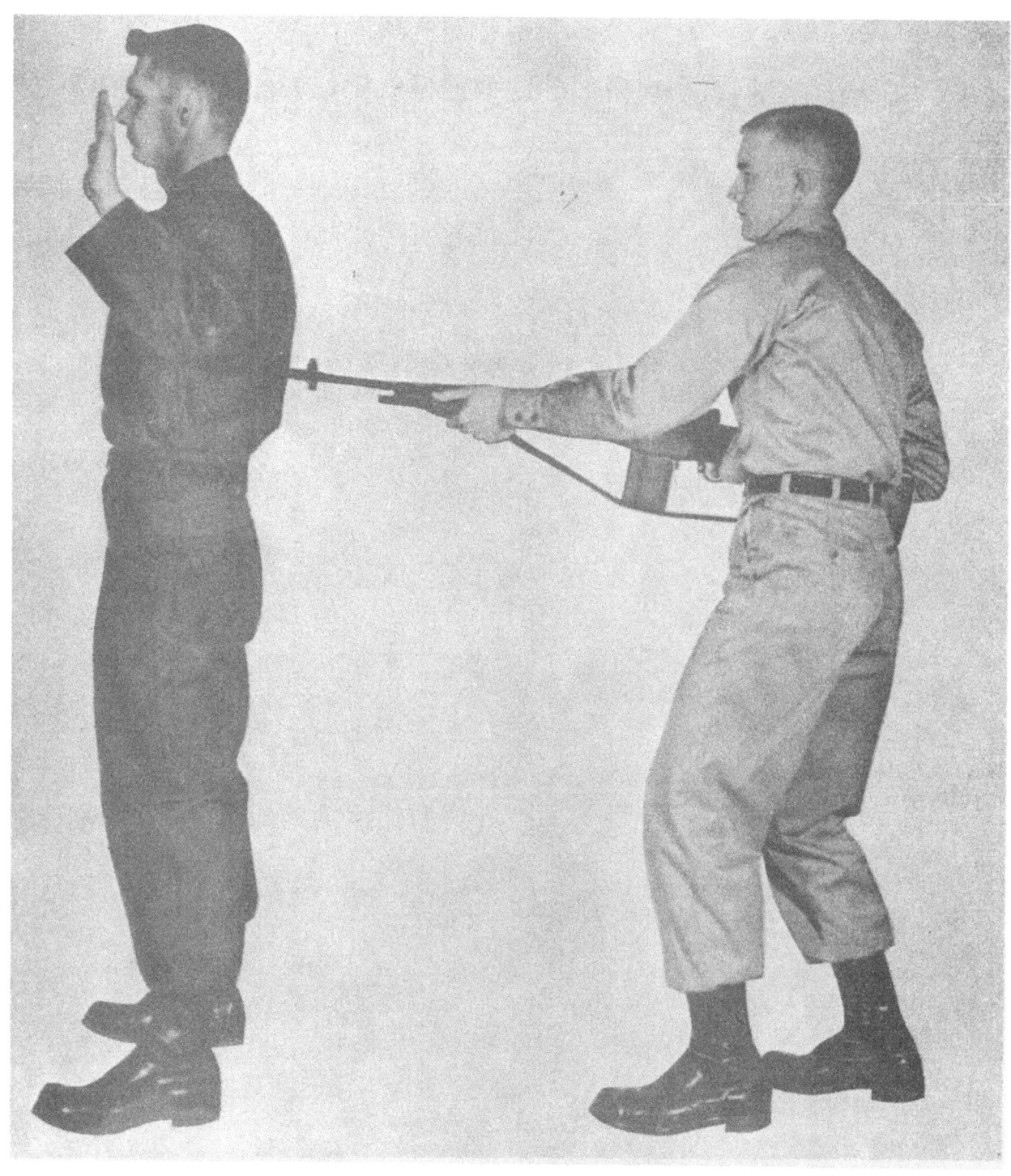
①
Figure 149. Counter against rifle in back.

Figure 149—Continued.

b. Now turn to the right by pivoting on your right foot. Face your opponent and bring your right arm under his rifle and over your opponent's left wrist. Place your left hand on your opponent's right hand where it grasps the stock, or grab the receiver from the top (3, fig. 149). This prevents him from executing a butt stroke.

Ⓑ
Figure 149—Continued.

c. Pull with your left hand and push with your right shoulder and arm, forcing your opponent to the ground and making him release his grip on the rifle (4, fig. 149).

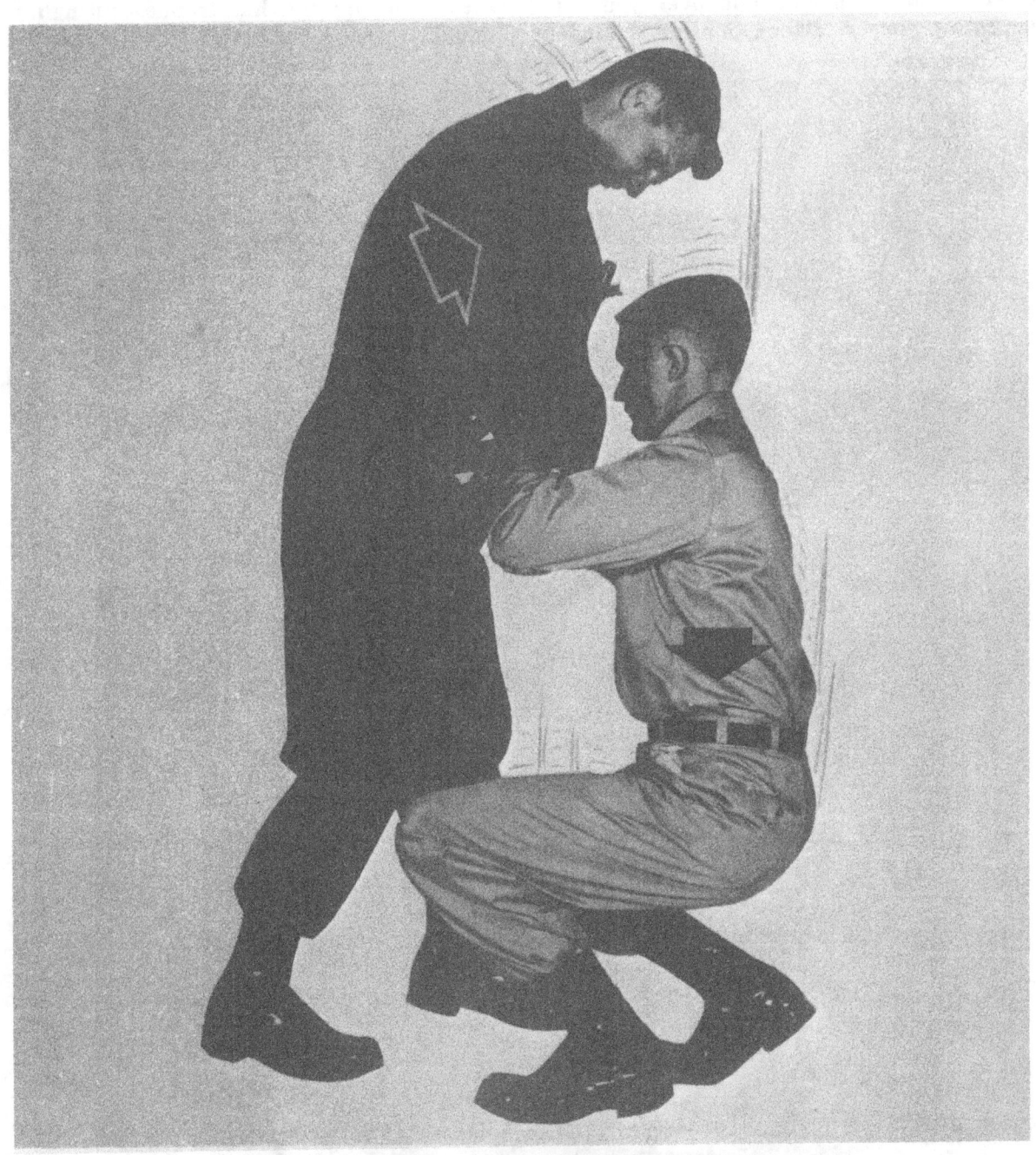

④

Figure 149—Continued.

89. Counter Against Pistol in Front

a. Your opponent orders you to raise your hands. As you do keep your elbows as low as possible (1, fig. 150). The twist your body to the right and strike your opponent's wrist with your left forearm (2, fig. 150).

①
Figure 150. Counter against pistol in front.

②
Figure 150—Continued.

b. Grab the pistol barrel with your right hand, making certain your hand is not covering the muzzle. At the same time, strike downward on your opponent's wrist with your left first (3, fig. 150).

Figure 150—Continued.

c. While applying pressure with your left fist, bend the pistol towards your opponent's body with your right hand, causing him to release his grip (4, fig. 150). If he retains his grip, his index finger will be broken. From this position, you can strike him on the temple with the pistol butt.

Figure 150—Continued.

90. Second Counter Against Pistol in Front

a. As you start to raise your hands bring them quickly forward and simultaneously twist to your left away from your opponent's line of fire (1, fig. 151).

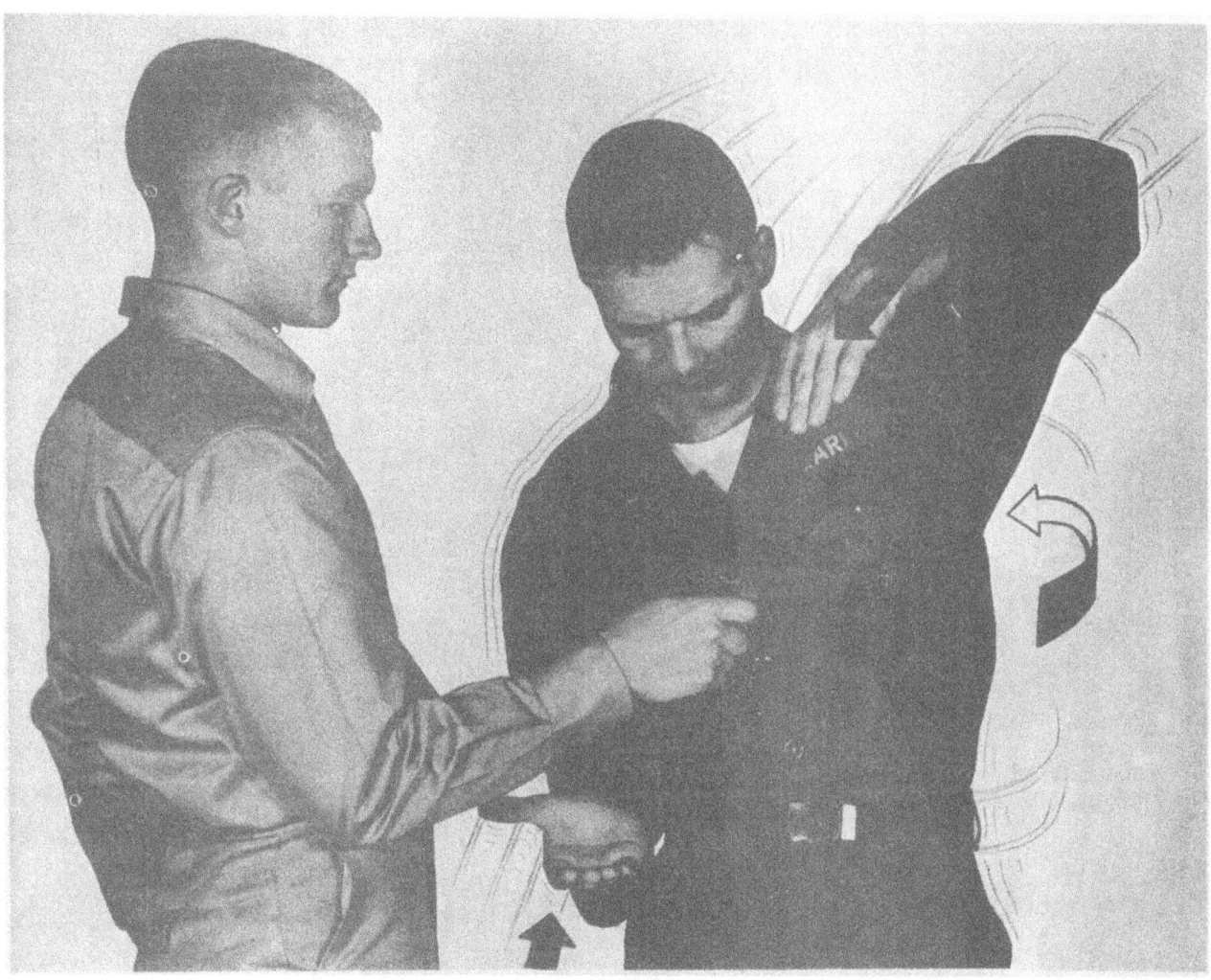

①
Figure 151. Second counter against pistol in front.

b. Bring your right hand under your opponent's wrist, either with a grasping or striking motion, and simultaneously grab the pistol barrel with your left hand (2, fig. 151).

c. Then you push up on his wrist with your right hand and push down and out on the pistol with your left hand (3, fig. 151). Your opponent will release his grip on the pistol.

Figure 151—Continued.

91. Counter Against Pistol in Back

a. This counter should be used only when you are certain that the pistol is in your opponent's right hand (1, fig. 152).

b. As you raise your hands, keep your elbows as close to your waist as possible. Twist your body to the right and simultaneously bring your right elbow against your opponent's forearm (2, fig. 152). Keep your feet in place.

c. Bring your right arm under your opponent's right forearm. Place it on his elbow joint so that his forearm rests in the crook of your right elbow (3, fig. 152).

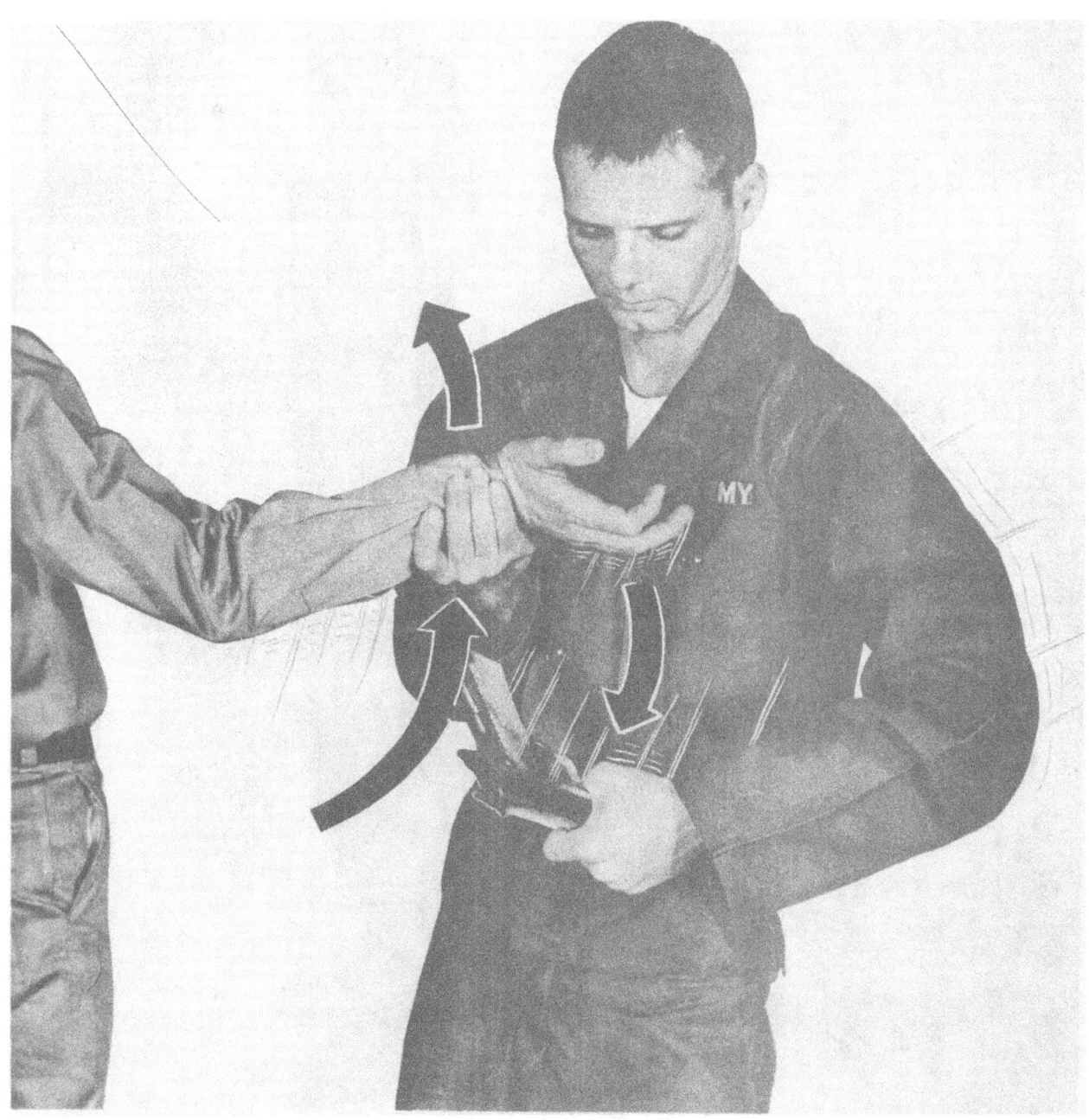

③
Figure 151—Continued.

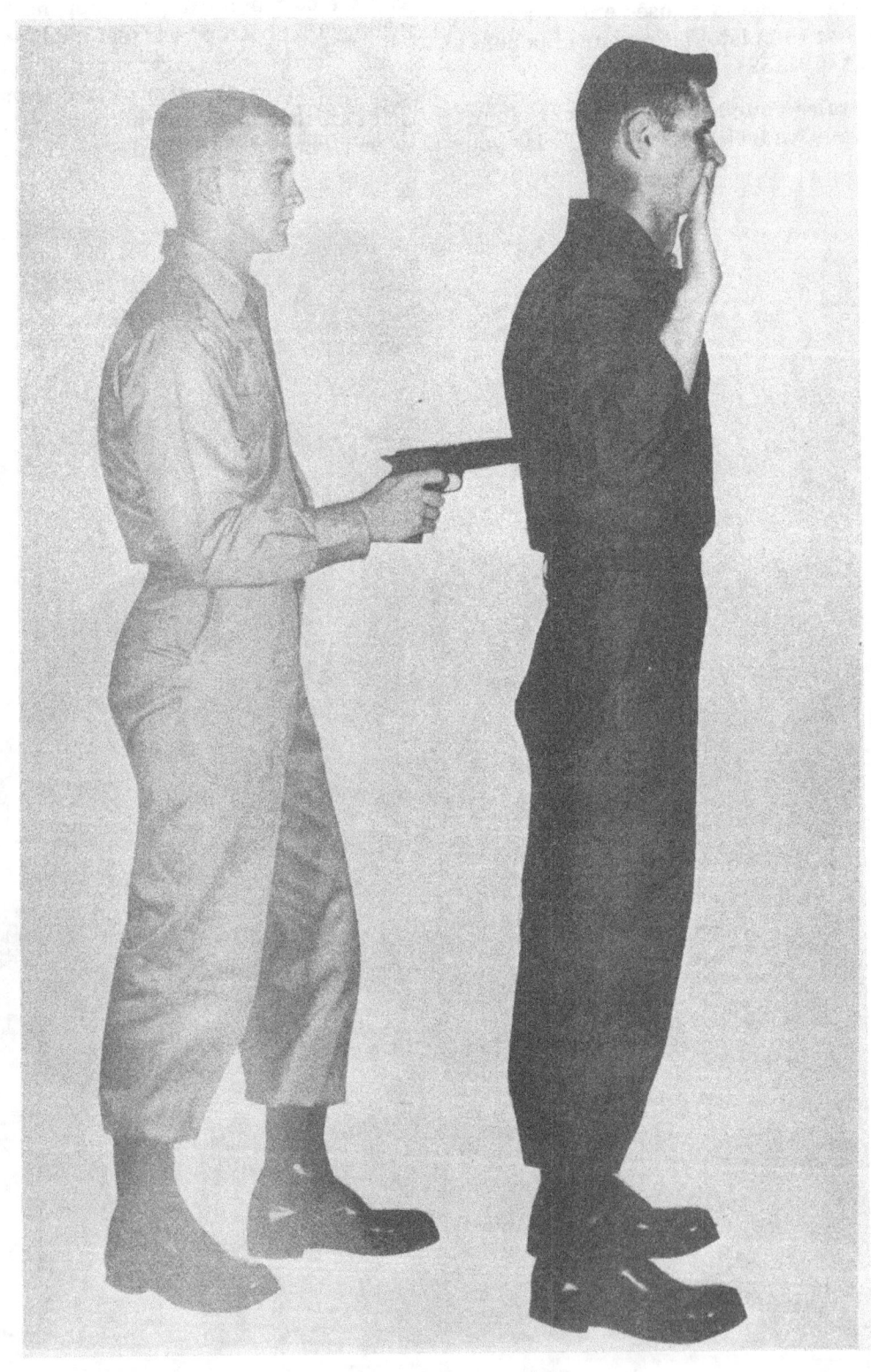
Figure 152. Counter against pistol in back.

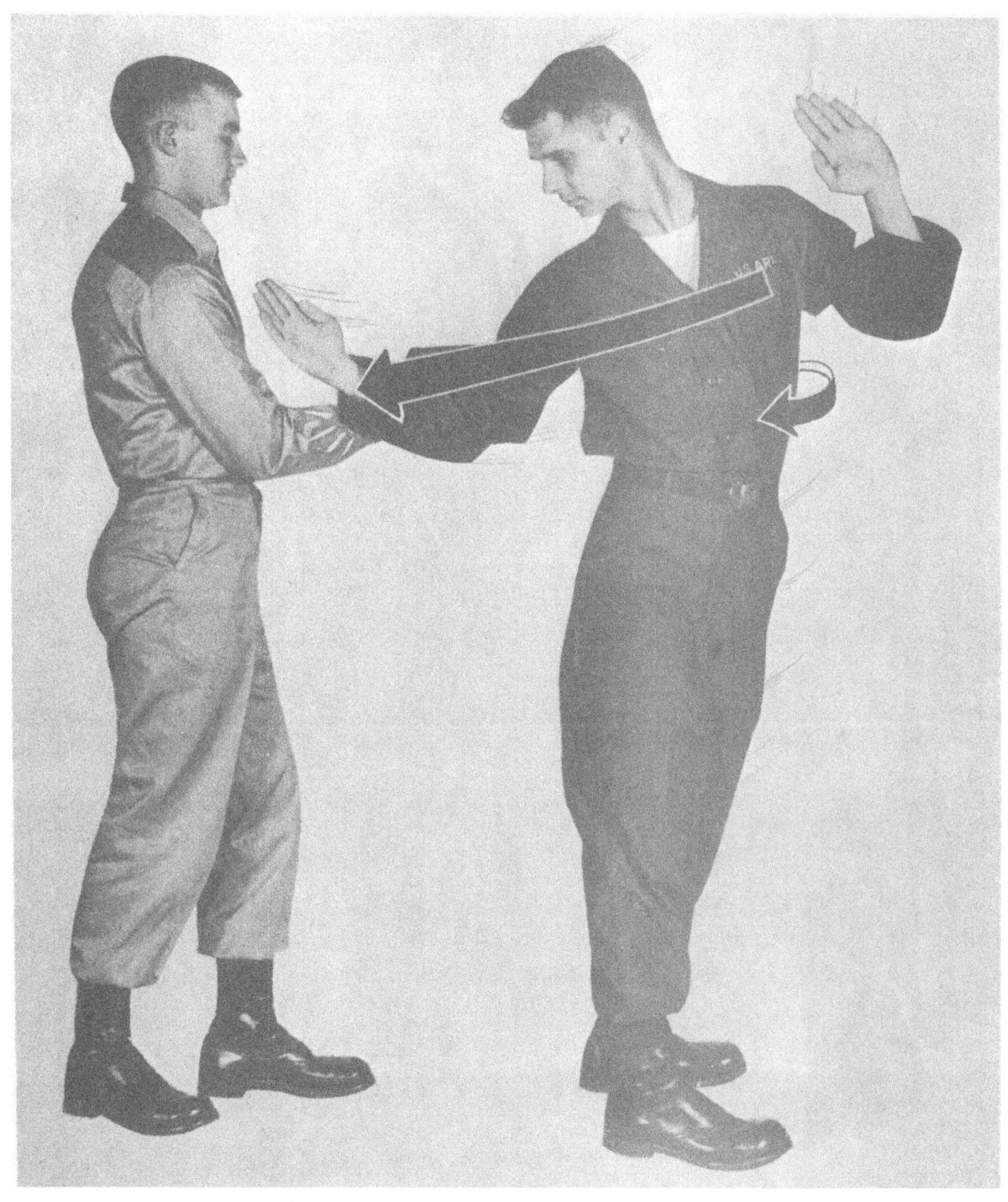

②
Figure 152—Continued.

③
Figure 152—Continued.

d. Grasp your right hand with your left hand and bend swiftly from the waist (4, fig. 152). By doing this, you force your opponent to the ground and cause him to drop his weapon.

92. Second Counter Against Pistol in Back

a. Use this counter when you are certain that your opponent is holding the pistol in his right hand. Keep your elbows as close to your waist as possible. Twist to the left striking your opponent's wrist or forearm with your left elbow (1, fig. 153).

b. Bring your left arm behind your opponent's right elbow so that his forearm or wrist rests on your shoulder or neck (2, fig. 153).

④

Figure 152—Continued.

Figure 153. Second counter against pistol in back.

Figure 153—Continued.

c. Grab your left hand with your right hand and press your left forearm against your opponent's right elbow (3, fig. 153). A swift twist to the front brings your opponent to the ground. With added pressure, you can break his arm. During this counter the muzzle of the pistol is always pointed away from you.

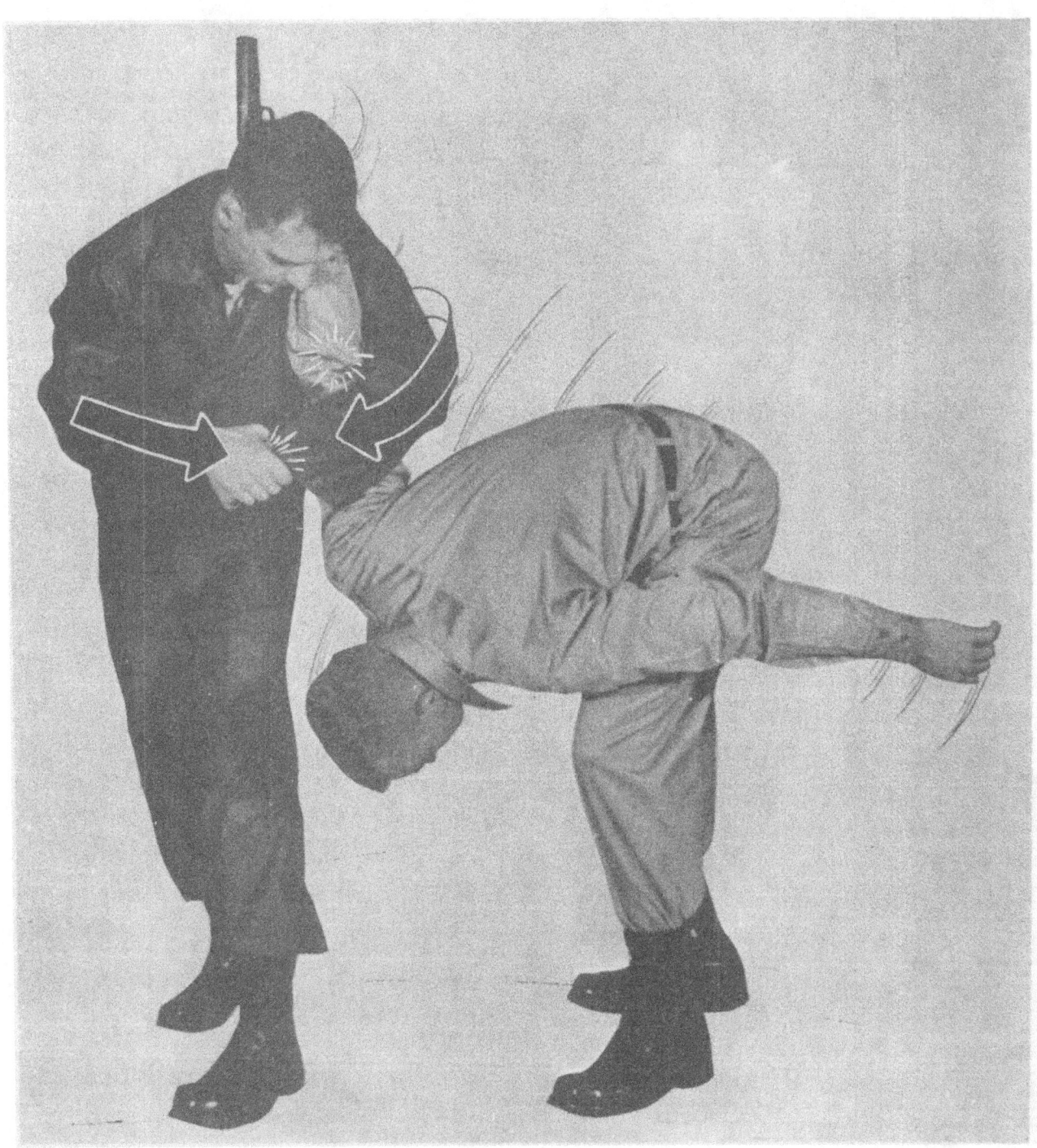

Figure 153—Continued.

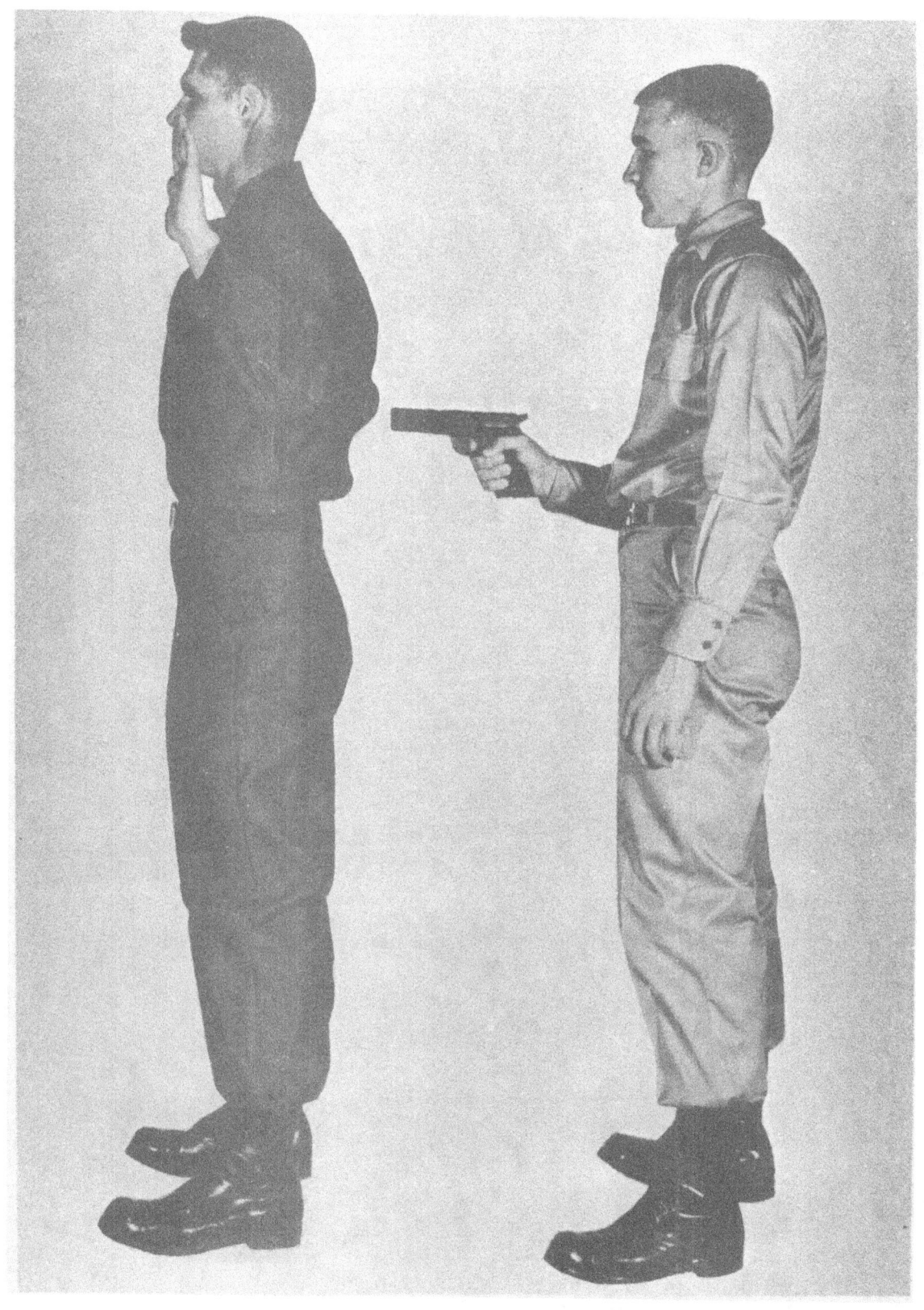
Figure 154. Third counter against pistol in back.

②
Figure 154—Continued.

Figure 154—Continued.

93. Third Counter Against Pistol in Back

a. In this counter it does not matter whether your opponent holds a pistol in his right or left hand because your actions are the same. The description given is to counter a pistol held in the right hand. The holdup is illustrated in 1, figure 154.

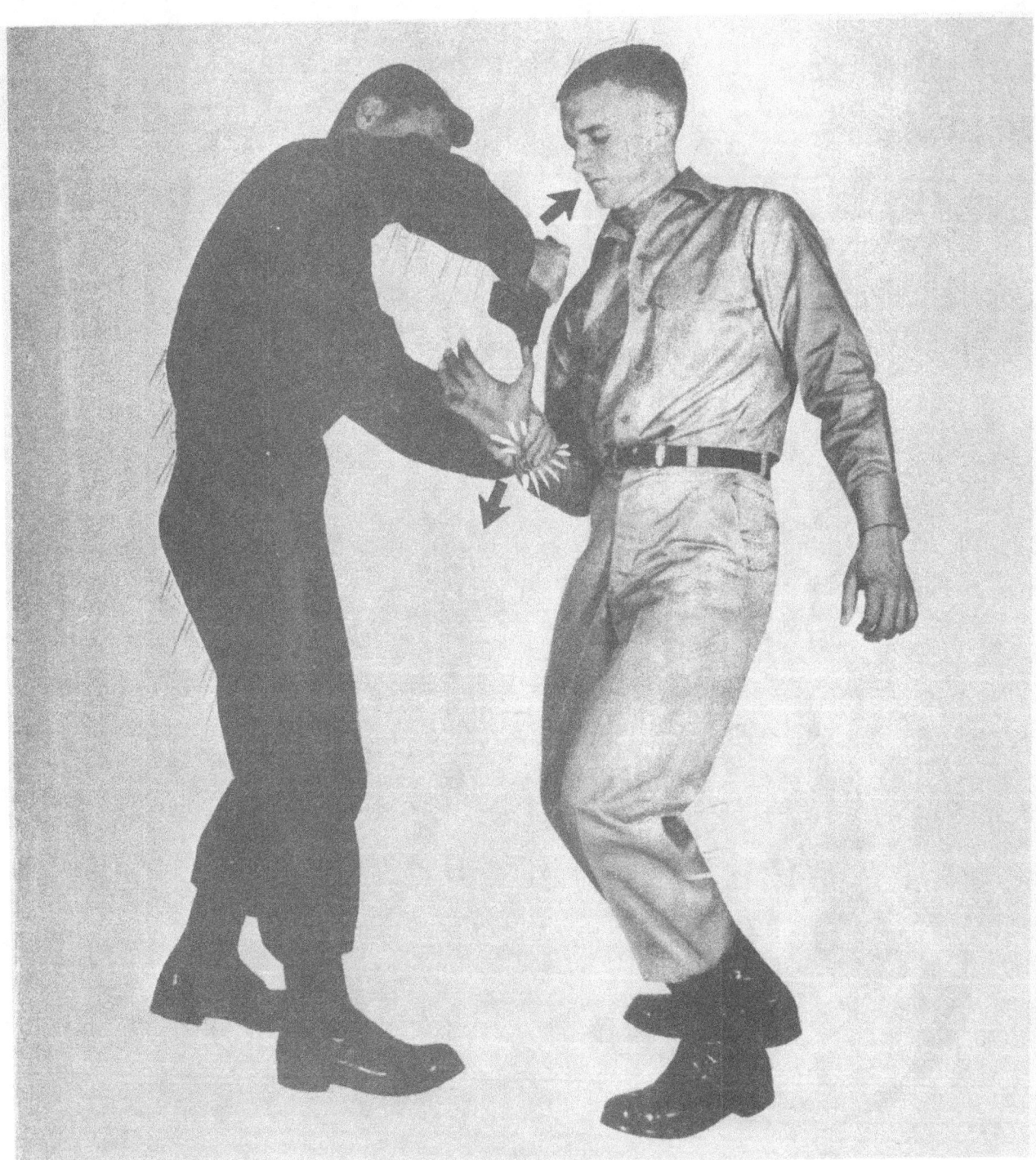

④

Figure 154—Continued.

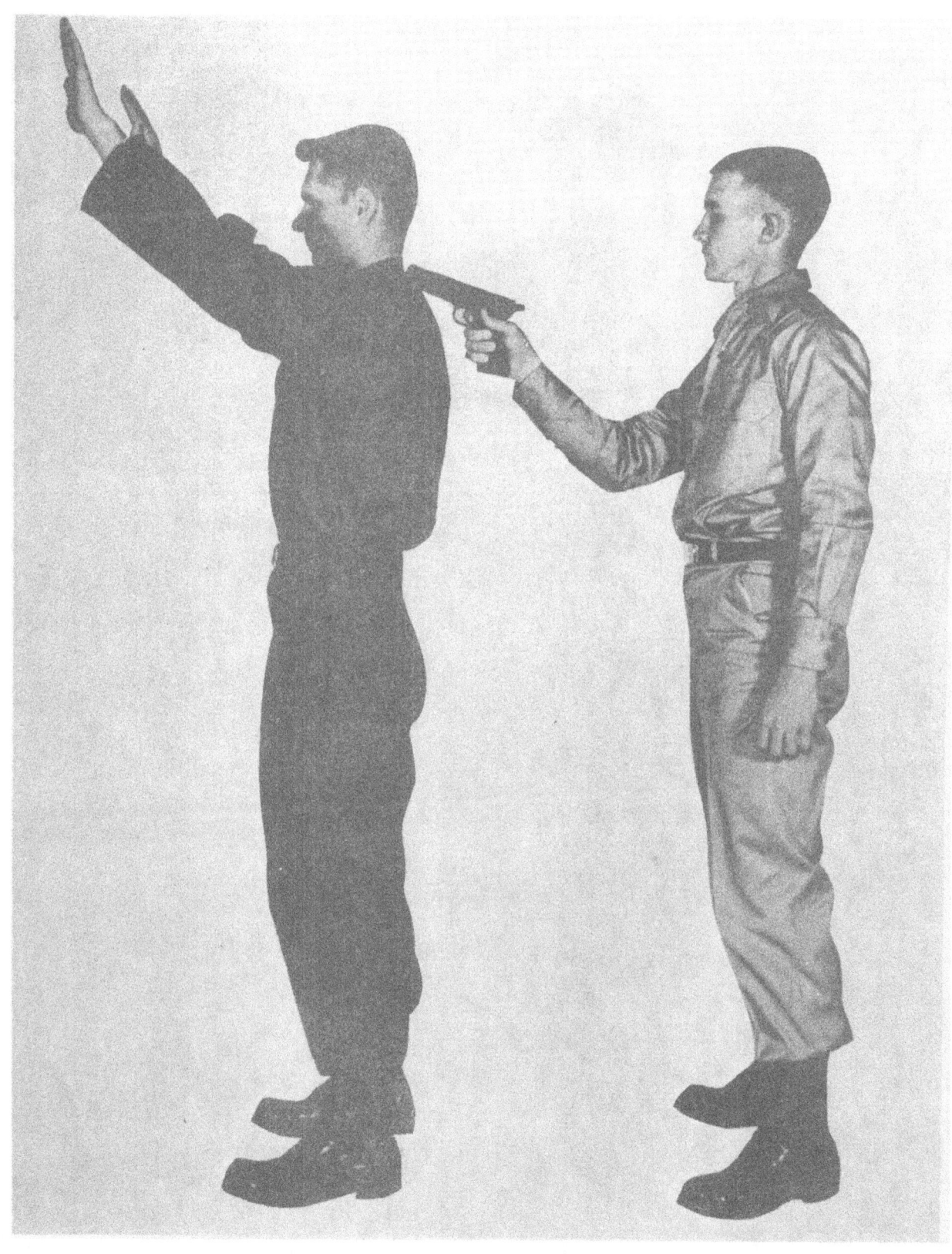

①

Figure 155. Counter against pistol in back of neck.

Figure 155—Continued.

b. Twist your body to the right striking your right elbow against your opponent's hand or wrist (2, fig. 154).

c. Pivot to the right and place your left wrist against your opponent's right wrist, grabbing the pistol barrel with your right hand, palm up. Apply pressure to his hand and trigger finger by pushing the barrel toward his upper arm. This releases his hold on the pistol and may break his index finger (3, fig. 154).

d. You should now have the pistol in your right hand, opposite your left shoulder. By twisting forcefully to the right, you can strike your opponent on the chin or neck with the pistol butt (4, fig. 154).

Figure 155—Continued.

94. Counter Against Pistol in Back of Neck

a. This counter is practical only when you are certain that the pistol is held in your opponent's right hand. When raising your arms, bring your elbows shoulder high (1, fig. 155).

b. Twist your body to the left and bring your left arm under your opponent's right elbow (2, fig. 155).

c. Reach across with your right hand and grasp your left hand. Twist forward and put pressure on your opponent's elbow with your left forearm. You can either break his arm or force him to the ground, causing him to release his weapon (3, fig. 155).

95. Second Counter Against Pistol in Back of Neck

Use this counter primarily for an attack when the pistol is held in your opponent's right hand. The initial move, however, can be used for a right or left hand attack.

a. Hold your elbows shoulder high when your opponent has the pistol in back of your neck (1, fig. 156).

b. Twist your body to the right and simultaneously bring your right upper arm over your opponent's right wrist (2, fig. 156). If the pistol is in your opponent's left hand, bring your right upper arm over his left wrist.

c. Pivot on your right foot and place your left foot close to your opponent's right foot. Hold your opponent's wrist close to your right side with your right upper arm. Cross your left arm under his right upper arm and grab the left lapel of his shirt or jacket with your left hand (3, fig. 156). Hold his right wrist close to your side and lift with your left upper arm, applying pressure to his elbow.

96. Third Counter Against Pistol in Back of Neck

a. Hold your elbows shoulder high when your opponent has the pistol in back of your neck (1, fig. 157).

b. The initial movement in this action is identical with that in the second counter shown in (2, figure 156). Twist your body to the right and strike your opponent's left wrist with your right arm (2, fig. 157).

c. Pivot on your right foot and place your left hand against your opponent's shoulder or upper arm. Bring your right forearm or wrist under your opponent's left elbow and lock it against your left forearm (3, fig. 157). Apply pressure and cause your opponent to drop his weapon. Severe pressure can break his arm.

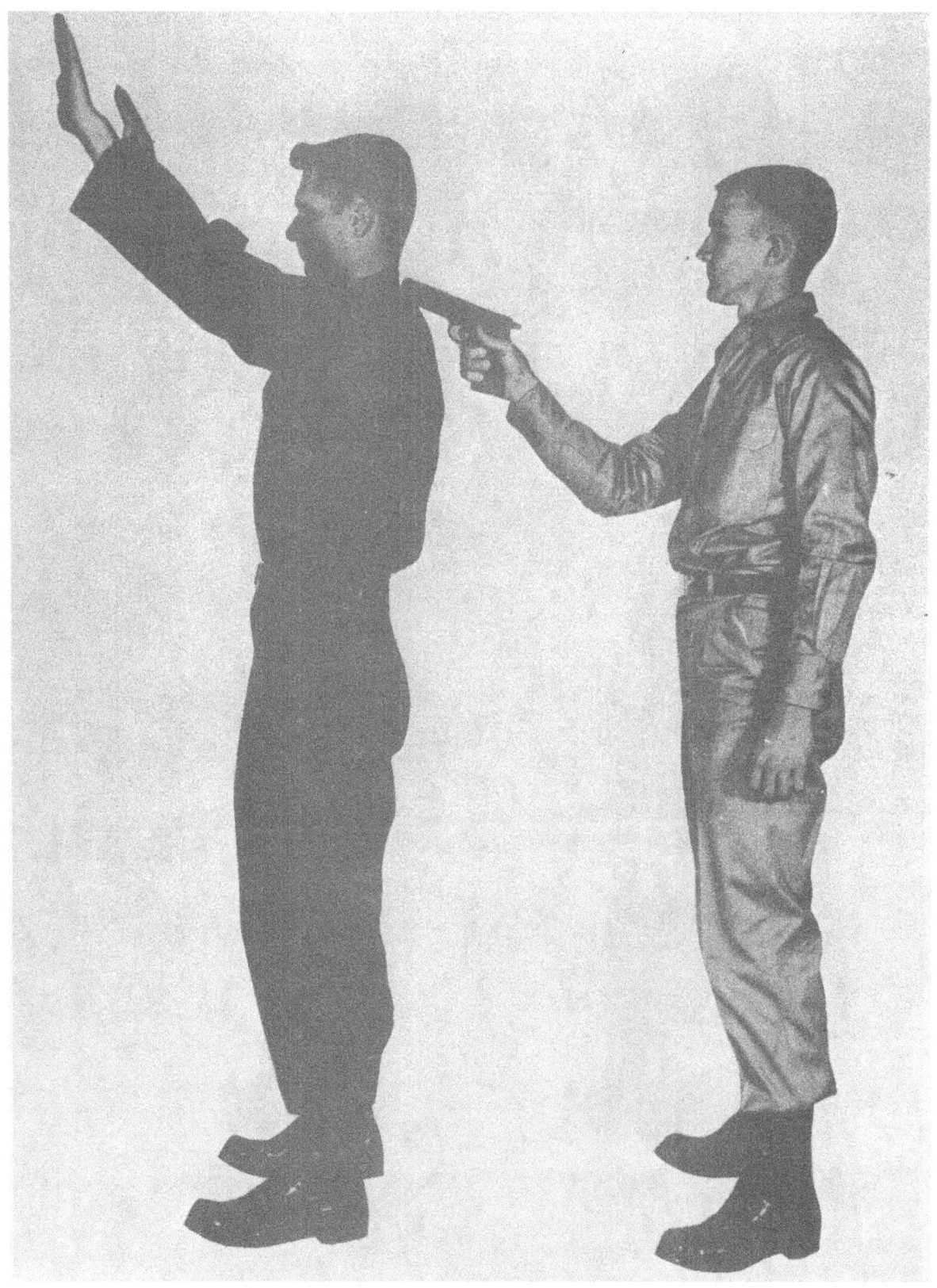

①
Figure 156. Second counter against pistol in back of neck.

Figure 156—Continued.

③
Figure 156—Continued.

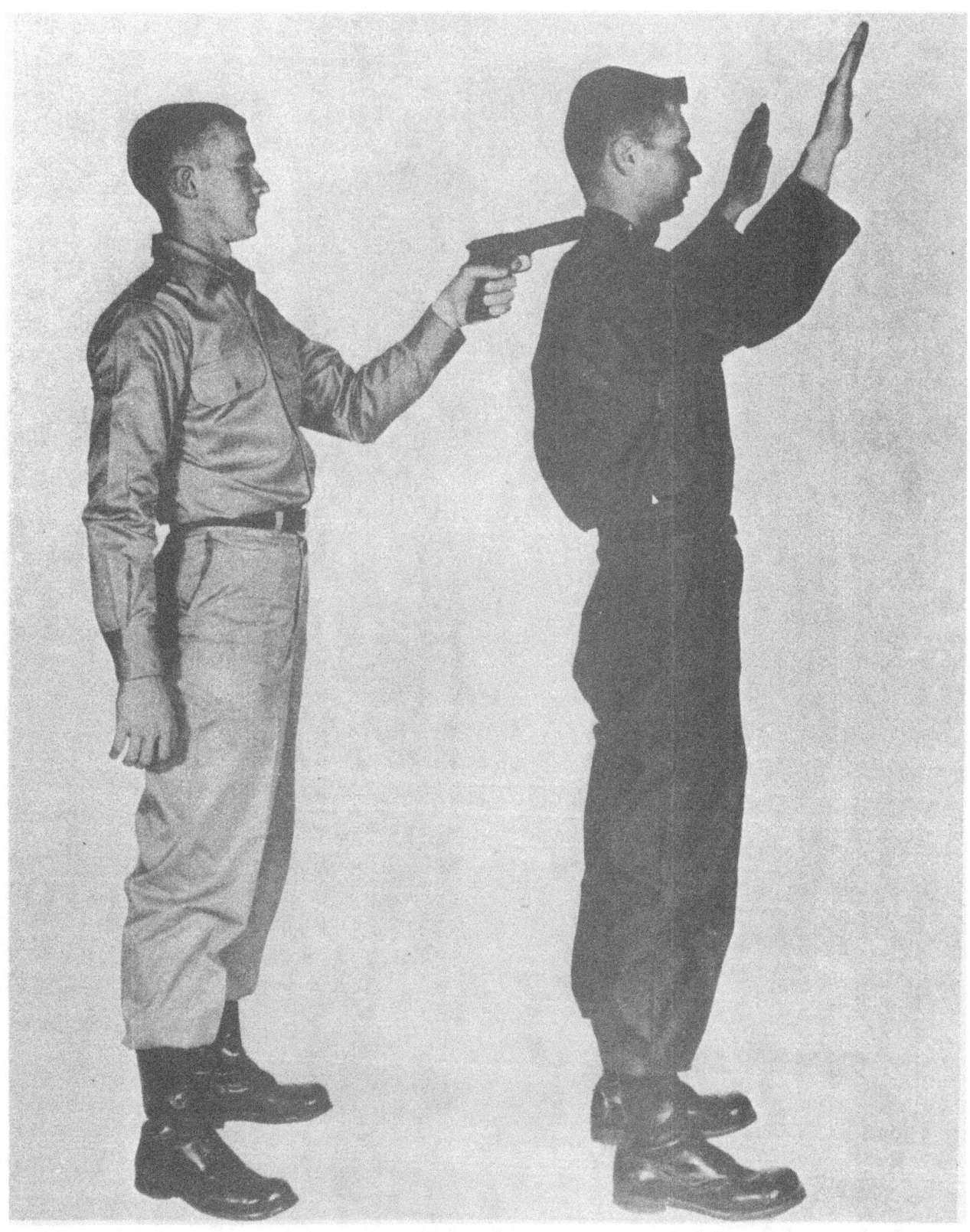

①
Figure 157. Third counter against pistol in back of neck.

②
Figure 157—Continued.

③
Figure 157—Continued.

97. Helping a Friend

a. When approaching an opponent from his rear, while he is holding a friend at gunpoint, carry your right hand low and your left hand shoulder high (1, fig. 158).

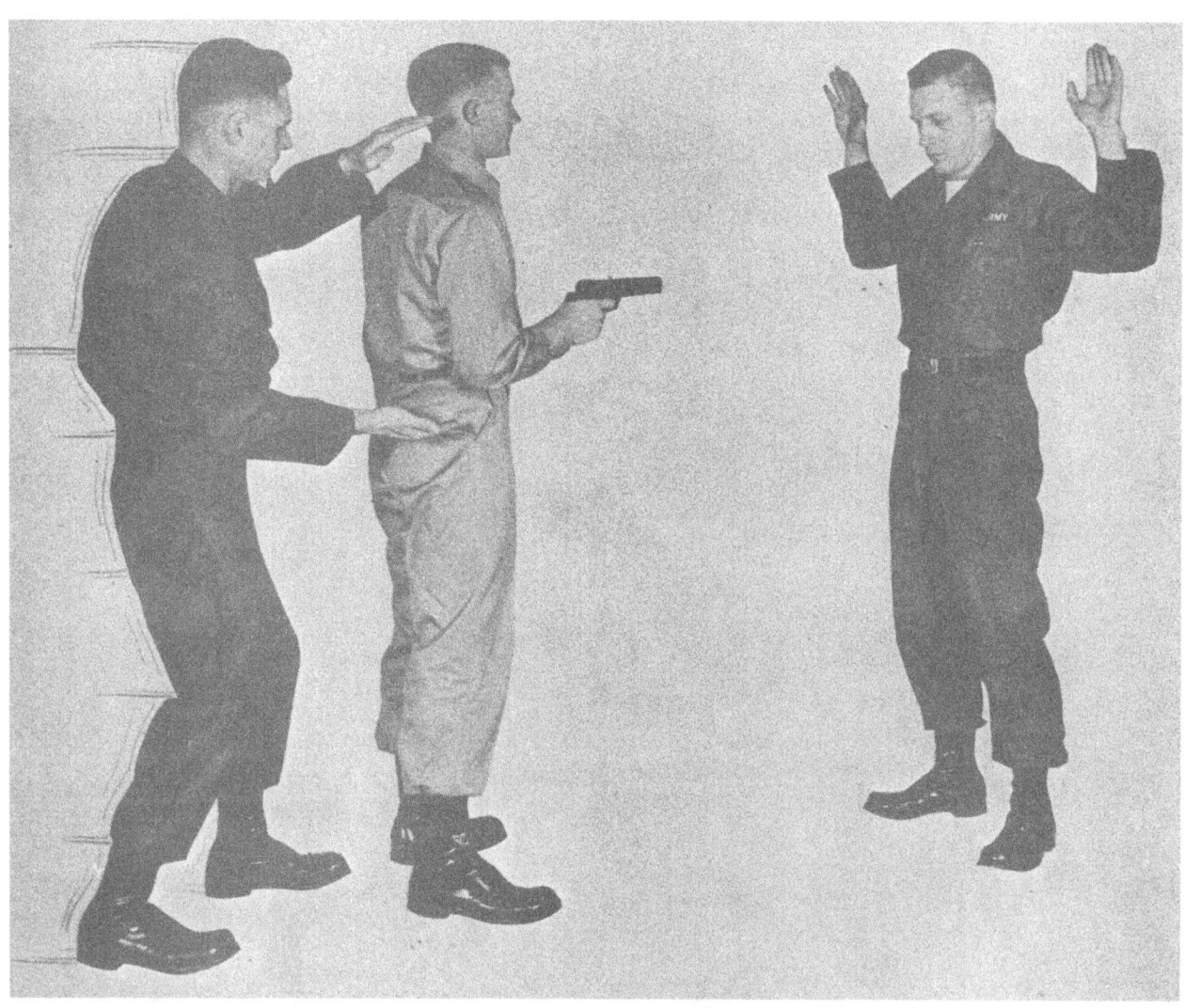

①

Figure 158. Attacking an opponent, who has a gun, from his rear.

b. You must grab your opponent with both hands at the same time. With your right hand, palm up, grab his pistol hand and lift it while using your left hand to push his right upper arm forward (2, fig. 158).

c. Turn your body to the left and continue to apply pressure by pushing with your left hand and pulling his right hand backward (3, fig. 158). This causes him to drop to the ground or suffer a dislocated shoulder.

③

Figure 158—Continued.

③
Figure 158—Continued.

98. Actions Against Opponent Who is Holding You and Your Friend at Gunpoint

a. The original position in this holdup is shown in (1, figure 159). The gunman is pointing the pistol at your friend, then at you back again to your friend. You are sta on your friend's left.

①

Figure 159. Attacking opponent holding you and friend at gunpoint.

b. As the weapon swings away from you, step forward with your left foot, place your left hand on the back of the opponent's gun hand, and push forcefully to his left (2, fig. 159).

Figure 159—Continued.

c. Take a step with your right foot and a quick, long step with your left foot. Your movement brings you in front of your opponent with your back to him. At the same time, twist his gun hand to his left, turning it so his palm is up and his right elbow comes in contact with your left armpit (3, fig. 159).

d. Bear down on his right elbow with your armpit and lift up on his hand causing him to release his weapon or suffer a broken arm (4, fig. 159).

Figure 159—Continued.

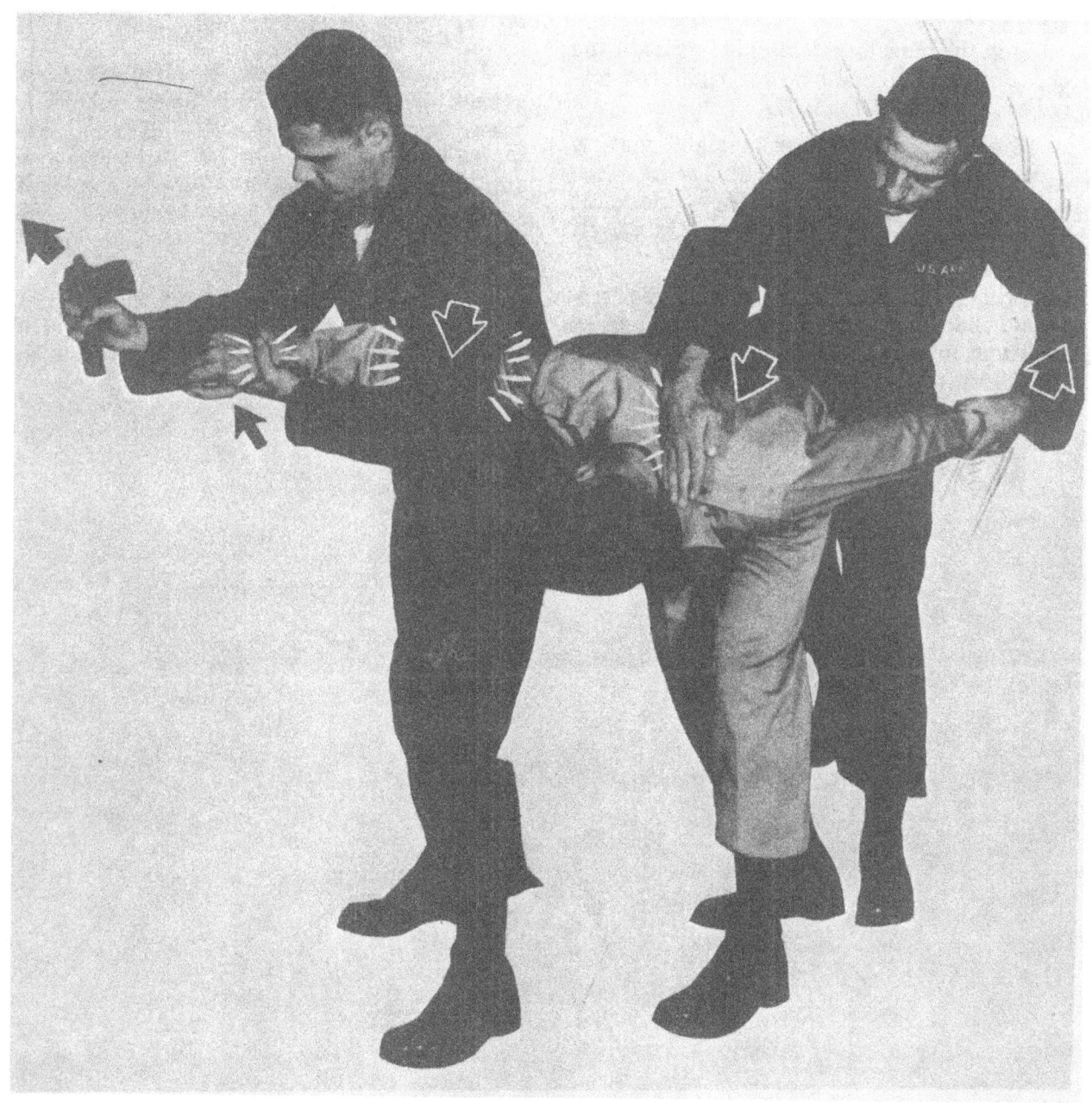

④
Figure 159—Continued.

Section XII. KNIFE DISARMING

99. Counter Against Downward Stroke

a. The following counter against a downward knife stroke is used if your opponent attacks you holding the knife higher than his shoulders (1, fig. 160).

b. Stop the blow by catching his wrist in the pocket formed by bending your right fist forward at the wrist (2, fig. 160).

c. Step through with your right foot to protect your groin area. At the same time, strike him sharply in the crook of his right elbow with your right forearm or wrist (3, fig. 160). This causes his arm to bend.

d. Bring your left hand behind his right forearm and underneath your right wrist, and grasp your right forearm. Bring your elbows close to your body (4, fig. 160).

e. Bend swiftly from the waist putting pressure on your opponent's arm (5, fig. 160). This causes him to fall backward and lose his weapon.

100. Second Counter Against Downward Stroke

a. Stop the knife stroke by catching your opponent's wrist in the pocket formed at your left wrist by bending your fist forward. Step through with your right foot to protect your groin area. Keep your left forearm horizontal to the ground. At the same time, bring your right hand underneath your opponent's knife arm and grasp your left fist (1, fig. 161).

b. Bend forward swiftly from the waist and put pressure on your opponent's arm (2, fig. 161). This causes him to fall backward and lose his weapon.

①
Figure 160. Counter against downward stroke.

Figure 160—Continued.

③
Figure 160—Continued.

④
Figure 160—Continued.

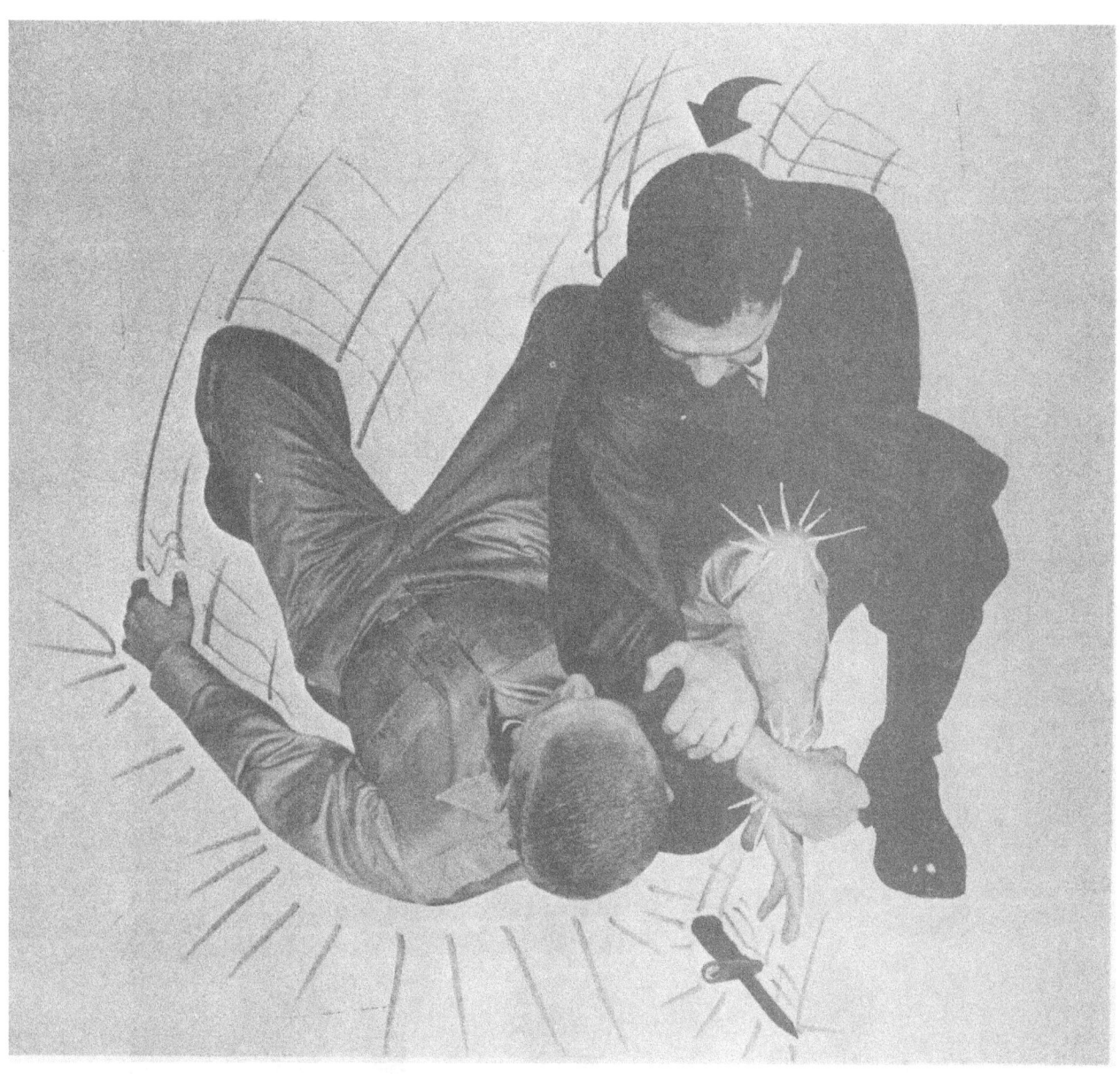

⑤
Figure 160—Continued.

Figure 161. Second counter against downward stroke.

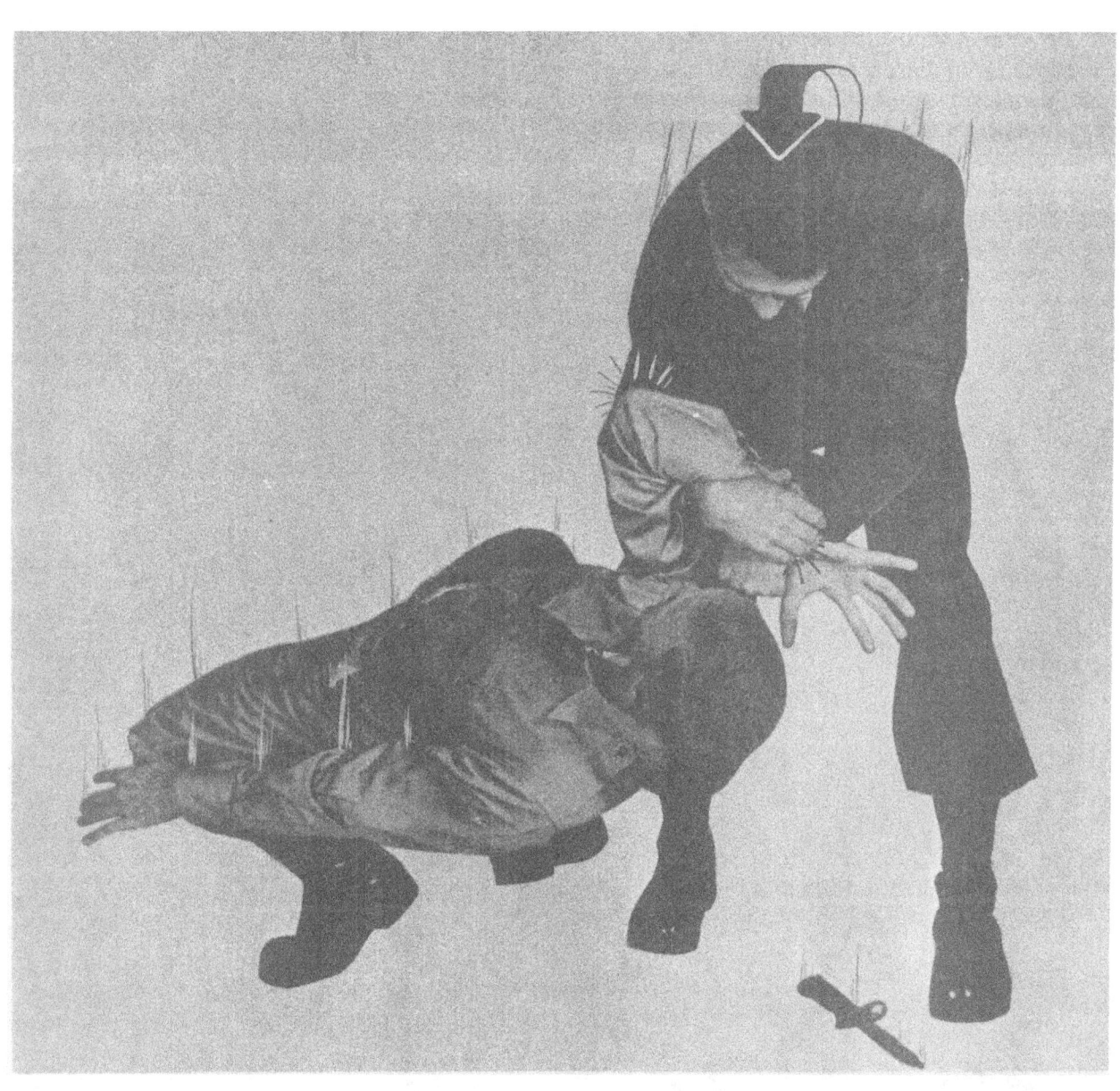

Figure 161—Continued.

101. Counter Against Upward Stroke

a. Block an upward knife stroke by catching your opponent's wrist or forearm in the V formed by crossing your arms at the wrist. At the same time, hop slightly to the rear to keep the knife from striking you in the stomach (1, fig. 162).

①

Figure 162. Counter against upward stroke.

b. As soon as you stop the blow, grab your opponent's right hand with your left hand and place your thumb on the back of his hand. Reinforce this hold by grabbing his wrist with your right hand and placing your left thumb on the back of his hand (2, fig. 162).

c. Twist his wrist to your left and bend his hand toward his forearm causing him to fall to the ground (3, fig. 162).

②

Figure 162—Continued.

102. Second Counter Against Upward Stroke

a. Another method of defending yourself against an upward stroke is to block your opponent's wrist or forearm in a V formed by your hands (1, fig. 163).

b. Keep your arms extended. Take a short hop to the rear as you block his thrust so your midsection is farther from the knife point (2, fig. 163).

c. Grab your opponent's wrist tightly with both hands and pivot to your left on the ball of your left foot. At the same time, raise your opponent's knife hand and step directly beneath his arm (3, fig. 163).

d. From this position, snap his arm forward and downward as you bend at the waist and simultaneously force him to the ground (4, fig. 163).

③
Figure 162—Continued.

103. Third Counter Against Upward Stroke

a. This phase is the same as that described in paragraph 102*a* and *b*.

b. Grab your opponent's wrist tightly with both hands and pivot to your right. Raise his hand and bring his arm down over your left shoulder (1, fig. 164).

c. Apply downward pressure on his arm. This will throw him to the ground or break his arm. This method can be varied by stepping under his arm and behind his back, forcing him to drop the knife by bending his arm (2, fig. 164). You must pivot quickly to prevent him from spinning out of the hold.

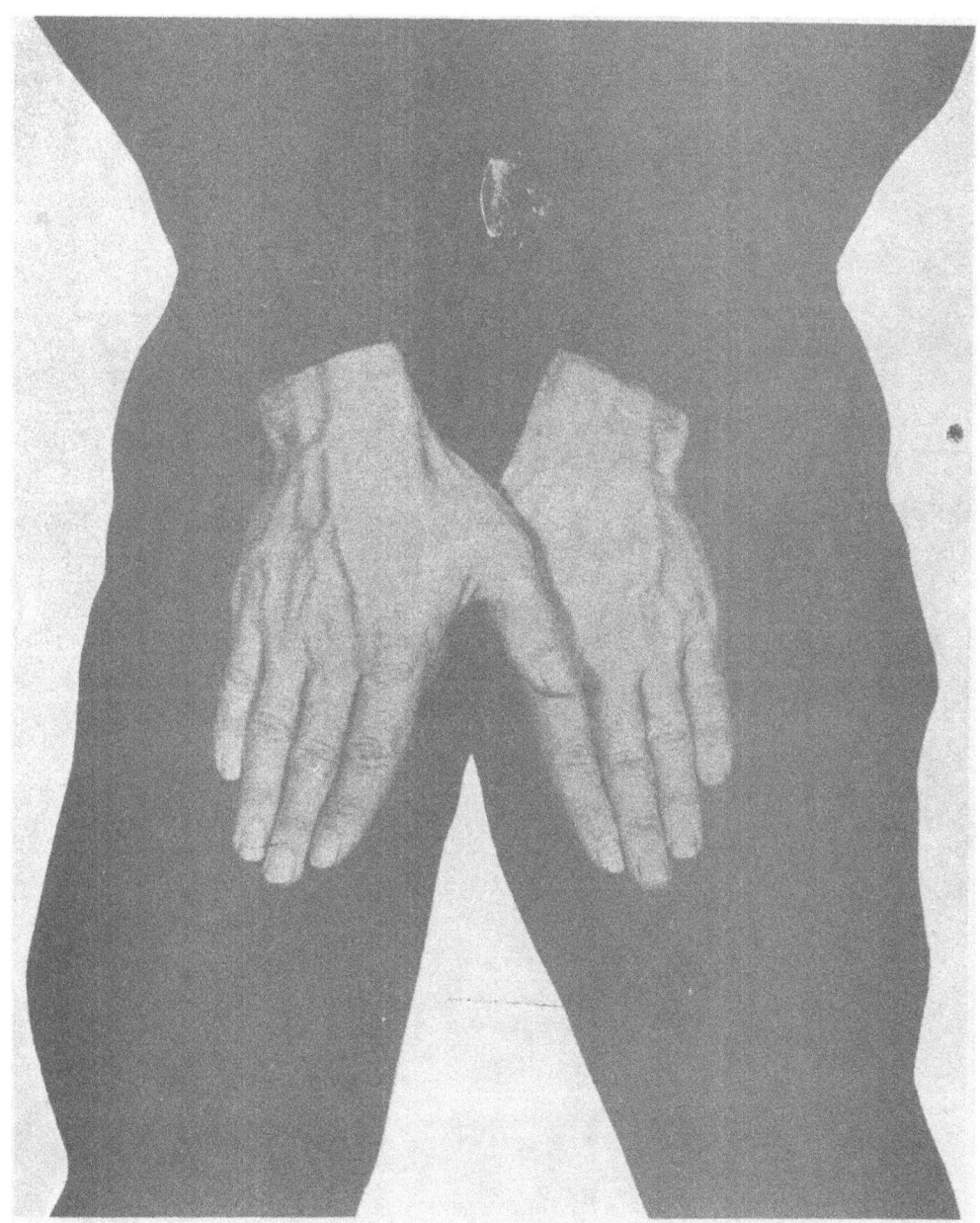

①

Figure 163. Second counter against upward stroke.

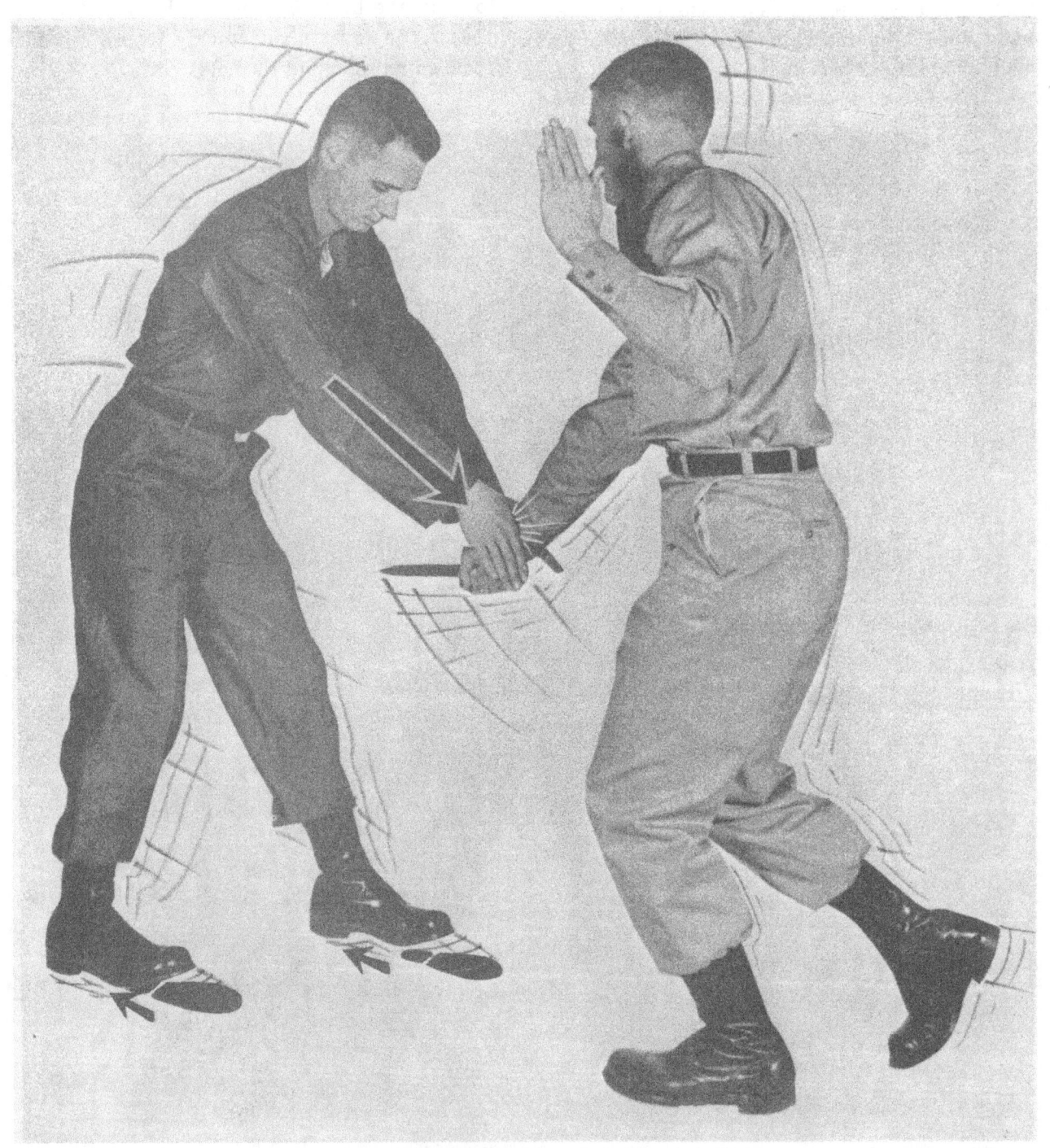

③
Figure 163—Continued.

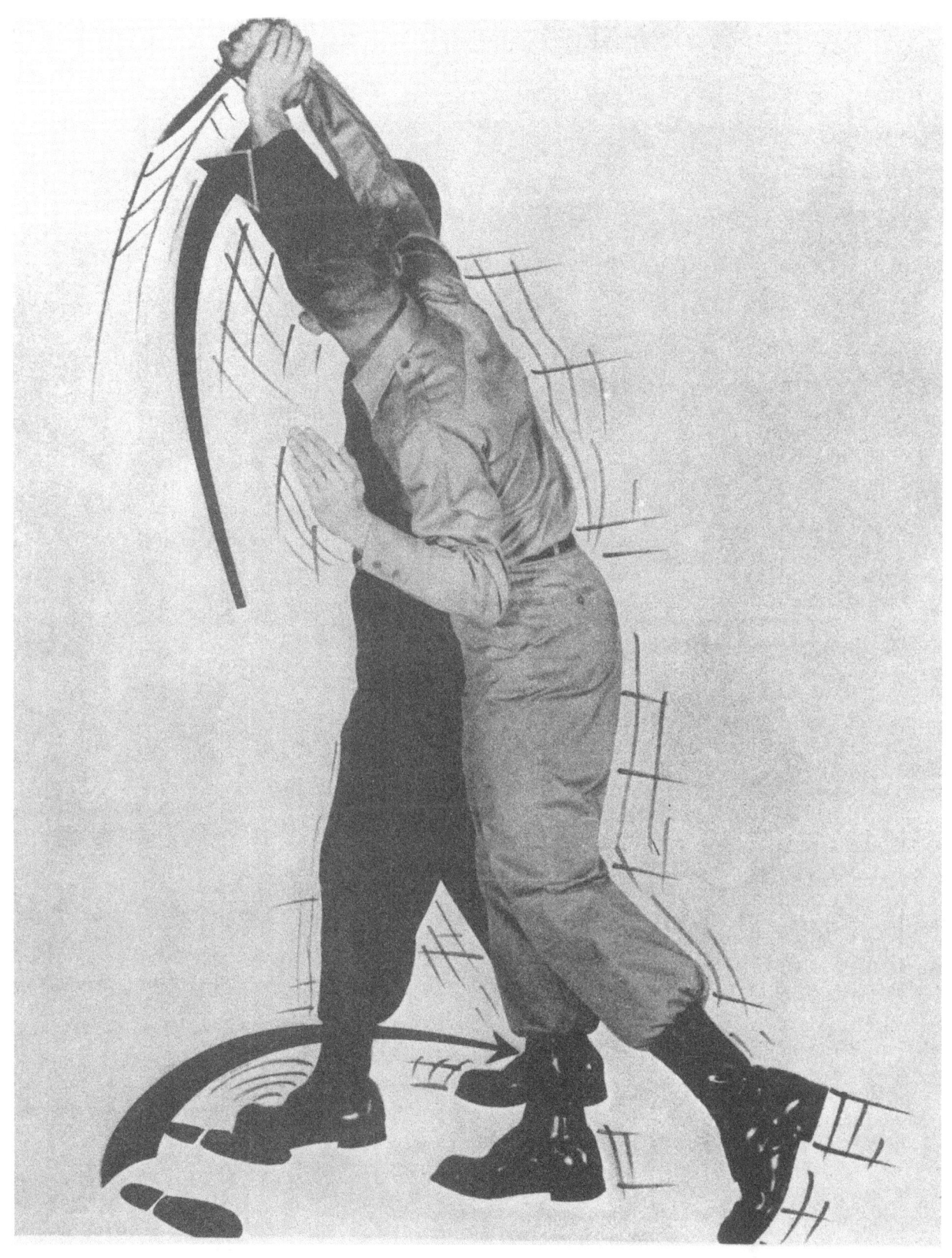

③
Figure 163—Continued.

④
Figure 163—Continued.

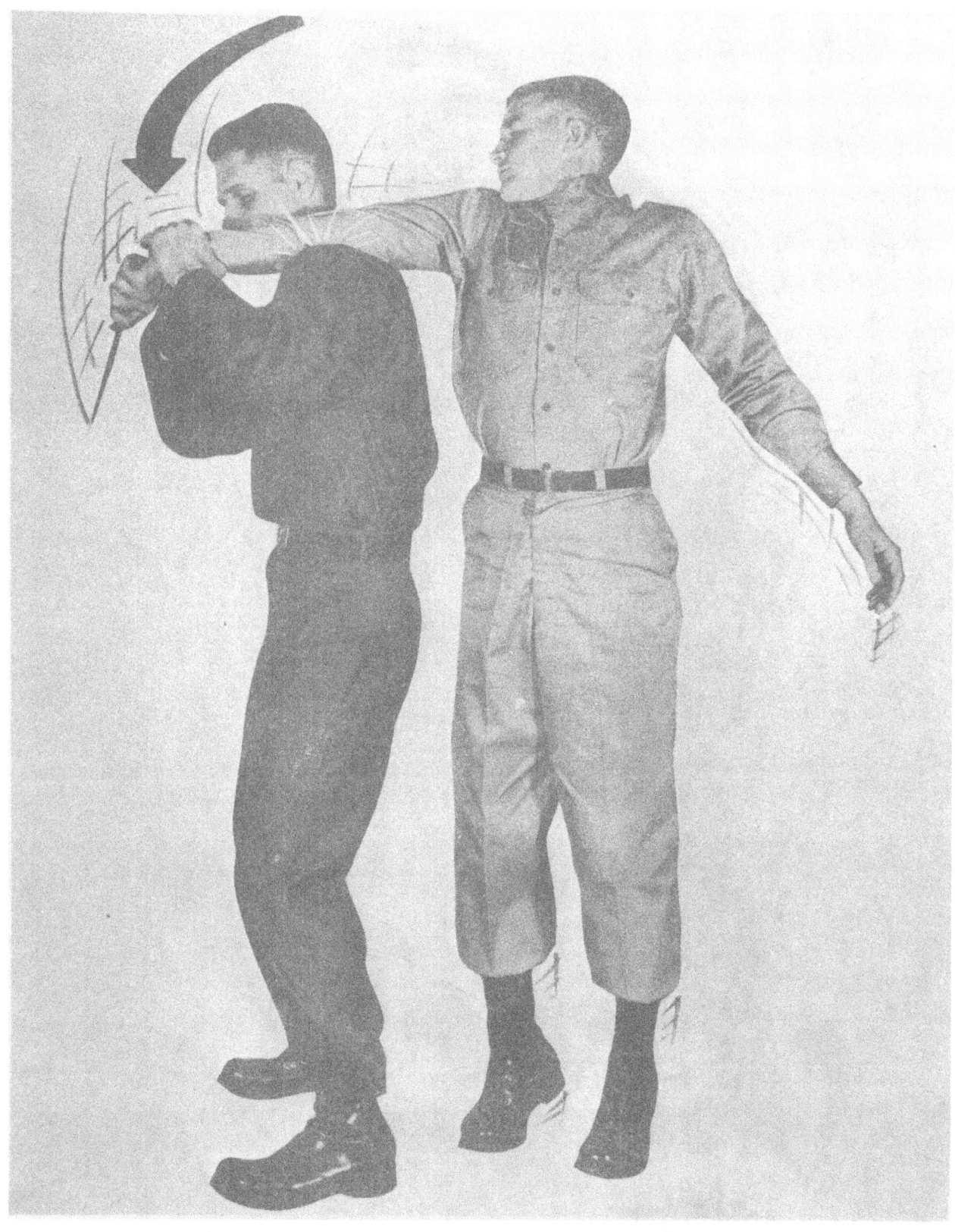

Figure 164. Third counter against upward stroke.

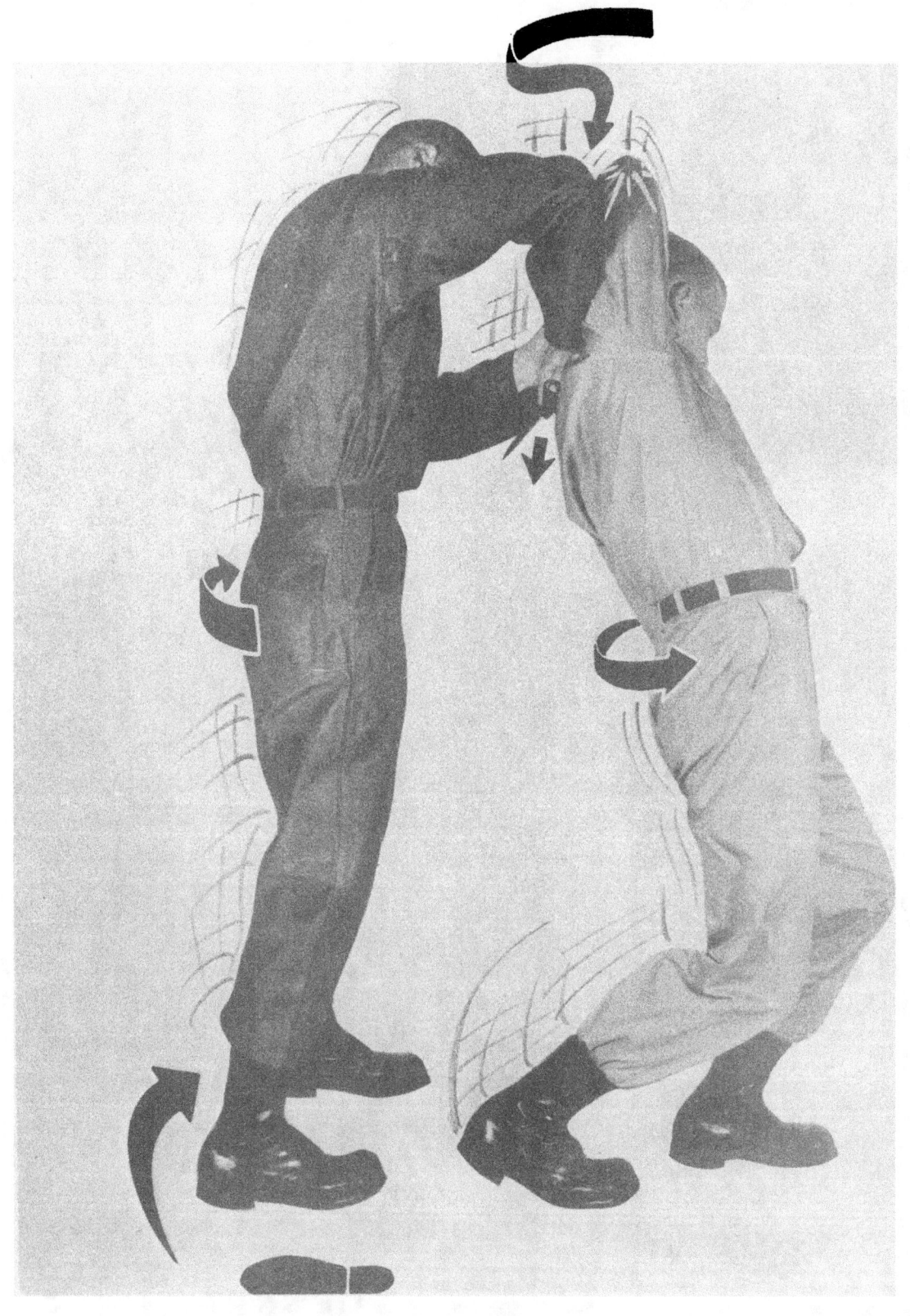

② Figure 164—Continued.

104. Counter Against a Cautious Approach

a. When your opponent attacks as shown in 1, figure 165, his left foot is forward and his left hand is extended to ward off any of your possible blows. He holds his knife hand ready to strike when an opening occurs. This is an extremely dangerous man. He is well prepared and trained and your actions must be perfect.

b. As soon as he comes within reach, spring off the ground throwing your body at him feet first and twisting to your left. Hook your left instep around his forward ankle and kick his knee with your right foot (2, fig. 165).

c. Break the force of your fall with your hand and arm. This maneuver knocks him on his back. When both of you strike the ground, quickly raise your right foot and kick his groin or midsection (3, fig. 165).

①

Figure 165. Counter against a cautious approach.

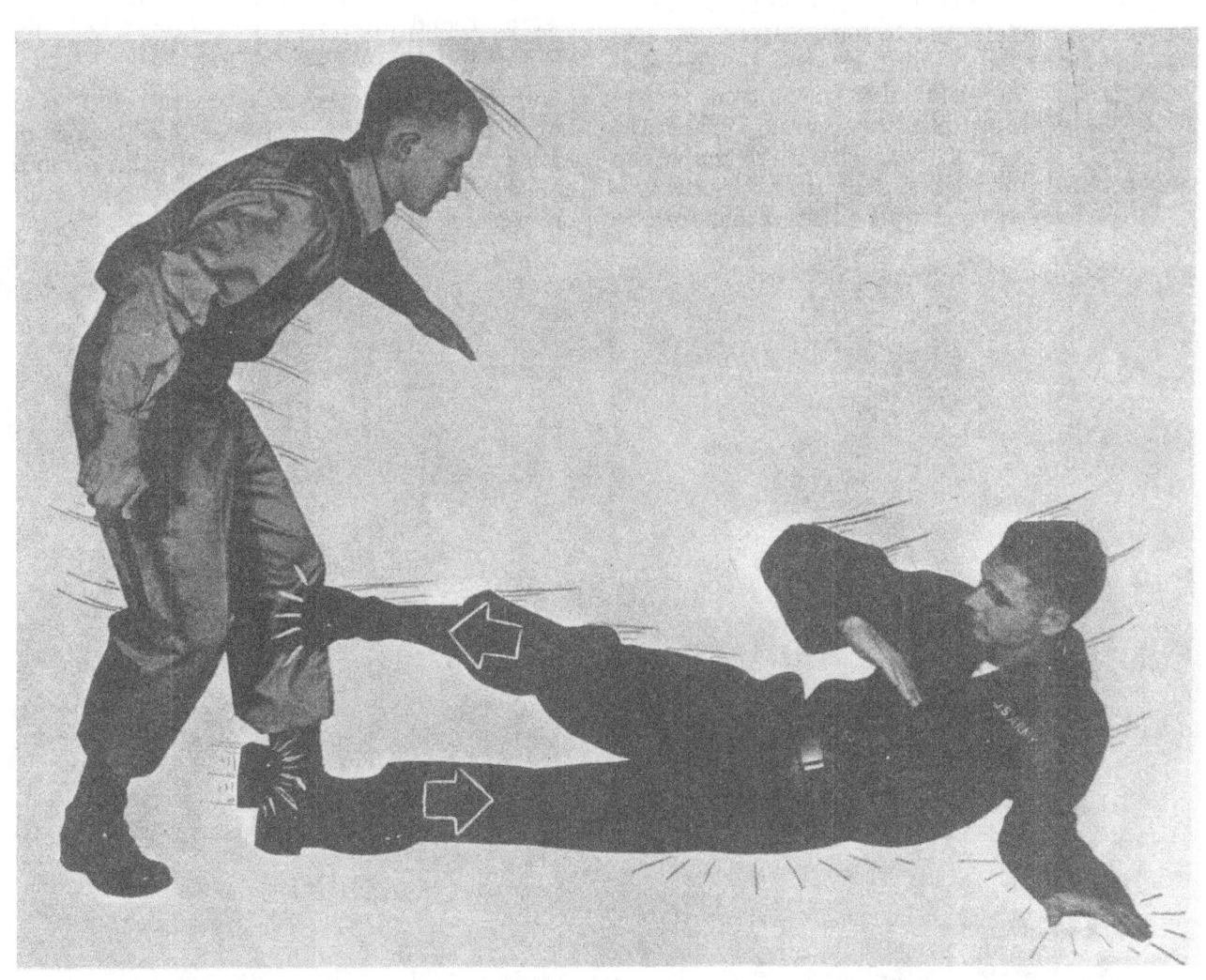

③
Figure 165—Continued.

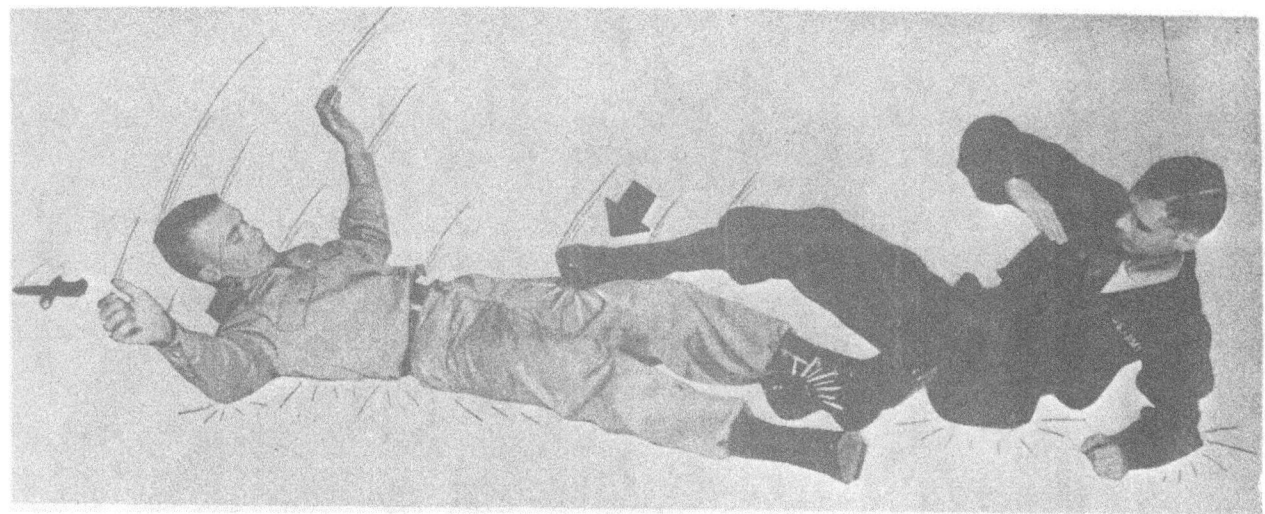

③
Figure 165—Continued.

Section XIII. SILENCING SENTRIES

105. General

Knowing the methods of silencing sentries will enable you to maintain surprise and to kill an unsuspecting opponent quickly and quietly from the rear.

106. Helmet Neck Break

a. Grab the front rim of your opponent's helmet with your right hand. At the same time, place your left forearm against the back of his neck and place your left hand on his right shoulder (1, fig. 166).

b. Holding firmly to the front rim of your opponent's helmet, pull his helmet up, back, and down, and drive your left forearm forward (2, fig. 166). Your left forearm, under the back edge of his helmet, acts as a fulcrum against which his neck is broken. This method is possible only when your opponent's helmet strap is fastened underneath his chin.

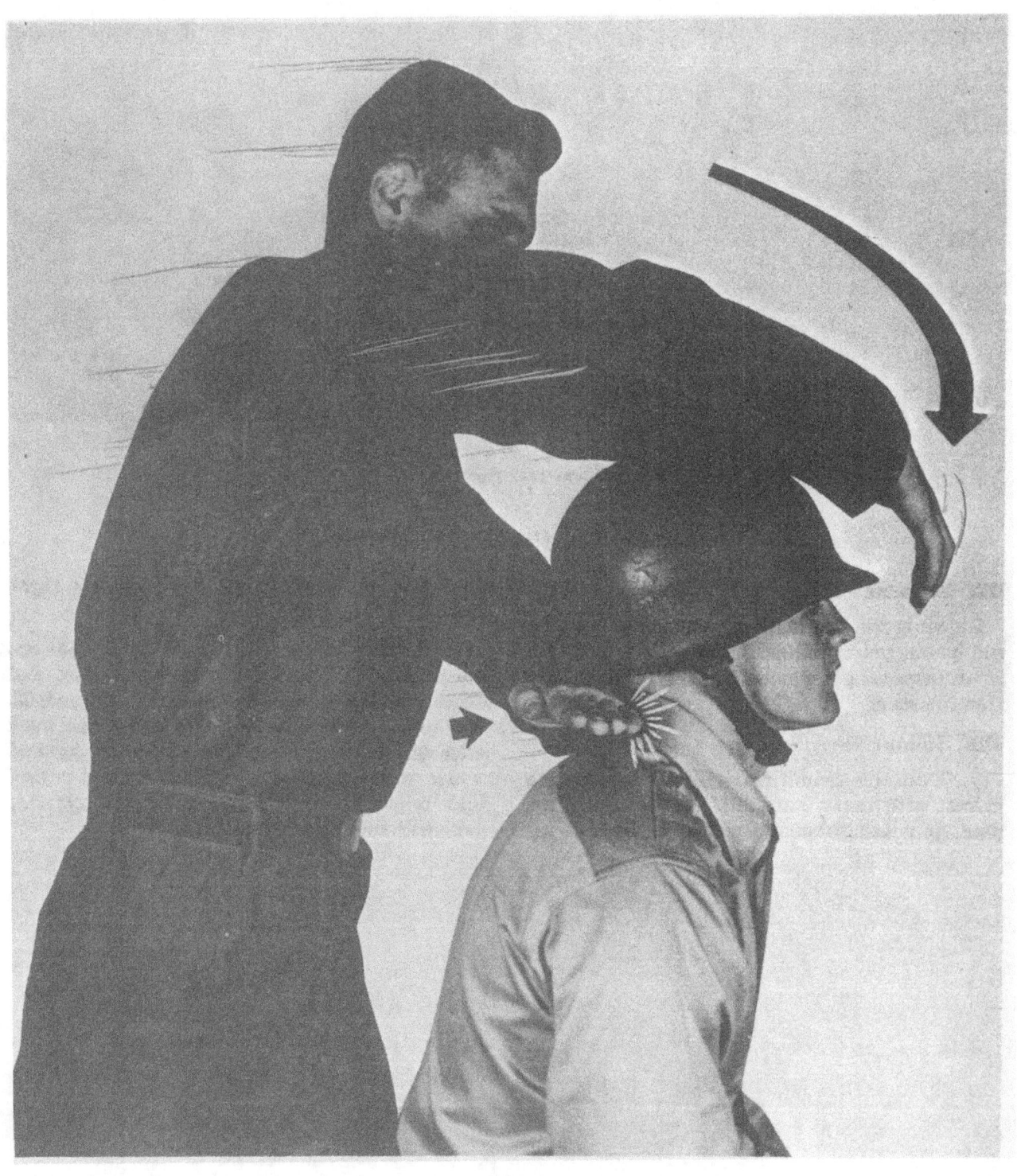

①
Figure 166. The helmet neck break.

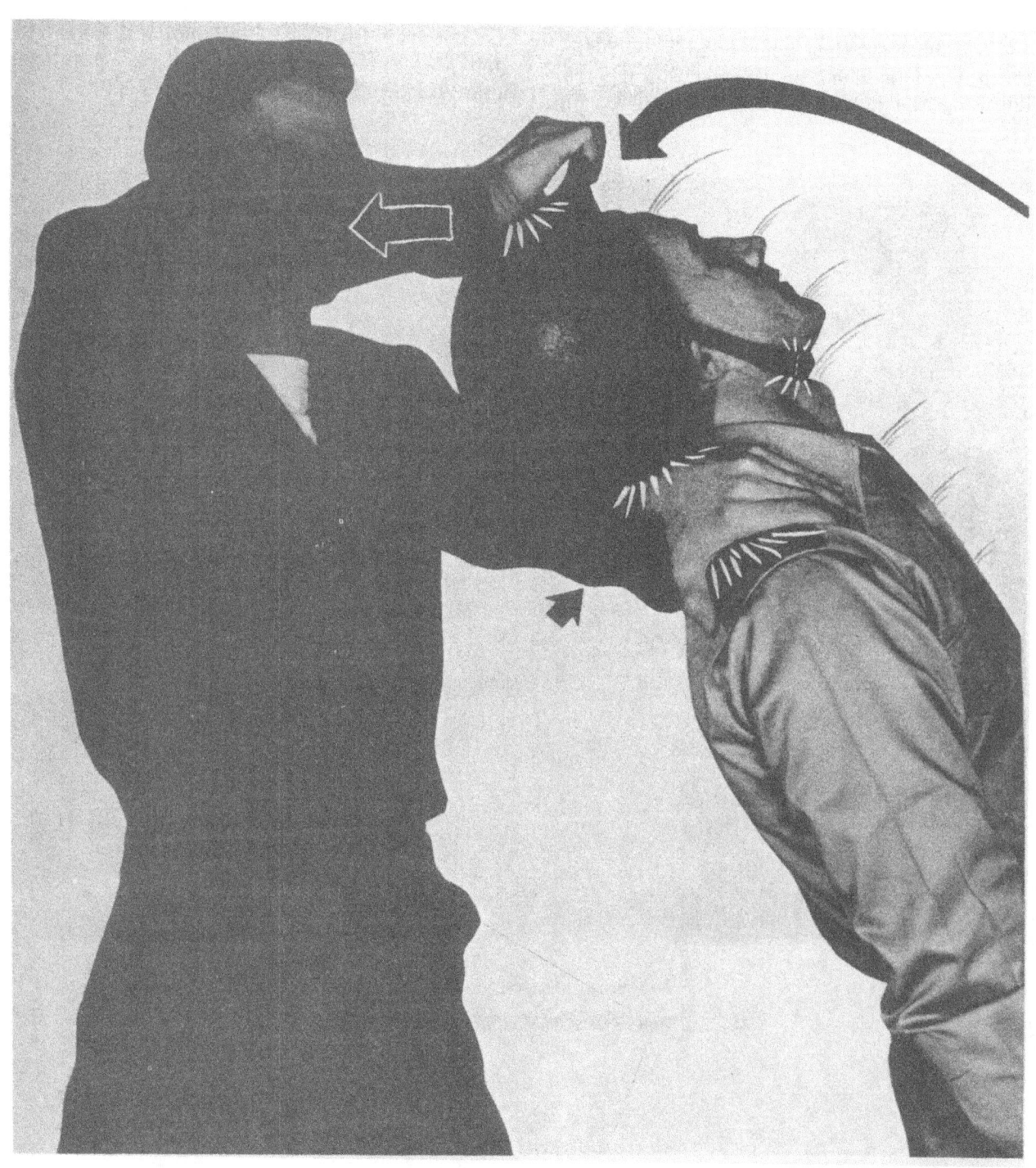

③
Figure 166—Continued.

107. Helmet Smash

a. If you see that your opponent's helmet strap is not fastened, or discover this when attempting the helmet neck break, silence him with a helmet smash. Snatch your opponent's helmet from his head. While doing this grab his collar or shirt with your other hand, jerking him off balance to his rear (1, fig. 167).

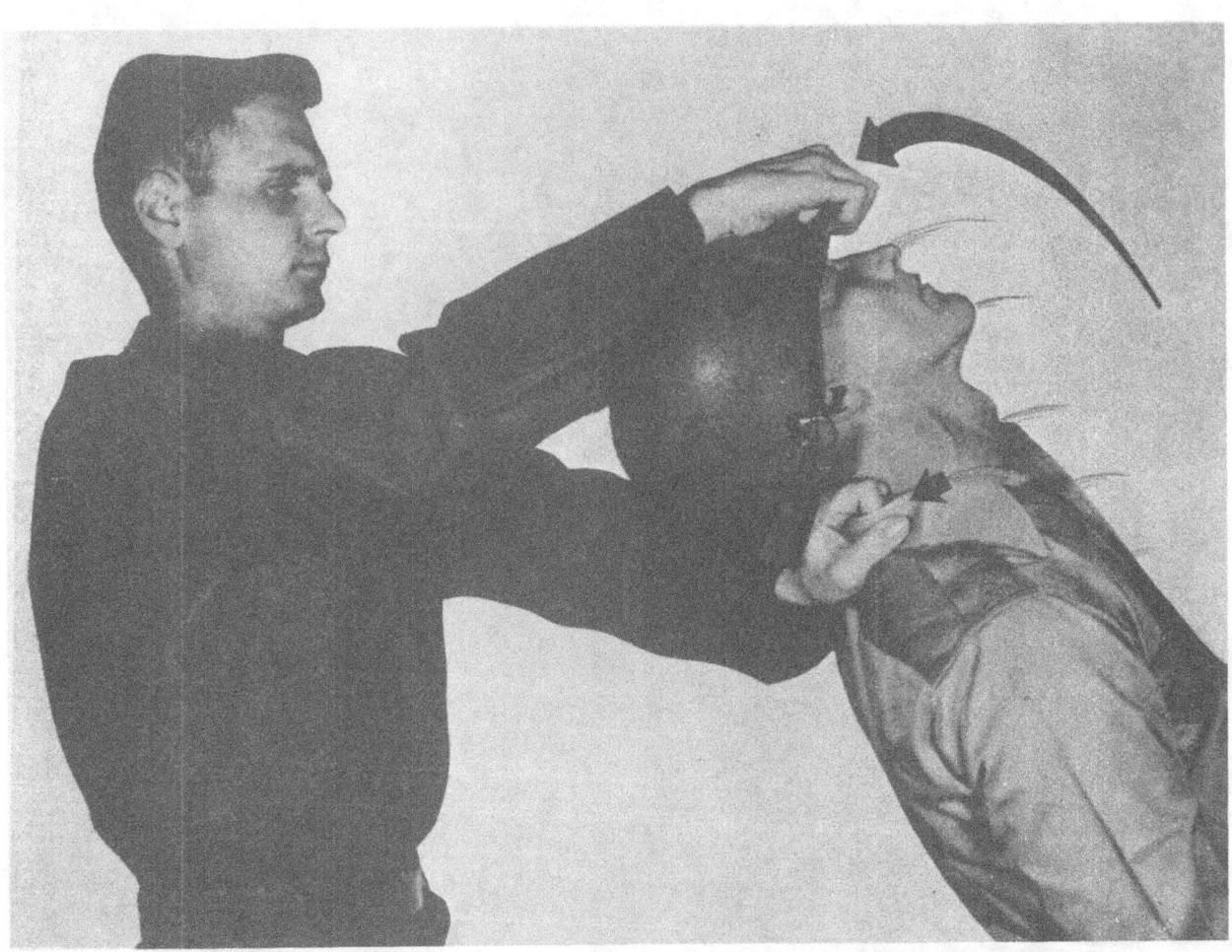

①
Figure 167. The helmet smash.

b. Now smash the helmet on the back of his head or on his temple (2, fig. 167). Your opponent may have a chance to yell when this method is used.

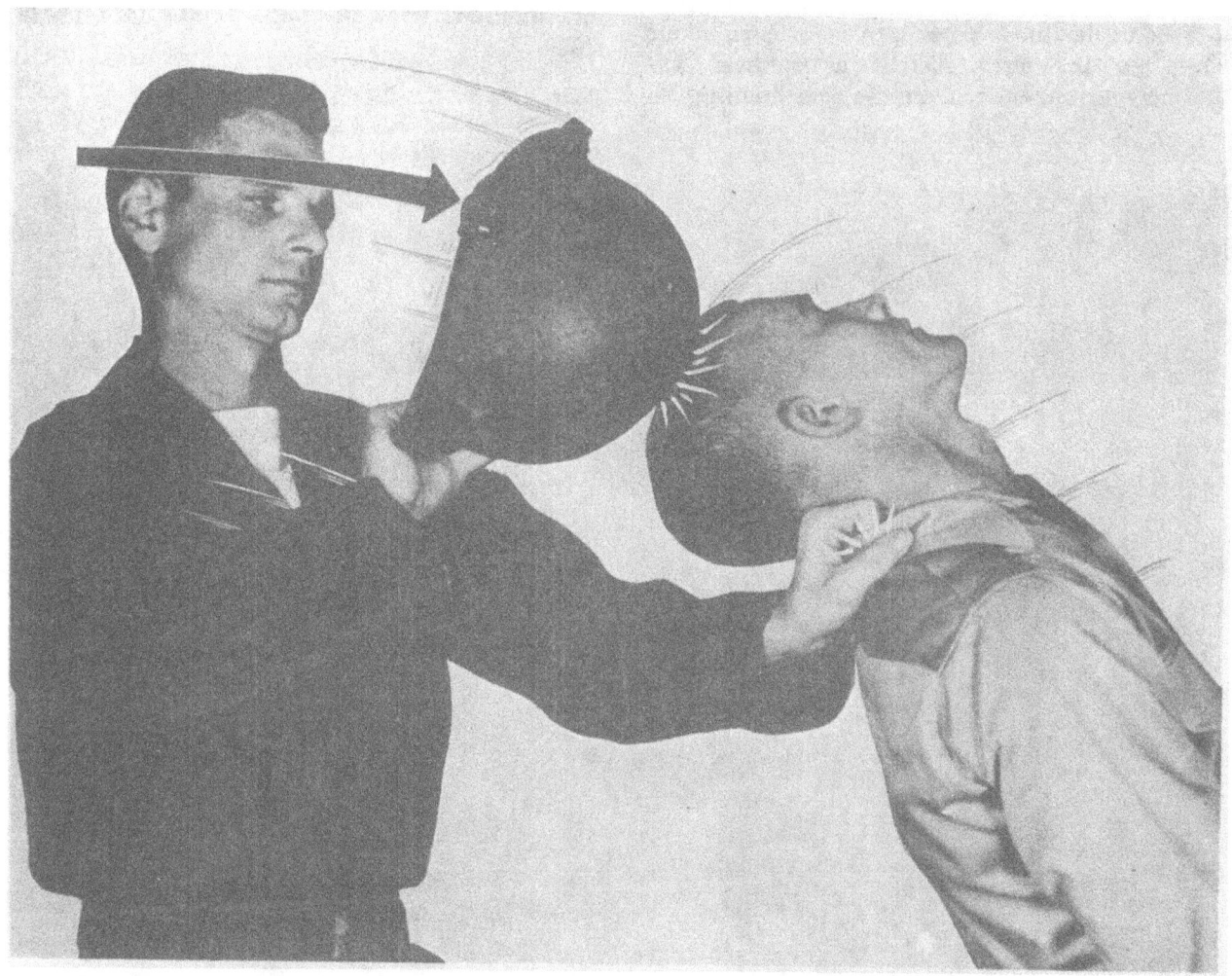

②
Figure 167—Continued.

108. Strangulation with Cord or Wire, One-Hand Loop

a. For this method of strangulation you need a piece of flexible wire or a piece of cord about three feet in length, such as a bootlace. Approach your opponent from the rear holding the wire or cord ends in each hand. Toss it over his head from his left and place the heel of your left hand, still holding the end of the cord, on his shoulder near the nape of his neck (1, fig. 168).

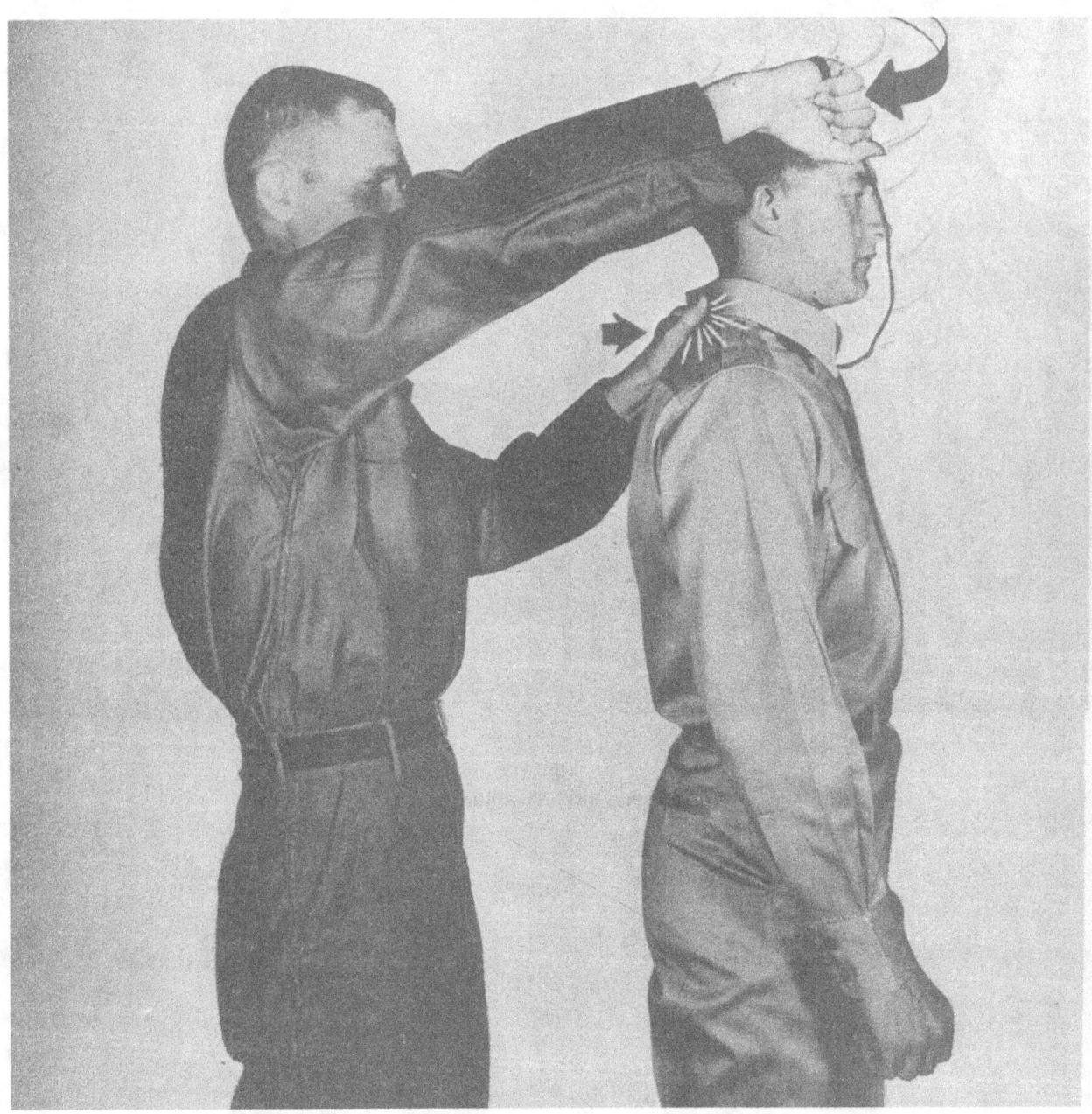

①

Figure 168. Strangulation with a cord or wire, one-hand loop.

b. At the same time, place your knee (either one) in the small of your opponent's back and yank the cord or wire with your right hand while pushing with your left hand (2, fig. 168). If this is done quickly, your opponent cannot cry out. You can tie the ends of the cord or wire around two short sticks for better handholds.

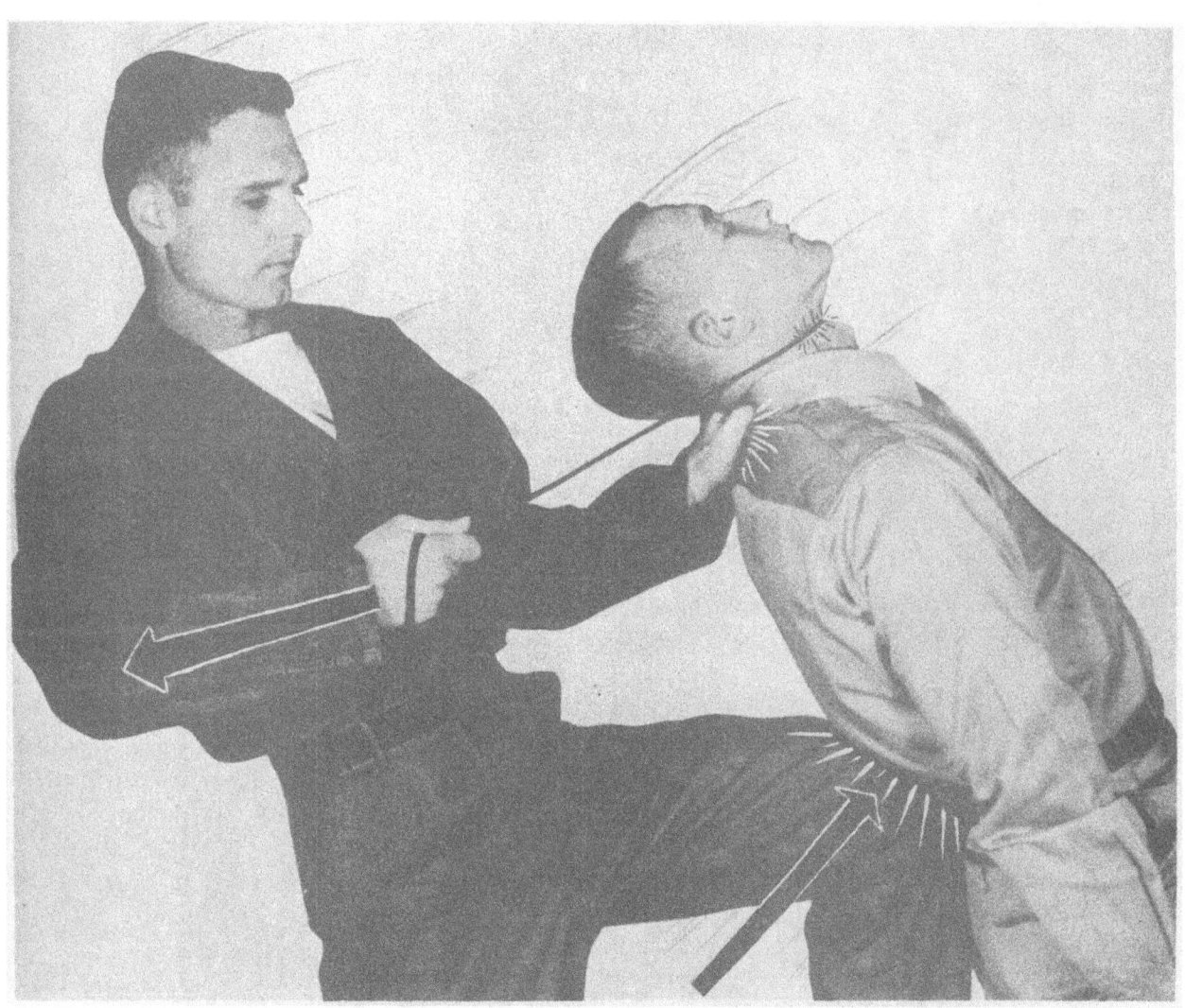

②

Figure 168—Continued.

109. Strangulation with Cord or Wire, Two-Hand Loop

a. Hold the wire or cord ends in each hand. Place your left forearm across the back of your opponent's neck. Swing your right arm over your opponent's head from his right, looping the cord in front of his throat (1, fig. 169).

①
Figure 169. The two-hand loop.

b. Complete the loop and jerk your arms sharply in opposite directions, tightening the loop and strangling your opponent (2, fig. 169). Quick application of this method prevents your opponent from crying out. You can cause unconsciousness or death, depending on the force used and the length of time the hold is applied.

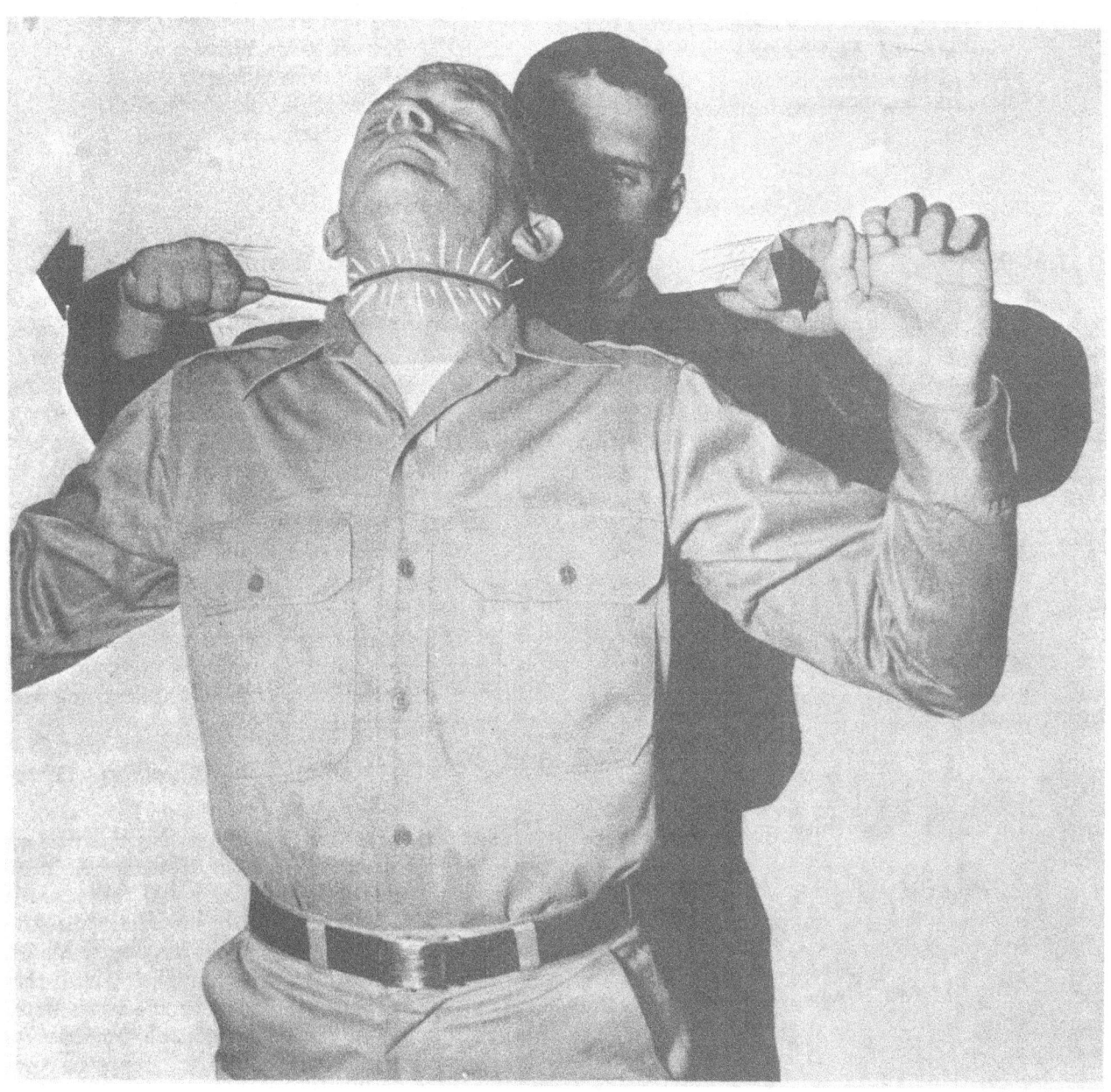

②
Figure 169—Continued.

110. Other Methods

Other methods of silencing sentries are listed below.

a. Available Weapons.
   (1) Striking an opponent on his spine with a blunt object to stun him and striking him with a sharp object to kill him (par. 34c).
   (2) Use of the homemade blackjack (par. 34b).

b. Natural Weapons. Striking an opponent on the base of the skull with the knife edge of your hand or the padded fist (par. 23b).

c. Holds.
   (1) Rear takedown (par. 49).
   (2) Rear strangle hold (par. 60).

d. Knife Attack (par. 79).
   (1) Thrust to the kidney.
   (2) Thrust to the side of the neck.
   (3) Throat slash.

Section XIV. PRISONER SEARCHING

111. General

If you capture a prisoner you should have assistance while searching him. Move him to a rear area where he can be covered by another soldier while you search. In extreme circumstances, however, it may be necessary to make a thorough search unassisted. Methods for an unassisted search are presented in paragraphs 112 through 118.

112. Rules for Searching

The rules you should follow when searching a prisoner are—

a. Indicate by speech and actions that you are confident and will shoot if necessary.

b. Do not let your prisoner talk, look back, move his arms, or otherwise distract you.

c. Never attempt to search a prisoner until you have him in an off-balance position.

d. Do not move within arm reach of your prisoner until you have him in an off-balance position.

e. If armed with a pistol, while searching a prisoner, hold it at your hip in a ready-position and keep it on the side away from him.

f. When you have assistance, keep out of your partner's line of fire. One soldier conducts the search while the other remains far enough away to observe the prisoner at all times.

g. Do not relax your guard after completing your search.

113. Technique of Search

a. The "pat" or "feel" method of searching a prisoner will reveal most weapons and concealed objects. Search the prisoner's entire body, paying particular attention to his armpits, arms, back, groin area, and legs. Thoroughly search the clothing folds around his waist, chest, and the top of his boots. Knives can be concealed on a string around the neck or taped to any area of the body. Be extremely cautious when putting your hand in a prisoner's pocket or in the fold of his clothes or he may grab your arm and throw you.

b. After the initial search, a detailed search of the prisoner is made when he is moved to a rear area. Force him to take off all clothing and thoroughly examine his body.

114. Prone Method of Searching When Armed with a Rifle

Make the prisoner lie down on his stomach so that his arms are extended beyond his head with his hands close together (fig. 170). His legs are also extended with his feet close together. Place the rifle muzzle in the small of his back, and keep the rifle upright. Grasp the rifle tightly around the small of the stock with your index finger on the trigged. After searching from the rear, order him to turn over and search him from the front. Place the rifle muzzle on his stomach. Twist the muzzle into the prisoner's clothing to prevent it from slipping. You can also use the prone search method when armed with a pistol, but keep the pistol at your hip while searching. You will have to use arm-and-hand signals for non-English speaking prisoners.

115. Kneeling Method of Searching When Armed with a Rifle

Force the prisoner to interlock his hands behind his head and kneel (fig. 171). He must bend forward until he is just able to maintain his balance. While searching his left side, hold

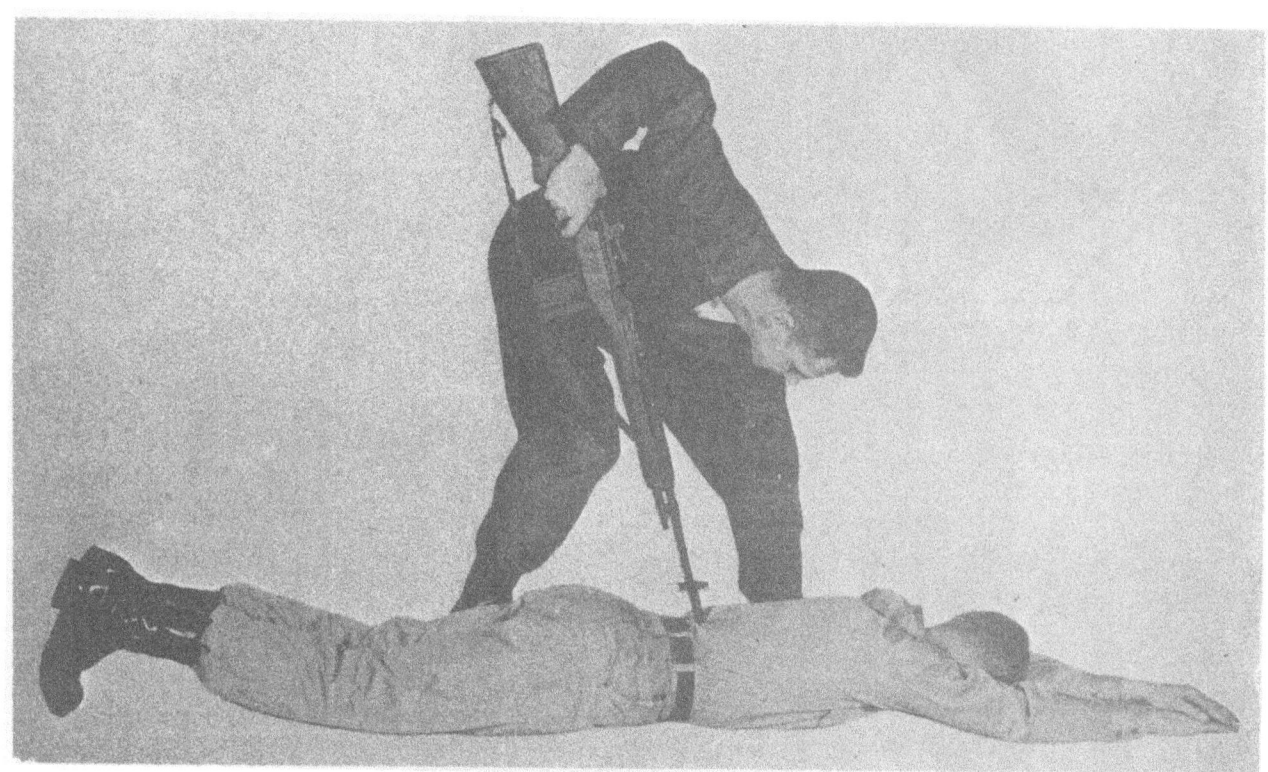

Figure 170. The prone search method.

the rifle in your right hand, muzzle jammed into the small of his back. Put your left leg between his legs and against his buttocks. In this position you can quickly knock him forward by thrusting with your left knee. When searching his right side, hold the rifle in your left hand and put your right leg between his legs with your knee against his buttocks. You can also use this method when armed with a pistol, but keep the pistol at your hip while searching.

Figure 171. The kneeling search method.

116. Lean-To Method of Searching When Armed With a Pistol

Have the prisoner lean against a wall, tree, fence, truck, or other upright object, one hand over the other, with his feet crossed and extended as far as possible to the rear. This puts him off balance. To search his left side, place your left foot in front of his feet and keep the pistol at your right hip (fig. 172). If the prisoner attempts to move, kick his feet out from under him. To search the prisoner's right side, switch the pistol to your left hand and place your right foot in front of his feet. For another lean-to method of searching see FM 19-5.

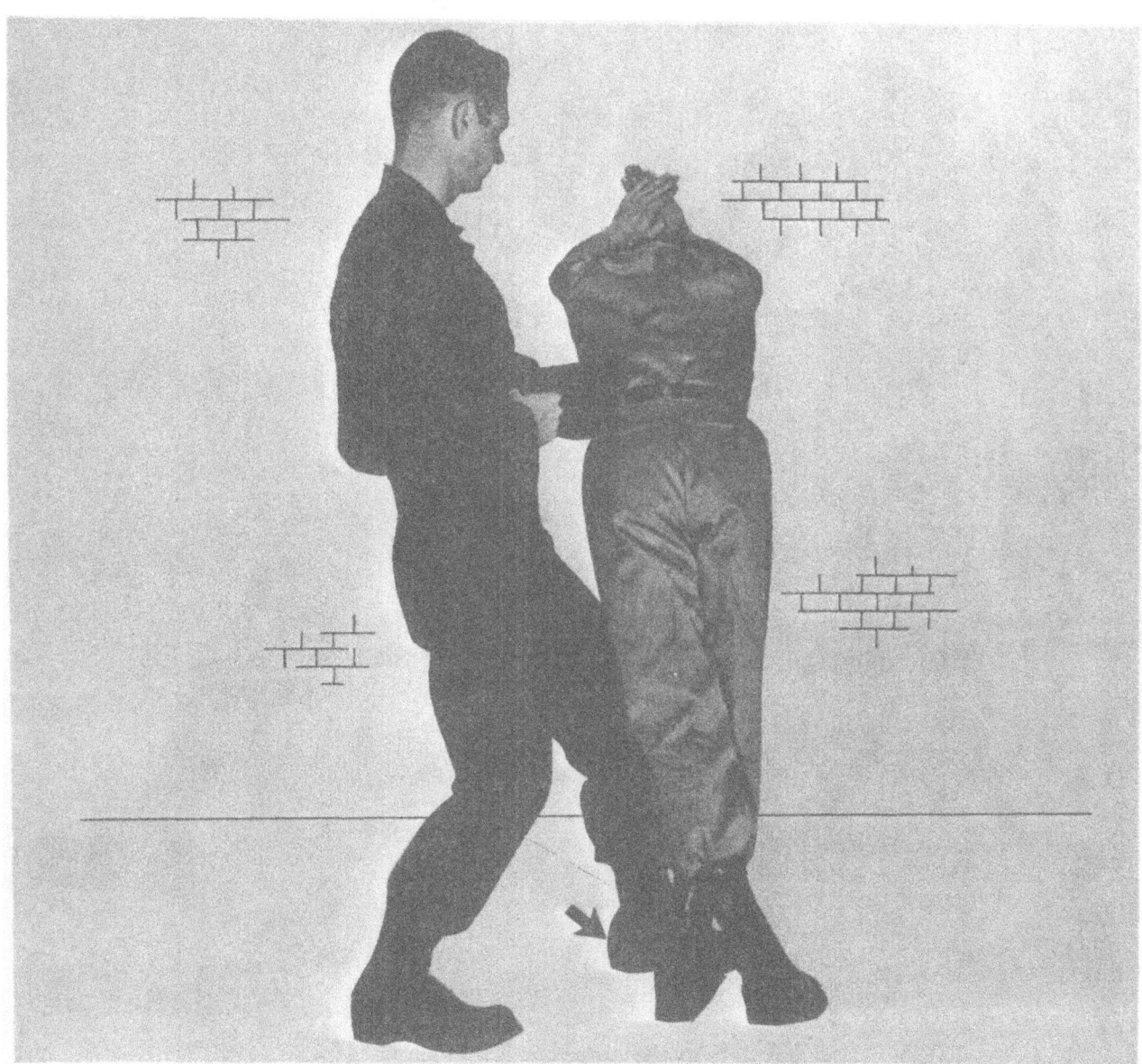

Figure 172. The lean-to search method.

117. Standing Method of Searching When Armed with a Pistol

a. Make the prisoner spread his legs far apart and place his hands on top of his head, fingers interlocked (1, fig. 173).

①
Figure 173. The standup search method.

b. When you move close to search his front, place your foot against his heel and turn your body to the side to protect your groin (2, fig. 173). Search thoroughly and be alert.

②

Figure 173—Continued.

118. Searching More Than One Prisoner

When armed with a pistol you can search more than one prisoner at a time by using any of the methods presented in this section. Remember, however, to watch all of them and do not look away as you search for hidden weapons.

a. The Lean-To Method.
  (1) When using this method keep the pistol in your right hand and search the left side of the first prisoner (1, fig. 174).

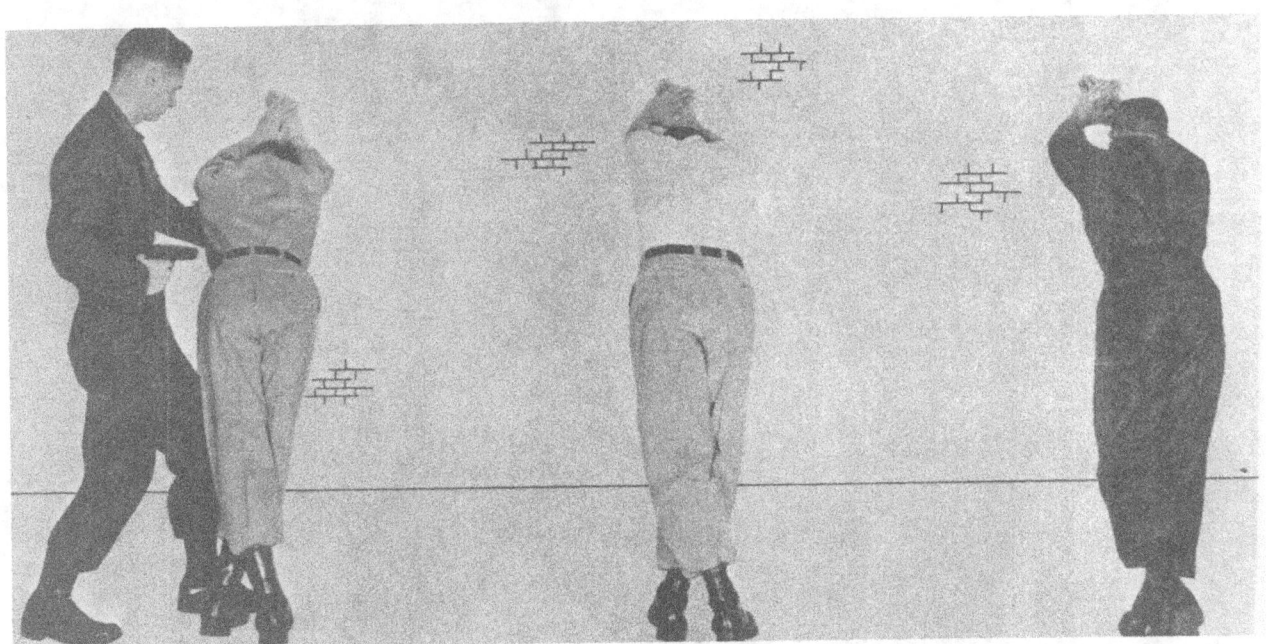

Figure 174. The lean-to search method for several prisoners.

(2) Step back and have the first prisoner move to the far end of the line and have him resume the lean-to position. Search the left side of the remaining prisoners in the same manner (2, fig. 174).

(3) After all prisoners have been searched on the left side you move to the right side of the line. Hold the pistol in your left hand and search the right side of each prisoner. As you finish searching each prisoner have him move to the far end of the line and resume the lean-to position.

b. *The Kneeling Method.*
(1) To search more than one prisoner using the kneeling method you make them all assume the same position in column about four or five feet apart (1, fig. 175).

(2) First you search the prisoner at the rear of the column and have him move to the front where he resumes the kneeling position (2, fig. 175). Search the remaining prisoners from the rear and move each over to the front as you finish with him. When you are alone and armed with a rifle, the kneeling search is the best method to use.

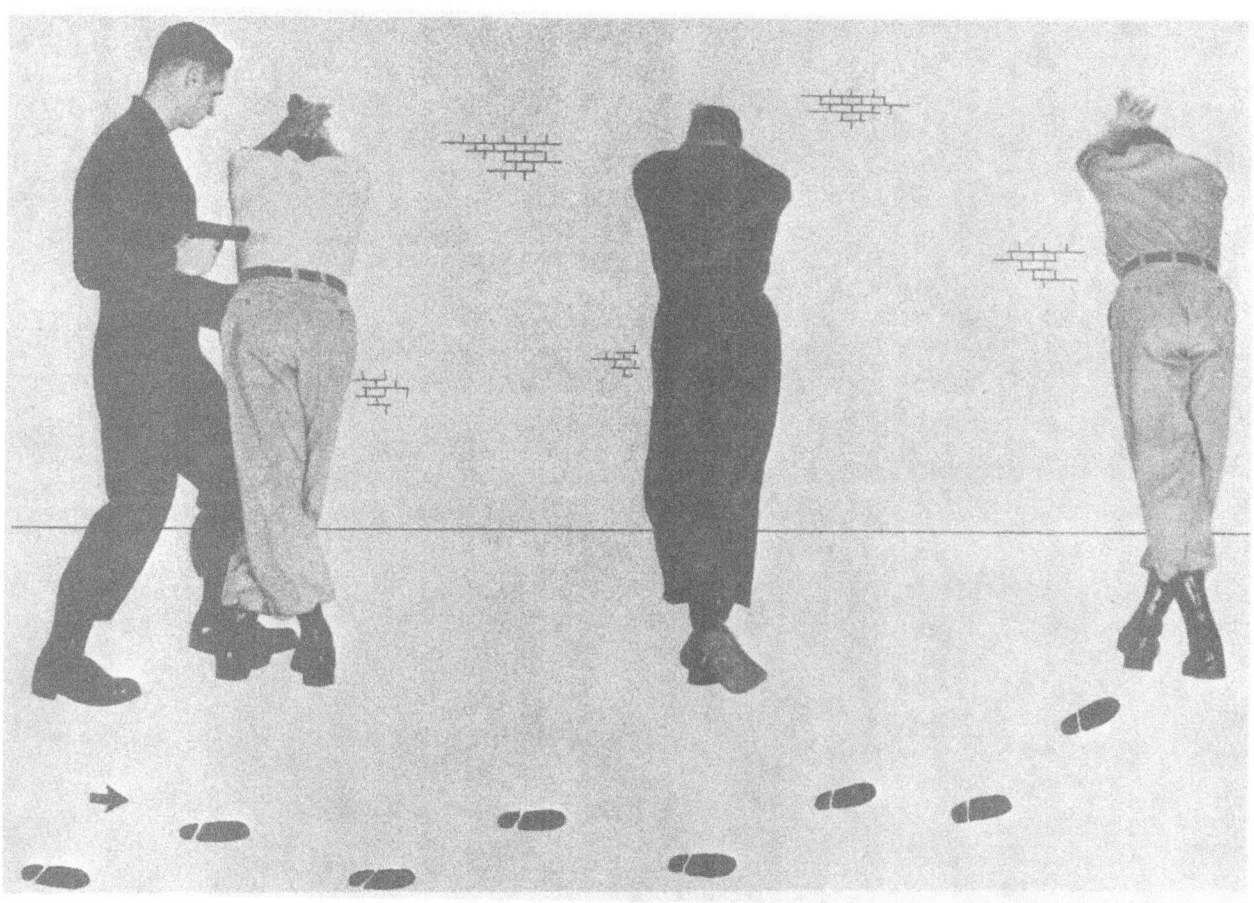

③

Figure 174—Continued.

Figure 175. The kneeling search method for several prisoners.

292

Figure 175—Continued.

Section XV. SECURING AND GAGGING PRISONERS

119. General

The most effective way to control a prisoner is to tie him. You can securely tie a prisoner with pieces of clothing or equipment such as shoelaces, leather or web belts, neckties, handkerchiefs, or twisted strips of cloth. If a patrol has the mission of capturing prisoners, it should always carry pieces of rope or flexible wire.

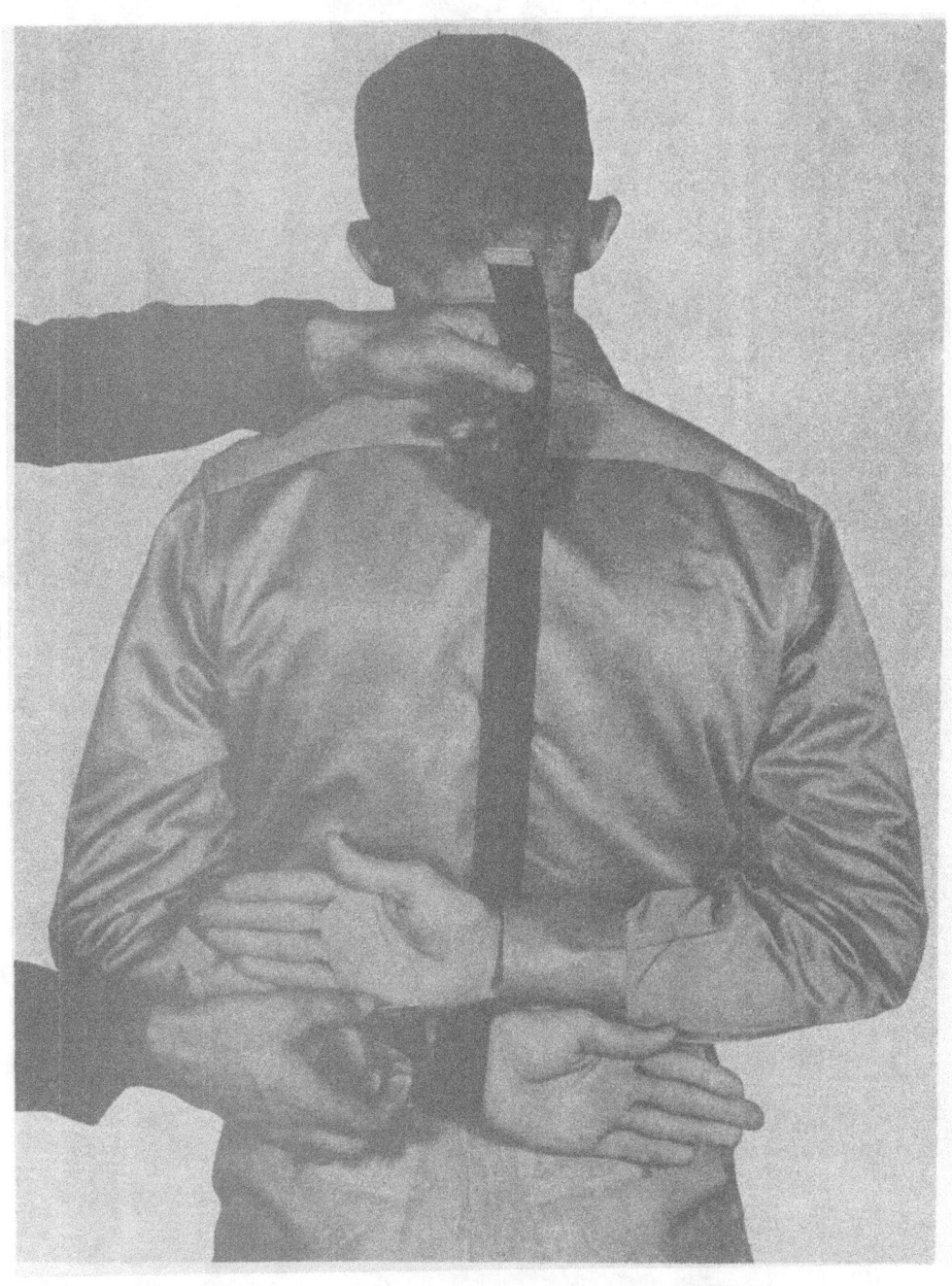

①
Figure 176. The belt tie.

120. Belt Tie

a. Take the prisoner's belt and order him to lie on his stomach. Cross his arms behind his back and place the running end of the belt toward his back and the buckle toward his feet. Hold the buckle on the wrist of his bottom arm and tightly wrap the running end of the belt around his wrist several times. Place the running end parallel with his spine and inside the wrist of his upper arm (1, fig. 176).

b. Now wrap the running end around the wrist of his upper arm several times. Be sure to keep the prisoner's arms as close together as possible and to wrap the belt as tight as possible (2, fig. 176).

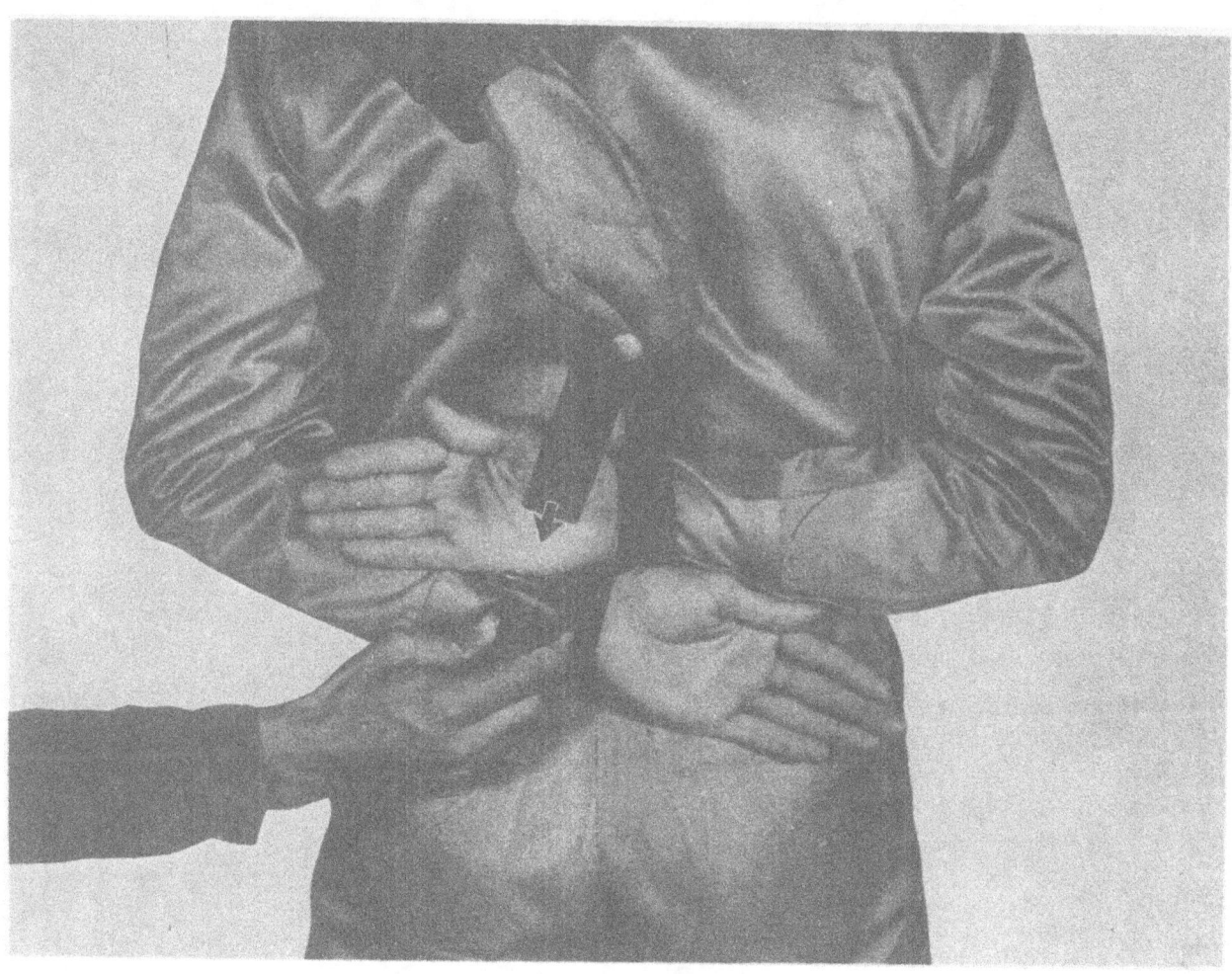

③
Figure 176—Continued.

c. Fasten the belt end in the buckle (3, fig. 176). Although this is an effective means of tying, you should use it only when the prisoner is under close surveillance.

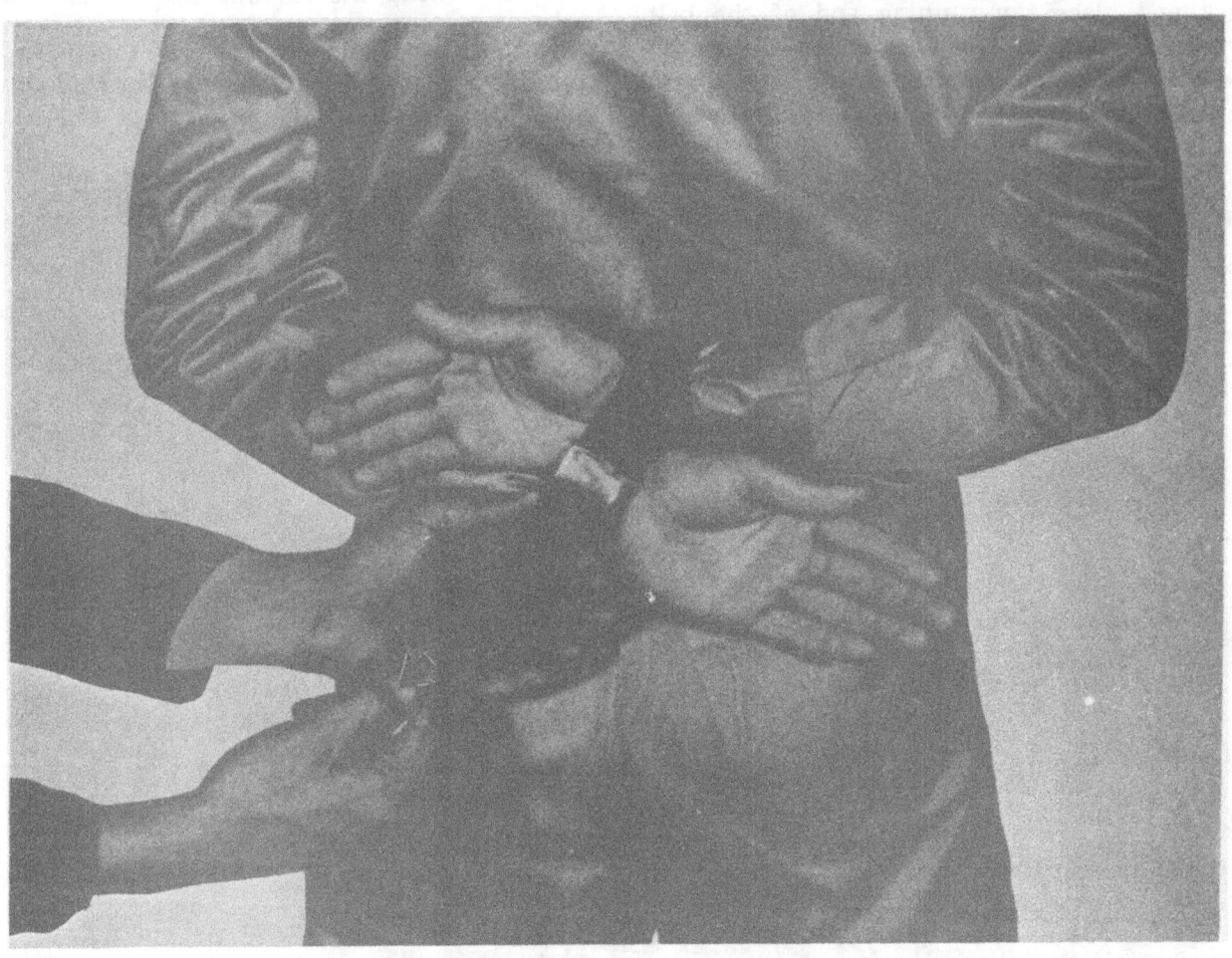

③
Figure 176—Continued.

121. Shoelace Tie

a. Two 27-inch shoelaces or one 72-inch bootlace is needed for this tie. Have the prisoner remove his shoelaces or bootlaces. You can make this tie with the prisoner's hands either in front of his body or behind his back, the latter being more effective. Place his hands back to back, wrists touching each other. Take one lace and tightly wrap it several times around both his wrists. Now, wrap the lace end around the lace between the insides of his wrists. This will further tighten the outside loops. Tie the ends of the lace together with any conventional knot (1, fig. 177).

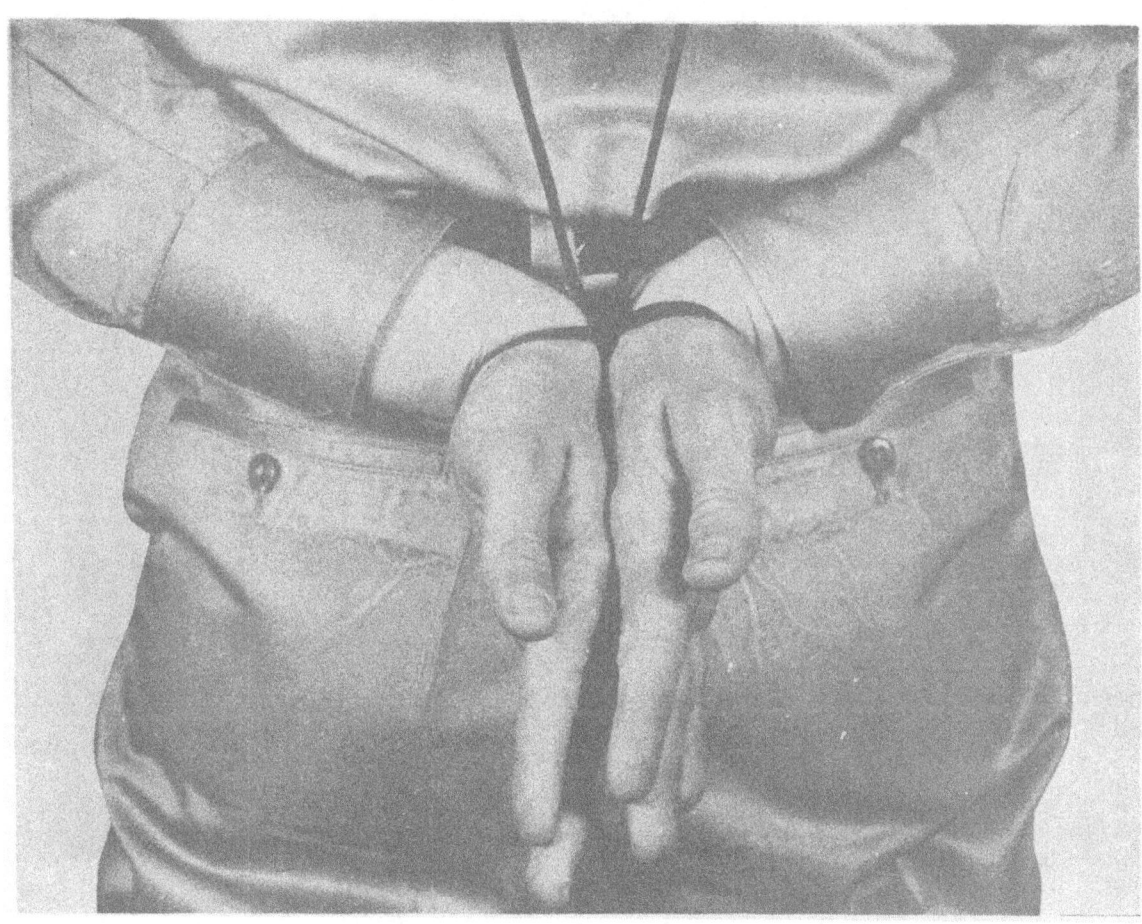

①
Figure 177. The shoelace tie.

b. Next, tie his two little fingers together using one end of the second lace. Pass the remainder of the lace over the loop around the wrists and tie his thumbs together. When you pass the second lace around his wrists be sure to pull it tight and keep it tight when tying his thumbs (2 and 3, fig. 177).

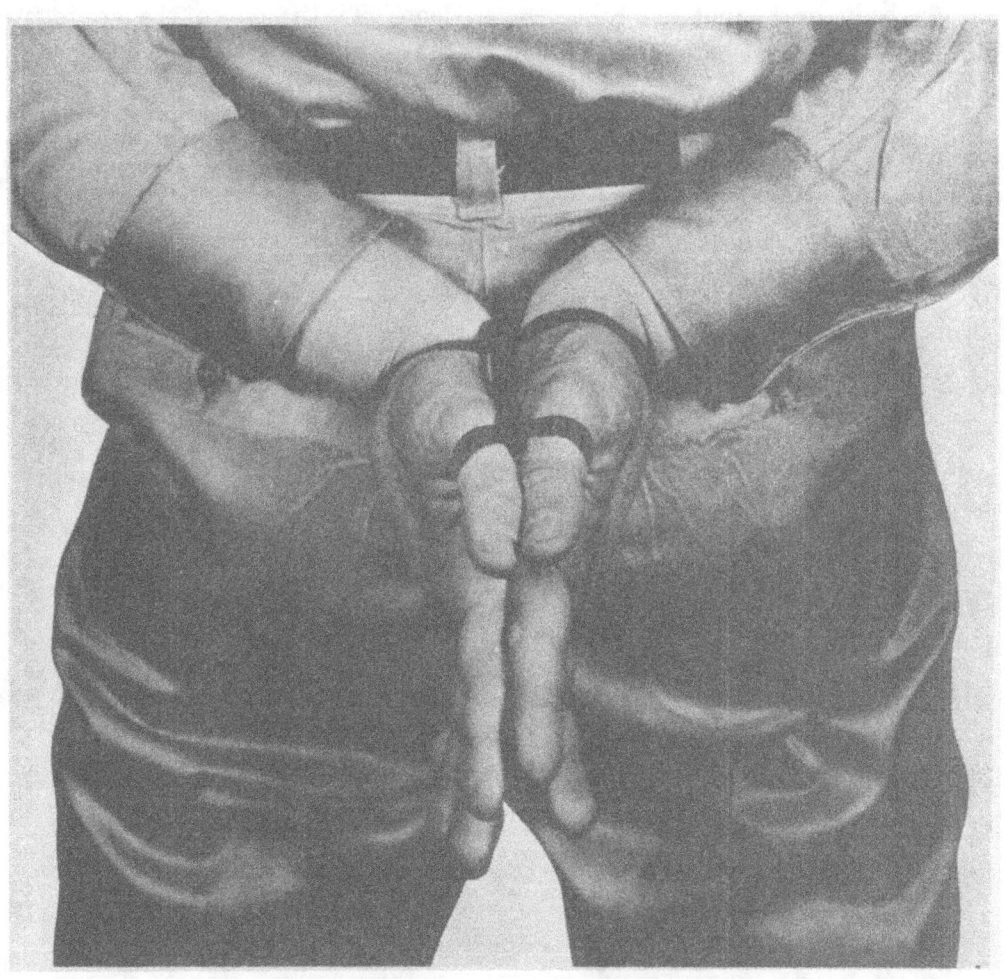

③
Figure 177—Continued.

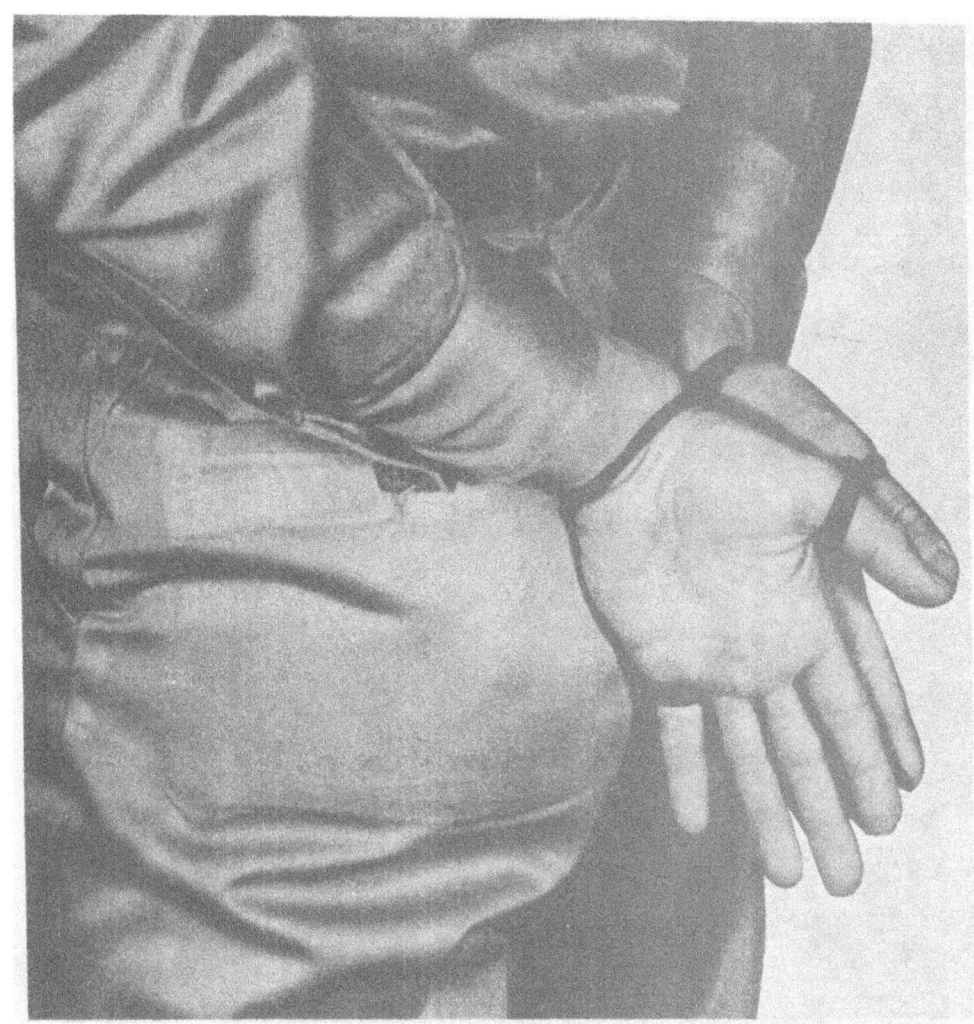

③
Figure 177—Continued.

122. The Lead Tie

A piece of rope or two long bootlaces are needed for this tie. Make the prisoner lie face down. Tie his hands behind his back using any conventional knot. Force his arms behind his back in a strained, up position. Pass the rope or lace around his neck and tie it around his wrists. The length of the loop around his neck should be short enough to force him to keep his arms in a strained position to relieve pressure on his throat (fig. 178). The prisoner can be subdued easily by jerking on the rope as you walk behind him.

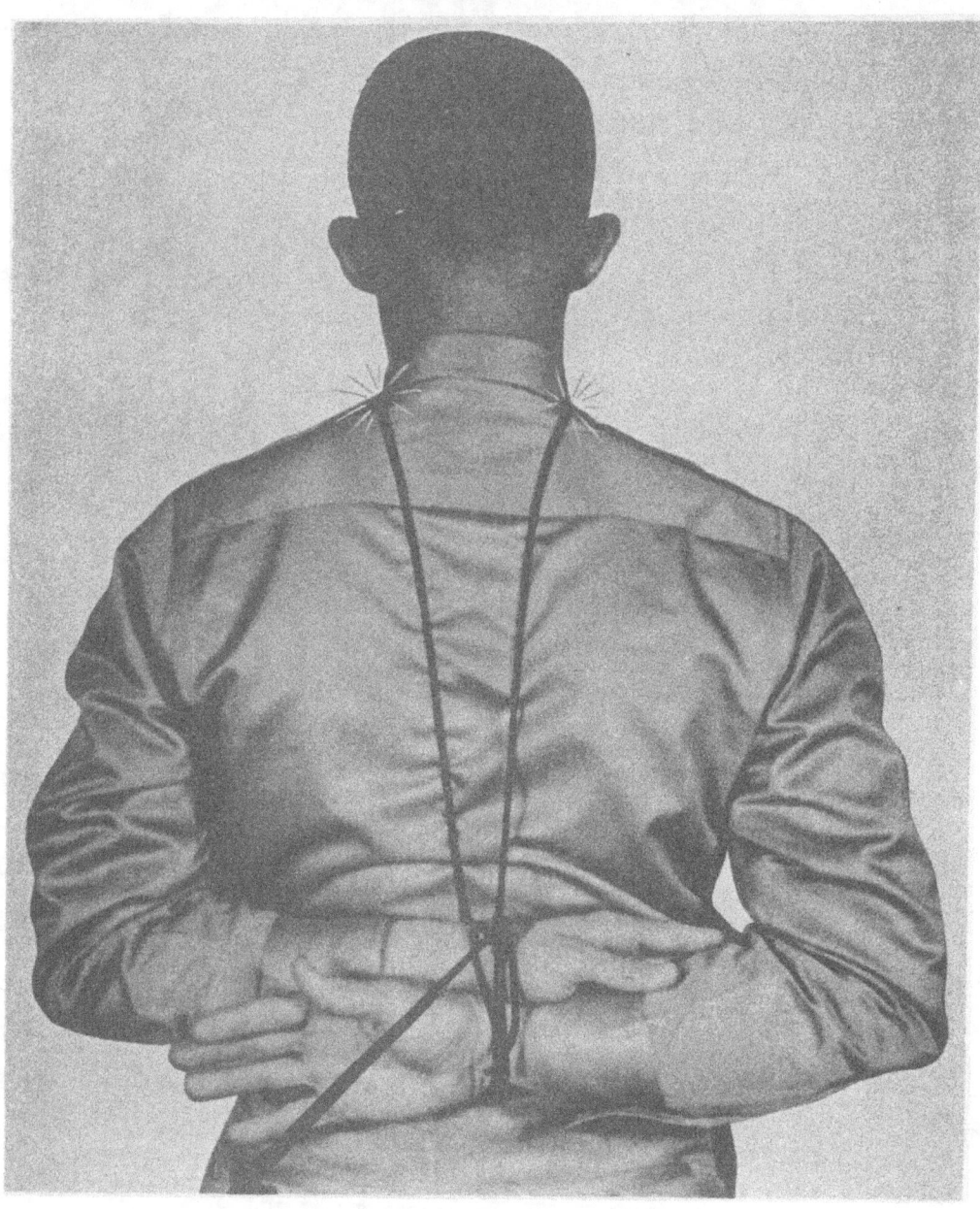

Figure 173. The lead tie.

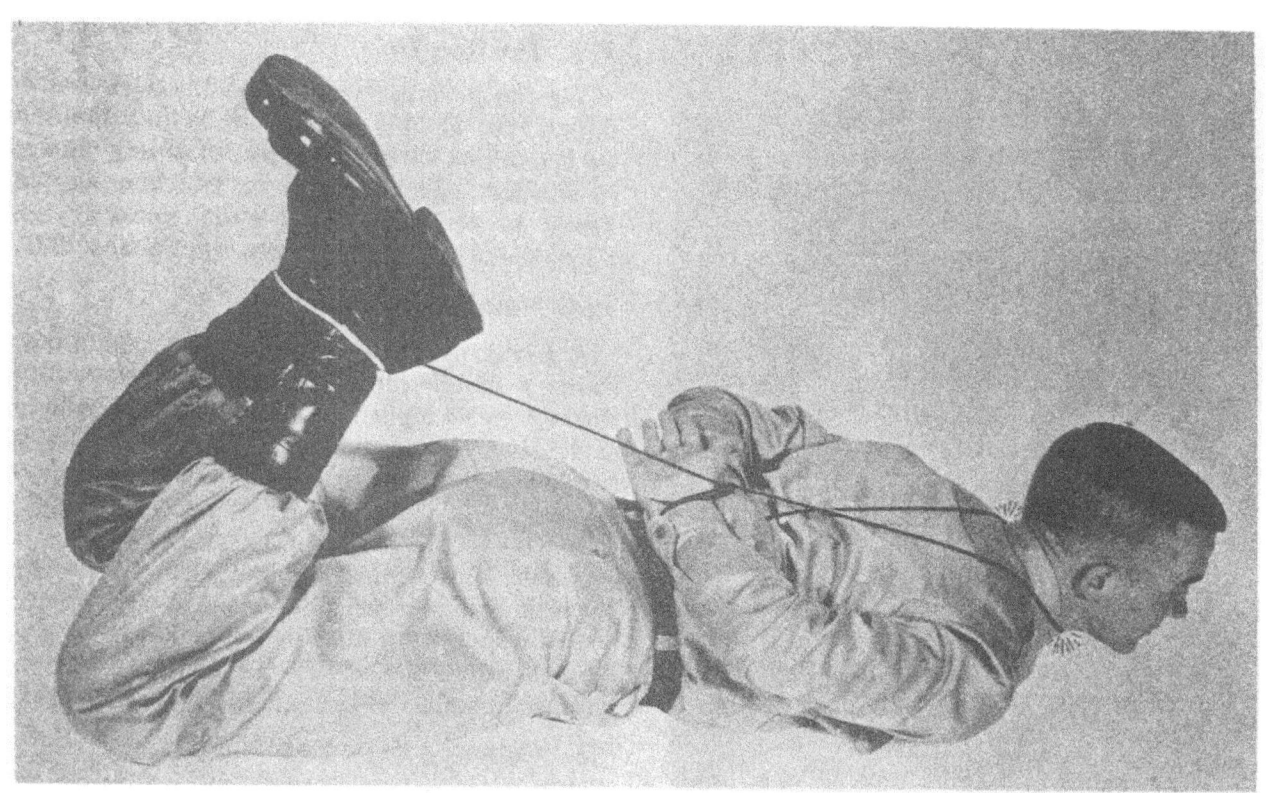

Figure 179. The hog tie.

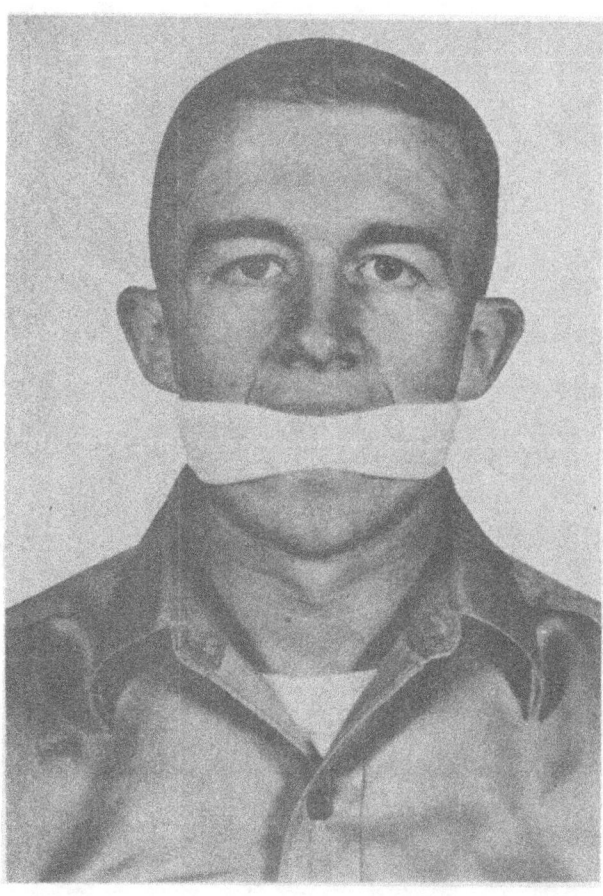

Figure 180. Handkerchief gag.

123. The Hog Tie

Tie the prisoner in the lead tie as shown in figure 178. Double his legs up behind him and tie his ankles with the rope so that they remain in position. Any struggle to free himself will result in strangulation. When correctly applied, there is no escape from this tie (fig. 179).

124. Handkerchief Gag

A gag prevents a prisoner from crying out. Force a handkerchief or a strip of cloth into the prisoner's mouth. A handful of turf will do if nothing else is available. Then tie a handkerchief around the prisoner's mouth (fig. 180).

125. Stick Gag

If a strip of cloth is not available, a stick can be used. Stuff the prisoner's mouth with a piece of turf. Force the stick between his teeth like a bit in a horse's mouth. Tie the stick with a shoelace around the back of his neck (fig. 181).

126. Adhesive Tape Gag

Place several strips of tape across the prisoner's mouth (fig. 182). The tape should be at least one inch wide and five inches long. Stuffing a handkerchief, a piece of turf, or a strip of cloth into his mouth first will make the gag more effective.

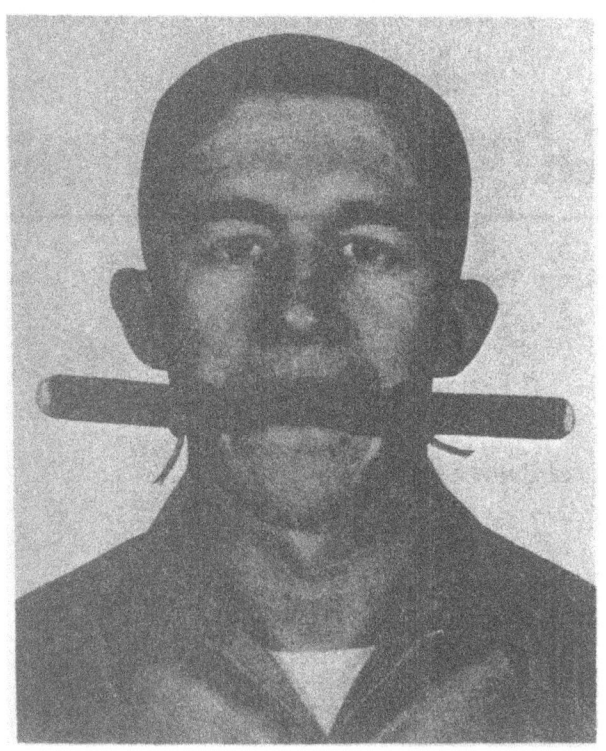

Figure 181. Stick gag.

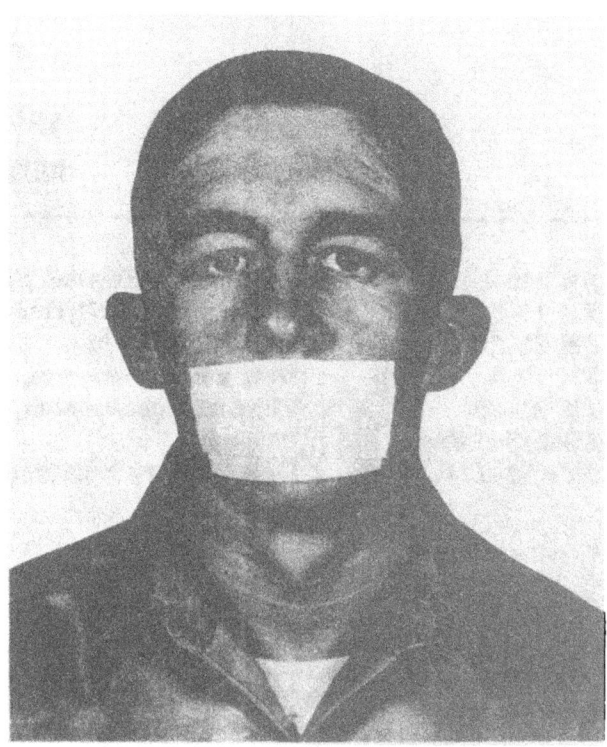

Figure 182. Adhesive tape gag.

APPENDIX I
REFERENCES

AR 320-5	Dictionary of United States Army Terms.
FM 19-5	The Military Policeman.
FM 21-20	Physical Training.
FM 22-5	Drill and Ceremonies.
TM 21-200	Physical Conditioning.
ASubjScd 23-28	Bayonet.
ATP 21-114	Male Military Personnel Without Prior Service.

APPENDIX II
BAYONET ASSAULT COURSE TARGETS, OBSTACLES, AND SCORESHEETS

1. General

For uniformity in training and consistency in scoring, all Bayonet Assault Courses should contain basic targets and obstacles. As an aid to construction, the dimensions and types of targets and obstacles are presented in this appendix.

2. Types of Wood

a. Pine wood, treated against rot, is used to construct the targets, and the front side of the thrusting target should be covered with sections of salvaged truck tires.

b. The parry stick should be made of knot-free hardwood, preferably hickory, ash, or oak.

c. The use of woods specified in *a* and *b* above will reduce maintenance of the targets and parry sticks.

3. Basic Targets

The four basic targets are—

a. The thrust target.

b. The parry thrust target.

c. The parry vertical butt stroke target.

d. The parry horizontal butt stroke target.

e. Photographs of each of the above targets are shown in figures 183 through 190 with diagrams listing target dimensions.

Figure 183. Thrust target.

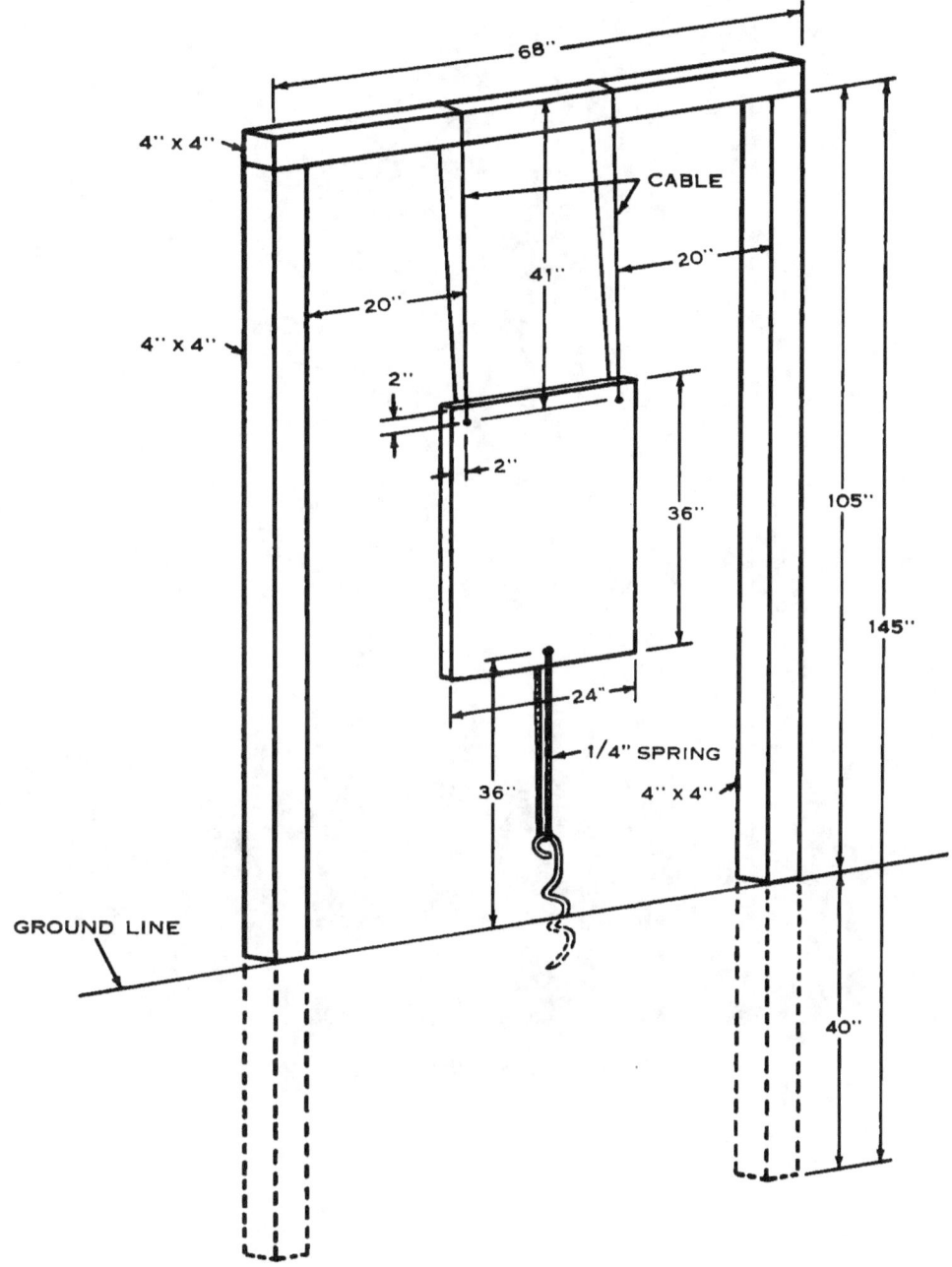

Figure 184. Construction details for thrust target.

Figure 185. Parry thrust target.

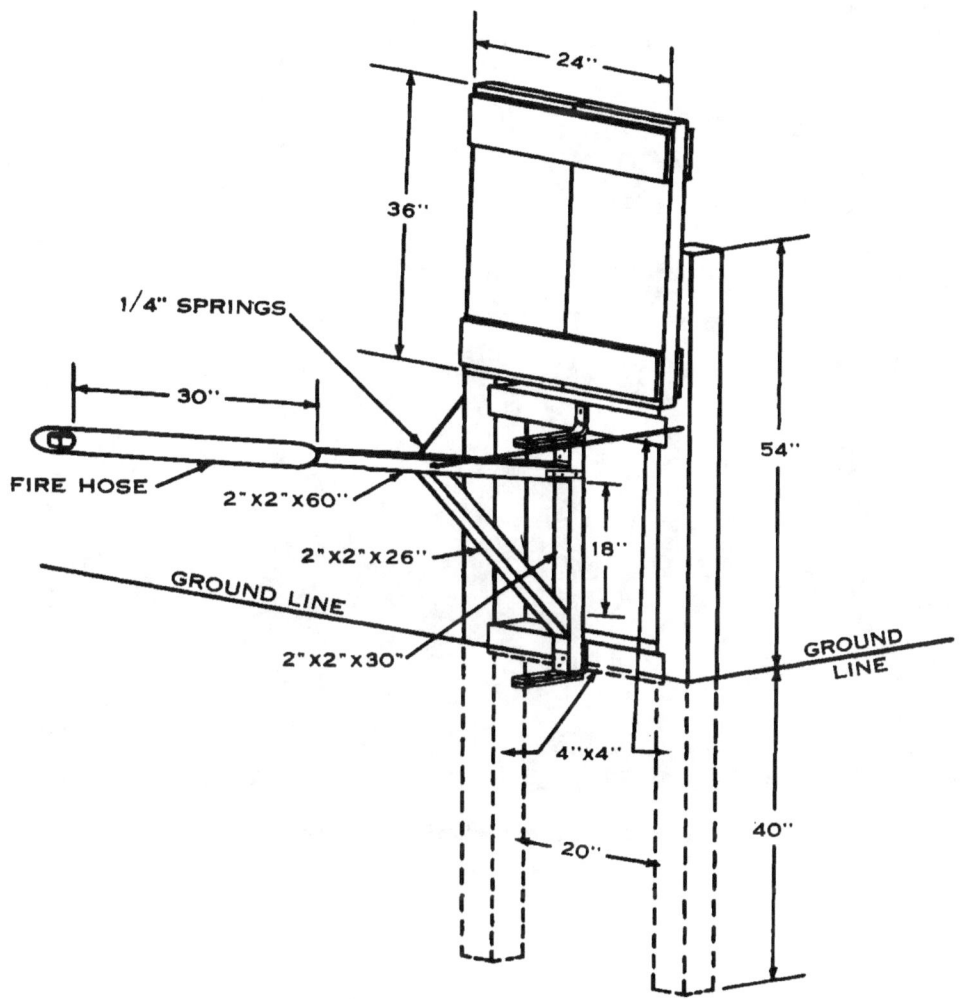

Figure 186. Construction details for the parry thrust target.

Figure 187. Parry vertical butt stroke target.

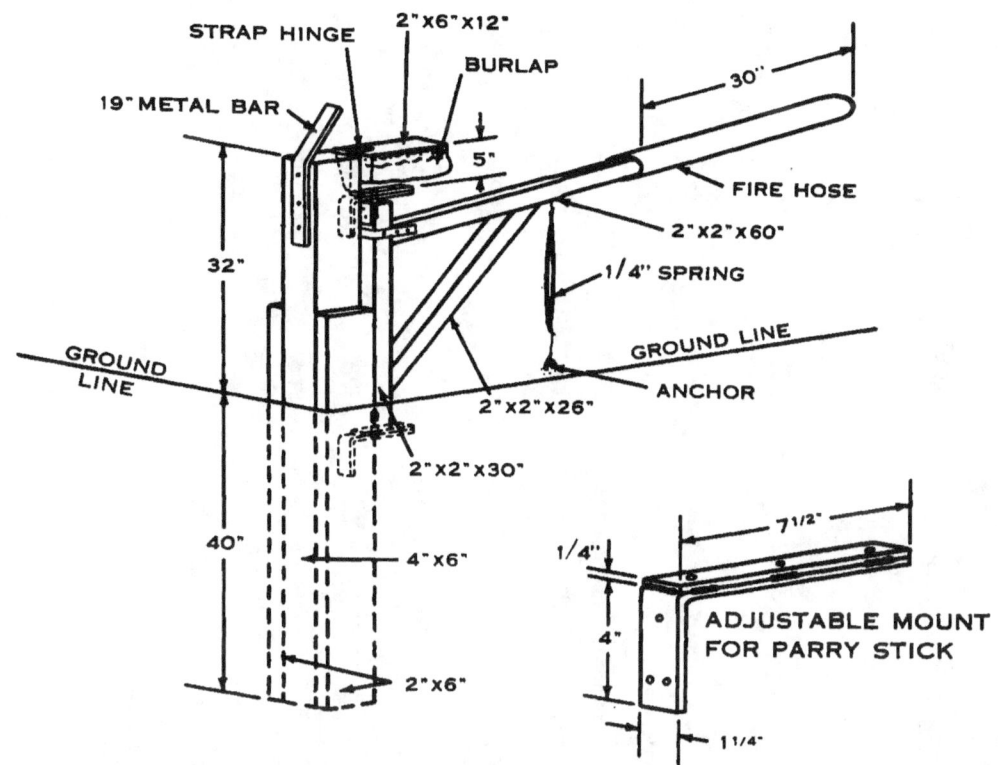

Figure 188. Construction details for the parry vertical butt stroke target.

Figure 189. Parry horizontal butt stroke target.

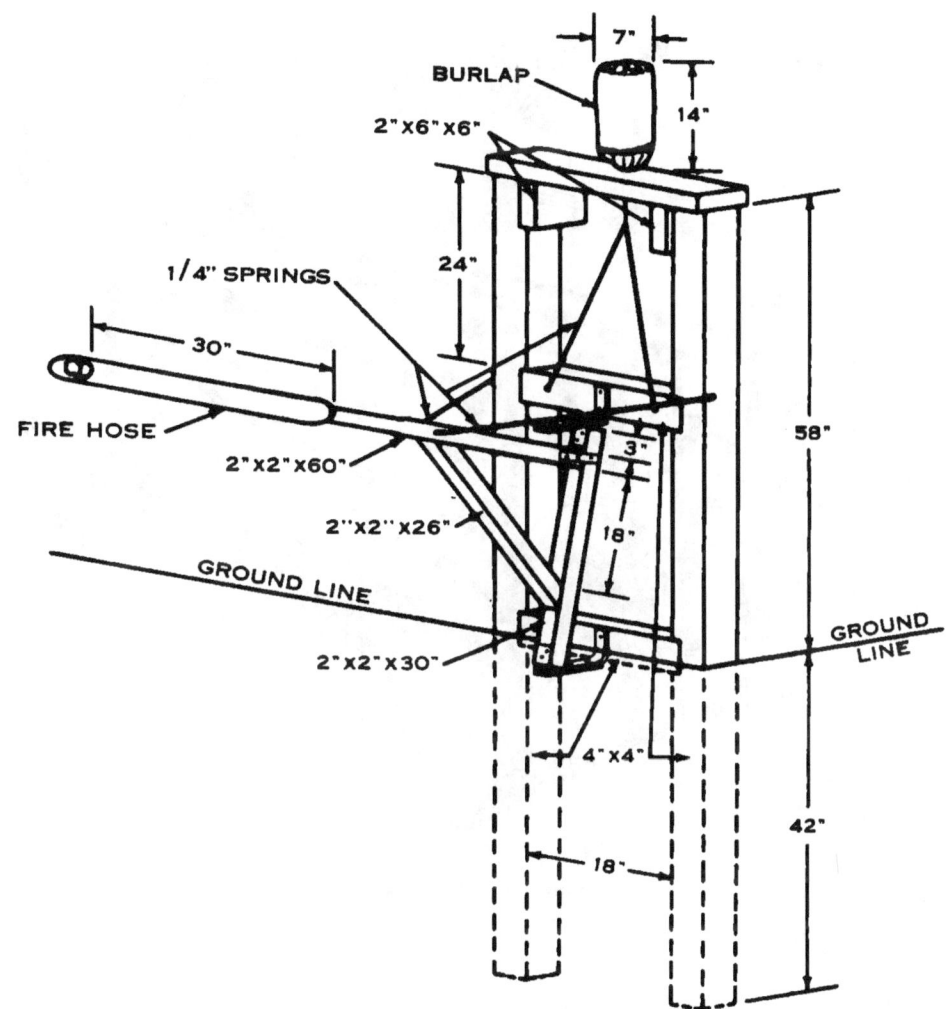

Figure 190. Construction details for the parry horizontal butt stroke target.

4. Obstacles

Figures 191 through 198 show the eight suggested obstacles and their dimensions.

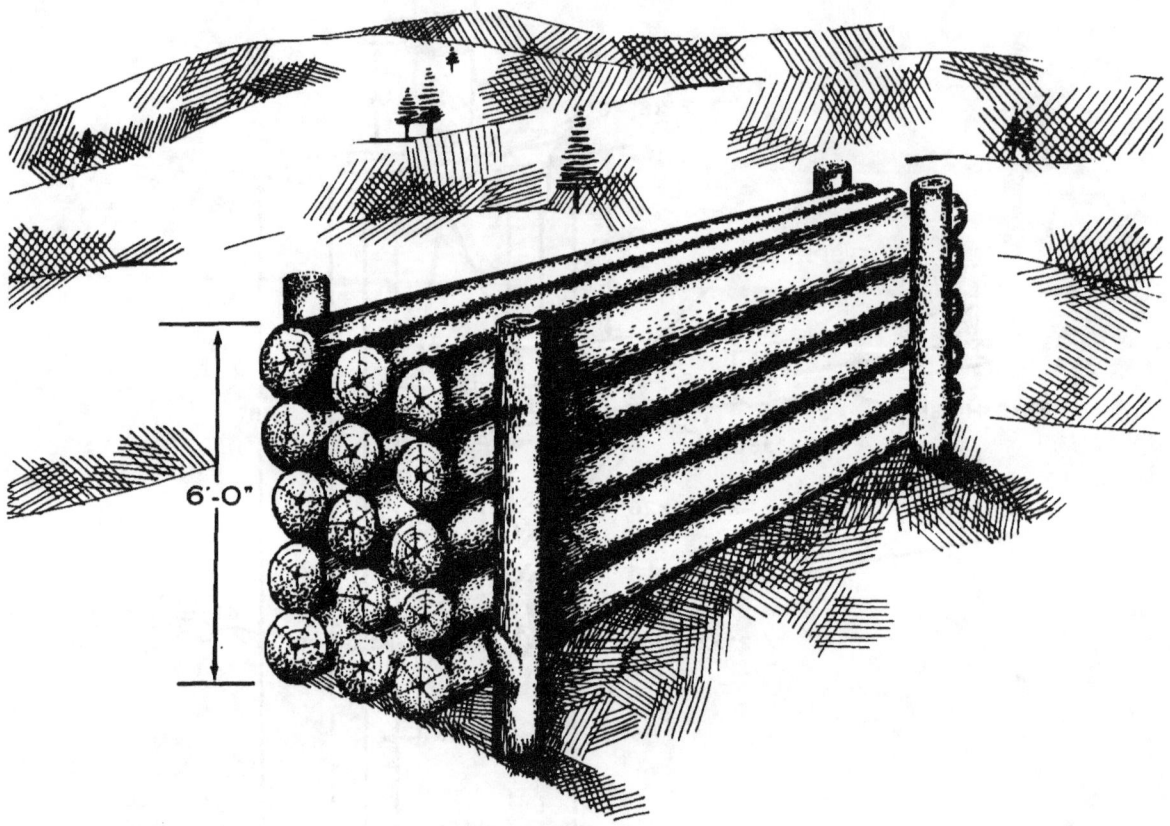

Figure 191. Log wall.

VARIABLE HEIGHTS - 27" MAX
VARIABLE INTERVALS

Figure 192. Hurdles.

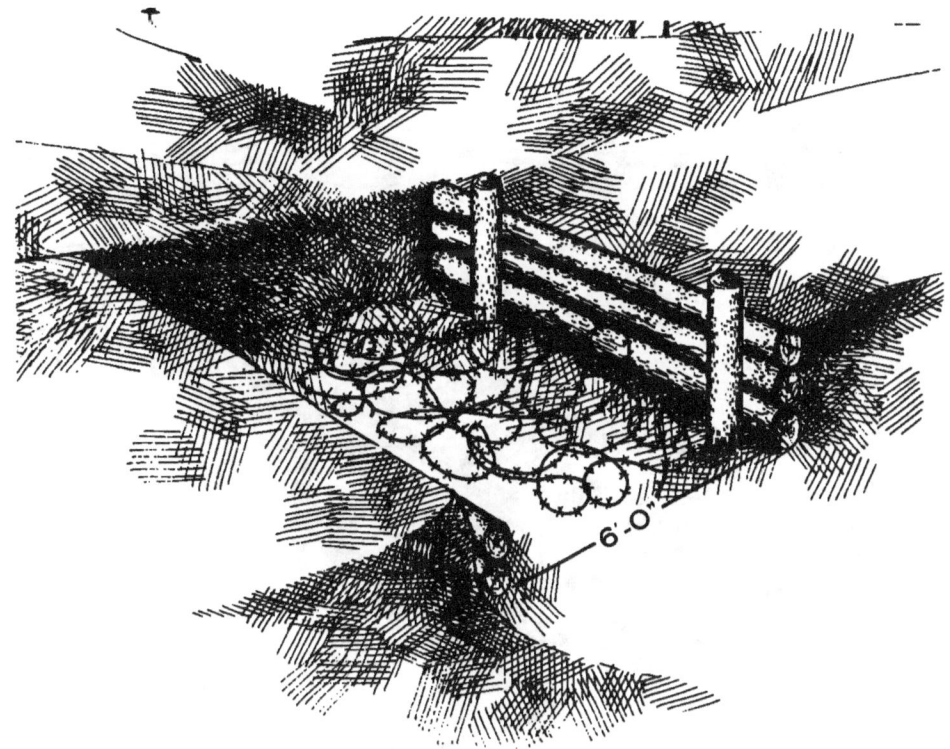

Figure 193. Ditch jump.

Figure 194. Prone target in crater.

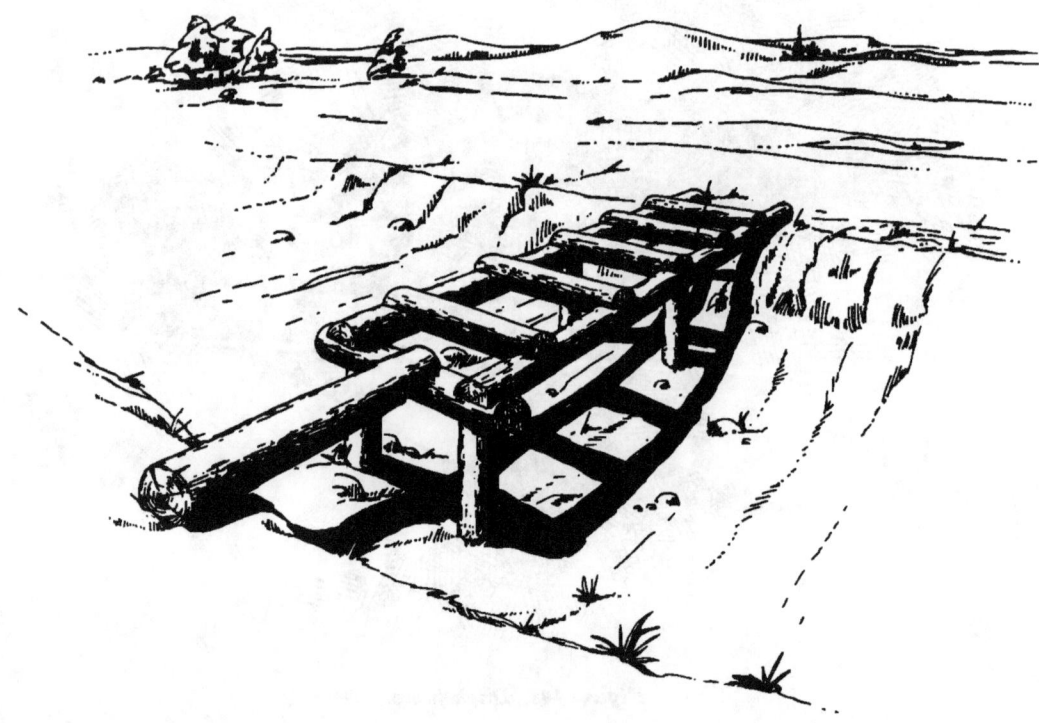

Figure 195. Log balance and horizontal ladder.

Figure 196. Tunnel crawl.

Figure 197. Fence vault.

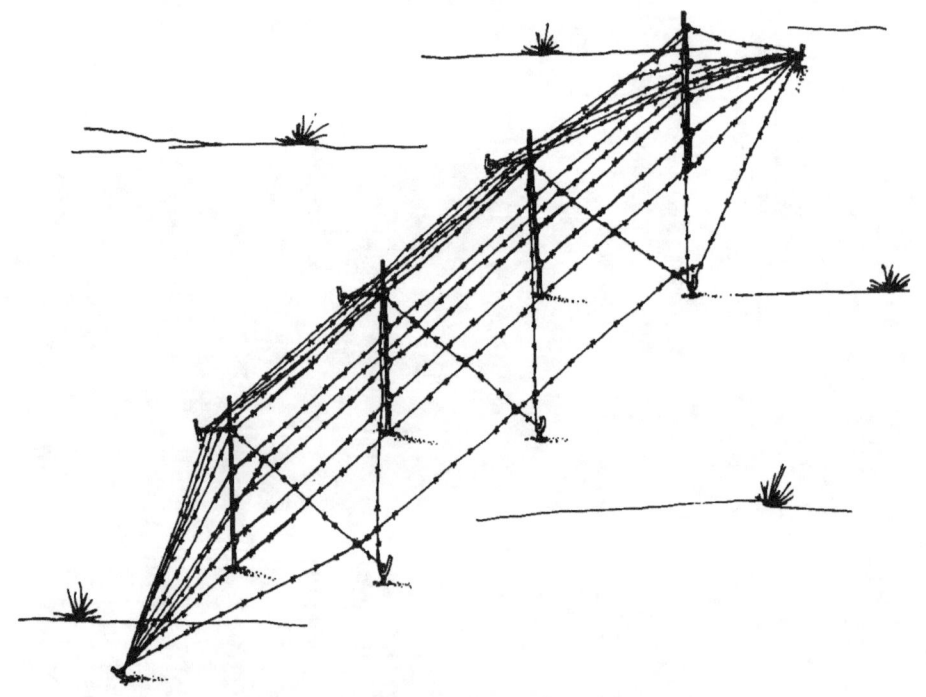

Figure 198. Double apron barbwire fence.

5. Scoresheets

The use of DA Form 1770–R (fig. 199) insures a standard scoring system for each fixed target on any Bayonet Assault Course. It contains the necessary criteria for scoring students on any of the targets. Figures 200 and 201 are sample scoresheets to illustrate scoring methods used when running a large group through the course at one time.

BAYONET QUALIFICATION COURSE SCORESHEET (FM 21-150)					DATE *1 Jan 64*	
TARGET POST NUMBER *4*	TYPE OF TARGET (i.e., Parry Thrust, Vertical Butt Stroke, etc.) *Parry Thrust*					
ELEMENT		POOR	GOOD	EXCELLENT	GRADE	
1. DID MAN PASS THROUGH GUARD POSITION UPON ATTACKING TARGET? (Total possible points - 3)		0	1	3	*3*	
2. DID HE SELECT PROPER MOVEMENT TO ATTACK TARGET AT THIS POST? (Total possible points - 5)		0	3	5	*5*	
3. DID HE EXECUTE MOVEMENT PROPERLY INCLUDING PARRY (if appropriate)? (Total possible points - 7)		0	5	7	*5*	
4. DID HE MAKE PROPER RECOVERY (i.e., withdrawal, return to guard position)? (Total possible points - 5)		0	3	5	*3*	
5. DID HE AGGRESSIVELY CONTINUE HIS ASSAULT TO NEXT POST? (Total possible points - 5)		0	3	5	*3*	
TOTAL (Maximum - 25)		0	15	25	*19*	
NAME OR ROSTER OF PERSON RUNNING THE COURSE *#96*		NAME AND GRADE OF SCORER *ROGERS, R. 1/Lt*				

DA FORM 1770-R, 1 Aug 63   Previous edition of this form is obsolete.

Entries in italics are for sample ONLY.

Figure 199. DA Form 1770–R.

BAYONET QUALIFICATION COURSE SCORESHEET			DATE 1 JAN 1964
LAST NAME DOE	FIRST JOHN	MI A.	ROSTER NO. 96
LANE NUMBER 2	ORDER NUMBER 8	UNIT A 1/66	SCORE
1. PARRY THRUST			21
2. PARRY VERTICAL BUTT STROKE			21
3. THRUST TARGET			25
4. PARRY HORIZONTAL BUTT STROKE			23
5. PARRY THRUST			22
6. THRUST TARGET			23
7. PARRY VERTICAL BUTT STROKE			20
8. PARRY HORIZONTAL BUTT STROKE			25
TOTAL			180
NAME AND GRADE OF SCORER ROGERS R. 1/LT			90%

Figure 200. Bayonet qualification course scoresheet.

LANE SCORER'S RECORD FOR E.I.B. BAYONET TEST							
LANE# 2	TARGET# 5	NAME JONES, F.B. PSgt					
ORDER	SCORE	ORDER	SCORE	ORDER	SCORE	ORDER	SCORE
1	20	18	25	35	19	52	23
2	17	19	25	36	25	53	23
3	20	20	23	37	25	54	20
4	15	21	20	38	20	55	21
5	19	22	21	39	21	56	25
6	18	23	19	40	21	57	25
7	25	24	25	41	18	58	24
8	22	25	25	42	25	59	25
9	25	26	25	43	19	60	20
10	24	27	23	44	23	61	18
11	20	28	24	45	23	62	24
12	17	29	21	46	22	63	24
13	25	30	25	47	23	64	19
14	25	31	25	48	19	65	20
15	20	32	25	49	19	66	22
16	25	33	23	50	20	67	23
17	18	34	20	51	25	68	24

Figure 201. Lane scorer's record for Expert Infantry Badge bayonet test.

APPENDIX III
ADVICE TO INSTRUCTORS OF BAYONET TRAINING

1. The Instructor

a. The instructor should encourage the students to growl. It will take their mind off footwork and develop a smooth series of movements. Noise, however, is no substitute for enthusiasm or ability. The instructor does not curse and discourages cursing among students.

b. Students should be in fairly good physical condition before they begin bayonet training. Physical conditioning should be gradual so the students do not become muscle sore.

c. The instructor explains and demonstrates movements briefly and clearly. He and his assistants first demonstrate the movements in slow motion and explain so that each movement is clear to the students. Then they demonstrate by the numbers so that each part of the movement is broken down and can be understood. This is followed by a demonstration of the movement at full speed.

d. Warmup exercises at the begining of bayonet training periods relax the students and help develop the muscle coordination used in bayonet combat. Five or ten minutes should be allotted for these exercises. The best warmup exercises are the basic bayonet positions such as guard, short guard, high port, at ease, moving from one to the other prior to actual training in the various advanced movements such as the long thrust. Calisthenics are not recommended as warmup exercises.

e. The instructor stresses speed, balance, timing, and distance judgment. Since a tense student cannot fight effectively with the bayonet, the instructor also stresses muscle relaxation.

f. Each student must think and act for himself. Therefore, the instructor should avoid the harmful practice of turning bayonet practice into a drill. Commands do not help students think for themselves or achieve the muscle coordination necessary for bayonet fighting. Thus, the coach-and-pupil method of training, which does not employ commands, must be undertaken as early as possible.

g. Teamwork is stressed during instruction in group assault tactics and on the assault course.

h. Prior to bayonet training (particularly before running the Bayonet Assault Course) students must remove the maintenance equipment from the butt stock of the rifle. This will prevent injuries should the stowage compartment door of the butt plate open and the equipment fly out and accidentally injure a student.

2. Conduct of Classes

a. Fix and Unfix Bayonets.
  (1) For safety reasons, these commands should be given by the assistant instructors with each group when the group is ready.
  (2) These movements are not executed in cadence.
  (3) On the command FIX BAYONETS (when the bayonet scabbard is on the belt), the muzzle of the rifle is moved across the body and grasped with the left hand below the gas cylinder plug. The snap on the scabbard is unfastened, the bayonet is grasped with the right hand, and it is drawn from the scabbard. The point of the bayonet is turned upward and the bayonet is fixed on the muzzle with a downward movement. After the bayonet is fixed, the position of attention is assumed.
    (*a*) The command UNFIX BAYONETS is given only when the student is at order arms.
    (*b*) At the command UNFIX BAYONETS, when the bayonet scabbard is on the belt, the rifle is moved to the left hand as when fixing bayonets. The student glances down

and grasps the handle of the bayonet with his right hand, the palm toward the body. The bayonet catch spring is pressed with the inside of the forefinger. The bayonet is raised vertically until the handle is approximately a foot above the muzzle of the rifle. Then, keeping his eyes on the point of the bayonet, the student returns the bayonet to the scabbard, reversing the movements of its withdrawal. The snap on the bayonet scabbard is fastened with the left hand and the position of order arms is assumed.

(c) When the bayonet is carried other than on the belt, it is fixed and unfixed in the most convenient manner possible upon receiving the commands.

(d) Safety precautions should be observed when fixing bayonets. While the rifle is held diagonally across the body with the left hand make sure the bayonet is secure by tapping *the base of the bayonet handle* with the heel of the right hand. If resistance is met when unfixing the bayonet, thrust the bayonet into the ground with the blade facing the right toe. Then press the bayonet release with the toe of the right boot and remove the rifle from the bayonet. The bayonet blade is not touched with the hands.

b. *Mass Formation* (fig. 202). A mass formation of not more than 200 men may be used during training in the fundamentals of bayonet techniques, positions, and movements. The formation is similar to that used in mass physi-

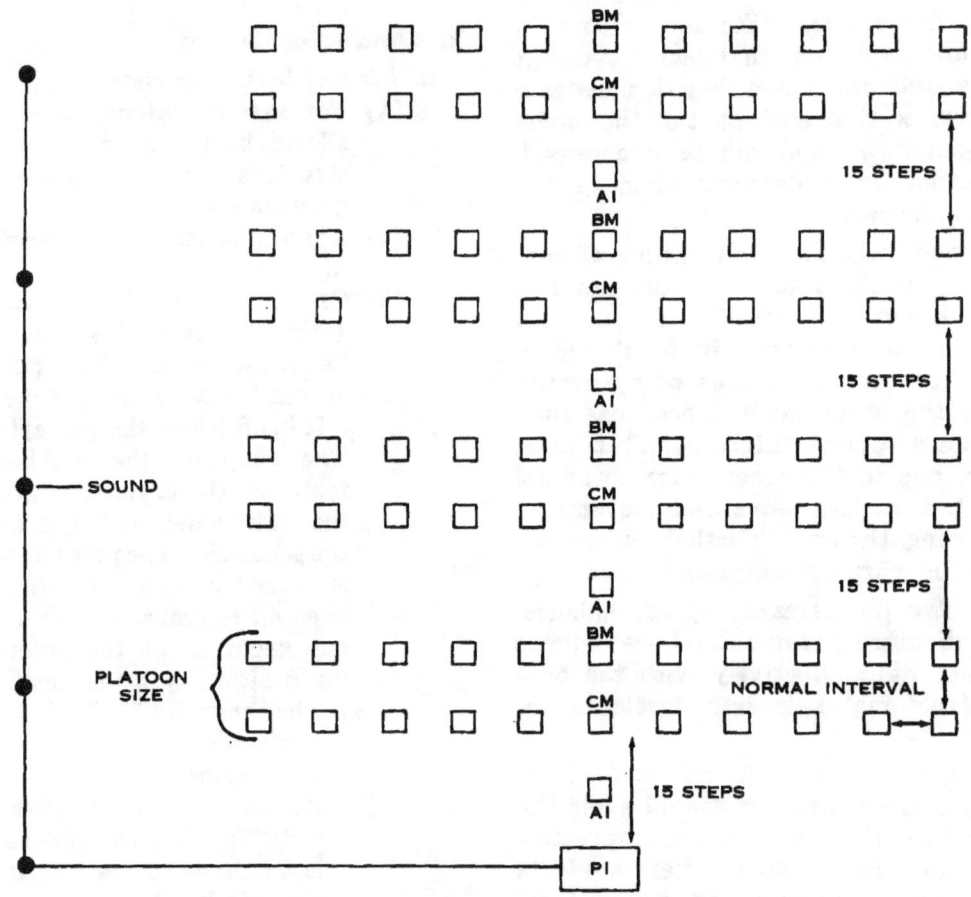

Figure 202. Mass training formation for company-size unit.

cal training except for an increase in the distances and intervals between men. Assistant instructors correct errors. Students who are slow to learn are taken out of the formation for individual instruction.

c. *Group Formation* (fig. 203).

(1) For bayonet training in platoons or smaller groups, the students form in two ranks at normal interval. The instructor designates one student in the rear rank as "baseman." This student immediately takes up the high port position. The instructor then commands FORM FOR BAYONET TRAINING, THIS MAN (pointing) BASE, MOVE. At the command MOVE, the baseman assumes the guard position. The other students in the rear rank run to the right and left respectively and take up a three-step interval. They face to the front and go into the guard position. Each front rank student runs to a position about 10 steps from and immediately in front of the student who was behind him and assumes the guard position. While moving into position, all students carry their rifles at the high port.

(2) To assemble the group, the instructor commands ASSEMBLE, MOVE. At the command MOVE, the baseman comes to attention. All others form on him at a run and come to attention.

(3) To form for more detailed instruction, the instructor stands in front of the two ranks and directs the flanks to close toward the center. This produces a three-sided formation which enables the entire group to hear the conference or see the demonstration. At the end of the instruction the instructor orders BACK TO YOUR PLACES.

3. Commands

The following commands may be used at the

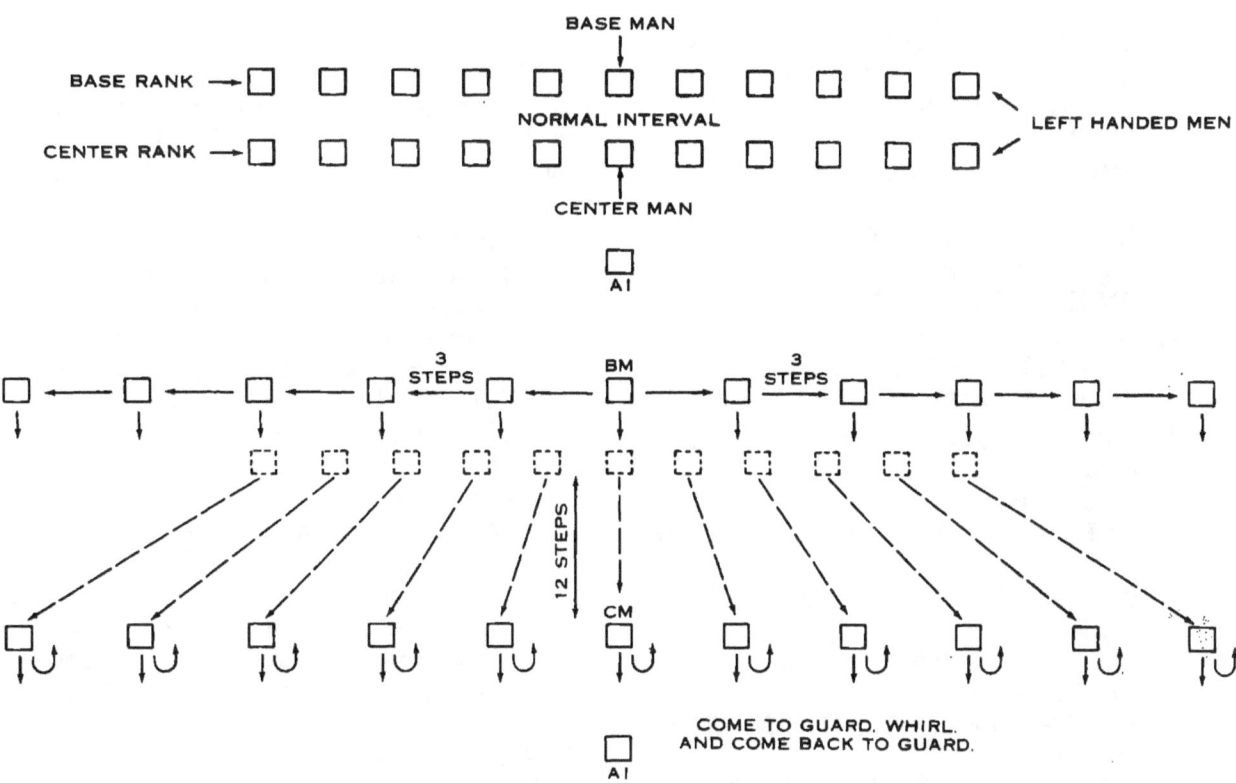

Figure 203. Group formation for platoons or smaller units.

beginning of bayonet training. (Commands given by the numbers should not be used unless the students show that they lack enough coordination to execute the movements while working from slow motion to normal speed.)

a. To form for bayonet training and to reassemble, the instructor commands
FORM FOR BAYONET TRAINING, THIS MAN BASE, MOVE.
ASSEMBLE, MOVE.

b. The commands used in assuming the basic positions are—
ON GUARD.
SHORT GUARD.
HIGH PORT.

c. The commands used in assuming additional positions are—
AT EASE.
RELAX.

d. The commands for the high port, crossover, and whirl are—
HIGH PORT AND CROSSOVER, READY, WHIRL.

e. The commands used in the thrust movements are—
(1) *By the numbers.*
LONG THRUST AND HOLD, MOVE.
RECOVER AND HOLD, MOVE.
WITHDRAW AND HOLD, MOVE.
ON GUARD.
SHORT THRUST AND HOLD, MOVE.
RECOVER AND HOLD, MOVE.
WITHDRAW AND HOLD, MOVE.
ON GUARD.
(2) *Without the numbers.*
LONG THRUST SERIES, MOVE.
SHORT THRUST SERIES, MOVE.

f. The commands used in the butt stroke movements are—
(1) *By the numbers.*
VERTICAL BUTT STROKE AND HOLD, MOVE.
SMASH, RECOVER, AND HOLD, MOVE.
SLASH AND HOLD, MOVE.
ON GUARD.
HORIZONTAL BUTT STROKE AND HOLD, MOVE.
SMASH, RECOVER, AND HOLD, MOVE.
SLASH AND HOLD, MOVE.
ON GUARD.
(2) *Without the numbers.*
VERTICAL BUTT STROKE SERIES, MOVE.
HORIZONTAL BUTT STROKE SERIES, MOVE.

g. The commands used in the parries are—
(1) *By the numbers.*
PARRY RIGHT, LONG THRUST, AND HOLD, MOVE.
RECOVER AND HOLD, MOVE.
WITHDRAW AND HOLD, MOVE.
ON GUARD.
PARRY LEFT, SHORT THRUST, AND HOLD, MOVE.
VERTICAL BUTT STROKE AND HOLD, MOVE.
SMASH, RECOVER, AND HOLD, MOVE.
SLASH AND HOLD, MOVE.
ON GUARD.
(2) *Without the numbers.*
PARRY RIGHT, LONG THRUST SERIES, MOVE.
PARRY, LEFT, SHORT THRUST SERIES, MOVE.

4. Sequence of Training

A suggested outline for a program of instruction in bayonet practice follows. (Training should not exceed one 50-minute period in any one day.)

a. First Period.
(1) Introduction to bayonet training.
(2) Bayonet training formation.
(3) Demonstrate and explain the basic positions and movements as follows:
 (*a*) Guard and short guard.
 (*b*) High port.
 (*c*) At ease and relax.
 (*d*) Whirl.
 (*e*) High port and crossover.
(4) Practical work in the basic positions and movements. The group is either in mass formation controlled by the instructor or in platoon or smaller groups controlled by assistant instructors.

b. Second Period.
(1) Review previous instruction.
(2) Teach short and long thrust series.

c. Third Period.
  (1) Review previous instruction.
  (2) Teach vertical and horizontal butt stroke series.

d. Fourth Period.
  (1) Review previous instruction.
  (2) Teach parry right and parry left series.

e. Fifth Period.
  (1) Introduce thrusting targets.
  (2) Practice the long and short thrust series using the thrusting targets.

f. Sixth Period. Run Bayonet Assault Course.

g. Seventh Period.
  (1) Substitute pugil stick for rifle and review previous instruction.
  (2) Conduct individual bouts in platoon-size or smaller groups.

h. Eighth Period. Teach group assault tactics using pugil sticks (two on one, three on two).

i. Ninth Period. Run Human Thrusting Target Course.

j. Tenth Period. Run Human Bayonet Assault Course.

5. Continued Training

a. Students need repeated periods of bayonet practice to remain alert bayonet fighters. These periods enable them to keep their form and alertness; 30 minutes of practice 3 days a week are necessary. Such periods will deal with the Bayonet Assault Course, pugil training, and other training procedures of a varied and vigorous nature.

b. To acquire the correct form and coordination, practice the movements first by the numbers and then in slow motion. Increase the pace in order to develop speed and aggressiveness.

c. Initial training in parries includes the actual parrying of an opponent's bayonet and rifle to develop a sense of distance, force, and timing. The coach-and-pupil method should be used in all practical work periods. Both students (coach-and-pupil) will have their bayonets fixed on their rifles. Scabbards are placed over the bayonets for safety purposes (fig. 204). The instructor directs the coaches to execute a thrust at half speed. The pupils parry right and thrust, parry left and thrust, or butt stroke at half speed. After practicing for one or two minutes, the instructor directs the coach-and-pupil to change places. He supervises and controls the exercise to point out errors, to avoid sparring tactics, and to give equal practice to both ranks. This exercise should be limited to brief periods.

d. Training with the thrusting targets develops distance judgment, balance, and force. Stress will be put on maximum extension of the body and rifle.

e. Practice in group assault tactics develops the important elements of teamwork.

f. Throughout bayonet training, students are trained to see and strike instantly at any opening. This training develops coordination between the eyes and muscles and produces mental physical alertness.

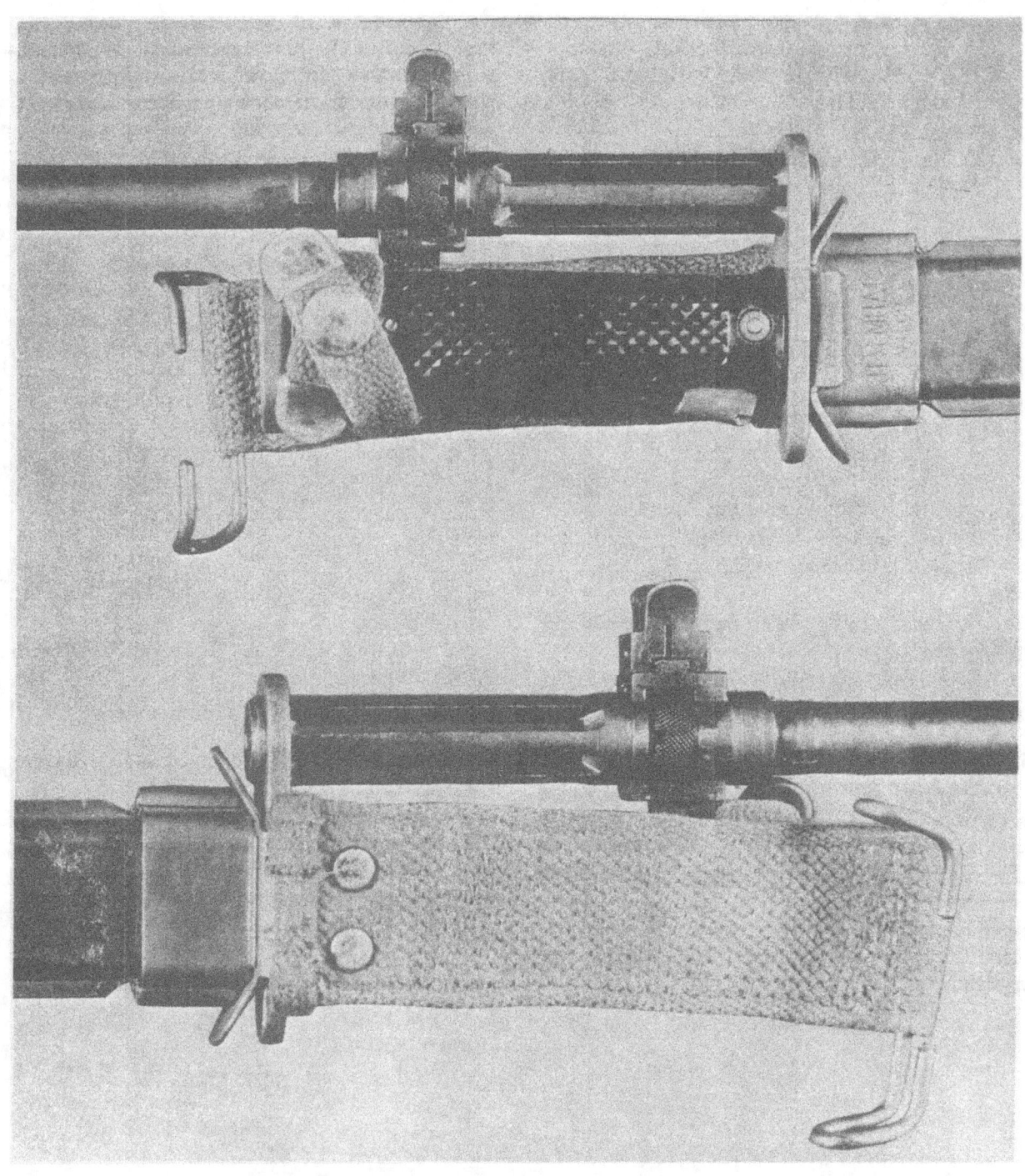

Figure 204. Securing scabbard strap around bayonet stud.

APPENDIX IV
ADVICE TO INSTRUCTORS OF HAND-TO-HAND COMBAT

1. The Instructor

The instructor should be in good physical condition and should be able to demonstrate all the maneuvers described in this manual. He must at all times display intense enthusiasm, vigor, and leadership qualities that will inspire the best efforts of the men being trained. He should train assistant instructors to closely supervise all practical work and to demonstrate advanced maneuvers.

2. General Safety Precautions

The following safety precautions must be strictly followed during all training in unarmed combat:

a. Supervise all practical work closely and constantly. Never leave a class unsupervised.

b. Familiarize the students with each maneuver by a complete explanation and demonstration before attempting practical work.

c. During the learning stages, do not let the students get ahead of your instruction. This prevents accidents.

d. During the stages of learning and perfecting techniques, the training partner offers no resistance. He should allow the maneuver to be executed freely.

e. Insure adequate space for all practical work. A space at least eight feet square is needed for each pair of students.

f. Have the students empty their pockets and remove jewelry, identification tags, or glasses before practical work periods.

3. Specific Safety Precautions

a. Vulnerable Points. Stress that only gentle blows are struck during the initial practical work. As students become more advanced, harder blows may be used. Students must always be cautioned against using excessive force in order to avoid injuries.

b. Fall Positions, Throws, and Holds.
 (1) Establish a signal that can be given by the individual student to stop the application of pressure when practicing holds. All students must know this signal, *particularly when practicing strangle holds.* This signal can be a handclap or a handtap on his training partner.
 (2) Be sure all students are warmed up before doing any practical work.
 (3) Teach fall positions before conducting practical work in throws.
 (4) Caution the students to apply very light pressure until they become familiar with the holds.

c. Disarming.
 (1) While the men are learning bayonet disarming methods, keep scabbards on the bayonets firmly attached to the rifles, as shown in figure 204.
 (2) Use tent pegs or bayonet scabbards to simulate knives while giving knife disarming instruction.
 (3) Caution the students who are to be disarmed not to place their finger in the trigger guard of their pistol or rifle while practicing disarming methods with these weapons.

4. Formations

a. Regulation physical training formations may be used for practice (FM 21-20). In the extended platoon formation have the first and third ranks face the second and fourth ranks so that each student will have a partner. Even numbered students do not uncover. It is recommended, when practicing throws, that twice the normal distance be taken between ranks.

b. To instruct disarming methods, it is recommended that you use a formation of two concentric training circles or a formation that employs only two well-extended ranks. In forming the concentric training circle, pair off the students so that each will have a partner.

5. Commands

a. Most of the maneuvers described in this manual can be divided into several steps or phases. To facilitate learning and to insure that the student learns each movement of an entire maneuver accurately, each maneuver is presented by phases.

b. For example, the right hip throw (par. 44) is a three-phase maneuver. In the first phase the student places his left foot in front of and slightly to the inside of his opponent's left foot. At the same time, he strikes his opponent on his right shoulder and grabs his clothing. The command for this movement is PHASE ONE OF THE HIP THROW, MOVE. At the command MOVE, the student executes phase one and holds his position until given subsequent commands. These commands are PHASE TWO (THREE), MOVE. When the student has become proficient in the movements, you can work for speed. The phases of the maneuver are combined into a continuous movement by commanding HIP THROW, MOVE. At first, the maneuver is executed slowly. Students gain speed through constant practice.

c. Paragraph 85 explains the counter against the long bayonet thrust. This disarming method is divided into three phases. For the first phase (par. 85a), the armed student is given the preparatory command LONG THRUST, and the unarmed student is given the preparatory command PARRY RIGHT. Since you want both students to halt their movements and remain in position for a subsequent command, you must command HOLD. The entire command for the first phase, therefore, is LONG THRUST, PARRY RIGHT, AND HOLD, MOVE. The next two phases of the movement are executed while the armed student is extended in the long thrust. The command for the second phase (par. 85b) is GROUND AND HOLD, MOVE. The command for the third phase (par. 85c-e) is DISARM AND HOLD, MOVE. The command for executing this disarming maneuver is DISARM FROM THE LONG THRUST, MOVE.

6. Exercise

a. *Recommendations for Warmup Exercises.* Use combative exercises, grass drills, and tumbling exercises to warmup your men. The aggressive nature of these warmup drills lends itself to the spirit of hand-to-hand combat (FM 21-20).

b. *Recommended Drill for Parry Exercises.* It is important that your students be trained in the bayonet disarming parry movements before practicing the disarming methods. To do this, have the paired students assume their respective guard positions with the chin of the unarmed man six to eight inches from the bayonet point. The armed student stands fast in the guard position during the entire exercise. The unarmed student, on command, parries the bayonet first to the right and then to the left. As he parries to the right, he sidesteps to his left oblique with his left foot, brings his right foot slightly to the rear of his left, and faces the side of the rifle. When he parries left, he sidesteps with his right foot to his right oblique.

7. Training Pit

a. The most suitable area for teaching fall positions, throws, and counters is a sawdust pit. You can obtain sawdust at most military installations. Figure 205 shows a training area with four sawdust pits surrounding an instructor-demonstrator platform. Each pit will accommodate 12 pair of students. If you need additional space fill in the area along the sides of each pit, as shown.

b. To construct a pit dig out the pit area to a depth of 18 inches or build a retaining wall of dirt or sandbags 18 inches high around the pit area. Fill the area with sawdust. Do not use wood shavings because they tend to settle and form a hard surface.

c. Build a platform, 14 feet square, in the center of the pit area. Construct retaining walls made of sandbags, four bags high, and fill the inside with sawdust. This platform is big enough to hold two demonstrators and the instructor.

d. The students gather around the platform to watch the demonstrations.

8. Other Training Areas

a. Any large grassy or sandy area is suitable for work in disarming methods and throws.

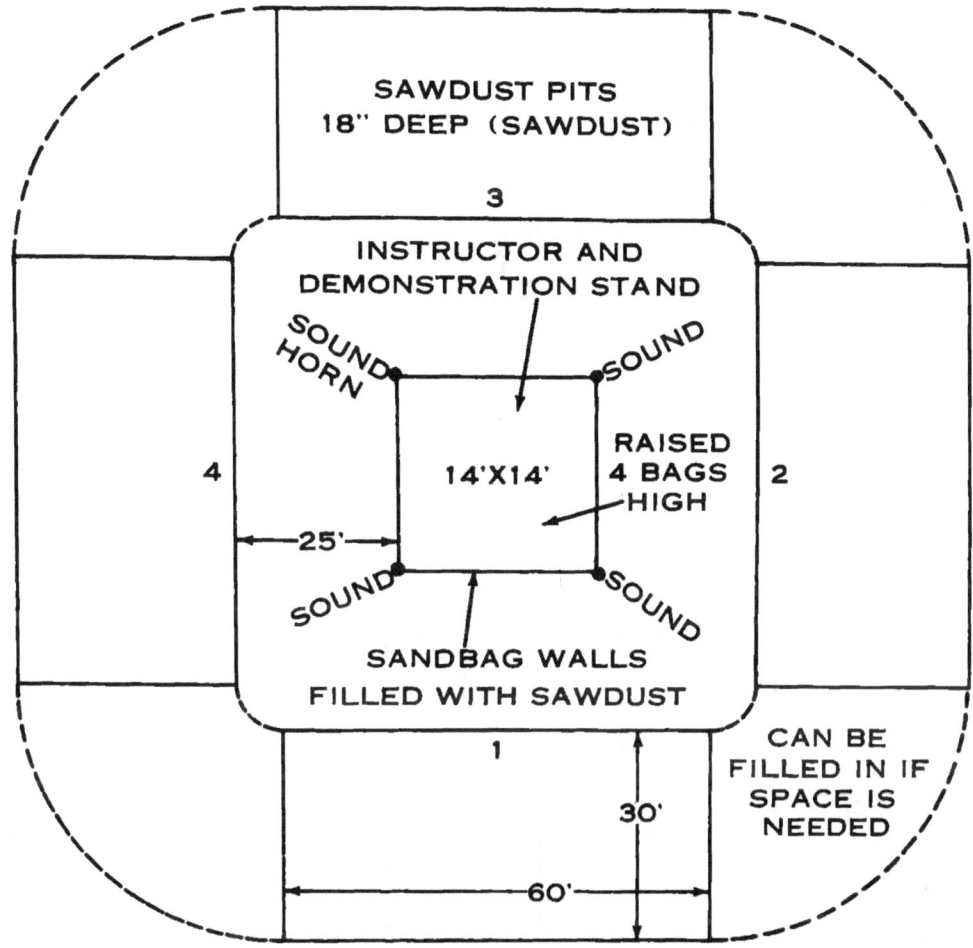

Figure 205. The training pit should be large enough to allow students to maneuver.

Students should be taught fall positions before performing throws on a hard, grassy area.

b. Classes in unarmed combat can also be conducted indoors, but the floor and walls should be matted. The difficulty indoors is that only a small group of men can participate at one time because an area eight feet square should be allotted for each pair of students.

9. Variation in Minimum Training Program

Periods eight and nine of the subject schedule (fig. 206) include work in throws, falls, and escapes from basic holds. These periods, however, may be spent in reviewing previous lessons if the instructor thinks the students need review. The throws, falls, and escapes can be included in the physical training program.

SUBJECT BREAKDOWN CHART FOR MINIMUM TRAINING PROGRAM *

PERIOD	SUBJECT	TYPE	AREA	STUDENT EQUIPMENT	REFERENCE
1	INTRODUCTION; FUNDAMENTALS: ATTACKING VULNERABLE POINTS.	CONFERENCE DEMONSTRATIONS PRACTICAL EXERCISES.	SAWDUST PIT	NA	CHAPTERS 7, 8, 9.
2	FALL POSITIONS: RIGHT SIDE, LEFT SIDE, AND REAR; HIP THROW.	DO	DO	NA	CHAPTERS 10, 11.
3	REVIEW SECOND PERIOD; REVERSE HIP THROW, OVERSHOULDER THROW, CROSS-HOCK TAKEDOWN, REAR TAKEDOWN.	DO	DO	NA	CHAPTER 11.
4	HOLDS: ESCAPE FROM HOLDS.	DO	DO	NA	CHAPTERS 13, 14.
5	REVIEW THROWS AND TAKEDOWN; KNIFE ATTACK GRIP, STANCE, ATTACKING VULNERABLE POINTS.	DO	DO	ONE TENT PEG OR BAYONET WITH SCABBARD PER TWO STUDENTS.	CHAPTER 15.
6	REVIEW KNIFE ATTACK; KNIFE DISARMING COUNTERS AGAINST DOWNWARD STROKE COUNTERS AGAINST UPWARD STROKE.	DO	DO	ONE TENT PEG OR BAYONET WITH SCABBARD PER TWO STUDENTS.	CHAPTER 18.
7	REVIEW FALL POSITIONS; BAYONET DISARMING, COUNTERS AGAINST SHORT THRUST, COUNTERS AGAINST LONG THRUST.	DO	DO	ONE RIFLE WITH BAYONET AND SCABBARD PER TWO STUDENTS.	CHAPTER 16.
8	REVIEW FALL POSITIONS: RIFLE AND PISTOL DISARMING.	DO	DO	ONE RIFLE AND ONE PISTOL PER TWO STUDENTS (CAN SUBSTITUTE STICK OR ANY SUITABLE ITEM FOR PISTOL).	CHAPTER 17.
9	SILENCING SENTRIES: PRISONER SEARCHING, SECURING AND GAGGING.	DO	DO	ONE STEEL HELMET AND ONE TENT ROPE PER TWO STUDENTS.	CHAPTERS 19, 20, 21.
10	REVIEW FALL POSITIONS: VARIATIONS OF HOLDS, THROWS, TAKEDOWNS, AND COUNTERS.	DO	DO	NA	CHAPTER 12.

* THIS PROGRAM IS USED TO GIVE STUDENTS A BRIEF ORIENTATION IN HAND-TO-HAND COMBAT. MUCH MORE TIME MUST BE SPENT TO BECOME PROFICIENT. IF MORE TIME IS AVAILABLE IT CAN BE USED FOR EACH OF THE PERIODS.

Figure 206. Training program.

INDEX

	Paragraphs	Page
Advice to instructors:		
Bayonet training	app. III	321
Hand-to-hand combat	app. IV	327
Attacking gunman from front	98	252
Attacking gunman from rear	97	249
Attacking the limb region	33	89
Attacking the neck region	31	71
Attacking the trunk region	32	81
Attacking with available weapon:		
Bayonet hilt	34	95
Homemade blackjack	34	95
Basic takedowns:		
Cross-hook	48	117
Rear	49	121
Basic takedowns, variation	53	131
Basic throws:		
Hip	44	104
Overhead	47	114
Overshoulder	46	110
Reverse hip	45	107
Basic throws, variations	50–52	124
Bayonet assault:		
Award	11	30
Course	app. II	305
Obstacles	app. II	305
Purpose	11	30
Scoresheet	app. II	305
Scoring	11	30
Supervision	11	30
Targets	10, app. II	30, 305
Bayonet assault course	app. II	305
Bayonet attack, rest positions:		
At ease	6	4
Guard	6	4
High port	6	4
Rest	6	4
Short guard	6	4
Bayonet, basic movements:		
High port and crossover	8	10
Horizontal butt stroke series	8	10
Long thrust series	8	10
Parries	8	10
Short thrust series	8	10
Vertical butt stroke series	8	10
Whirl	8	10
Bayonet, counters against:		
Long thrust	84, 85	202, 208
Short thrust	81–83	192, 199
Bayonet fighter	4	3
Bayonet, fighting principles	3	3
Bayonet group assault tactics:		
One against two	19	54

	Paragraphs	Page
Bayonet group assault tactics—Continued		
Three against two	19	54
Two against one	19	54
Two against three	19	54
Bayonet, uses	2	3
Body, vulnerable parts	29	69
Counters against rifle:		
Back	88	216
Front	87	214
Counters against pistol:		
Back	91–93	227
Back of neck	94–96	242
Front	89, 90	221, 225
Fall positions:		
Left side	37	99
Rear	40	102
Right side	36	98
Fall positions, practice:		
Left side	39	99
Rear	41	102
Right side	38	99
Fall practice, advanced:		
Left side	42	103
Rear	42	103
Right side	42	103
Hand-to-hand combat, available weapons:		
Boot kick	23	66
Heel of hand	23	66
Knife edge of hand	23	66
Padded fist	23	66
Pointed fist	23	66
Small fist	23	66
Hand-to-hand combat techniques:		
Accuracy, speed	27	69
Balance	25	69
Momentum	26	69
Holds:		
Cross collar strangle	57	135
Double wristlock	61	142
Front strangle	55	132
Full nelson	58	136
Hammerlock	59	139
Rear strangle	60	140
Side collar strangle	56	132
Holds, escape from:		
Choke hold	63, 64	146
Front strangle	65	150
Grip on both wrists	69	158
Grip on one wrist	68	157
One-arm strangle, rear	70	163

	Paragraphs	Page
Holds, escape from—Continued		
Overarm bear hug	66	151
Overarm body, rear	71	164
Underarm bear hug	67	155
Underarm body, rear	72, 73	170, 174
Human bayonet assault course	17	51
Human thrusting target course	16	40
Knife:		
Grip	75	176
Stance	76	180
Stance, modified	77	181
Knife attack, frontal:		
Heart	78	182
Leg	78	182
Stomach	78	182
Throat	78	182
Upper arm	78	182
Wrist	78	182
Knife attack, rear:		
Kidney	79	186
Side of neck	79	186
Subclavian artery	79	186
Throat	79	186
Knife attacks, counter against:		
Cautious approach	104	273
Downward stroke	99, 100	256
Upward stroke	101–103	264
Pugil stick construction	13	32
Pugil training	14, 15	34, 37
Pugil training equipment:		
Face mask	13	32
Gloves	13	32
Groin gear	13	32
Headgear	13	32
Searching prisoners, methods:		
Lean-to	116	287
Kneeling	115	285
Prone	114	284
Stand up	117	288
Searching prisoners with:		
Rifle	114, 115	284, 285
Pistol	116, 117	287, 288
Searching several prisoners	118	290
Securing prisoners:		
Adhesive tape gag	126	302
Belt tie	120	295
Handkerchief gag	124	302
Hog tie	123	300
Lead tie	122	300
Shoelace tie	121	297
Silencing sentries with:		
Helmet neck break	106	275
Helmet smash	107	278
Wire, cord strangulation	108, 109	280, 282

Department of the Army Field Manual 21-150, edition of September, 1963. This volume supercedes FM 21-150, 14Jun54, including C1, 7May58, and FM 23-25, 22Jun53, including C1, 16Jul56. Commercially reprinted by Normount Technical Publications, Wickenburg, Arizona, 85358. See catalog for listing of additional titles of similar inerest.

Second reprinting, August, 1975

A Selection Of Classic Instructive Titles Relating To The Art Of Pugilism & Self Defence In Both War & Peace
Find our entire selection @ naval-military-press.com

ALL-IN FIGHTING

The distilled knowledge of W.E. Fairbairn, legendary SOE instructor in unarmed combat, and inventor of the Sykes-Fairbairn knife, who learned his deadly skills in 30 years on the Shanghai waterfront. Fully illustrated.
9781847348531

ART OF BOXING AND SCIENCE OF SELF DEFENCE

Former Lightweight Champion Billy Edwards shares the techniques and strategies of the sweet science in his beautifully illustrated boxing guide. Explore boxing's transition from bare knuckle spectacle to today's Marquis of Queensbury ruleset.
9781474539548

SELF DEFENCE OR THE ART OF BOXING

Ned Donnelly was a pioneer of boxing training during the late Victorian era. Explore the strategies and techniques used by this trainer of champions via a series of easy-to-follow illustrations and clear, concise coaching steps.
9781474539562

JACK GOODWIN'S BOXING

This 1920's boxing masterpiece by Jack Goodwin puts you in the shoes of a coach in that era. Uncover the best ways to run, manage and train boxers as taught by Jack Goodwin, a champion and trainer of champions in the noble science.

9781474539586

ART OF WRESTLING

George de Relwyskow Army Gymnastic Staff

In the appreciation to this book Captain Daniels, V.C., M.C., Rifle Brigade, states: "In adding a word to this book on the style of wrestling as taught at the Headquarters Gymnasium of the British Army, and having had personal experience in the various holds and throws taught, I consider it has been of great value in the training of the soldier, and the bringing out of those qualities of grit and determination which have been seen in all ranks who have taken an active part throughout the greatest war in history." 1919.

9781783313563

THE COMPLETE BOXER

Gunner Moir provides detailed instructions on the techniques he deployed to become British Heavyweight Champion. Taught in a series of easy to learn techniques, combinations, and boxing strategies.

9781474539609

BOXING (V-Five)
The Aviation Training Office of the Chief of Naval Operations

The game-changing V-Five suite of training manuals helped get a generation of American aviators fit for war. Here we explore how the airmen of the US navy trained in boxing as part of their military fitness regime.

9781474539623

WRESTLING (V-Five)
The Aviation Training Office of the Chief of Naval Operations

The game-changing V-Five suite of training manuals helped get a generation of American aviators fit for war. Here we explore how the airmen of the US navy trained in collegiate wrestling as part of their military fitness regime.

9781474539685

THE TEXTBOOK OF WRESTLING

Get your wrestling skills matt-ready from wrestling champion and world-renown trainer Ernest Gruhn. Replete with detailed holds, throws, pins and strategies for success in a wide range of wrestling rulesets.

9781474539647

MANUAL OF PHYSICAL TRAINING 1914
(United States Army)

Published just prior to the outbreak of World War 1, this beautifully illustrated guide was designed to revolutionise the combat fitness and readiness of the US Army covering a wide range of gymnastic and combat calisthenic exercises.

KILL OR GET KILLED

Rex Applegate's "kill or be killed" helped prepare America's marines, soldiers, sailors, spies and airmen for the realities of war. This highly shared and respected work provides all you need to know about unarmed combat and close quarter engagement with the enemy.

9781474539661

HAND-TO-HAND COMBAT

Bureau of Aeronautics U.S Navy 1943

This is one of the best combative manuals from World War 2, developed by the US Navy V-Five Staff, that included the renowned American wrestler Wesley Brown. It is then not especially surprising that wrestling skills predominate in this manual, and form the base skill-set for this combative system.

9781474537391

ABWEHR ENGLISCHER GANGSTER METHODEN DEFENSE OF ENGLISH GANGSTERS METHODS – SILENT KILLING – FULL ENGLISH TRANSLATION

In 1942 the Wehrmacht published a training manual with the goal of countering the "silent killing" tactics used by the British commando units. The manual was – much in line with typical National Socialist terminology –titled
"Abwehr Englischer Gangster-methoden" or "Defence Against English Gangster methods".
This book was compiled due the Wehrmacht intelligence operatives uncovering of a British hand-to-hand course for the SOE, Commandos, et al, on methods of quick and silent killing (undoubtedly developed by W. E. Fairbairn and E. A. Sykes). They correctly assessed that their troops in general and particularly the Geheime Staatspolizei (Gestapo), Sicherheitsdienst (SD), their security guards, and sentries would be in grave danger when confronted by men trained in these methods. This manual/program was the Wehrmacht's response.

9781474538336

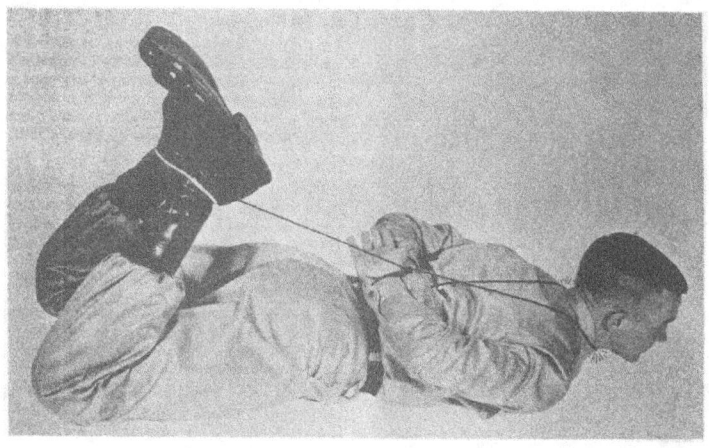

HAND TO HAND COMBAT

Francois d'Eliscu taught thousands of U.S. Army Rangers how to fight down and dirty in World War II. d'Eliscu doesn't get the press that Fairbairn and Applegate do, but he did a commendable job writing this book. It is basic, meant for training raw recruits in a short amount of time before sending them to the front, but simple is good when you are in combat, as most combative experts' will tell you.

9781474535823

WE Fairbairn's Complete Compendium of Lethal, Unarmed, Hand-to-Hand Combat Methods and Fighting In Colour

All 844 images of Fairbairn and his assistants can now for the first time be seen in full colour, lending a clarity to the practical methods of mastering the manner of dealing with an assailant, both in time of war and when placed in difficulty during unpleasant modern urban situations. These various holds, trips, kicks, blows etc, allow the average man or woman a position of security against almost any form of armed or unarmed attack.

Captain W.E. Fairbairn would have approved of this new colour version, that gives an illustrative clarity to the original that was lacking in previous monochrome reprints of his work.

All six of W.E. Fairbairn's works in one binding to create the ultimate colour compendium: Get Tough-All-In Fighting-Shooting to Live-Scientific Self-Defence-Hands Off!-Defend

9781783318735

BOXING FOR BOYS
Regtl. Sergt.-Major E & B Dent Army Gymnastic Headquarters

A successful system of boxing instruction for large classes, to allow tuition with no detriment to the "backward or shy pupil". Covers Kit-On, Guard-Sparring-Advance-Point & Mark-Ducking-Medicine, Bag-Left & Right Hooks etc. The author considered that boxing systematically taught to the youth was beneficial exercise, and would have a marked elevating influence on the national character.

9781783314607

HAND-TO-HAND FIGHTING
A System Of Personal Defence For The Soldier (1918)

A tough book on the art of hand to hand fighting in the trenches of the Great War. Demonstrating techniques utilised to "do away with the enemy", many of which are barred in clean wrestling, the book includes good clear photographic illustrations presenting important attack methods including the "Hammer Lock", "Kidney Kick", "Head Twist", "Knee Groin Kick", and the "Knee Break", all very important in a man to man, life or death encounter, when fighting in the mud of the trenches.

9781783313983

www.ingramcontent.com/pod-product-compliance
Lightning Source LLC
Chambersburg PA
CBHW080421230426
43662CB00015B/2179